Leo Ornstein

Leo Ornstein

Modernist Dilemmas, Personal Choices

MICHAEL BROYLES
AND DENISE VON GLAHN

INDIANA UNIVERSITY PRESS
Bloomington and Indianapolis

This book is a publication of

Indiana University Press
601 North Morton Street
Bloomington, IN 47404–3797 USA

http://iupress.indiana.edu

Telephone orders   800–842–6796
Fax orders   812–855–7931
Orders by e-mail   iuporder@indiana.edu

The paper used in this publication meets the minimum requirements of American National Standard for Information Sciences—Permanence of Paper for Printed Library Materials, ANSI Z39.48–1984.

Manufactured in the United States of America

LIBRARY OF CONGRESS CATALOGING-IN-PUBLICATION DATA

Broyles, Michael, date
    Leo Ornstein : modernist dilemmas, personal choices / Michael Broyles and Denise Von Glahn.
      p. cm.
    Includes list of Ornstein's works (p.   ), bibliographical references (p.   ), and index.
    ISBN 978-0-253-34894-4 (cloth)
    1. Ornstein, Leo, d. 2002. 2. Composers—United States—Biography.
I. Von Glahn, Denise, date II. Title.
ML410.O67B76   2007
780.92—dc22
[B]   2007022611

1 2 3 4 5   12 11 10 09 08 07

FRONTISPIECE: Leo Ornstein. *MSS 10, The Leo Ornstein Papers, Irving S. Gilmore Music Library, Yale University.*

To families . . . whose power to shape us cannot be measured.

CONTENTS

ACKNOWLEDGMENTS

Over a period of eight years authors accumulate many debts. We have tried to keep track, but apologize in advance for the almost certain oversight of important people who have assisted our project. We want to thank Gayle Sherwood Magee, formerly Music Sponsoring Editor at Indiana University Press, for her enthusiastic encouragement of this book, and Jane Behnken, who picked up where Gayle left off. Our copyeditor, David Anderson, has been a quiet force in clarifying our prose, and Peter Pohorence and Keith Ramsey have provided invaluable service setting musical examples. We are grateful to our home institutions, Penn State and Florida State universities, for granting us each a sabbatical leave to pursue this work, and for the librarians at our schools who have contributed their time to helping Leo Ornstein once again come to life: Amanda Maple, Music Librarian at Penn State, and Dan Clark, Head Music Librarian in the Allen Music Library at Florida State. We thank our students, those continuing and others long graduated: Amy Dunning, Amy Keyser, Nicole Le Blanc, Steve Leinbach, Paul Moulton, John Packard, Sean Parr, and Peter Reske for the varied research and editing projects they took on and the elusive bits of information they tracked down.

Among librarians and archivists across the country who have helped in our work we are especially grateful to George Boziwick, Chief of the Music Division at the New York Public Library for Performing Arts; Suzanne Eggleston Lovejoy and Kendall Crilly at Yale University's Irving S. Gilmore Music Library; John Pollack and Lynne Farrington at the University of Pennsylvania Rare Book and Manuscript Library; Kile Smith and Linda Wood at the Philadelphia Free Library; Jean Morrow, Director of Libraries at the New England Conservatory; Jane Gottlieb and Jeni Dahmus at the Juilliard School; and Vivian Perlis at the Oral History American Music project at Yale University, who shared invaluable video archives and her own personal recollections of Leo Ornstein with us.

We are indebted to a host of experts ranging across a number of fields including Gary G. Roth, former project manager of the Statue of Liberty/Ellis Island Project with the U.S. Department of the Interior National Park Service, for his insights into the varied processes by which immigrants first stepped foot on shore; Valerie Langfield, Roger Quilter's biographer, for helping us understand the scope and importance of the Ornstein-Quilter relationship and for sharing essential correspondence between the two men; Charles Amarkanian for his time and resources; Tom Winters and his student Matthew Trojanowski at West Chester University for locating and making available difficult-to-access materials; Desmond Scott, son of Cyril Scott, for his e-mail correspondence; Scott Paulin for sharing his work on the Edmund Wilson–Leo Ornstein collaboration *Cronkhite's Clocks*; Chris Sreeves of the Peter Warlock Society, who directed us to correspondence that shed light on Ornstein in England; Sue Niemoyer for sending, unsolicited, information about an early Ornstein concert; L. Douglas Henderson of ARTCRAFT Music Rolls for sharing his expertise on Ampico; Carol Oja, who encouraged us from the perspective of a scholar who has already done considerable work on Ornstein; Judith Tick and Gail Levin, who first made us aware of the William Zorach portrait of Leo Ornstein that graces the cover of this book; and Jonathan Zorach for permission to use his grandfather's painting.

We are grateful to the Art Institute of Chicago, and especially Aimee Marshall and Sue Meyer, for allowing us to reproduce Leon Kroll's painting, and Norma Marin for sharing her home and recollections of John Marin's relationships to the Stieglitz circle and Leo Ornstein. We appreciated the opportunity to talk with former Ornstein students Andrew Imbrie, Lily Friedman, and Elizabeth Kessler, who helped us understand Leo Ornstein in his role as teacher, and Cedric Elmer, who shared letters and programs from his mother, who was also a student. A number of people in Blue Hill and Deer Isle, Maine, provided information or helped us locate records, particularly Ellen Werner, Executive Director of the Kneisel Music Festival, Christina Shipps, Evelyn and Jan Cook of Stonington, and members of the Deer Isle–Stonington Historical Society and the Blue Hill Historical Society.

We are grateful to a number of musicians who have shared their talents and ideas with us and who have given Ornstein's music new life: Sarah Cahill, Daniel Stepner, Marc-André Hamelin, Joshua Gordon, Jeanne Golan, Randall Hodgkinson, Bonnie Hampton, William Westney, Marthanne Verbit, and Janice Weber. From the beginning, it was their music making that inspired this project.

While authors regularly thank their own families for support both practical and intangible, we must first thank another family without whom this biography could not have been written. Starting in March 1998 and continuing to the present, Leo and Pauline Ornstein's son and daughter, Severo Ornstein and Edith Valentine (and Severo's wife Laura Gould), have been exceptionally helpful in supplying materials, offering hospitality, sharing thoughts, and answering what must have seemed like endless questions. They have patiently responded to phone calls and e-mails, and with grace and humor have endured the lengthy process of our writing their father's life story. Where the active involvement of ones so close to the subject could easily have compromised our work and the outcome of the book, Severo and Edith offered their insights with no strings attached. They accepted our decision not to show them what we had written until the book was in the last stages of production, when things couldn't be changed. They gave us permission to quote from materials and never forbade us access to anything in their possession. We appreciate their trust and hope that upon reading this book they decide it was well placed even if our interpretations of events differ from their own.

The family's involvement didn't stop with Leo's children. Other Ornstein family members including Severo's daughter Jude Ornstein spent considerable time speaking with us about intergenerational family dynamics as she observed them as a child. Holly Carter, Leo's grandniece, shared materials and many hours of her time helping us understand the role that her father, Peter Ornstein, played in the Ornstein revival of the 1970s. Robert Titiev, grandson of Jacob Titiev, spoke with us at length about the extended Ornstein family and helped us piece together his grandfather's journal, which anchors the first chapter. Ben Schwaid, husband of Madeline, who was the daughter of Leo's twin sister Lisa, shared insights regarding Leo's birth date. We have enjoyed working with them all.

Our own families have shown remarkable amounts of interest, patience, and tolerance as we brought our all-consuming biography project to holiday dinner tables and casual phone conversations. We thank them for making room for Leo, and for everything else.

INTRODUCTION: VIRTUOSO ON THE FRINGE

It's 8:00 P.M., Tuesday, March 26, 2002, and the weather in Manhattan is miserable; large puddles of water at curbsides make standing broad jumpers of everyone braving the elements. Umbrellas are helpless against the windy torrents. Despite the deluge, the Miller Theatre of Columbia University at Broadway and 116th is packed with enthusiasts eager to hear a concert showcasing music of the "Hidden Russian Avant-Garde" and to witness the keyboard wizardry of Marc-André Hamelin. No amount of rain is going to dampen their excitement. The hall buzzes amid the distinctive smell of wet wool.

Hamelin is not your ordinary modern touring virtuoso, and the crowd knows that. On the one hand, he continues in the tradition of the nineteenth-century composer-pianist who dazzled crowds with impossible feats at the keyboard. On the other hand, rather than serve up a steady diet of warhorses, and guarantee full houses and a career, the forty-year-old elects to champion "all those musical genies and lepers" who, without his efforts and extraordinary talents, could and do easily slip between history's cracks.[1] Dozens of recordings tell the tale, and tonight's concert continues his mission "to agitate for more music he believes in."[2]

The biggest name on the program is Alexander Scriabin, and Hamelin inspires everyone with his execution of the mystic composer's sixth and seventh sonatas. The music alternately shudders and shimmers. Hamelin is in his element. The rest of the first half of the program consists of the "knuckle-busting" preludes and etudes of Nikolai Roslavets, a turn-of-the-century Ukrainian composer, who in spite of Hamelin's efforts has not yet become a household name.[3]

But by and large the crowd hasn't really come to hear the works of either of those composers; they've come to the Miller Theatre to hear Hamelin take on the music of Leo Ornstein, the Russian-American pianist-composer who, between 1915 and 1920, was the most notorious musician on the American arts scene. It was Ornstein the futurist, Ornstein the anarchist, Ornstein the advocate for all things modern who once again claimed the attention of the audience. Hamelin dedicated his recital to the memory of Leo Ornstein, who had died just the month before at the age of 108.

Why the affinity by the French-Canadian for the music of a Russian Jew born in the Pale more than a century earlier?[4] Backgrounds and temperament stand 180 degrees apart: Hamelin, solidly built, calm, poised, and almost casual; Ornstein, waiflike, intense, artistic, and given to emotional outbursts. Hamelin seeking after fame; Ornstein shrinking from it.[5] But their sense of the piano, its ability to both sing and stomp, and their ability to navigate it with blurring speed and apparent ease make them soul mates. More importantly, Ornstein's music flows from Hamelin's being as if he wrote it himself. For years, Ornstein was alone in possessing the combinations of skills and musicianship needed to perform his original compositions. When he withdrew from a public performing career, his music went with him, much of it not written down, and even more of it beyond the comprehension or patience of other able performers. With Marc-André Hamelin, Ornstein has found someone up to the task of leading the charge. While certainly not the first pianist to advocate on behalf of Ornstein's music, Hamelin's timing, reputation, recording contract with Hyperion, and continuing presence in the public eye have caught the attention of the press, and Ornstein is the beneficiary.[6] It has taken a while, but Leo Ornstein, that early-twentieth-century "bad boy" of music, is back.[7]

III

Where did he go? Why did he suddenly abandon an immensely successful concert career in the mid-1920s? Why did it take so long for his music to reemerge? Would Ornstein have been better treated by history if he'd died young, or at least younger than 108? Did he outlive his own relevance? It is likely that had Ornstein died soon after his meteoric rise to fame (or infamy), or at least sooner than eight decades later, there would have been numerous articles assessing his life, career, and contributions, and more efforts to get his music published and recorded. But Ornstein outlived all of his colleagues and associates, anyone who had experienced first-hand the thrill of one of his concerts. Over the years there was little motivation to track down a person who appeared so determined to remain in the shadows.

Perhaps Ornstein was like a Fourth of July sparkler, brilliant and attention-grabbing, but designed to be short-lived, disposable, merely a moment's experience. Was he one of the twentieth-century's earliest pop phenoms generously granted his "fifteen minutes of fame" by a public that regularly craved novelty? If that were the case, then his obscurity was likely predictable, maybe even deserved.

Questions regarding Ornstein's perplexing disappearance are only part of the intriguing story. Another set of questions surrounds his inexplicable stylistic epiphany, which came to him sometime in 1913. Suddenly the young musician, whose sole claim to fame, like so many other Russian-born pianists, had rested squarely upon his prodigious technical gifts, became the sign and symbol of musical modernism in America, a country that lagged well behind Europe in this domain. With no advance warning, no paper-trail proof, and nothing to explain what happened but vague references to sounds that had come to him out of nowhere, Ornstein began composing and performing solo piano works that rivaled the most dissonant and harmonically advanced pieces by Schoenberg, the most pounding and rhythmically driven works by Bartók. Two concerts in London in 1914, and then a series of four recitals in New York in the winter of 1915, turned audiences on their collective ears: these events made him famous.

What were the circumstances surrounding his change of musical heart? To what degree was his stylistic shift merely a detour in a still-developing aesthetic? After all, by 1916 he had renounced the direction his most extreme works appeared to be taking him. To what extent was the detour driven by sincere aesthetic values? Or was Ornstein a remarkably savvy manipulator of public opinion using what some labeled "antics" to distinguish himself from a thick crowd of touring virtuosi and gather a following of his own?

A final set of questions revolves around Ornstein's personal life and the choices he made there. In 1918, quite without warning, Leo Ornstein married Pauline Mallet-Prevost, a fellow student from Bertha Feiring Tapper's piano studio. She was an extraordinarily sheltered New York debutante, her background seemed completely at odds with Ornstein's own humble beginnings and flashy performing career. How did she impact the course his life took? To what degree did her implacable nature balance his temperamental outbursts? To what degree did her own needs to have Leo all to herself direct the course his life would take? To what degree did Ornstein hide behind Pauline and use her as a foil to extract himself from a life he'd grown tired of? To what degree did he find he'd given up more than he had intended?

The story of Leo Ornstein is larger than an exploration of a single, brilliantly talented pianist who composed. It is the story of the last one hundred years, especially as they were played out in America. It intersects with the stories of millions of immigrants who arrived in the United States in the opening years of the twentieth century. It reveals the power of World War I and the flu pandemic to alter the course of individual lives as much as international boundaries. It records the insidiousness of national hysterias, in this case the Red Scare, that have their roots in political machinations more than citizen sentiment. It is the story of new aesthetic values, modernist ones, appearing on the American scene.

In tracking Ornstein's life we find that he was not alone in 1915 in advocating modern music. Quite the contrary, musicians and artists talked and exchanged ideas early in the century, and he was one of a group of well-placed, like-minded women and men in the arts who worked tirelessly on behalf of the cause. If the International Composers' Guild (ICG) and League of Composers of the early 1920s have gotten the lion's share of credit for establishing American musical modernism, it is perhaps because their members posted mission statements, organized themselves formally, named officers, appointed advisory boards, sponsored concerts, and wrote themselves into history. But Ornstein, bolstered by many of the same people in the late teens, was doing much the same, except he was also on the front line, taking the music, himself, to thousands of eager listeners.

Let us be clear about one aspect of Ornstein's career. While he composed music that clearly deserves hearing today and, as Marc-André Hamelin's concert demonstrated, that can arouse classical music crowds into a frenzy of excitement usually reserved for football games, Ornstein's place within the pantheon of Western composers is circumscribed. He is not, as his wife believed, the greatest composer since Bach, and this study will not try to argue that he was. As a composer he had immense talent, but also serious limitations, imposed in part by his own aesthetic philosophy, from which he never wavered. Yet for other reasons Ornstein was a key figure in the development of American musical modernism, and just how central he was is a story that has not been told. In many ways Ornstein was a man of his time and a man who shaped his time. A typical Jewish immigrant who came to the United States atypically from the salons of St. Petersburg, who struggled for years with uncertainties about his own identity, who at the height of his fame responded in complex ways to World War I and its aftermath, and who became unwittingly a central figure in the anti-Semitic backlash of the 1920s, Ornstein embodied and affected many currents of the first three decades of the twentieth century. This book is not an analytical study of Ornstein's music, although the music will be there. It is a study of early-twentieth-century America, as seen through the life and career of an extraordinary individual.

The story of Leo Ornstein reveals how one person responded to the historic moment. At a time of unprecedented uncertainty and weariness, he promised energy, vitality, and youth. His insistence upon the supremacy of instinct and intuition was a welcome antidote to a world that was teetering on the brink of extinguishing itself using science and technology. In many ways, the very quality of Ornstein's music, so bold and powerful and certain, heightened the disappointment many felt when he turned away and retreated. Like the youths killed in the trenches of World War I, he too seemed to be cut off at the peak of his powers. *Leo Ornstein: Modernist Dilemmas, Personal Choices* explores the ways one man's life and music are inextricably intertwined. And both are mirrors of their age.

Leo Ornstein

FIGURE 1.1. The Avremele Ornstein
family, ca. 1895. Seated: Jacob Titiev,
brother-in-law, Rosa Titiev, Sarah (in
lap), Clara (mother), Avremele (father),
Manus, Paulina. In front, Lisa (twin
sister), Lazar; in back, Aaron, holding
Leo. *Photo courtesy the Ornstein family.*

1 ||| Jacob Titiev's Story

Patching together the early life story of a Russian Jew coming to America at the turn of the century, even one as famous as Leo Ornstein, is no easy task. The disdain for Jews in nineteenth- and early-twentieth-century Russia, and the numerous and successful efforts to eliminate them through a series of pogroms, means that most public records normally available for consultation simply do not exist. There are few birth certificates, records of businesses owned, inventories of personal property, or official accounts of this dispossessed people.

In the case of Leo Ornstein, there is no extant official document that states the month, day, or year of his birth. On the contrary, there are various and contradictory references to his age, which seemed to change depending upon circumstances and memories. It is likely that he was made older than his years to qualify for admission to the conservatory in St. Petersburg. Later on, in keeping with the tradition of eternally youthful child prodigies, he would be identified as younger than his actual years. The only official document we have discovered that illuminates the year Leo was born is a birth certificate for his niece Madeline, the daughter of his twin sister Lisa. The place on the certificate that lists the mother's age establishes her year of birth as 1893. Traditionally, one feels comfortable assuming that twins are the same age, but even this expectation is problematized by another document.

The manifest for the Campania, *the ship that transported the "Gornstein" family from Liverpool to New York in February 1906, lists Ornstein's parents, Abram (musician) and Claire (wife), ages forty-nine and forty-two, and six of their seven children; the oldest daughter, Rose, traveled with her husband Jacob Titiev and their children, and so she is listed separately on the manifest. We can account for Leo's brothers Aaron (who is identified as a pianist), Manus, and Lazar, and his sisters Pauline (gymnast) and Lisa. A nine-year-old "child" named Judka, however, presents difficulties as the Ornsteins had no such child. Additionally, Leo is not listed anywhere. We assume that Judka was the name assigned by the bursar of the ship to the young Leo, who as a child went by the name Leova, which may have been misunderstood as Judka.*

Immigration rules of the time required families to be in possession of $50.00 for each family member twelve years or older who was sailing to this country. As the facsimile of the manifest shows, the Ornsteins presented $300.00 and declared Lazar and Judka to be ten and nine, respectively. Miraculously, Lisa is listed as fourteen, a full five years older than Judka. Given Leo's extremely small stature and childlike visage, it would have been quite easy for him to appear younger than his age. Lisa, on the other hand, an adolescent girl of twelve, may have presented greater difficulties for parents or family members trying to shave off a few years. The rest of the children were much too old to pass for under twelve, and so Lazar and Judka became the two family members under twelve, thus saving the family $100.00. No mention was made of any of the children being twins.

LICENSED OFFICE
Form Line A.

SALOON, CABIN, AND STEERAGE ALIENS MUST
THIS SHEET IS FOR SECOND-CA

LIST OR MANIFEST OF ALIEN PASSENGERS FOR THE U. S.

Required by the regulations of the Secretary of the Treasury of the United States, under Act of Congress appro
Officer of any vessel having such passengers on board upon

S. S. *Campania* sailing from *Liverpool* *Feby 17th 1906*

No. on List.	NAME IN FULL	Age Yrs. Mos.	Sex	Married or Single	Calling or Occupation	Able to—Read. Writ.	Nationality (Country of last per-manent residence.)	Race or People	Last Residence (Province, City, or Town.)	Final Destination (State, City, or Town.)	Whether having a ticket to such final destination	By
1	Broadlane William	24	M	S	Gutter building	Yes Yes	G Britain	English	Rochdale		Yes	Se
2	Bennett Philip		M	S					London	Winnipeg		
3	May E.	46	F				Canada					
4	Behrsen Axel P.	36	M	S	Baker		Denmark	Scandinavian		Rodney 24	No	
5	Byers William	34	M	S	Marine Engineer		G Britain	English	Toronto Can		Yes	Se
6	Clarke Thomas	23	M	S	Iron Mason				Birmingham	N. Y.		
7	Changood Kaji Katia	22	F	S	None		Russia	Hebrew	Kremengag	Vancouver B.C.		A
8	Lincoln	11	M	S	child				Hebrew	Kremengag		
9	Davies John Charles	21	M	S	Carpenter		G Britain	English	Newford		Yes	
10		18	M	S	Solicitor							
11	Donnstein Abram	49	M	M	Musician		Russia	Hebrew	Kremengag	N. Y.		Ka
12	Chane	42	F	M	wife							
13	Aron	23	M	S	pianist							
14	Paul	19	M	S	gymnast							
15	Diana	17	F	S								
16	Lisa	14	F	S								
17	Lazar	10	M	S	child							
18	Judka	9	M	S								
19	Hansen Emma Cath.	19	F	S	none	Yes Yes	Germany	German	Hannover	Merden	No	Se
20	Higham Hugh	20	M	S	Labourer		G Britain	English	Chorley	Philadelphia	Yes	
21	Houghton Davies	22	M	S	Brick Layer				Wigan	N. Y.		
22	Jacobson Philip M.	30	M	S	Merchant		Russia	Hebrew	Libau	N. Y.		
23	Johnstone Sarah	27	F	M	wife		G Britain	Scotch	Edinboro	Seattle		
24	Grace Ethel G.	9 mos	F	S	infant							
25	Kobal Max	20	M	S	Butcher	Yes	Germany	German	Bremen	N. Y.		
26	Lade Charlotte Elis	30	F	S	Lady's maid		G Britain	English	London		No	
27	Lee William Damois	42	M	M	Jeweller				Sheffield			
28	Emily	42	F	M	wife							
29	Linscott John	30	M	S	Jeweller				London	Chicago		
30	Macmaster William	20	M	S	Gardener		Irish	Glasgow	N. Y.		Yes	

* "Race or People" is to be determined by the stock from which they spring and the language they

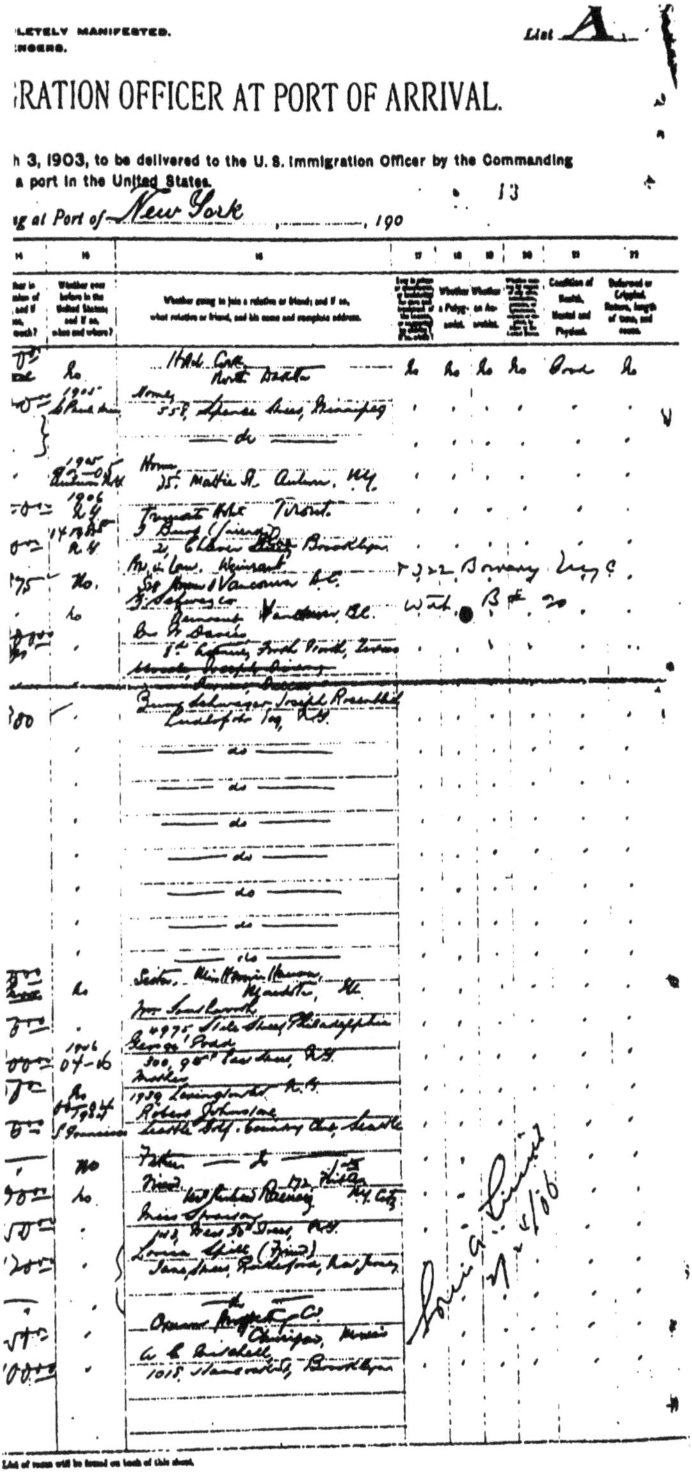

...LETELY MANIFESTED.
...NGERS.

...RATION OFFICER AT PORT OF ARRIVAL.

...h 3, 1903, to be delivered to the U. S. Immigration Officer by the Commanding
...a port in the United States.

13

...g at Port of _New York_ _____, 190

FIGURE 1.2. Manifest
of the ship *Campania*.

The question of Ornstein's age becomes all the more tangled when within two months of arriving in the United States and enrolling at the Institute of Musical Art the nine-year-old is listed as twelve (his real age according to his niece's birth certificate). By this time the "G" of Gornstein has been dropped, and his last name appears on the registration form as Orenstein. This spelling held for a time and is how Leo is listed on Institute recitals from 1907 through spring 1909.[1] By December 1909 the spelling was standardized to what we know it as today: Ornstein.[2] Identity morphed. Thousands of refugees and immigrants poured into the country, many of them with minimal possessions and no trace of their history except that which was burned in their memories.

With these conditions being the rule rather than the exception, the discovery of an account written by one of those immigrants, regardless of when it was created, sends biographers into paroxysms of joy. Its rarity confers special meaning upon the document. In the early 1930s Leo Ornstein's brother-in-law, Jacob Titiev, husband of Leo's sister Rose, wrote such an account. It chronicles the journey of one Jewish immigrant family to America and supplies the only record of Ornstein's years in Russia written by someone who was there with him.[3] We have chosen to have Jacob tell the story in his own words, interrupting him only to clarify or contextualize his remarks.

Jacob Titiev was born in 1877 to a wealthy, land-owning family in the vicinity of Kremenchug. I distinctly remember our big house, which was the main house for some miles. It was separated from a few neighboring little peasant dwellings by a trench surrounding our domain from all sides. Our yard must have taken up a couple of miles. Apart from our big house there were several buildings of very large proportions. There was one house, where in the summer time, there were sleeping quarters for two or three hundred men, and one of about the same size for women. There were stables for an enormous quantity of horses, also for cows, and even a separate stable for sheep, and one for goats. Then there were quarters for chickens and other fowl, one big house being occupied by pigeons. There were also dog kennels for shepherd dogs, and other dog kennels just for watch dogs. . . . My father owned two thousand acres of land, and in the summer time we had about five or six hundred people working in our fields and in the yard.[4]

Jacob's father saw to the education of his offspring by hiring a teacher from the city for [his] brothers and sisters. Jacob, too young for formal schooling, paid full attention to [his siblings'] studies during the week and learned much by overhearing their lessons.[5] His intellectual interests and gifts resulted in being pressed in to the study of the Bible before [he] had reached the ripe age of five![6] The death of his father when he was just five, however, and the dispersal of his family's possessions resulted in a significant change of status for young Jacob and his family. His mother took Jacob and his seven siblings to live with a relative, and Jacob was placed in a school. For the first two terms I was tutored in Krukow, but after that it was admitted by all the teachers of Krukow that they were not able to teach me any further. Therefore, I was compelled to walk every morning, summer and winter, from three to four miles before 8 A.M., and the same distance back again every evening after 8 P.M. . . . This was the only way I could get some instruction.[7] *When Jacob was twelve he was bar mitzvahed.[8]*

Jacob's intellectual gifts were acknowledged by the Kremenchug rabbis who decided that it was time he go to a Yeshibot (that is the highest school of learning similar to a University) and to the best one of its kind. Volosin was the Yeshibot chosen for me because of the head of that institution "Reb Hersh-Leib," who was a great genius.[9] *And so, at just twelve years of age Jacob was sent to Volosin. By his own accounting, he was an exceptional student.* How well I remember my first session when studies began. I was called upon to recite in front of the whole assembly—we were ninety-two in all—and I was the third one called upon. I managed to include as many commentaries as possible, almost without error. When I had finished the Rabbi turned to the class and said, "That is the way I want you all to prepare your lessons, that is to say, it is almost a thorough study."[10]

But his much older classmates had little use for a boy five or six years younger than any of them in their midst:[11] They did not even recognize me, one step out of the Yeshibot. I still was a mere baby to all of them. The result was that I had no one to play with or exchange a word not pertaining to studies. I had no enjoyment of any kind, and I grew morose. I started to hate people. I saw their falsehood. They praised and even flattered me in order to have me prepare the lectures with them, and immediately discarded me as a shameful thing. It came even to the point that I refused to prepare the lectures with them under any consideration. They would come and beg me and entreat me to make friends, real friends, with them, but I noticed that even if they stopped to greet me in the street, they always had an urgent mission to perform—this being an excuse to leave me at once.[12]

Although he was friendless other aspects of his schooling appeared to be going quite well for Jacob until he questioned two apparently contradictory passages in religious texts that had been assigned. When he noted the discrepancy to his teacher, the rabbi reprimanded him severely: Before I even finished my sentence, I received such a smack in the face that I saw stars. And I heard the Rabbi say, "You fool. You must ask no questions." From that time on, I became a perfect non-believer.[13]

Soon after the incident, the head of the school, acknowledging that Jacob was never going to use his Hebrew studies in any professional capacity, encouraged him to pursue Russian, a foreign language for young Jewish children, and then after a while to learn double-entry bookkeeping, thus preparing Titiev for a career in business.[14] Because he and the head rabbi shared great mutual respect and affection, Jacob's lack of religious belief was not an impediment to his staying at the Yeshibot. He mastered Russian. In every way Jacob was a model student. Upon the death of his brother-in-law, however, when Jacob was just fifteen-and-a-half years old, he left his formal studies to support his sister and her three children. Using the skills he had learned, he became the bookkeeper to two merchants in Kremenchug.[15] *Leaving school would be the first of many sacrifices Jacob made to nurture and support his extended family. Later on, Leo Ornstein would benefit from his generosity as well.*

During the next few years Jacob made the acquaintance of Rose Ornstein, the daughter of the Cantor of the Great Synagogue, Avremele Ornstein.[16] *Their courtship was difficult.*[17] *Jacob also met her youngest brother, Leo:* In time I started to notice that Leo—that is one of the twins—was very attentive to music. In fact, on Sunday he climbed up on the piano stool to the piano, and started banging on the keyboard. I noted that if he struck a discord, he kept on trying another and another combination, and that he never stopped on a discord. But if he happened to strike an accord, he kept on striking the same accord many a time. Then he wandered off again and did not stop until he struck a proper accord again. I immediately recognized the genius in him.[18]

At one time Jacob played a tune on the violin for the young prodigy who mimicked it easily at the piano, even creating an accompaniment for the melody. I was like a drunk! When his father and a basso who sang in his chorus for a number of years entered the house, I asked them to keep quiet and to listen to something. I took my violin once more and played the same few simple bars before Leo, asking him right after to play them for me. He did it with the accompaniment! They could not believe it was his own work, as they thought that I had shown him the fingering.[19]

That incident was a defining moment in his life and in Leo's: From that day on, all my attention was concentrated on that child. When he grew up to be five years of age I started to teach him music. Soon enough I felt that he needed really good instruction, and I started to search for a good teacher, against the will of his parents, who used to curse and abuse me, and call me crazy for it.[20] The first teacher I brought him to was the wife of one of our prominent physicians. She was a graduate of Rubinstein's Conservatorium of Music. She declared to me after listening to his playing, "I can not be bothered with such babies!" The next one was the wife of a well-known dentist. She was a graduate of the Moscow Conservatorium of Music. She taught him for about six months, but I did not like the method she used in her teaching. She was lacking expression, which I tried to instill in him from the outset. I changed her for another who was still worse. At that time, there came to our city a very young lady. She was the wife of a captain of a boat. She was a very fine musician. On hearing about her I went with Leo to see her. As soon as she heard him play, I could not take him away from her. The greatest progress he ever made in so short a period of time was under her tutelage. But she soon had to leave town on account of her husband's appointment. Meanwhile Leo reached the

FIGURE 1.3. Avremele Ornstein in
Russia. *Photo courtesy the Ornstein family.*

age of almost seven years. At that time it was announced in the newspapers and by posters that Josef Hofmann was coming for a concert. I decided to have Leo play before Josef Hofmann, and to get the opinion of so great an authority.[21]

When Jacob learned where Hofmann was staying, he convinced the virtuoso to consider listening to Leo. Hofmann responded: If that is the case, take him over to the Concert Hall. There you will find my tuner who is a graduate of Moscow Conservatorium. Tell him that I sent you. Let him listen to the child, and if he will report to me anywhere near what you think, you don't have to worry. I'll listen to him.[22] *Jacob went to the hall and explained that Hofmann had sent them, and* the tuner took Leo up to the piano at once. But the child could not reach the keyboard, so we put our coats on the stool and set him up on top. Then he could reach the piano keyboard all right.[23]

Leo played for the tuner and a nurse who accompanied Hofmann on his tours; before he was done they took our address and promised to let us hear from them soon! We went home and rested up a bit and had some refreshments.

No sooner were we done with our little party than a phaeton—that is a two-horse carriage—stopped near our door and from it there emerged Hofmann's nurse, his manager, and his tuner. All of them were dressed in the height of theatrical fashion. They came into the simple house of my father-in-law to invite us to the concert.

I remember myself blushing like a schoolgirl. I saw the impresario holding tickets and asking me how many there were in the family. I was ashamed to tell him how large a family it was, so I told him a couple of tickets would do.

"Oh! Take a least a half a dozen, you can give them to your friends," he said. "You and the little boy don't need any tickets. When you come in, look for any one of us. We will take you to your place. Mr. Hofmann has ordered two seats to be made on the stage. You and the little boy will sit there because Mr. Hofmann wants the boy to be able to see his hands while he is playing."

I thanked them very much for their kindness.[24]

Leo's attendance at Hofmann's concert would mark the beginning of his eventual move away from home. Towards evening I took the child with me to the concert. As soon as we entered, the impresario met us and took us up on the stage. We sat there the first half of the concert until intermission. At intermission time the impresario came over to us, and rushed us, against my protest that the artist would surely need that time for rest, into a room where we found Josef Hofmann reclining on a couch.

On seeing us enter he turned to Leo and asked "Do you know Beethoven?"

Leo—as a child naturally would—replied, "Yes I do know Beethoven."

Josef Hofmann then took him up on the couch, looked at his little fingers, at the shape of his ears, and in general at his entire appearance. Then, getting up to go back on stage to continue his concert, he said to me, "You and the child had better stay here. The public was devouring the child with their eyes. I'll not close the door, I'll only let down the curtains, so that you can hear everything."

We remained in the room till after the performance. When Mr. Hofmann finished, the applause broke out thunderously and kept up for quite a time.

Mr. Hofmann did not feel like playing any more, but on entering the room he noticed little Leo applauding him and he then turned to Leo and asked him, "Did you like it?"

"Yes. Very much."[25]

"Would you like to hear me play some more?"

"Yes."

"All right, I'm going to play for you!"

He went out and played Mendelssohn's Wedding March. When he came in, Leo was applauding with more vigor than ever.

In the meantime the packers started to take away the piano. On hearing that noise, Mr. Hofmann rang for the impresario. When he came in Mr. Hofmann asked, "Are they going to take away the piano?"

"We must send off the piano at once to Odessa. You have to play there tomorrow evening."

"I'm not going to! I remain here over night!"

"And how about the concert?"

"Are there no cables in Russia? The concert is postponed for one day!"

The public meanwhile had cleared out of the hall. Then Mr. Hofmann turned to Leo and said, "I played for you. Now you have to play for me."

"Certainly," he said, "I'll play."

We all went to the concert room—Josef Hofmann, his nurse, the impresario, the tuner. All sat in the first row.

I went up on the stage with Leo.

Josef Hofmann asked me to have him play the same Beethoven he had played in the afternoon. As he finished Josef Hofmann got up and asked me if I would permit him to test him in his own way.

I said, "Surely!"

He then asked the impresario and me to take Leo in between the two of us and obstruct his vision.

When we did this, Josef Hofmann went over to the piano and struck a chord with all his ten fingers. He asked Leo if he had heard it.

"Yes."

"Can you sing it?"

"Yes." And Leo sang it.

"Release him now," said Hofmann.

We did.

"Go and try to find it on the keyboard."

Leo went over and struck all the ten keys at once.

Josef Hofmann was quite taken by that feat of a child. He then told me, "He has absolute pitch! I would invite you for supper, but it is late. The child must go to sleep. I am sorry I cannot invite you. Put him to bed at once. But tomorrow morning at nine o'clock be sure to be at my hotel. I have something to tell you, and something to give you."

I took the child home. At that time I lived next door to my father-in-law and I brought Leo to my own house, figuring "Why should I wake up everybody. I have a very comfortable place for him to sleep."

Early the next morning, my father-in-law came in cursing me and saying, "That crazy nut, he keeps on dragging the child around."

I said, "Josef Hofmann listened to him play."

"What of it?" he asked. "I'll bet he already forgot that Leo exists."

I, seeing that there was no use in saying anything, left the house.

At nine o'clock sharp I was at the hotel, the Palonira [?]. On entering the hotel, before I reached Josef Hofmann's door, the hotel man told me, "Hurry, he has been looking and asking for you several times. Every once in awhile he opens his door and inquires if you are here."

I rushed on, but before I reached his door he opened it. As soon as he saw me he grabbed me by the arm, led me to a soft chair, and made me sit down, saying "Please be seated. I'll be with you in no time." Then he disappeared into the next room.

In a couple of minutes he reappeared holding in his hand a photograph of himself, near the face of which was written in German, I believe, "I wish you luck in your studies my little colleague." On top of the above writing he wrote, "To Leo Ornstein, Kremenchug," then he dated and signed it.

On handing that to me he said, "Be careful it is wet yet," and then he added, *"This will open the doors of the whole musical world for him!"*

To describe to you people what I lived through in the space of that quarter of an hour or so is physically impossible. My heart palpitated, my eyes were dim, my knees and my hands were shaking, my voice failed me, my head was floating around. In a word I experienced a sensation that is rarely given to earthly beings!

I even forgot to be happy! While I went from the hotel to my office, I stepped in to a picture frame place and ordered an elaborate frame to be made ready in a couple of hours. When I went home for lunch, I first went to the frame maker to get my picture. I took it unwrapped under my coat.

When I arrived home the door of my house was locked. I knew that Rosa . . . must be at her mother's and so I went there too. I found not only the whole family there, but also some members of the chorus. All were in deep discussion of Josef Hofmann's concert, and also of the hearing he gave Leo.

One tenor had hidden himself behind a door, and when all of the public had left the hall, he had sneaked in unseen by anybody to a remote corner of the big hall and from there he had watched all the proceedings of the trial.

The old man still insisted "What of it! I dare say he has already forgotten that a Leo Ornstein exists!"

Just at that point he saw me. "Oh! Here is that crazy nut! Dragging around the child at all hours of the night!"

While he was advancing that tirade, I unbuttoned my coat, took out the photograph and held it up against my breast, without saying a word.

On seeing that, only one exclamation escaped the lips of everyone present!!!

My father-in-law turned crimson red, and purple in turn. He lost his speech for a while.

I still was mum. Not a word did I say. From that time on I found no opposition as to my behavior with Leo. I found myself all wrapped up in Leo and to him I gave all of my time.

At this point Jacob turns away from telling Leo's story and focuses more specifically upon his own progress in business. His story occasionally provides insights into Kremenchug, the town where Leo was born, as when, in passing, he mentions that there were three rabbis in the city of approximately 40,000 Jews. We learn also of the impact of the Russian-Japanese war upon young men, Jacob included, and the various ruses they concocted to avoid military service.[26] Although the near complete absence of dates in Jacob's story makes pinpointing the precise moment of particular activities impossible, Leo next emerges as a central subject in Jacob's narrative what appears to be two years later:

Leo meantime was progressing by the hour. Ossip Gabrilowitch gave a concert in our town. I took Leo to see him. He gave me a letter of introduction to his teacher in Rubinstein's Conservatorium in St. Petersburg, now called Leningrad.

About that time Leo reached the age of nine years. His father then obtained a letter from one of the wealthy men in our town addressed to his daughter, who resided in St. Petersburg. He took Leo to St. Petersburg, where Leo was accepted as a scholarship student in Rubinstein's Conservatorium.[27]

According to the narrative Leo is now safely in St. Petersburg. But extremely disturbing events begin to occur throughout Russia. Jacob's lengthy and detailed account helps us understand why the Ornsteins and thousands of others eventually fled Russia:

At that time rumors started going around that there was going to be a "Pogrom"—that is a massacre of the Jews. One quite often heard it spoken of by peasants, by city bums, and from all kinds of degraded people.

It was on a Friday I believe. A proclamation came out whereby the tzar granted his subjects a Duma—that is something similar to a congress. Students came in to my office, carrying these proclamations, still wet, just off the printing press. The students were dancing, and rejoicing, and were hilariously happy!

I get hold of one of the proclamations and read it carefully. I then said to the students, "I really do not see what you are so happy about. If you would take the trouble to really understand thoroughly what it says in that proclamation, you would see that there is nothing to rejoice about. At any moment it can be turned to a weapon against the people!"

The students laughed at me, saying "You are an incurable pessimist."

About four o'clock in the afternoon a bunch of working people came to the corner of our street, one of them had a whistle. He whistled while the others shouted at the top of their lungs, "Zakrivfai"—that means "close up!"

FIGURE 1.5. Leo in Russia, probably at the time he was in St. Petersburg. *MSS 10, The Leo Ornstein Papers, Irving S. Gilmore Music Library, Yale University.*

Every one started to close their stores or offices. On arriving home I found that my sister-in-law Pauline was not home.

"Where did she go?" I inquired.

"To the Auditorium," I was told.

The Auditorium was a newly constructed building that held a crowd of 6,000 people.

"There will be revolutionary speakers, and she went there to listen to them speak," I was told.

I turned on my heels to go for her.

My father-in-law took his coat. He wanted to go too.

I went there by myself as quickly as my legs could carry me. On arriving at the building I looked inside. It was packed to capacity with people. By sheer luck I recognized my sister-in-law in the crowd. I forced my way in and reached my sister-in-law's arm. I took hold of it, as though with iron bars. I pulled her out by force telling her she must go home at once. I did not let go of her arm for a single moment.

As we turned the first corner from the Auditorium we saw regiments of damn Cossacks coming from every direction towards the building, urging on their horses to make haste. We went home almost on the run.

On our way we passed by the city hall. In the city hall yard we saw the police on horses and on foot filling the big yard. I knew every one of them, and they knew me. Some of them were even seemingly my good friends. Now when I greeted them I received no answer, as though I were a perfect stranger to them.

On seeing that, I urged our company to make haste to reach home, though I did not see what protection home could offer against organized—as you can see—massacre.

Anyway we reached home and closed ourselves in. No body dared to step out that night. In the morning I went to my office. Every one I met on my way was panicky.

I saw on every corner two, three, or four people together speaking in a whisper.

I went over to one of such little groups and in a whisper they told me that last night the Auditorium was surrounded by Cossacks, and police. They let no one go out.

They held a consultation among themselves as to what would be the most advisable way of inflicting the greatest torture to that mass of humanity. Some suggested to spill on the building some kerosene oil and then put a torch to it. Others suggested to bring up a few cannons and demolish the building with all in it by a few shots of the guns. Others again thought it wise and more fun to cut the electric wires off, then let the Cossacks on horseback into the building with blazing swords and let them trample the human mass under the hoofs of their horses, and at the same time cut them with their swords. The last suggestion was the one accepted!!

They cut the electric wires and let their horses go in to the beating of drums. That was to stifle the wild agonizing cries of men, women, young girls and boys that issued forth from that frenzied horror-stricken mob of humanity wriggling in the agonies of death, packed in a comparatively small space, with no way of escape!!!

Many of them were killed. A greater number injured badly. The greatest number of all were the maimed and the insane as a result of the excessive fright that came over them so suddenly, as from a clear sky!

All the people that walked the streets that next day, were like moving shadows. Life had thus left all of us unfortunates, who remained to tell the story. . . .

The Saturday that followed that prominent Friday, dragged through lifeless, and listless. You could feel the calm before the oncoming storm.

On Sunday morning the same kind of feeling, yet somewhat intensified, prevailed. We all walked around in some kind of uncertainty.

At this point Jacob tells of a chance encounter he has with one of his workers, who is drunk. The man recalls what he saw in Mishzenko's wine cellar: "the tzar's portrait with a hole in it. You can go over and see for yourself, if you don't believe me. . . ."

"The Jews shot at the tzar's portrait?" "Yes. I tell you. I have seen the portrait myself."

"I don't believe it."

"But it is there in Mishzenko's."

In that manner he kept on while I felt like dropping to the ground. Then he said, "I am a good friend of yours."

"Yes" I replied.

"You better hide yourself."

"Cross my heart. They are going to rob and kill the Jews. Yes you better hide."

With that he turned away and staggered back again.

How I ever reached home I cannot tell. I had my whole life flown out of me. But I did not lose my presence of mind. The first thing I did on entering the house was to inquire if every member of the family was present. I found two of them missing. I also found a Christian woman hired by my mother-in-law in the house. I made the woman go, paying her off liberally, for work she had not done.

Soon my sister-in-law Pauline—she was one of the missing members of the family—made her appearance.

I went out in the yard with a hammer, and loosened one board in the fence to an adjoining yard. This yard was owned by a man who was the buyer of tobacco for the B. Klerman factory, to which I came as bookkeeper and then shortly was promoted to the full power of attorney. We had always been the best of friends.

In the front building of his yard, that is, the main building—the bottom floor was occupied as an official office of the Cossacks. The top floor of the building was occupied by my friend himself. To him I went, and asked him to take my family in. He at once consented.

I went back to my house through the loosened boards, and sent the family up one by one. The older ones, each one carrying a child with him, crept to the house of my friend.

During that time my oldest brother-in-law Aaron came in on the run. He had been the only member of the family that was missing.

He was just as pale as a wax figure. All his blood was gone. In a word he was just like dead. His first words were, "They are murdering the Jews!!! I have seen one all covered with blood!!! Blood!!! Blood!!!"

He was all shivering. I had a hard time to quiet him and send him off to the house of my friend. At first he could not grasp what I was talking about.

On arriving at my friend's house, I found it filled to capacity with men, women, and children. Filled so that there was no more than standing room for everybody. There in that congestion we stayed for three days and three nights, in constant fear for our own lives and the lives of our wives and children! We heard all the time the drunken masses rejoicing after every noise that came from a big rock hurled into a window breaking the glass! Each crash of a piano thrown down from a third or fourth story, called an outburst of hilarity from the throats of a multitude of drunken beasts!!!

If the children got frightened from these hilarious outbursts and began to cry, we had to stifle the cries and smother them with our hands pressed against their mouths!

We had been forewarned by the officers of the Cossacks, though we paid them ten rubles an hour for having placed a sentinel near the door, that if any outcry should be heard coming from that house, they would not be responsible for the consequences.

So we were living a living death there. At night time I and one of the sons of the owner of the house used to steal out of the house, and through the loosened boards in the fence we used to reach our cellar, where we could find some potatoes and flour.

That was cooked, and everyone could have at least a mouthful to keep body and soul together.

Those drunken bums used to give off from time to time such frightful out-cries that the blood in our veins used to curdle.

At time we could also hear the heart-rending cries of some one of the victims. Everyone wished to be dead rather than to hear those outrages. In fact I know that I had that wish.

So we remained for three long, endlessly long days and still longer nights. I am sure that every one of those present lived through a whole lifetime and more during those cursed three days!!! I could not imagine living to tell the tale.

That state of affairs might have kept up no one knows how long, but the Colonel of the Cossacks was craving very much to be promoted, and now if he proclaimed martial law he would immediately be promoted to the rank of a General. That was why, on the morning of the fourth day, martial law was pro-claimed and posters appeared everywhere on the walls, and the massacre stopped as if by the lifting of a magic wand.

I remember very well that morning after the pogrom. I was absolutely listless. I had no ambition and no desire to move about. I was in a state of inertia. Young men of my own age came running in from the street. They had seen that both of my factories and my store had remained untouched by the dirty hands of the hooligans. They were congratulating me, but I was passive to all their rejoicing. I took the keys of all my places of business and told them, meaning literally every word I said, "If all I have can save the life of a single Jew here willingly do I give away all my possessions to save that single life!!!" And I added, "I am no longer a Russian."

Beginning with the first night after the Pogrom, a series of provocations started, which served as a pretense to take away from the Jew all he possessed. At first posters appeared stating that if the shot of a pistol or gun were fired from any building, that building was to be demolished by a cannon, and the owner of the building was to be fined three thousand rubles.

On that first night two homes of wealthy Jews were demolished under the pretense of a shot being heard coming from the vicinity of those houses. One of these houses was demolished with two living beings in it. No warning was given, that they were going to destroy these houses, and certainly no shots had ever been fired from them. All kinds of the dirtiest sneaky tricks were played on the God-forsaken, miserable Jews![28]

The pogroms of 1905–1906 resulted in an unprecedented surge of immigration by Eastern European Jews to the United States.[29] Although it would take some time for the elder Ornsteins to accept the idea that leaving Kremenchug was very likely their only chance for survival, and while intricate plans had to be made to collect Leo from St. Petersburg, shortly after the massacres began, Titiev started making arrangements for the extended family to sail to America. It is impossible to know how much or what the young pianist knew of the events transpiring in Kremenchug; we have no reports or correspondence. But certainly the journey to America would become part of family lore and Leo's own story as it was repeated over the years. Jacob explains:

At that time my family consisted of three children. My mind was made up to leave Russia for the United States of America. I first spoke it over with my wife who said she was willing to go if her parents consented to go. I started to speak to my father-in-law. He advanced all kinds of arguments for remaining in Russia, the main reason being that there he had a life position of cantor of the main synagogue. How quickly that life could be shortened by a Russian Cossack or a plain hooligan he could not see.

I, on the other hand, actually could not live there any longer. It took me four months to make them see the light; to make them go with us. During those four months not one single night did I sleep through. Life had no more charm for me there! Constant fear for the lives and welfare of beloved ones can drive one crazy.

Business also went topsy-turvy. A customer who was a good friend would come. The first thing he would do would be to look around and see that nothing had been disturbed during the Pogrom. He would say; "Thank God, they have not touched you!"

"No, they did not! Fortunately they stopped breaking into places about four stores away."

"I was robbed to the skin, and what the drunken mob did not take away, they set fire to. In a word they left me and my family plain naked. Fortunately we were hiding in the woods for over a week, otherwise they surely would have killed us. Now I want to start in business again, and I have come to ask you to extend me a credit of a couple hundred rubles."

Now, the reader must know that the man who was speaking already owed me five or six hundred rubles, which were wiped out by the Pogrom. It is true it was not through his own fault, but in regular times that man would have brought me that money or a great part of it which enabled me to pay off my obligations, or buy reserve stamps for the merchandise he himself was taking. But without receiving any cash, I had no possible means to continue my business.

Perforce I had to explain my position to him and why I was compelled to refuse him the credit.

The customer could not possibly see that! All he saw was that he was robbed of everything while I, on the other hand, was not robbed at all, and was simply a heartless creature with whom he did not care to associate.

There were over four hundred customers of mine robbed, owing me any-where from fifty to eight hundred rubles. The loss I had to carry was far greater than my possessions. So not only did I lose everything I had ever earned, but in addition I lost my friends. They would not even speak to me after being refused credit, which went beyond my possibilities.[30]

After four months of hard and constant talk, I succeeded in making my wife's family see that there was nothing left for them in Russia. I paid a sum of over eigh-teen hundred rubles for second cabin transportation for the family. I put them all on a train for Libova, the port from which we were supposed to embark for Hull, England. There they were supposed to await my coming, as I had to finish the liquidation of my business, and then go to St. Petersburg—now Leningrad—to fetch Leo from the Conservatorium.

As we had been told that Russian paper money was valueless in the U.S.A. I changed all my money into gold. We made two wide belts, and filled them with gold coins. One of the belts Rose, my wife, put on, and the other one was put on by my father-in-law.

I gave them, besides, over six hundred rubles as pocket money in case any unforeseen need should arise during their travel, even though all expenses were paid for by the transportation co[mpany]. I then went to St. Petersburg to fetch Leo. At that time no Jew was permitted to enter the city, and if one was caught entering he was sent to jail. Knowing that, I made friends with a couple of soldiers who were also traveling to St. Petersburg. They were returning to their regiments from a furlough. The trains in Russia at that time used to stop even at the smallest stations, for fifteen minutes; and larger ones, for one hour or one hour and a half.

At almost every station I managed to get hungry and thirsty—mostly thirsty, and usually I led the two soldiers down with me to help me drink and eat. In that way we became close friends during the three-day journey. When we were nearing St. Petersburg I said to them, "Do you want to earn five rubles a piece easily?"

"Sure!" was the answer.

"Then," I said, "When we arrive at the station let each one of you take me under one arm, and lead me through the station to the other side. There I'll say goodbye to you, and pay you each a five ruble bill."

They did this with pleasure and once I got out of the station I called an izvogechik. As I jumped in I slipped the bills into the soldiers' hands while saying good-bye to them, and to the driver I said "Drive!" and he drove off in a fury.

The purpose of having the two soldiers lead me through the station was to deceive the gendarmes that were snooping around the station looking for victims. They stopped every new-comer. I was sure that it would be no hardship for them to recognize me as a Jew. I think that it was enough to spot my nose! But being led under the arms by two soldiers in uniforms meant that I was already arrested. In that case they no longer cared.

The fact is that the trick worked, and I entered the city without any trouble.

The izvogechik asked, "Where shall I drive?"

I knew the name of the most important street so I said drive to "Newsky Prospect"!

He did.

After driving on for about an hour, the driver turned again to me asking, "Where do you want me to drive now?"

I consulted my watch and saw that it was a few minutes after eight o'clock. I figured that by the time he would reach the Conservatorium it would be somewhere around nine o'clock, and that that must be the time for Leo to come to the Conservatorium, so I directed the driver to drive me there.

The reason for having him drive me around all the time was that they could not arrest me while driving.

Sure enough, I did not have to wait very long. Leo showed up on the stairs leading to the Conservatorium. I told him my errand, and without entering the building we turned back to the sleigh, and drove up to Leo's rooming place. We took some of his music and some of his clothing, and from there we drove right to the railway station where I bought tickets to Libova. Once you are at the station with tickets to show that you are leaving, they can arrest you no more.

From St. Petersburg we made the next big stop in Vilno. Vilno was one of the biggest Jewish centers in Russia. There we stopped over night.

In the morning after breakfast we went down to a barber shop, as I needed a shave badly. While in the barber shop we heard that all the talk was that they were expecting a Pogrom to break out at any moment. All kinds of frightening rumors were circulating.

Though at first we had intended to walk around a bit and see that ancient cradle of Judaism, we soon changed our minds and went to the train instead. We took the first train for Libova, arriving there about midnight of the second day.

Before leaving the station at Vilno, I had sent a telegram to the transportation company in Libova informing them the exact time of our arrival. Now, on arriving to Libova, we found at the station a man with a carriage awaiting us. We entered the carriage, and the driver started to drive. He drove on for a long while, till we passed the whole of the city.

Somewhere not far from the waterfront he stopped, near a peculiar building surrounded with a brick wall about eight or ten feet high. We stopped near a door covered with iron. It looked just like an old time prison!

"Here you are," called out the driver, stopping his horses.

I looked out of the carriage and noticed the glass spread around that God-forsaken place. Even in the night time you could easily single it out from any other human habitation. I could not imagine it to be a second cabin resting place, and I doubted the driver's honesty.

I told him then, "Make open that door, or else drive us back to the station."

The driver started to put up an argument saying that he was not supposed to drive us back!

But I had in my hands my walking stick made of Japanese black wood. It has the weight of iron, if full of knots, and if you strike somebody with it, once is enough, you don't have to repeat it. . . .

I lifted my stick, saying to him harshly, "Do as I say and I'll pay you for it. Or else!!!"

Seeing that I meant to enforce my orders with the stick, the driver went down, and with the handle of his whip he started to pound on that iron-covered door. Every blow resounded in the quietness of the night like a cannon shot!!!

It took quite a while, but at last the rusty hinges gave out a shrieky sound. The door opened and out came a woman resembling the best description of a witch, with yellow disheveled hair, half-closed sleepy eyes, and an open bosom, from which were protruding two enormous breasts. Her face and body were besprinkled with large-sized freckles, and she held a burning candle in her hands.

"What is all that commotion for?" she asked.

Then I stepped forward and asked her if the Ornstein family was stopping there.

"Sure, sure, they are, and they are waiting for you," she said. "Come, I'll lead you to them."

She went on, and we followed her all the way through the house that was overfilled with human bodies spread out all over the floor, most of them half naked. Men, women, and children in such a chaotic state, that it surpasses all imagination. Legs, legs, and more legs, everywhere, and one had to be somewhat of an acrobat and a juggler to go through that human mass without stepping on someone! In addition there was such an unbearable stench, that it made me rush ahead with all my might, the quicker to get out of it!

Well, somehow we walked through the house till we reached the yard. In the yard there was a wooden staircase. On that staircase, she went up to the very roof. There was a door leading to an unfinished attic. There our family had found an abode. They were all lying on boards supported by wooden horses, or on boxes. On top of the boards were straw mattresses.

On my entering that improvised sleeping chamber, everyone cried out, "Bend down, bend down!" I did so without knowing why. But soon enough I found out the reason. The attic being an unfinished one, had rusty ugly long sharp nails sticking down from the roof, and if you didn't bend down they might penetrate your scalp or blind you!

That was the place for which I had paid somewhat over eighteen hundred rubles for transportation!

"Are there no hotels in the city?" I asked my father-in-law.

"The hotels are all taken up," he told me.

The remainder of the night passed away in conversation, and eating because they all seemed to be famished, and I had brought with me from Vilno, delicious wurst, pastrami, and salami. I had brought a large quantity of food but they were so hungry that they finished it all up right there and then.

The next day, early in the morning, I got up and taking with me a couple of my brothers-in-law went strolling to see what kind of a city Libova was.

We had not walked more than a couple of blocks when I saw an impressive hotel. I went in and asked the proprietor if he had any rooms to let.

"Yes." He said. "Come in and I'll show them to you."

He took me into a very large beautiful light room with two enormous beds in it and then showed me another one just like it.

I asked him the price. He said, "Two rubles a room per day."

I immediately hired the two rooms, took the keys with me, and returned back to the family. I told them that I hired two spacious beautiful rooms, and asked them to come with me. Here only the truth started to come out. My father-in-law suddenly got a notion that he wanted a Kosher place. That means a place where the food is prepared strictly according to the orthodox traditions. It was on account of him that the family had been placed with all the steerage passengers. Now, after my finding such lovely quarters, he refused to go there.

I left the old couple to enjoy their Kosher filth, and took all the children away to the hotel. It is hard to describe the happiness of the children when they entered such cheerful bright rooms, after that gloomy, unlit, unfinished attic. It was worth anything to see, with what kind of appetite they devoured the food served on immaculately clean linen, with shining silverware.

The manager of the transportation company came to see me and took over all the hotel bills on his own account. He also returned to me one ruble and twenty-five kopecks per day for each member of the family, this being the difference between second and third cabin. He told me that he had wanted to place the family on a second cabin footing, but the old man had insisted on Kosher, and that was the only place that kept strictly orthodox Kosher rules.[31] We stayed there four more days, during which time the transportation company was rigging up a vessel for us to go to Hull, England. As the vessel had no special quarters for second cabin, they fixed up one, by dividing our compartment from the rest of the passengers. They tried in every way to be nice to us, to make up for the poor quarters allotted to the family before I came.

Even in buying the provisions for our three days' journey, they showed great care. They bought food and fruit enough to feed a regiment a whole week, and everything was of the best obtainable!

The storage room where all the provisions were kept had a door opening into our quarters, and the door was never locked. Therefore I had free access to it at any time during the voyage. Seeing that our people were all seasick and could not enjoy any food, I used to take out of the storage room quantities of fruit and other food that was prepared for our party but which remained untouched by any member of our family, but me and the small children; and bring that food over to the third cabin passengers who used to gobble it up in a jiffy!

At this point in the narrative Jacob catches himself getting ahead of actual events, so he backtracks and takes readers through the experience of leaving Libova, Russia, which occurred prior to sailing for the United States from Hull, England. According to Titiev, this first journey was literally, but more importantly emotionally the real departure from Russia!

How others of the extended family understood, experienced, or interpreted all that Jacob recounts is not clear. Readers already know of the elder Ornstein's initial reluctance to leave Kremenchug, and their eventual consent. For Leo, who had been separated from his family and the events in Kremenchug for perhaps as many as two years, and who had been enjoying life as a young darling of St. Petersburg's salon society, Jacob's appearance at the conservatory doors might have appeared less a rescue than a kidnapping.[32] Over the course of those two years, while Jacob was becoming increasingly estranged from Russia and from the Jewish community, Leo was learning about Russian culture for the first time. The St. Petersburg Conservatory was a bulwark of Russian musical achievement. He learned the language and heard chant at the Russian orthodox churches in the city. His later identification with and championing of Russian composers suggests a different relationship to his native land than Jacob enjoyed. It is therefore quite possible that Leo did not share all of Jacob's enthusiasm about leaving and may even have found it a source of distress. Even so, the young pianist could not possibly have anticipated the life that awaited him in the United States or the fame that would be his a mere ten years after his Atlantic voyage. And much of that was directly attributable to the actions of Jacob Titiev. Titiev's description of the family's exit from Russia follows:

It was on a gloomy drizzling day that our departure took place. In the morning, around ten or eleven o'clock, carriages came to take us to the sea shore. There they put us all into a dreary unheated barn that was giving way to the fancy of the wind outside. Police officers were mingling with the crowd, and spotting one of higher rank I took him aside, and shoved into the palm of his hand a few rubles telling him that I had the passports of all the members of our family, and that it was absolutely useless to keep the women and children in the cold. I asked him to let them go into the boat, while I with all the passports remained in the bureau as long as necessary.

It worked just like money would on any servant of the law at that time in Russia, under the leadership of the czar. They let all the family in on my say-so without counting them or verifying by the passports that they were the ones described and named in the documents. I could have smuggled through several others if I had had them there. I really regretted the fact that I had nobody to smuggle through.

The day, as I said before was very gloomy, and a storm was brewing. It seemed to be gathering strength from time to time as the day progressed. I, being a privileged character was allowed not only to stay in the doorway of the bureau, but even to walk out of the bureau entirely, which I did. I walked over to a nearby grocery store and bought a freshly baked small bread and a small box of sardines. Then I walked over to a government liquor store and bought a "Monopolka"—that is a very tiny bottle of vodka, which contains only one drink. It used to cost only six kopecks. In this way I prepared to have a bite as soon as I entered the boat, because I was actually starving. Meanwhile the storm was raging. The waves were increasing in their velocity and strength. It was nearing night when the bribed officer came over and asked me to show him the passports. He tore out the parts that had to remain on record, shook hands with me, and let me go in.

By that time the waves were surely four stories high! I saw them reaching up a stone wall, with a fury that could demolish anything but a stone wall! It was really a stunt to walk on a couple of boards for about two hundred yards with the wind tugging at one's clothes without any mercy.

Only by unusual luck no accident happened to me while walking up the plank. As soon as I entered—I was the last to enter the boat—the sailors pulled up the anchor and the boat started to shake and dance in a great horrible frenzy. I only had time to uncork the Monopolka, and to open the sardines. But no sooner did I place them on the table than the whole boat went topsy-turvy, and the Monopolka as well as the sardines and the bread landed on the floor under a bench on the other side of the boat. That was the end of a perfect foodless day for me, in addition to being all the day through almost eaten up by a dreary cold.

One of my brothers-in-law, who always tried to show himself heroic offered to play a pinochle game with me. But he could go no further; he became as pale as a ghost, and I had to assist him to his bunk. They all got sea sick at once, and I had my hands full attending them, running around from one to another, trying to hold up their heads, or trying to give them some water. I was the only one of the grown-ups not affected.

When a little lull came, my mother-in-law said to me, "You must be starved."

I said, "Yes, I am. But I am afraid to eat. Everyone is vomiting!"

"Don't be foolish. Eat as long as you have a desire for it," she said.

I went over to the chef and asked him if we were going to have supper. He said "No! because everyone on the boat is sick." But he gave me something to eat. He made up a tremendous sandwich of black bread, and filled it with assorted cuts of meat. I relished every bite. When I finished that sandwich my mother-in-law asked me if I was still hungry.

I admitted that I could do away with one more sandwich, but that I was in real fear of getting seasick. She again told me not to be foolish, and if I felt like eating, I should. Once again I went to the chef and got another sandwich from him. That appeased my hunger.

Of all the people that suffered seasickness, my wife was the worst. She really almost passed out. The captain and I carried her out on deck, placed her near the chimney and covered her with all the fur coats I could get hold of, and still she was shivering! I sat through the whole night with her. All of the three days of our voyage she suffered.

On the fourth day, in the morning, we arrived at Hull. As soon as we landed splendid carriages were awaiting us, and they brought us to a magnificent hotel where a long table was set with fresh flowers, and an army of uniformed waitresses were lined up to give us service. Soon we had a delightful repast. Every body ate with a very good appetite. They forgot about the sea-sickness entirely.

While we were eating, the Rabbi and a delegation of Jewish citizens came to greet us. They walked us to the station, where we took a train for Liverpool. That same day towards evening we arrived at our destination. There again carriages were awaiting us. My wife, our children, and myself entered one carriage, the rest of the family were taken in other carriages.

We were brought to a first class hotel where at the time of supper a small band was playing and several artists were performing some lovely dances. Right after supper I inquired about the other members of the family. The answers I received did not sound right to me. I insisted on being led to the place where they were. After a long and persistent demand on my part, we were taken to see them.

Again we came up to an iron-covered door, built into a high brick wall, just like a prison. The door was unlocked by inserting a twelve-inch key into it. We found them just as they had finished their supper, which had consisted of three-cent boxes of sardines and boiled potatoes.

The tables that were numerous in that basement, consisted of long boards, supported by wooden horses, covered with spreads that had not seen a laundry for the last three or four months, or may be still longer. From the ceiling was dripping a dirty moisture, yellowish in color. I knew immediately whose work that was so I did not even question anything, but I was provoked to the quick. All that was missing was to have some member of the family take sick. From such filth we could easily fall sick. I turned to the man from the company and said, "Get us out of that prison." The man did not feel like letting us go.

I repeated my request, adding, "If you don't do it at once, I'll do it myself, by first knocking your stupid head off with that stick of mine!!!"

My mother-in-law, knowing my temper, quickly grabbed my arm, meanwhile imploring me to quiet down. The man representing the company understood that I really meant business so he thought it best to unlock the door for us, and to let us go free.

The similarity of this account to the earlier one may call into question Jacob's memory. Is he conflating both experiences, or did his father-in-law's actions, as he implies, result in two comparably unpleasant situations for the Ornsteins? Regardless of the accuracy of the particulars, it becomes clear that there are significant differences between members of the traveling party, and these will continue when everyone gets to America. While Jacob appears to get along well with his mother-in-law and easily follows her advice, his opinion of Abraham Ornstein is none too high, and he takes advantage of every opportunity to point this out. Now, having bullied his family's way out of prison-like lodgings, Titiev sets about finding them better accommodations. Jacob never explains why the transportation company seemed intent on cheating him out of what he had paid for, so readers are left to imagine.

At once we started out in search of a hotel. We passed by three hotels but we found them all claiming to be filled up. But I also noticed that a uniformed man from the transportation company was preceding us into every hotel. On seeing that trick I thought "Well, I'll outwit you."

I told my people to proceed at a very slow rate of speed, on the same street, without turning off. I myself and one of the boys went down a side street.

As soon as we saw a hotel we entered. I asked for one large room with two big beds. I was shown to such a room. I hired it, paid for it, and took the key with me. We ran quickly to catch up with our people, and led them to the hotel. We slept there over night as best we could.

The next morning, early, the manager of the transportation company came over to our hotel. I gave him what was coming to him, for leading them to a concentration camp and then trying to detain me there too! He again paid me the difference in rate between second and third class, he also paid me for the hotel, and he took us all back to the same hotel where my family and I had had supper the previous night. They had everything Kosher for the old couple right there. Later on in the day the head Rabbi came to visit us. We had to stay there until Saturday.

On Saturday the biggest boat of that time, the Campania, was leaving for New York, and we as second cabin passengers left the shores of England for the coveted Golden Land.

It is while sailing to America that Leo reappears in the narrative.

The ocean passage was a delightful thing for me, and the young children. Not so well did all the adults of our family fare. Most of the time, they were in their bunks sick. I found a piano in the first cabin salon. I asked the captain's permission for Leo to practice on the piano. My request was granted with pleasure. The captain, on finding out about Leo's playing, asked me if I would permit Leo to play a concert, the proceeds of which should go to a fund for widows and orphans of sailors lost at sea. I certainly consented to Leo's playing for such a worthy cause. The concert was announced for Wednesday night.

On that Wednesday towards evening the ocean became very stormy, to such an extent that the captain ordered all the doors leading to the platforms to be closed. No passengers were permitted to pass out of any door. I saw men and women trying to get up the iron stairs from one floor to another, and on nearly reaching the top of the staircase they fell down to the ground.

In one parlor, two elderly gentlemen were sitting and playing chess on a specially devised little table, which was attached to the floor of the boat by iron bolts. The boat was shaking so badly that the table's iron legs broke, and one of the two old men started to roll and could not stop himself until he reached the opposite wall.

My son Oscar held a banana, and while the boat shook fiercely he dropped it. He tried to catch it, but every time he put his hand over it, the boat shook anew and the banana would roll away a couple of feet. He had to follow it. He did not succeed in catching it, till he landed at the opposite wall under a bench. It was very amusing to see all these performances.

The time of the concert came and the storm was raging with such enormous strength that they had to rope the piano to the wall of the salon and the piano stool had to be roped to the piano; and with all that, both the piano and the stool were sliding around on the floor, and Leo with them.

Almost all of the passengers were sick. Only about thirty people were able to attend the concert. Though so few people attended the concert, the donations reached two hundred and forty two dollars. Leo's playing was superb.

Nothing more of great importance happened to us during the voyage.

Jacob's proprietary attitude toward Leo, which was first evident in relation to finding Leo a suitable teacher, and then the meeting with Josef Hofmann years earlier, emerges again. By "consenting" to the concert, Titiev wasted no time positioning himself as Leo's champion cum agent. What Leo's parents thought about the concert, or whether they were even consulted, remains unknown. According to Titiev's account, once the Campania landed, it was just a matter of days before he made arrangements for Leo's musical studies in America. According to the Institute's records, Leo began his studies in April 1906, two months after the family disembarked.

On arriving at New York we were met on Pier 51 surely by three hundred people. The people came to meet us because about two weeks before our arrival it was announced in the Jewish press that we were due to come to New York. We were let off at Pier 51 while the boat took all the rest of the passengers to Ellis Island. *Such special treatment was likely the result of Leo's concert for sailors' widows and orphans, and Titiev's ingratiating himself and the young prodigy to the captain. Ship captains could use their discretion and allow those in his favor to be processed onboard ship, thereby eliminating the need for the regular processing at Ellis Island. This would account for no records of the Ornstein family's entry into this country at Ellis Island.*

Among those that came to meet us was my wife's cousin Nadya and her husband Benny Giventer—who is now Dr. Giventer, Superintendent of one of the biggest hospitals in Boro-Park, New York.

They hired temporary rooms for us on the corner of Ave. C. and Seventh St.

We also found a ready cooked supper on the stove.

The rooms were furnished with beds, tables and chairs.

We came as though we left home for some vacation, and then returned home again.

But we were very tired from the ocean trip.

So on arriving, we went early to bed.

Jacob tells of his first morning in New York and his attempt to negotiate Manhattan's elevated train system without speaking any English. Taking Leo with him "for company sake" he wandered for hours in search of Eighth Avenue and 114th Street to deliver a letter entrusted to him by the man who had sheltered the family during the pogrom in Kremenchug. While the two walked many extra miles and hours than were necessary, they eventually

found the address. Jacob quickly learned the necessity of knowing the language. Having
dispatched with this errand his next task was to see to Leo.

During that first week Jacob sought out "the best institution of music for Leo," purchased
a piano for his practice, "the first object bought by me on this soil," and "on the tenth day of
my being in this country, . . . took Leo, and . . . went to 14th St. and 5th Ave.," the address
of Frank Damrosch's newly established Institute of Musical Art. The lengthy excerpt that
follows offers a glimpse into Leo's first musical experience in America and Jacob's role in
bringing it to pass.

On ringing the bell a negro appeared.

He said something, I don't know what.

But the motion of his hand meant to me to enter, and so we did.

Several of the people in there went up to us.

They all tried to understand us, and to make themselves understood.

But in vain.

Till one lady started to speak German.

Her, I understood perfectly, and to her I told that I want to see Mr. Frank
Damrosch.

She told me to be seated, he is due in another ten to fifteen minutes.

It did not take long and Mr. Damrosch made his appearance.

The German-speaking lady went up and related to him all about us, offering
her services as interpreter, but Mr. Damrosch dismissed her, telling her he will
attend to us himself.

When we were left alone Mr. Damrosch started some inquiries, and being
told the exact purpose of my errand, he explained to me, that here is not like in
Russia.

In Russia when one is extremely talented the Government pays his tuition.

But here are private institutions, and everybody is supposed to pay his or her
own tuition, and seeing that Leo is talented he needs all kinds of subjects like:
harmony, solfeggio, counterpoint, and languages, his tuition would run up to
about $1,600 a year.

"Well" I said, "It seems to me that in America geniuses have to take great care
to be born only into millions, otherwise they must be lost. . . ."

He got kind of colored in his face, and asked me:

"Do you really think him so great?"

"Would I dare to approach you, if not?"

"What does he play?"

I took out a long list of over one hundred composers, and showed to him.

On seeing the list he said: "That is more than I can do! Does he play anything
of Tchaikowsky?"

"Sure, What would you like to hear of Tchaikowsky?"

FIGURE 1.6. Frank Damrosch. *Photo Courtesy Music Division, The New York Public Library for the Performing Arts, Astor, Lenor and Tilden Foundations.*

"The Autumn."

I could not understand what the word Autumn meant.

He then explained to me in German that he wants him to play "die Herbst."

I then said to Leo in Russian: Play for him Tchaikowsky's "Autumn." But play so that all the devils should take a hold of him.

Leo said: "I understand!" And he started to play.

Damrosch could no longer sit in his place.

He got up, and on tip-toe he went over to the piano.

He stood there motionless till Leo finished.

Then he turned around towards me, and by sign he let me know, that it is grand.

He went back to his desk, took Leo on his lap, and asked me a few questions about Leo.

Took my address, and told me "you can go home now."

"I'll call a meeting of the directors, and I'll get in touch with you soon."

We went home, and had our lunch.

No sooner did we complete our repast, than a negro came with a letter.

Not being able to read or speak English, I motioned to the negro to sit down, and I went to canvas all the tenants of the five story apartment we lived in. In an effort to find any one person who could read and translate to me the contents of the letter.

I succeeded in finding a young lady, who was able to read and translate the letter to me.

It said that I should take Leo with me to the Institute of Music Damrosch at once.

A carriage is waiting for us down stairs.

That was the only time in my life that I did ride in a carriage where the driver sits in the back, and drives the horse over our heads. . . .

The streets all around were kind of deserted a couple hours ago, no sign of life was seen for blocks around.

Now the same neighborhood was all bristling with life.

All kinds of cars surrounded the building for blocks and blocks away.

You could not recognize it as the same place at all.

The doors of the Conservatorium spread wide open, and Mr. Damrosch met us at the door with outstretched hands, he welcomed us into his office, there he told me, that the directors are assembled in the concert hall, where we shall proceed.

On arriving there, I shall go up with Leo on stage, in order he should not get frightened, and make him play the same "Autumn" by Tchaikowsky.

So we did, and when he finished a thunderous applause broke out.

Mr. Damrosch tried to quiet the applause, but it was impossible.

On parting Mr. Damrosch told me that Leo is accepted, and I'll hear from them very soon.

This is how I placed Leo in Damrosch's Conservatorium, and I was completely forgotten by Leo, and especially by his father, who used all his influence to make him forget me.

Jacob's narrative details the steps he took helping Abraham secure a position as a cantor, and then his own varied experiences finding employment and eventually establishing himself in business. On the way we learn of Jacob's fluency with a number of languages—Russian, Yiddish, Hebrew, German, although English was not among them—and his seemingly indefatigable energy, which he directed at carving out a place for himself in his new country. Titiev's difficult relationship with Leo's father appears as a rondo theme throughout the story influencing the events he reports and the tone of their telling, but he seems not to miss an opportunity to remind readers of the deepening divide that grows between the two men. No dates are given for the incident that follows, but one may assume that it occurs sometime in spring of 1906 after the family had been in the country for several months. It sets up conditions for later events. We've edited Jacob's telegraphic and fragmentary English prose to aid comprehension:

The Ornsteins, as soon as my father-in-law signed a contract with one of the congregations that were after him, moved out of the house one day while I was at the shop, taking away all the furniture, [thus] leaving my wife, and the children without even a single chair on what to sit! Though he got that position through my efforts and money.

Given the likely size of their quarters and the number of people trying to live there together—five in Titiev's family, and perhaps as many as eight in the elder Ornstein household—it seems reasonable that Abraham would want to find lodgings for his own family just as soon as he was financially able to do so. In addition the elder Ornstein's preference for a kosher household, and Jacob's avowed atheism and secular interests, would have made cohabiting extremely difficult for both men.

A number of years pass before Leo and his family appear again in Jacob's story. Leo has been studying with Mrs. Thomas Tapper at the Institute of Musical Art in New York City where, after his graduation, she is preparing to take him to Vienna to play for her teacher, the world-famous pianist and pedagogue Theodor Leschetizky. Although the full story is impossible to piece together, in what appears to be a misunderstanding Jacob receives a panicked phone call from the Ornsteins informing him that Mrs. Tapper wants to adopt Leo. (In the spring of 1910 Leo would have been sixteen, although given the confusion about his birth date it is possible some people thought he was much younger.) According to the narrative, Jacob untangles the mess to everyone's satisfaction. Although he provides no dates for these events, we know that Leo played for Leschetizky sometime in the summer or fall of 1910, and he performed with the Volpe Symphony on March 5, 1911. Titiev's account compresses the time frame, making it sound as if the series of events occurred in close succession. In reality, they must have been spread over a period of almost ten months.

One evening on coming in to the drug store to work, [*Titiev by this time had become a pharmacist*] Mr. Giventer said: "There was a telephone call for you."

"For me?"

"Yes."

"From whom was the telephone [call]?"

"From the Ornsteins" he said.

"What do they want?"

"Oh, there is trouble. They want to adopt Leo."

"Who wants it?"

"His teacher. A Mrs. Tapper. They are all crying. It is there, just like a funeral!"

"Well," I said, "If that is the case, you will have to work yourself tonight. I have to go there."

"Are you crazy?" He said. "Haven't you got enough of them yet?"

You must not forget that man Benny [Giventer] was related to them.

I said: "It concerns Leo, and I must go there!"

"You crazy nut, I ought to split your head! Go, Go to hell!!!"

I went.

On entering the Ornstein apartment, Leo and his sister Pauline fell on my shoulders crying.

"They want to tear the family apart."

I asked them to stop their crying, and tell me coherently what is happening.

Leo brought out the adoption papers. I looked over a part and asked Leo for the address of Mrs. Tapper. As soon as his father heard that, he came in to the room saying: "Oh, he'll go and quarrel with her and spoil the whole thing!" I said, "All you can do is go with me."

It is high time to remind the readers that from the moment I placed Leo in the Damrosch Conservatory the old man pulled him away from me with all his might. Therefore I never met his teacher Mrs. Tapper.

Mrs. Tapper lived in the exclusive Riverside Drive section. Aside from being the wife of the editor of Philadelphia's newspaper the *Ledger*, who is a millionaire, she had millions of dollars of her own.

When we reached her home my father-in-law being acquainted with her was asked to sit down. I remained standing near the door.

He did not introduce me.

Mrs. Tapper started to ask him what brought him there?

He, not being able to speak English, started to mumble incoherently, pointing towards me.

I, seeing that he is not able to make himself understood, spoke up. I said, "We come here about the adoption papers."

She took me to be a lawyer, therefore she disregarded me [completely].

She turned again to my father-in-law. "Who is that man? I don't know him at all!"

I answered, though I have not been spoken to at all. I said:

"I'll tell you who that man"—meaning myself—"is! I am the man who recognized Leo from [the] cradle as a genius! I brought him before Josef Hofmann when he was not quite seven years old and got him his picture, [which] you surely saw. I had chosen all his teachers. I took him from the steps of the Rubinstein Conservatorium and brought him here where I placed him in Damrosch's Conservatorium, where you found him!!! Now as I understand, he needs to go for accomplishment to Vienna to Leschetizky! I can take him there without any-body's aid at all!!!"

During my narrative Mrs. Tapper got as pale as a ghost. She got up from a piano stool she was sitting on, [and] stretched her hand out to me, saying: "I am Mrs. Tapper and am very glad to know that Leo has one like you. You can easily understand I could not entrust him to a thing like that"—pointing to my father-in-law.—Then she asked me: "Have you got the papers?"

"Yes" I said.

She said: "Change in it anything you want, I'll sign it."

I said: "I am sorry. I know nothing about law. But if you permit me to have the papers till tomorrow about noon time, I'll have everything changed to your satisfaction, except adoption. If it is money, I'll put it the way you want."

She started to laugh. "I don't need any money, I have more than I am able to use.

"All I want is to be the recognized teacher of his. That is all I am after."

"Alright" I said, "I'll see you tomorrow at about noon time."

The next day around the noon hour I had the papers changed already. I come to my father-in-law saying: "Well the papers are ready. Come with me." He then said: "Go! Go! She will throw you down all the stairs."

"All right." I said. "To be thrown down the stairs I have to go! But to receive the applause, there is where you come in! I know that well enough!!!"

On seeing Mrs. Tapper, she asked me to make an appointment with her to go and meet Mr. Arthur Brisbane, editor of all the Hearst newspapers. We arranged there for a tea party to be held at the house of Mr. Brisbane's fiancée, in Cedarhurst, N.Y. at which Leo is to play.[33]

While Leo was playing, Mr. A. Brisbane and myself were closeted for one hour and one half in their library, and Mr. Brisbane was jotting everything I told him about Leo.[34] He then wrote out three editorials out of what I have been tell-ing him.

He also made my acquaintance with Beatrice Fairfax, who wrote five full pages in the society column from what I have told her.[35]

Then we hired the New Amsterdam theatre. I also hired the Volpe Symphony for a concert with Leo, at which concert more than two thousand people were turned away.[36]

Whether it was the Volpe Symphony concert in March 1911, or an earlier one, Jacob's description of Leo's nervousness about going on stage, which follows, became part of the early

Ornstein legend. As the excerpt demonstrates, Titiev's chronology is often not particularly reliable.

But to get a clear idea of Leo's nervousness, and what I had to go through I must give you a slight description of what happened. In the first place for a few days before the concert, I had to go with Leo to the theatre to hear him rehearse, and creep around in the galleries, to every corner of them, and listen to the sound, how [it] carried, if the piano is sounding in different places. Then to rehearsals with the symphony. At last the very day of the concert arrived. Leo became frantic. About three hours before the concert he was already dressed and started to rush me to go to the theatre. When we arrived to the theatre, he wanted to go away. I suggested that we go in, in some restaurant in the vicinity of the theatre, and order some tea or coffee, and sit there and talk for a while. We walked for a while then he spotted a restaurant and said: "Let us go in here."

We went in, and I ordered tea and some cookies, that is what he said he wanted to have.

But before the waiter returned he wanted me to pay for it. Not to have it! But to go away back to the theatre.

In the theatre he found back stage under a pile of dust, an old upright piano, and wanted to practice on it. I got some water and towels. I cleaned it a bit, then spread out towels over the keyboard and let him practice on the towels.

About one half an hour before the appointed time, he started to nag me, that he wants to go out already to play. Naturally I did not let him. But when the time came to go out, he refused to go! No coaxing could persuade him to go. I got somewhere a whisk broom and told him that he was all in cobwebs—which was a truth—and I started to brush him, and turn him around. All that I did right near the opening to enter the stage, and when I had him facing the stage, I gave him a strong push. He found himself at once in the midst of the symphony players, and the applause broke out thunderously. He could not back out. So he went right straight to the piano and started to play. The concert was performed most beautifully. We cleared, after paying all the expenses, $4,800.00. With that money he went to Vienna for accomplishment, to Mr. Leschetizky. There he remained for a period of about four years. During that time he played before a number of crowned heads of Europe. He got contracts to play in Europe for two years. During that time, I never heard of him.

In truth, Leo Ornstein went to Europe in the summer and fall of 1910 for no more than a few months. A second trip, begun in summer of 1913 and lasting through April 1914, was the last of his sojourns to the continent. Neither one was a concert tour. Leo's final appearance in Jacob's autobiography recalls a time following his return in 1914, and after plans for a lengthy European tour had been canceled by the outbreak of World War I.[37] It will be taken up in a later chapter.

Jacob's account, even with its clear biases, missing dates, and occasionally questionable data, provides insights into the conditions and events of Leo Ornstein's early life that are unavailable anywhere else. Readers get a taste of the kinds of experiences shared by hundreds of thousands of immigrants, and a glimpse of the rare opportunities enjoyed by an extraordinarily gifted young musician in Russia at the end of the nineteenth century. Leo was at the center of a large family, many of whom harbored their own desires for his development. This situation would be duplicated in the years that followed as his teacher, and numerous writers, critics, agents, friends, and family members, attempted to shape the pianist-composer to suit their own agendas and needs.

2 ||| From Institute to Bandbox

In February 1906 when Ornstein and his extended family arrived in New York City, it was just four months after the Institute of Musical Art had opened. The Institute was the realization of a long-held dream of its founder, Frank Damrosch, who with his father Leopold, the conductor, his mother, Helene von Heimburg, a singer, his younger brother Walter, also a conductor and later a radio commentator, and his sister Clara, later a cofounder of the Mannes School of Music, constituted one of the most influential German musical families to immigrate to the United States.

The Institute, which eventually merged with the Juilliard School of Music in the mid-1920s, became only the most well known of Frank's many bequests to musical culture in his adopted country. The People's Singing Classes and People's Choral Union, organizations he started in 1892, designed specifically to involve students and workers in music making, were his first systematic attempts to bring music education and concerts to those with limited opportunities and financial resources. Buoyed by their overwhelmingly positive reception, Damrosch created the Musical Art Society in 1893. This professional a cappella vocal ensemble specialized in Renaissance and Baroque repertoire and paved the way for a revival of interest in early music decades before the movement gained real momentum in the United States.[1]

It was Frank Damrosch's passion for music, a belief in the moral uplift it provided, a commitment to social welfare, and his confidence that he knew best how music should be taught that made him such a powerful force in all the organizations with which he was associated. Leo Ornstein would be one of the thousands of young people who benefited from Damrosch's fervor and devotion. Many others who studied at the Institute, including Claire Raphael (Reis) and Pauline Mallet-Prevost (Ornstein), carried his convictions regarding the high calling of music teaching into their own professional endeavors: Raphael Reis founded the People's Musical League in 1912, which sponsored concert series aimed especially at immigrant populations, and played an essential administrative role in the International Composers' Guild and then the League of Composers throughout the 1920s; Pauline Mallet-Prevost Ornstein along with Leo founded the successful Ornstein School of Music in Philadelphia in 1934.[2] Pauline became especially identified with teaching young people and their teachers.

Initially the Institute was housed in the leased Lenox Mansion at 53 Fifth Avenue on the corner of 5th Avenue and 12th Street, not far in actual distance

FIGURE 2.1. Institute of Musical Art.

from where the newly arrived Ornsteins lived in the Lower East Side, even if the cultural distance was enormous.[3] The placement was ideal, however, for the constituency Damrosch sought to reach. In the early decades of the twentieth century immigrants poured into this lower Manhattan enclave. It was a first stop for hundreds of thousands of people fleeing Europe. As historian Andrea Olmstead noted, safe and easy access to the Institute was a priority for Damrosch; before signing a lease, he needed assurances of its proximity to subways and trains. The Lenox Mansion, with its location just two blocks from the 14th Street Union Square Station, provided just that. A 1910 move by the Institute uptown to 122 Street and Claremont Avenue was precipitated by the owner of the Lenox Mansion, Thomas Fortune Ryan, who terminated the lease agreement and reclaimed the property. A newly built facility near the Union Theological Seminary, Barnard College, and Columbia University in present-day Harlem put the Institute in another area known for its diverse population, and one that Damrosch characterized as "the educational center of the city."[4] It opened there November 5, 1910, the fall term after Ornstein graduated and while he was on his first trip to Europe since arriving in the country four years earlier.[5]

In 1906 the diminutive immigrant Ornstein no doubt appealed immensely to Damrosch, who would not only have recognized the youth's prodigious talents and valued his association with the prestigious St. Petersburg Conservatory, but would also have welcomed the opportunity to uplift this seemingly poor, newly arrived musical soul. Throughout his tenure Damrosch interviewed and auditioned every student who applied to the Institute, so his personal attention to the child Ornstein was not exceptional, although the extent of his advocacy, as Titiev describes it, certainly would have been.[6] Whether Damrosch's being half-Jewish played any role in the enthusiastic reception he accorded Leo, we can't know.[7] Given the school director's own religious heritage, his immigrant experience years earlier, and his commitment to teaching students of all races and backgrounds, it might be that Ornstein's ethnicity allowed Damrosch to empathize with Leo. But at this point in the Institute's history religious or ethnic background or citizenship would not have resulted in preferential treatment.[8] More likely Damrosch recognized Leo's talent.

Without question, however, as a male student Ornstein would have been especially prized. In the Institute's first years females dominated student rolls and graduating classes even though opportunities for their placement in professional organizations were severely limited, as was made clear by James Francis Cooke in an article written for *Etude* magazine in 1906.[9] Although, according to Olmstead, Damrosch was critical of the narrow opportunities for females studying at European conservatories—"they were mostly limited to voice, piano, and harp"—at his own institution, while females made up a full 38 percent of the faculty (nineteen of fifty), they were a force in only three fields: they represented five of eight voice teachers, eleven of fifteen piano teachers, and two of three language teachers.[10] The lone female string teacher taught harp. All theory and composition faculty as well as teachers of orchestral instruments and all lecturers were male. While opportunities for female *students* would be equalized in Damrosch's American Institute, the division of labor among the faculty remained similar to what he found in Europe: a condition that most likely reflected inadequate numbers of trained female instructors outside the three traditional areas.

Aware of the gender imbalance in professional musical organizations, Damrosch kept careful statistics on male-female enrollment at the Institute. His advocacy of careers in teaching and his conviction that such were professions of the very highest calling, eclipsing by far the value of a career as a virtuoso, became a recurrent theme in his graduation speeches. In fact, however, Damrosch's beliefs coincided with the reality of the contemporary situation. At Leo's 1910 commencement exercises Damrosch made his feelings clear: "The glittering promise of a successful virtuoso life leads many to think that the teacher's profession is

FIGURE 2.2. Attorney Street in 1908. *Photo Courtesy New York City Municipal Archives.*

but a small and contracted one, but those who know, *those who know*, realize that the highest, the noblest, the most beautiful profession of all in the world is that of teaching, and only in so far as the performing artist is a teacher does he fulfill his best and noblest mission."[11]

Without questioning Damrosch's sincerity, such sentiments may well have been informed by his realization that teaching was the most likely career choice available to his graduates. Very few of the Institute's earliest students were poised to enjoy immediate fame as performers; Leo Ornstein would be an exception. His uniqueness among the Institute's graduates is attested to by his featured place in the June 6, 1910, commencement program, on which he played the complete Concerto for Piano in G Minor, Op. 25, by Mendelssohn; Frank Damrosch conducted the Institute Orchestra.[12]

In his 1918 biography of Ornstein, Frederick H. Martens referred in passing to a review of his performance written by Arthur Brisbane that appeared June 11, 1910, in the *New York Evening Journal*. Brisbane, however, was no simple reporter. He was the president of the *Journal*, and his remarks were, in fact, more than simply a review of this public concert. His lengthy story provided the very first public snapshot of Ornstein, "a boy of extraordinary promise," and introduced images that would become part of the proverbial publicity packet. Material for his narrative had come directly from Jacob Titiev, and it highlighted the dramatic nature of Ornstein's journey out of the Pale and into the spotlight. The prose leans toward purple: "This lad, fifteen years old, lives in a humble quarter of the East Side. To this poor quarter the boy's family came from the horrors, the persecution and murders of Russia only a few years ago. He has lived through poverty, through the horrible scenes of Russian religious persecution—but within him burns the fire of true genius that nothing can quench."[13]

Only after setting the scene does Brisbane comment upon the concert itself: "Leo Ornstein plays with extraordinary power, and with true appreciation.... To praise his work adequately would seem friendly exaggeration. The piano, usually so cold, so mechanical, so hopelessly 'black and white' sings with strange power and sweetness under the touch of this Russian boy. Those that have heard him and that know music compare him already with the greatest artists that the world has known." That such predictions could be made based upon a single public performance of a single concerto speaks likely of *both* Ornstein's work and a generously inclined writer. Brisbane was a close friend of Tapper's.

A part of early reviews seemed always to include a description of Ornstein's physical presence and his shyness, although it must be kept in mind that he was still young, just sixteen. At his full adult height Ornstein stood only 5'4" tall. As an adolescent, his diminutive size and frame made his accomplishment seem all the more startling.[14] "The boy is as simple as any child of his age could be. He walks upon the platform, bashful, with his head hanging. It is a beautiful head, a fine, noble face, full of power, and reflecting true inspiration. When he plays it is with the strength and feeling of a grown man. His face is all spirit and light, and love of music carries him far off. There is change also in the duller faces of those that hear him."

Brisbane's story continued with paeans to both music and teaching, praising Mrs. Tapper by name and drawing some pretty heady comparisons: "It was pleasing to watch the happy face of this devoted teacher, delighting in the triumph of the boy who owes her so much. Michel Angelo could not have looked with greater pride and joy upon his young David, or his old, bearded Moses, after the last stroke of the chisel.

"We believe that this boy, providentially saved from Russia, brought up in the poverty of an overcrowded city, will stand with the great musicians of the world, on a par with the greatest *interpreters* of musical genius, and perhaps among the great musical creators." After a warning that those in positions of power not exploit Leo, Brisbane closed with words of advice: "Remember the name of Leo Ornstein. You will hear it again."[15] Given the effusiveness of Brisbane's comments, one wonders if Damrosch's 1910 graduation remarks regarding virtuosity had been directed specifically at Leo in anticipation of such a reception.[16]

The course of study fashioned by Damrosch for the Institute reflected late-nineteenth-century German musical values and his own sense of what was best, and it was thorough according to those standards.[17] As Damrosch explained:

> You come to us and place yourself absolutely into our hands—into the hands of the ladies and gentlemen of the faculty and myself. I hear you play or sing and I say, "My friend, you are fit to study because nature has endowed you with a certain amount of musical talent, and I will assign you to a teacher because that teacher is best able to direct your studies, and if at any time I shall find that you need another teacher to develop other sides of your musical work, I shall transfer you." You are absolutely in our hands and you must come here with confidence that we will seek to do whatever is best for you. I not only say to you: "You shall study with such and such a teacher," but "You must study such and such a thing."[18]

As a result, regardless of an entering piano student's playing ability, he or she was required to take three years of technique, three years of dictation, two years of sight-singing and sight-playing, and one year each of ear training, elements of music, notation, counterpoint, musical form, and musical analysis. Compulsory lecture, rehearsal, recital, and concert attendance rounded out each year's curriculum. As Olmstead explains: "Lectures were an important and required part of the course study: A certificate-holder had to have three years of these courses." Lecture topics included "The Physiology and Dynamics of Singing," Beethoven's Sixth Symphony, and music history, among others.[19]

Of particular interest to a study of Leo Ornstein is Dr. Thomas Tapper's position among the lecture faculty of the Institute. Dr. Tapper (1864–1958) was married to Leo's piano teacher and was a respected lecturer, writer, and music scholar in his own right. He had written books on music biography and history, melody writing, harmony, and counterpoint that were published between the 1890s and 1916.[20] Among the courses he taught was "Music as a Culture Study."[21] Although this particular course was offered in 1906–1907, Leo's first full year at the Institute, he was excused from these afternoon lectures to attend classes at the Quaker School.[22] Damrosch's iron-clad grip on student requirements seems to have allowed for some flexibility although eventually Leo would be officially "encouraged" to attend more lectures.[23]

Prior to his affiliation with the Institute, Thomas Tapper had been associated with musical activities in Boston and at New York University both as a student and as a teacher.[24] He was also associated with Oliver Ditson's *The Musical Record and Review* and from 1903 to 1907 edited *The Musician*. He later worked for *The Etude*. In the summers of 1907 and 1908 Tapper organized an experimental two-week summer session for public school music teachers to be held at the Institute. Such an abbreviated course of study was contrary to Damrosch's thinking that "sound musical education could not be obtained by the study of small sections in small doses." Damrosch discontinued the program after two years.[25] But Tapper had other projects in the works. Between 1907 and 1909, simultaneously with his duties at the IMA, Tapper directed the Music School Settlement in New York City. With his numerous connections to the media and his high standing among the music education community, Thomas Tapper was an ideal associate for Frank Damrosch, who was careful to involve potentially influential writers and critics in the operation of the Institute. Such contacts were likely to keep Institute events in the public eye and speak favorably of what transpired there. Dedicated to music education in the broadest sense of the term, cultivating Leo would initially be a family affair for both Thomas and Bertha Feiring Tapper.[26]

Ornstein's two years of studies at the St. Petersburg Conservatory (1903–1905) likely included much that he was required to take at the IMA. One can imagine the indulged, precocious youth who became the intuitive, instinctive, antiformalist pianist-composer in later years bristling at such compulsory requirements. Having coached musicians many years his senior while a child in Russia, being made to take basic musicianship courses with classmates lacking his skills must have seemed a waste of time. In her *Reminiscences*, Pauline Mallet-Prevost Ornstein recalls the ease and speed with which her peer, the young Leo, accomplished dictation exercises or sight-read:

> As pupils of the same teacher we necessarily met in competitive areas. I was inclined to be furious with his ability to outstrip every effort I could make. I remember an ear-training examination in which, the moment the dictation had been finished he got up and handed in his paper while I continued, hectically to check and recheck mine. When the piano examination followed I was prepared with a movement of a Mozart Concerto over which I had labored for weeks. While we were waiting for the examiners to arrive he took my music to look at it. He then proceeded to sit down at the piano and rip it off as if he had studied it longer than I had.

Generously, Pauline concludes: "This was not bravado[,] it was quite a matter of course to satisfy his curiosity about the piece." She admits, "such experiences were very frustrating," but they did not deter her from pursuing his friendship.[27]

Writing in 1918, Martens characterized the student Ornstein as being "naturally impatient of year-long harmony and theory courses along the traditional lines; he questioned authority, he kicked against the pricks instead of deferring to them. But he graduated in due time and is now, no doubt, more tolerant in retrospect as regards possible differences of opinion he may have had with his teachers in harmony and theory, Dr. Percy Goetschius and R. Huntington Woodman."[28] Given that Martens based his biography on personal interviews with Ornstein, it is probably fair to say that Ornstein was not the most dedicated or agreeable student. As will also become clear from numerous interviews with Ornstein's former students, he was not particularly devoted to studio teaching either, although he was apparently interested enough in writing about teaching to publish a number of articles on piano technique, usually, however, in a context of the technique needed to perform his own works. When it came to making a living, he was first and foremost a pianist, and second a composer, although his compositions brought audiences to his piano recitals. Throughout much of his life he thrived in the spotlight, he enjoyed the attention. In spite of Damrosch's admonitions, Tapper had groomed him for a public career.[29]

Starting in October 1906, Bertha Feiring Tapper (1859–1915) took on the prodigy and became "the greatest individual influence in his career, [a] guide, philosopher and friend, rather than mere teacher." As Martens tells it, Ornstein spoke of her always "with reverence and affection. She was unwearied in his training, not alone in a purely musical sense, but in her cultivation of his mind along broader educational lines."[30] In *Reminiscences*, Pauline's unpublished memoirs, she speaks of the "devoted relationship" between teacher and student and concludes "No child of her own could have commanded more dedication than Mrs. Tapper gave to young Leo."[31] Pauline's choice of words suggests that she was unaware that Mrs. Tapper did have children, a son and a daughter, from her previous marriage to Louis Maas. A full-page obituary written by A. Walter Kramer that appeared in *Musical America* on September 25, 1915, three weeks after her death and one in the October 1915 issue of *The Musician* provide the fullest accounts of this dedicated woman.[32]

Bertha Feiring was born in Christiania (now Oslo), Norway, and studied piano with Johann Svendsen and Agathe Bäcker-Grondahl in her native country before attending the Leipzig Conservatory beginning in 1874 at age fifteen. There she was a student of Carl Reinecke, Ernst Friedrich Richter, and Louis Maas; the last named she married. At some point she traveled to Vienna to work with the famous piano pedagogue Theodor Leschetizky. Feiring distinguished herself not only as a teacher, but also as a pianist, composer, and editor. A close friend of Edvard Grieg, her homeland's most famous composer, she edited two volumes of his piano works. Both Maases would have known the American composer George Whitefield Chadwick from his student days at Leipzig in 1877–1878. In 1882 Chadwick accepted a position with the New England Conservatory. Just a year later, Louis and Bertha Maas came to Boston and taught at the NEC, he from 1883 to 1890, and upon his death, she from 1890 to 1895. When Chadwick took over the directorship of the Conservatory in 1897, he invited other Leipzig colleagues to join his faculty. Study at Leipzig and other German universities had become a regular feature of American musicians' training in the closing decades of the nineteenth century. Whether it was Chadwick in the last decade of the nineteenth century, or Damrosch in the first decade of the twentieth, enticing Europe's students and teachers to come to the United States was how the nation's first conservatories stocked their faculties.[33]

In addition to providing incalculable amounts of emotional support, smoothing Leo's way in a foreign country, mentoring him in his piano work, accompanying him on his only two European trips, and introducing her young charge to Leschetizky, Bertha Feiring Tapper was the active patron of Ornstein, promoting him in myriad ways and making sure he met those who could advance his career. She used her home on Riverside Drive as the stage. Writer, social activist, and modern music aficionado Waldo Frank (1889–1967) devoted a lengthy passage in his memoirs to a description of a private recital that Tapper hosted the autumn after Leo had returned from his 1913–1914, second, European visit:

> The long room with a façade of windows giving on the Hudson was astir like a convention of birds with the elegant gentlemen and ladies perched on their camp stools, and facing their twitter stood the silent black Steinway grand. Now a youth, not much over five foot, in his late teens, sidled past the rows of seats; and as he came close to the piano his head seemed to sink into his shoulders. He crouched rather than sat on the piano stool and placed his large, beautiful hands on the keyboard. The noise lessened. His long head rose, and his body straightened; he seemed suddenly a foot taller. With a single finger he struck a single note; and as if it were a signal, the silence became perfect.
>
> He played a Debussy Prelude, making the music an overtone of his own strong seclusion. The music died, the applause burst, and the pianist took it as an almost unbearable invasion of the music. As if to stop it, he touched the keys again and played a piece by Ravel, whose wavery arabesques he hardened into springs of steel. When the applause came now,

he faced it, turning his head barely, his body not at all, and continued at once with a composition by Albéniz.

Mrs. Tapper stood up and announced to her guests that Leo would now play some of his own music. Leo responded with a voluminous, cacophonous broadside of chords that seemed about to blow the instrument in the air and break the windows. Chaos spoke. Ladies laughed hysterically. The music growled like a beast, clanged like metal on metal, smoldered before it burst again, and suddenly subsided. Leo drooped over the keys, like a spent male after coitus, his head down as if he were praying. The audience shot to their feet, unconsciously determined perhaps that the ordeal be over and they need hear no more horrors. Claire [Raphael Reis] and I shouldered through the throng to the piano which might have been a guillotine. I noted that there was blood on the keys. I looked close at the small ghetto-bred body . . . the strong masculine head, and threw my arms about Leo Ornstein, loving him at once because I loved the music.[34]

Waldo Frank's very first publication would be a brief story on Ornstein, which appeared in the April 1915 issue of *The Onlooker*.[35] Ornstein was drawn into Frank's literary and artistic circles. He was a valuable commodity, a true modernist musician, exotic, inspired, and with a talent for attracting attention: a breed in very short supply in the second and third decades of the twentieth century. His interactions with the city's modernist movers and shakers will be taken up in a later chapter.

Prior to connecting with that progressive group, however, Ornstein had enjoyed the community of large numbers of established musicians who regularly spent their summers along the coast of southern Maine. Starting in 1902 while still a member of the Boston Symphony Orchestra and busy with his famous quartet, Franz Kneisel began his summer chamber music school in Blue Hill, Maine.[36] Around the same time, Horatio and Anna Parker and Thomas and Bertha Feiring Tapper built summer cottages close by Kneisel's in Blue Hill. Countless other musicians, writers, and artists came by ferry and railroad to take advantage of the nurturing quietude they found in the woody enclaves that dotted the coastline. Thus began a close-knit colony of music and arts lovers.[37]

Starting while still a student at the Institute, and continuing for years after his graduation, Ornstein accompanied the Tappers on their summer sojourns to Blue Hill and spent months working with his mentor while enjoying the close associations that the musical colony provided. The Parker and Tapper houses were just across the road from each other, no more than 800 feet apart. Old Kneisel Hall was a third of a mile away. Frank Damrosch had his own summer retreat in Seal Harbor. It was in Blue Hill that Leo got to hear parts of Horatio Parker's opera *Mona* still in their draft stages.[38] It was here too that Ornstein experienced the intimate artistic interactions that characterized informal chamber music making among old friends.[39] As an observer and as a participant Leo got to enjoy duet, trio, and quartet playing at their finest. In the years after Mrs. Tapper's death, and until his marriage to Pauline, Ornstein returned to Maine and spent his summers in Deer Isle, just south and west of Blue Hill, and visited Seal Harbor, south of Bar Harbor and to the east of Blue Hill.

Deer Isle boasted a number of resort/summer colonies, most famous perhaps "The Firs" (opened in 1905) and "Felsted," formerly the estate of Frederick Law Olmstead and a somewhat more exclusive establishment providing "absolute privacy and quiet without isolation." Unlike much of the Penobscot Bay region, where large numbers of summer visitors had significantly (and negatively) impacted both the culture and geography of the coastline, Deer Isle took a certain pride in its having "been less exploited than most sections of the Maine coast." A publicity letter drafted by Mr. and Mrs. S. B. Knowlton, proprietors of the The Firs and Felsted, explained: "Scattered cottages and summer colonies are found here and there, but the island as a whole retains much of its primitive character." By the 1920s, the Knowltons ran a summer school program that drew a "faculty of experts from some of the best preparatory schools in the country." A list of colleges and universities attended by former residents of The Firs and Felsted Summer School proved the success of their program.[40]

An undated postcard whose recipient is unknown includes a hand-scrawled note by Leo with an arrow pointing to a house on the edge of Sylvester's Cove in Deer Isle: "This is where I work." The house, although much renovated, still stands today.[41] A photograph likely taken in 1915 of a smiling, youthful, rested Leo enjoying boating in a cove is testament to the restorative powers of these summers away from the city.[42]

III

Active participants in the music scenes of Boston, New York, and Maine, Kneisel, Parker, and Tapper also had close ties to Europe—Tapper and Kneisel by birth, and Parker through his training in 1882–1885 with the famous composition pedagogue Joseph Rheinberger in Munich.[43] As it had been in the closing decades of the nineteenth century, a European imprimatur was still highly sought-after proof of one's musical achievement in the first decades of the twentieth century.[44] It was likely with this in mind, as well as a desire to show off her famous student, that Bertha Feiring Tapper arranged trips to Europe in both 1910 and 1913. Once again, Tapper took on the roles of mentor, confidant, and promoter. In Europe Ornstein made another set of contacts and expanded his reach.

According to Martens, the first trip in 1910 was a brief but important one. "Leo heard Saint-Saëns's *Samson et Dalila* at the Paris Opéra, attended various concerts, the playing of the late Raoul Pugno in particular making a deep impression on him, and encountered modern music for the first time in the shape of the César Franck *Sonata* for violin and piano." From Paris, the pair traveled to western Austria where Leo experienced "a taste of mountain climbing in the Austrian Tyrol," and then "a visit to Vienna, where Leschetizky played Chopin and Schumann for him." The pair attended "the Salzburg Festival, where he heard Mozart's *Don Giovanni*, with [Lilli] Lehmann and Geraldine Farrar." The last stop was "Dresden, where he played symphonies for four hands and in this way became acquainted with those of Brahms, in his opinion 'superior to Beethoven's.' . . . From Dresden he returned to New York and gave his first public concert in that city at the New Amsterdam Theatre on March 5, 1911."[45]

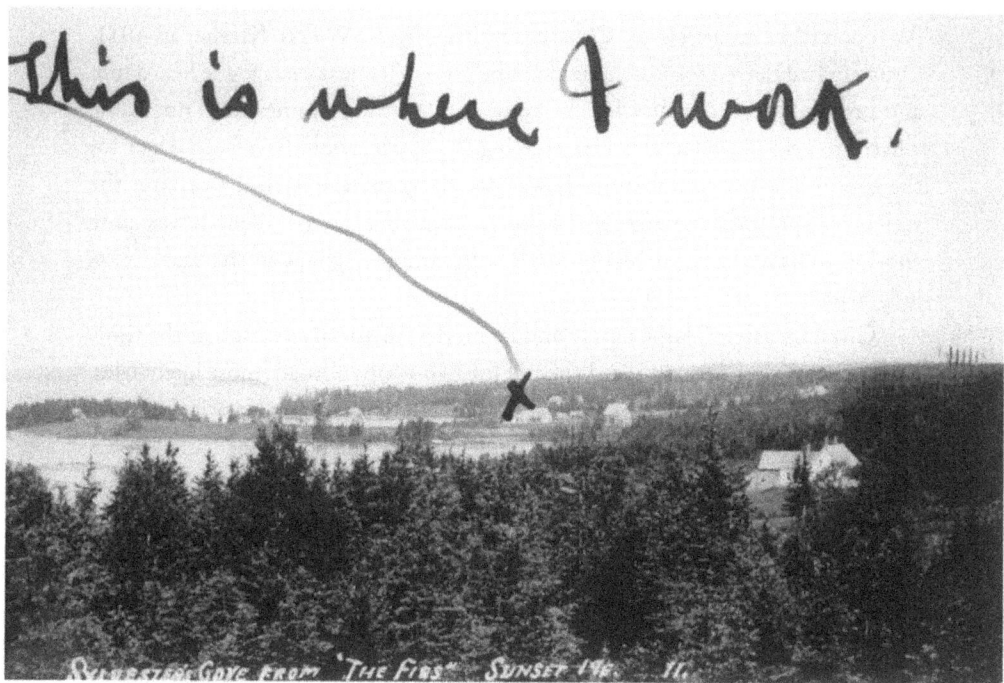

FIGURE 2.4A. Ornstein postcard of Sylvester's Cove. *MSS 10, The Leo Ornstein Papers, Irving S. Gilmore Music Library, Yale University.*

FIGURE 2.4B. Ornstein in boat. *Photo courtesy the Ornstein family.*

As reported in an article on Ornstein written by A. Walter Kramer in 1911, Ornstein had played for Leschetizky: "The great Viennese pedagogue heard him and pronounced him ready for the concert platform." Kramer does not name what Ornstein played at this first meeting.[46] Tapper would have been eager for the approval of her own mentor. It was one thing to have Arthur Brisbane, the widely read progressive newspaper editor, enthuse over your student, it was quite another to have the most highly respected piano pedagogue in the world pass judgment.

Given Ornstein's large family and its modest financial situation at the time, it is probable that others footed the bill for Leo's trips abroad, most likely Mrs. Tapper. The Institute had a generous scholarship program, many of its benefactors anonymously supported worthy students, and Bertha Tapper was known to provide personal scholarships for her pupils. Whether other family members accompanied Mrs. Tapper is unknown; none is ever mentioned. She performed a great service to her student by exposing him to composer-pianist Raoul Pugno (1852–1914), who was at the peak of his powers in 1910. The same can be said for the performance of *Don Giovanni* with the legendary Lilli Lehmann (1848–1929) and her most famous student, Geraldine Farrar (1882–1967). Lehmann was a driving force in the Salzburg Festivals and in 1906 had organized and performed *Don Giovanni* to enormous acclaim. A 1910 production of the same opera proved even more noteworthy given Lehmann's age and the increasing rarity of her performances. The sporadic nature of the Salzburg Music Festival Weeks prior to 1920 made this trip an especially timely and fortuitous one in Ornstein's musical development. It is likely that Tapper had planned this crossing for some time to coincide specifically with these opportunities.[47]

With Leschetizky's coveted sanction and Arthur Brisbane's enthusiastic editorial as calling cards, Ornstein spent much of 1911 and 1912 attempting to establish a foothold as one of New York's resident virtuoso pianists. The assorted and unexpected venues, the variety of programs, and often their occurrence at the tail end of the concert seasons (most of Ornstein's performances occur in March and April) suggest a concerted effort to get in front of the public eye, but only after the 1911 and 1912 seasons had already been set. Or perhaps Ornstein simply needed time to prepare and chose dates that would give him the longest lead time; given his December 1893 birth date, in March 1911 he would have been only seventeen years old and in the country just five years.[48]

On March 5, 1911, display ads in the *New York Times* announced: "Tonight at 8:15, Piano Recital—Debut" at the New Amsterdam Theatre on 43rd St. West off Broadway. Ornstein will be "assisted by the Volpe Symphony Orchestra."[49] A review that appeared the next day, unsigned but later identified as written by

Carl Van Vechten, noted the unusual location of the theater as the venue for a piano recital, perhaps suggesting late arrangements for the performance.[50] It also speaks of the program and critiques Ornstein's execution:

> The New Amsterdam Theatre is a strange place for a recital of piano-forte music, but one was held there last evening when Leo Ornstein, the latest wunderkind to claim metropolitan attention appeared before a very large audience to contribute his interpretation of a programme which would have tested any fully grown-up talent.
>
> It began with Bach's Chromatic Fantasy and Fugue, included Beethoven's "Sonata Appasionata" [sic], six Chopin numbers, and finally Rubinstein's D-minor concerto, in which the young Ornstein was assisted by the Volpe Symphony Orchestra. To say that this boy has great talent would be to mention the obvious, but to say that as yet he is ripe for such matters as he undertook last night would be stretching the truth. It should be stated, however, that his command of tone color is already great and that his technique is usually adequate for the demands which the music made, although in some passages in the final movement of the Beethoven sonata his strength seemed to desert him.[51]

An announcement in the *Times* on Thursday, March 30, 1911, advertised a Sunday afternoon concert taking place at Carnegie Hall the 2nd of April.[52] It appears among a raft of announcements for recitals by Isadora Duncan ("Farewell Performance"), Mary Garden, and the Kneisel Quartet. The Philharmonic Society of New York with Gustav Mahler conducting would present Tschaikovsky's "Pathétique" and an unidentified work by Wagner. Leo Ornstein is listed as "soloist," although no piece is named. A follow-up announcement the next day reiterated the ad.[53] A subsequent story entitled "The Philharmonic Society," however, clarified the program as consisting of Wagner's *Tannhäuser* Overture, the "Good Friday Spell" from *Parsifal*, the "Magic Fire Scene" from *Die Walküre*, and the "Kaiser Marsch." Ornstein would play Rubinstein's Concerto No. 4 in D Minor, a piece that quickly became a staple in his repertoire.[54] Performing at the same concert with the famous conductor was no doubt an auspicious way to launch a career. One can only wonder what opportunities might have existed had Mahler lived to champion the young pianist both in the United States and abroad; Mahler would die just a few months later.[55]

The anonymous review that appeared on April 3 was respectful if not laudatory: "The concerto was played by Mr. Leo Ornstein, a young man who made his first New York appearance a few weeks ago. He is a player of evident talent and considerable accomplishment, and his playing of the concerto was creditable. The accompaniment of the orchestra was not of the best, and for a moment or two near the end of the last movement disaster was imminent, if, indeed, it had not already arrived."[56]

Ornstein's repertoire was traditional by contemporary standards—Bach, Beethoven, Chopin, and Rubinstein—with little in it to distinguish him from other pianists on the circuit at the time, except his youth. In an interview with Van Vechten years after the debut Ornstein confided: "My ambition then was to play the concertos of Rubinstein and Tschaikowsky . . . and I satisfied it."[57] While other artists were wrapping up their season's performances, Ornstein continued. An announcement that appeared in the *Times* on May 14, 1911, finds him assisting at a Carnegie Hall recital by the baritone David Bispham scheduled for May 21 that showcased Walter Damrosch's 1898 setting of Rudyard Kipling's poem "Danny Deever."[58] Ornstein's precise role in the event is unclear, as according to the announcement Mr. Harry M. Gilbert accompanied Mr. Bispham on this particular number. A review of the recital that appeared in the *Times* on May 22 clarifies that the event was part of a "series of concerts for wage earners" being offered "in spite of the fact that the real music season ended over a month ago." Frank Damrosch's concern for education and social uplift through music was shared with his brother Walter and may have been passed along to Ornstein. Regardless of motivations, the recital was another opportunity to get in front of the public. In this review there is no mention of Mr. Gilbert.[59]

The 1911–1912 season opened with two announcements of Ornstein's future engagements, one with the Volpe Symphony and a second a special recital honoring Franz Liszt. On October 1, in the *Times*'s "News of the Music World," the Volpe Symphony Society of New York described its plans for its four subscription concerts to be given on Tuesday evenings in November, January, February, and March. Ornstein was slated to appear in the final one. In the same block of announcements readers learn that the Kneisel Quartet "returns to New York today" from Blue Hill, Maine, where they had been rehearsing throughout September.[60] It's likely that Ornstein had not left Maine long before them.

With 1911 the centennial year of Franz Liszt's birth (1811–1886), many musical groups planned special concerts and tributes, and Ornstein participated in the earliest of them. A *Times* announcement of a concert set for October 15, 1911, explained: "The People's Symphony Orchestra, which will give a concert this afternoon at Carnegie Hall, is the first of the large organizations to offer a Liszt programme. A painting by Joannes de Tahy, a Hungarian painter, depicting 'Liszt Composing the Second Hungarian Rhapsody' will occupy a place of honor on the stage. Leo Ornstein will be the soloist."[61] It is likely that Ornstein had spent his own summer in Blue Hill under the watchful eye of Mrs. Tapper preparing the

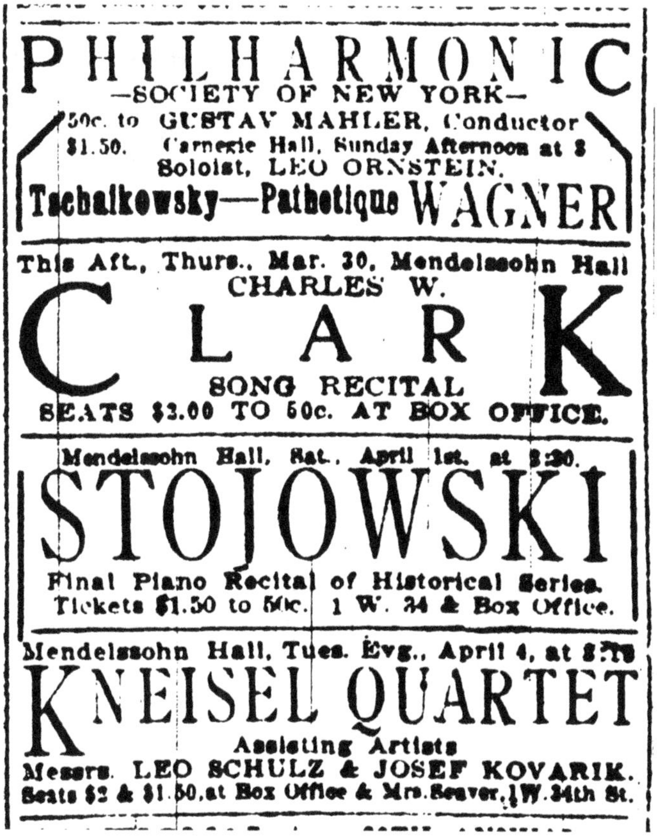
PHILHARMONIC
—SOCIETY OF NEW YORK—
50c. to GUSTAV MAHLER, Conductor
$1.50. Carnegie Hall, Sunday Afternoon at 3
Soloist, LEO ORNSTEIN.
Tschaikowsky—Pathetique WAGNER

This Aft., Thurs., Mar. 30, Mendelssohn Hall
CHARLES W.
CLARK
SONG RECITAL
SEATS $2.00 TO 50c. AT BOX OFFICE.

Mendelssohn Hall, Sat., April 1st, at 3:30.
STOJOWSKI
Final Piano Recital of Historical Series.
Tickets $1.50 to 50c. 1 W. 34 & Box Office.

Mendelssohn Hall, Tues. Evg., April 4, at 8:15
KNEISEL QUARTET
Assisting Artists
Messrs. LEO SCHULZ & JOSEF KOVARIK.
Seats $2 & $1.50, at Box Office & Mrs. Seaver, 1 W. 34th St.

FIGURE 2.5. Ornstein, Mahler, and competing events from *New York Times*.

Liszt for the event. This year, for the first time, Ornstein would be a presence in the New York concert scene at both the opening and the closing of the season.

The Volpe Symphony was an orchestra of young professional players founded in 1904 by Arnold David Volpe, a Lithuanian immigrant who had come to the United States via the St. Petersburg Conservatory. Like Frank, Walter, and Carrie Damrosch and many others, Arnold Volpe was dedicated to music education. For ten years, the Volpe Symphony was a reliable forum for showcasing young talent; in the spring of 1912 it would be the perfect home for the eighteen-year-old Ornstein.[62]

Commitment to music education was just one of Volpe's missions. Starting with the 1910 season, Volpe included "at least one American composition in each [symphony] programme"; this plan was implemented for a second season, as the October 1911 announcement made clear. A list of American pieces was included: "'Christmas Overture' by Percy Goetschius, 'The Mystic Trumpeter' by Frederick S. Converse, and 'Comedy Overture' on negro themes by Henry

Gilbert."[63] Missing was the piece Ornstein would play in March: Edward MacDowell's Second Concerto for Piano and Orchestra, another large work that became a staple in his repertoire.

Closer to the actual concert date, a March 3, 1912, announcement named the MacDowell as the work to be played by "the young Russian pianist."[64] Throughout the early teens Ornstein would be identified as "Russian." Given the rich national tradition, the term obviously carried cachet for musicians, perhaps for pianists especially. By spring of 1912, however, Ornstein would have spent nearly a third of his life in the United States and believed he was an American citizen. As will be seen, Ornstein's identity remained fluid throughout the 1920s and morphed as people and conditions required. The issue of his citizenship would surface as late as the 1950s.

Eager to build his repertoire, Ornstein spent the late months of 1911 and early 1912 perfecting the MacDowell. His efforts paid off. On March 27, the *New York Times* critic took note with a brief but positive review: "Mr. Ornstein is a youth who has been heard several times in New York in the last two seasons. He played MacDowell's second concerto in D minor in excellent style, with a real musical feeling and brilliant and secure technique. The performance indicated a substantial progress on the young man's part that was gratifying."[65] In 1912 the recently deceased Edward MacDowell was considered the most important American composer of his time, and a modern among moderns; his highly lyrical, romantically inflected music was wholly acceptable to large audiences. By adding this work to his growing concerto repertoire and then playing the work multiple times over the next ten years, Ornstein paid homage to MacDowell's position in American musical culture and linked himself with a highly regarded and much beloved composer.

Throughout 1911 and 1912, Ornstein continued to devote significant effort to establishing a name for himself as a serious pianist with an impressive repertoire. But as the somewhat patronizing March review made clear, Ornstein was still considered "a youth," a "young man" who according to the writer had made "substantial progress"; changing that perception was going to require something more than additional public appearances. Although Ornstein benefited enormously from the friendship of some of the most important musical personalities in the city—the Damrosches, the Tappers, and the Kneisels, and, as will later become clear, both Mr. and Mrs. Arthur Brisbane, A. Walter Kramer, and Frederick Martens—all of whom were able to advocate on his behalf, his career needed management.

In the February 7, 1912, issue of *Musical Courier* an ad appeared naming Kuester and Richardson of 25 West 42nd Street as exclusive managers of Leo

Ornstein. On the surface, the relationship seems to be short lived. Just three months later in the same magazine, Mr. Walter R. Anderson announced "Leo Ornstein, The Russian Pianist" as available for the 1912–1913 season. The similar graphics and print of the two ads, however, suggests that perhaps they were the same firm. Unfortunately attempts to track down Kuester and Richardson have proven fruitless.[66] A larger announcement by Anderson in the same issue listed ten other "well known artists" whom he represented, including Mr. Paul Althouse of the Metropolitan Opera and the American String Quartet. "Mr. Leo Ornstein" was identified as "Russian Pianist."

According to newspaper reports, Ornstein performed just twice more in the late spring of 1912, once in what appears to be a mixed recital at the Hotel Plaza on Tuesday, April 9, for which no information is available, and two weeks later playing a fuller program during "Stroud Week" at Aeolian Hall on April 23. The Stroud piano was the Aeolian Company's low-priced, upright piano that according to its publicity "had successfully passed the tests of concert pianists and musicians of the highest rank."[67] An advertisement included encomiums from Arthur Nikisch, Maurice (Moritz) Moszkowski, Moriz Rosenthal, and Mlle. [Cécile] Chaminade. The program, which included Mr. Roy William Steele, tenor, who sang four songs, clearly showcased Ornstein. He played four works by Chopin, a "Barcarolle" in A minor by Leschetizky, "Valse Caprice" by Rubinstein, and four of his own *Lyric Fancies*, Op. 10. This may well be the first public concert on which Ornstein played his own music; as the title suggests, these pieces are of a lighter nature and appropriate for a free Tuesday mid-afternoon recital.

The four original works came from a larger set. Arthur P. Schmidt published Ornstein's *Six Lyric Fancies*, Op. 10, in 1911, which would have been well before Leo had achieved any fame as a pianist or gained a reputation as a radical composer. None of them is particularly difficult, and beyond the occasional curious harmonic progression or use of quintuplets, none of them suggests the dissonant or daring style for which he became famous. On the contrary, they easily fit into the tradition of parlor music for the polished young lady. Four of them, in fact, are dedicated to young women, including No. 2 "Coquetry" to "Miss Irene E. Schwartz," No. 3 "At Twilight" to "Miss Katherine F. S." (Katherine Faulkner Swift, later to be named Kay Swift by George Gershwin), and No. 6 "Capriccietto" to "Miss Mallet-Prevost," who later married Ornstein. These three were fellow students with Leo of Bertha Tapper, and after her death all would become founders of the club named in her honor. Miss Millicent Almy, the dedicatee of No. 1, "Romance triste," is not listed among Mrs. Tapper's students.[68]

The summer of 1912 found Ornstein back in Blue Hill, working with Mrs. Tapper and enjoying the atmosphere of the summer music camp that was coastal

Maine.[69] Although no journal records his activities, it is likely that Ornstein spent his time learning new repertoire for what he hoped would be an increasingly busy concert season. But evidence of performances in 1912–1913 is scant. A single sentence in the *Times*'s "Music Here and There" column on November 24, 1912, announces a piano recital to be given in Aeolian Hall on Saturday evening, December 7. Three pages later a display ad provides the time and identifies W. R. Anderson as his manager. Finally, a week before the event, Ornstein's program is listed: the first and last movements of Schubert's Op. 42 Sonata, Franck's *Prélude, chorale et fugue*, three waltzes and six etudes by Chopin, Liszt's *Au bord d'une source* and Rhapsody No. 12, and Ornstein's own *Suite russe*, "In modo Scarlatti," the fourth of his *Six Lyric Fancies*, and a Mazurka in B-flat minor.[70]

Like *Six Lyric Fancies*, *Suite russe* shows no signs of what is to come. The seven pieces contained in the Suite are each very brief, focus upon a single melodic idea, and either repeat material immediately after it is introduced with just the slightest of variation or are in ternary form. "Chanson pathétique," the seventh and last of the group, is the most technically demanding and breaks away from the predictability of the ABA formal scheme with a more creative return of the opening material. The works are intimate character pieces, similar to those composed by Grieg. Given Tapper's close association with the composer, Ornstein probably was familiar with them. The works are accessible to an intermediate-level pianist.

Only the final piece with its *Allegro con forza* tempo and *forte* arpeggiated passages and octaves suggests a concert hall. It is uniquely dramatic in the set with a final passage that begins *fortissimo* and expands *con forza* to a triple *forte* E minor chord. No doubt, Ornstein could make even this relatively simple suite sound virtuosic with his dazzling speed and gift for voicing and color.

At a concert on February 17, 1913 with the Jewish Philharmonic Society of New York Symphony Orchestra Ornstein played Mendelssohn's Piano Concerto No. 1, the work he had performed at his commencement recital, Rubinstein's "Melody in F," the Mendelssohn-Liszt "Wedding March," a piece that would appear on dozens of his programs, and his own "Scherzino," later published in 1918 by Breitkopf & Härtel. The last-named work closely resembles the sixth of his *Lyric Fancies*, "Capriccietto," in key, tessitura, its *sempre staccato* instructions to the pianist, and overall mood. Based upon extant records, it appears that Ornstein did not perform the Mendelssohn Concerto again until 1919.

At a recital on April 3 at Wanamaker Auditorium in New York Ornstein programmed some of his old-reliables: Bach's Chromatic Fantasy and Fugue, brief solo works by Mendelssohn and Beethoven, and the now-to-be-expected set of Chopin pieces, as well as "Improvisata" by Grieg, "Marche grotesque" by Christian Sinding, Rachmaninoff's Prelude in G Minor, Liszt's Rhapsody No. 12, and his own "In modo Scarlatti." Given the suggested modeling of the last-named piece upon the piano music of Scarlatti, Ornstein's is remarkable for the complete absence of any counterpoint. The fifty-eight-measure piece showcases a single, minimally varied, repeated rhythmic-melodic motive. Its motoric qualities would have made a blisteringly fast performance, which is likely the kind Ornstein delivered, all the more impressive.

As late, then, as the close of the concert season in spring 1913, Ornstein's recitals were noteworthy not for their radical content, but for their virtuosic quality; he was "the Russian *Pianist.*" Two recordings that he made for Columbia on May 10, 1913, speak to his focus on nineteenth-century repertoire. As might be expected he played Chopin ("Impromptu," Op. 29; and Etude in G-flat, Op. 10, No. 5), Grieg's "Butterfly," Op. 43, No. 1, and Eduard Poldini's "March Mignonne."[71] Sometime over the next several months, however, things changed, and radically so: both his repertoire and his primary identification. Ornstein became the ultramodernist *composer* par excellence, the futurist flagman, the most infamous musical spokesperson for all that was new and daring, and all of this happened before he turned twenty. Gone were the character pieces that had comprised his programs and his compositions. Works with such evocative titles as *Danse sauvage (Wild Men's Dance)*, *Three Moods*, *Dwarf Suite*, and *Suicide in an Airplane* embodied a different sensibility. While audiences still came to hear his virtuosic pianism, for a period of time their real interests would lay more

FIGURE 2.7. Leo Ornstein, "At Twilight," in *Lyric Fancies*, mm. 24–44.

often with his boundary-pushing compositions. Why, when, where, and how the change occurred is one of the central and most perplexing sets of questions in Ornstein's life.

Contradictory accounts report Ornstein's composing his first radical works either just prior to his second trip to Europe, which began in the summer of 1913 when opportunities to hear radically modern music in New York were nearly nonexistent, or very soon after he got to Paris. Depending upon the account, the pieces differ as well. As will become apparent in the explanations that follow,

FIGURE 2.8. Leo Ornstein, "Chanson Pathétique," from *Suite russe*, fig. 2.10 page 1 of Scherzino.

the primacy, provenance, and inexplicable nature of Ornstein's futurist works combine to form an essential trope of the Ornstein legend.

The first published reference to the emergence of Ornstein's "new musical style" appeared in a lengthy article in *Musical America* on December 12, 1914. A. Walter Kramer, Ornstein's most dedicated champion, reported:

FIGURE 2.9. Scherzino.

Before he had left America . . . his creative powers had undergone a complete metamorphosis. . . . One morning he went to the piano and played a chord which he had mentally heard. He was skeptical of its significance at first; then he sat down and wrote an entire composition following on this chord. It was unnamed then, but it is now the "Funeral March of the Dwarves." He assured me that he was quite dissociated from himself, as it were, for several days, for he realized, judging this new piece by the standards of music as he knew it and also by comparing it with what music he had himself written before, that it was something quite new.[72]

While quite different from the *Six Lyric Fancies* and the *Suite russe* in its chordal rather than purely lyrical texture, and in its overall gravitas, Ornstein's Op. 11, No. 6, alternately referred to as "Funeral March of the Gnomes" and "Funeral

FIGURE 2.10. Leo Ornstein, "In modo Scarlatti," from *Six Lyric Fancies*.

March of the Dwarves," resembles Grieg's "March of the Trolls" in its title,[73] and a funereal piece by another composer with whose works Ornstein was intimately familiar, Franz Liszt. Although it is impossible to document Ornstein's specific knowledge of Liszt's *Funérailles*, the seventh piece of *Harmonies poétiques et religieuses* written in 1849 as an homage to Chopin, Ornstein's programming of other works by the nineteenth-century composer-virtuoso, and his attendance at a recital given at the Institute that included *Bénédiction de Dieu dans la solitude* from the larger *Harmonies* set, beg the question.[74] Liszt's much larger work may have acted as an unconscious influence upon Ornstein, suggesting registral placement, chord types, and more general proportions of internal sections one to another. Ornstein's work has more chords built on varieties of seconds, although Liszt's opening left-hand vamp stretches a minor ninth, and the right hand commences with sonorities that showcase minor, major, and augmented seconds. Perhaps it was enough to be writing a piece that attempted to convey a similar mood to guarantee some kind of shared traits.

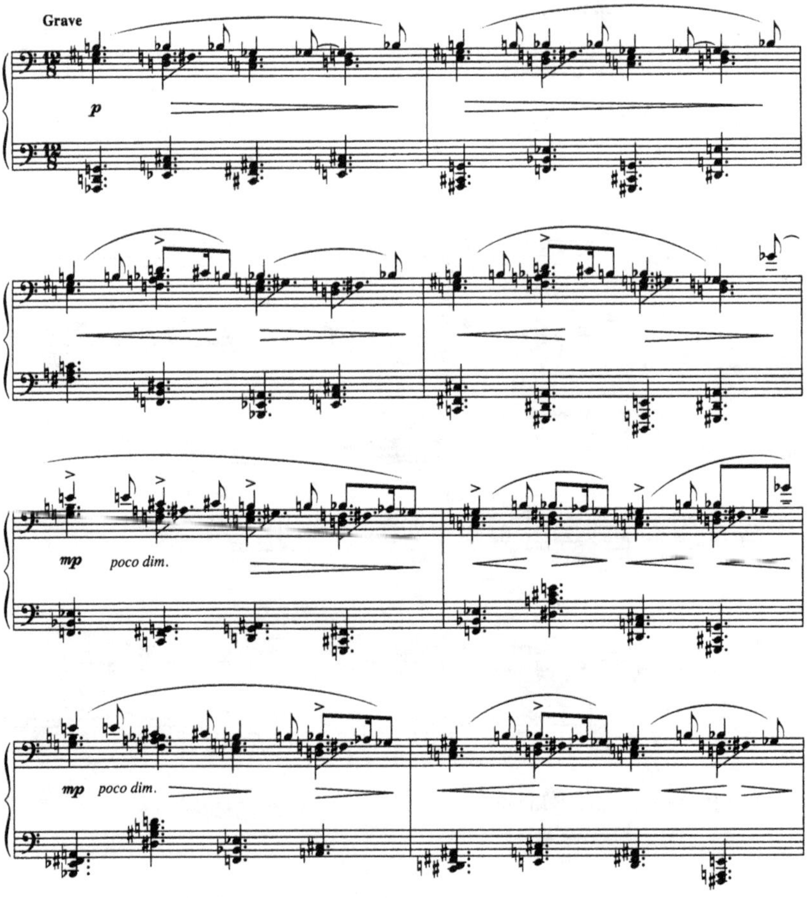

FIGURE 2.11. Leo Ornstein, "Funeral March of the Dwarves," from *Dwarf Suite*.

A second account of the Ornstein epiphany appeared in *Musical Courier* on April 14, 1915. The anonymous writer assured readers, as did Kramer, of the primacy and provenance of that "the strange new impulse," which he reports "evolved in New York." His efforts "manifested traits similar to those character-izing the music of Schoenberg and Stravinsky as if through some mysterious community of spirit—for Mr. Ornstein was quite unacquainted with their work." Clarifying the order of the experimental pieces, the writer concluded: "Out of the first arose new harmonies, which revealed themselves to him through his 'Dwarf Suite.' Obtaining gradually a surer grasp on his means, he wrote the 'Wild Man's Dance' and a number of other works, including the 'Impressions of Notre Dame,' which, though they defer to a logic of their own, are written quite independently of customary conventions."[75] In later accounts "Impressions of Notre Dame" will be cited as the first piece Ornstein wrote after his arrival in Europe, which does not contradict the American provenance of the other works.

Still other reports emphasized different aspects of the emergence of Ornstein's new style. An anonymous July 1916 article entitled "Leo Ornstein Hoists the Banner of Musical Futurism" that appeared in *Current Opinion* characterized his "conversion . . . which savors strongly of the occult." The account begins identically to that which Ornstein had given Kramer in 1914. It continues, however, as follows:

> "I could not stop to analyze it, however," Mr. Ornstein said, "for there were more things in my head that I simply had to write down. So I wrote a number of compositions. They were all in this new style—it must be labeled. And before I was really aware of it I was completely inured to it and my old manner of composing was gone. Since then I have worked steadily on my *real music.*"[76]

Within a few years, Ornstein would reassess what constituted his "real" music and take up a more expressive style.

Another article that appeared in July 1916 in *The Independent* written by Charles L. Buchanan and entitled "Futurist Music" seized upon the inexplicable, mystical nature of the stylistic change: "it is possible to conceive that Ornstein is what he claims to be: a kind of passive transmitter thru which a bleak, shrill, screaming kind of sound finds its way to us. But," Buchanan explains, "the fact that this music is an unpremeditated music, a sort of spontaneous combustion, so to speak, does not necessarily justify it."[77] In this instance, Buchanan seems not to be concerned with the provenance of the metamorphosis or its predating Ornstein's second trip to Europe. There is no time, place, or work named at all. By 1916, it is highly likely that the Ornstein name and story would be known by those in the circles who read this article; he wouldn't have had to make the case.

In 1916 Carl Van Vechten devoted an entire chapter of his book *Music and Bad Manners* to Leo Ornstein, and within that chapter a lengthy section to a description of Ornstein's stylistic metamorphosis and his second trip to Europe. In this telling the chronology and location of events are not so clear. There is no insistence upon the new style emerging in New York or prior to his Atlantic crossing. In Van Vechten's quoting of Ornstein, the time between his New Amsterdam Theatre debut in March 1911 and his return trip to Europe starting in the summer of 1913 seems to be compressed. Referring to Ornstein's debut concert, Van Vechten quotes his explanation:

> My ambition then was to play the concertos of Rubinstein and Tschaikowsky . . . and I satisfied it. Soon after that concert I went abroad.

FIGURE 2.12. Liszt, *Funérailles*, from *Harmonies poétiques et religieuses.*

> ... Suddenly the new thing came to me, and I began to write and play in the style which has since become identified with my name. It was music that I felt and I realized that I had become myself at last, although at first, to be frank, it horrified me as much as it has since horrified others. Mind you, when I took the leap I had never seen any music by Schoenberg or Strawinsky. I was unaware that there was such a generality as "futurism."[78]

Van Vechten's ellipses in the middle of Ornstein's quote are troublesome, but the chronology seems clear: the "new thing" came to Ornstein after he "went abroad." Depending upon exactly when he wrote his first futurist piece, it could easily have been after his arrival in Europe but prior to his "seeing" any Schoenberg or Stravinsky, as there is no evidence of his familiarity with their works prior to his second European sojourn.

The most dramatic account of events, and that which has been repeated most often in recent years, is the one told by Ornstein himself in 1972. According to the composer, he had been studiously perfecting his traditional repertoire in the spring of 1913, having no experience with ultramodern music (which his programs would support), when he suddenly heard new sounds that he couldn't ignore. Ornstein provided the following recollection of the time:

> *Danse Sauvage* was written by a young person with no experience whatever with modern music. I still wonder at the age of eighty, why should I have thought of that? A boy that had been sitting at the piano practicing the *Twelfth Rhapsody* to try to astonish the ladies with the speed and accuracy of the passages, and blind the audience with the terrific glissandos and what

not. Why suddenly that thing came into my head—I'll be blessed if I know. And as a matter of fact, I really doubted my sanity at first. I simply said, what is that? It was so completely removed from any experience I had ever had.[79]

Expanding upon the story, and summoning the name of the only person who might have shared his experience, Ornstein noted that Mrs. Tapper questioned his sanity as well, and it was not until she had heard him play *Danse sauvage* identically multiple times that she allowed that his new music was not some prank or sign of madness.[80]

Ornstein may have muddied the waters later in life, as compositions and events became conflated in his memory, or he may have been trying to defend primacy, originality, and independence of influence, which for modernist artists were badges of honor. Three of the earliest accounts are in agreement: the sounds of radical, dissonant harmonies, which identified many of Ornstein's early "new manner" pieces, occurred first in New York, and "Funeral March of the Dwarves" was the first composition in this new idiom. It was likely conceived in New York. "Impressions of Notre Dame" and *Danse sauvage*, written later, were more likely composed in Europe. There is little to contradict that summary other than Ornstein's own account, which came more than fifty years later when Ornstein was seventy-nine years old. Buchanan's and Van Vechten's accounts are both clouded by ambiguity, Buchanan's with an overall vagueness and Van Vechten's with those disturbing ellipses.

One unpublished biographical account of Ornstein does support the assertion that the new style appeared before he left for Europe in 1913, and that the "Funeral March of the Dwarves" was the first composition in that style. The account, probably the earliest record of the event, seems to place Ornstein's dissonant breakthrough in 1912. In the Ornstein collection at Yale University there is a brief undated biographical sketch, probably an insert for a program, by "A.C.L." In crayon this person is identified as "Landsberg." That would be Albert Clinton Landsberg, better known as Bertie, who lived in Paris at the time Ornstein was there. Landsberg was a good friend of composer Roger Quilter, who had met Ornstein in Paris in 1913 and invited him to England. Landsberg's sketch states that Ornstein began writing music in the new style "about two years ago" and that he was unacquainted with the music of Schoenberg and Stravinsky at that time. He further states that the pieces that make up the *Dwarf Suite* were "the first compositions in which he made use of altogether new harmonies," and *Danse sauvage* was "the first work in which he expressed himself, unhampered by conscious observance of technical tradition." "Impressions of Notre Dame" was written next.

While Landsberg's sketch is undated, it was probably written at the latest in February 1914, when Ornstein was in Paris and just before he went to London. In a letter from Ornstein to Roger Quilter, dated February 14, 1914, Ornstein adds a P.S.: "I'm also sending you the programme and will later send a little biography written by Bertie." One may assume that this is the biography in question, for it is unlikely Bertie would have written more than one. Landsberg's implicit dating of early 1912 ("about two years ago") may be stretching matters, but his general description and his chronological ordering of pieces do point to an early date for at least the "Funeral March."

Even later Ornstein placed the inception of both "Impressions of Notre Dame" and *Danse sauvage* specifically in Vienna, although he did not comment on "Funeral March":

> I remember that when I first began to hear the inklings of the *Danse sauvage* and the "Impressions of Notre Dame," I happened to be in Vienna. I was going to play for Leschetizky. I began to hear these things. I remember that actually the start of the "Impressions of Notre Dame," I began to put down the notes. The trunk had just been put in. There was no piano or anything. The trunk had been put in, and I had some music paper that I always carried with me, and I began to notate that. Then the man that had the hotel reserved the upper floor, and part of the upper floor for himself. He had a grand piano. They said he was away on his holiday in Switzerland or in the Tyrol, but they gave me the key, so I could go up there. And that was the first time that I heard, that I played the "Impressions of Notre Dame" for myself, and then made a few changes, but rather few. I was very fortunate to have heard it completely. [81]

Once again any account reconstructed over sixty years after the fact must be approached cautiously, and it is not clear whether Ornstein was discussing both pieces, or only "Impressions." If the former, then Ornstein clearly contradicts what he had said five years earlier to the same interviewer. If the latter, it also contradicts what Ornstein told Martens in 1918. In a trip that went from Paris to Switzerland to Vienna, it is easy to confuse where that middle stop—Switzerland—ended, and where the final goal—Vienna—began. None of these accounts speaks with certainty. Additionally, not knowing whether one of the earlier authors based his article on information contained in that of the other, thus repeating a story rather than hearing it anew from the composer and thereby confirming issues for himself, makes the question of which piece in which place an impossible one to solve with certainty. A picture does emerge, however. The *enfant terrible* took root in New York sometime in spring 1913, but only blossomed somewhere in Europe later that year.[82]

Was this turn of events another reason to head back to Europe? Foregoing Blue Hill in the summer of 1913, Mrs. Tapper accompanied her student across the Atlantic once again. While Tapper returned sometime in the fall, this would be a much longer trip for Ornstein; he would stay through April 1914. According to Martens, the two went directly to Paris. Other accounts have slightly different itineraries, but all agree upon the basic outline of the trip.

Martens reported the powerful effect Notre Dame Cathedral had on Ornstein, who upon seeing it for the first time immediately wrote two "Impressions of Notre Dame": "It was here that the sudden and overwhelming projection of Notre-Dame on his consciousness had such an effect on the composer that it evoked the two *Impressions* which bear its name. For three weeks after he had set them down on paper the composer had no chance to play them."[83] He eventually dedicated the first, "Moderato sostenuto," to Roger Quilter and the second, "Andante," to pianist Harold Bauer, both of whom he would meet just weeks later during his sojourn. Martens's choice of the word "evoked" reflects back on earlier references to the inexplicable appearance of Ornstein's second style.

Like *Danse sauvage*, the *Impressions* show a preference for clusters of notes, for chords whose outer limits span a major seventh, for steady levels of dissonance, for irregularly varying meters, tempi, and moods, for episodic though vaguely ternary form, and for moments of virtuosic display. The *Impressions* enjoy a more varied dynamic palette, one that encompasses a range from *pp* to *ff*, compared with the *f* to *ffff* that characterizes *Danse sauvage*. There are no signs, however, of the composer who wrote the well-behaved and predictable *Six Lyric Fancies* or *Nine Miniatures*. Whether the European environment was the cause of the stylistic shift, or merely reinforced nascent tendencies, what can be said with certainty is that a new voice gained strength over the coming months. Personal experiences often motivated Ornstein to compose; sometimes, however, external events got his creative juices flowing, as is the case with *Suicide in an Airplane*, whose title and overall sonic palette were inspired by an article that appeared in the *New York Times* on April 2, 1913 (see fig. 2.14).

Frederick Martens provides the most detailed account of Ornstein's second European trip including the basic itinerary of his several-months-long visit: the places he visited and the people he met. Martens explains that after the initial visit to Paris Ornstein went to Switzerland, "whose scenic beauties inspired another set, *Quatre impressions de la Suisse*, for four hands, and where he wrote a quartet and a quintet for strings." It was in Switzerland that Ornstein got to play his "Two Impressions of Notre Dame" for the first time. Ornstein then went to Vienna, where, according to Martens, "he first realized that, aside from his earlier, more conventional style and his new manner, he was in addition the possessor of a third, and began the 'Vannin' *Waltzers* and *The Night*."[84] The idea of Ornstein "realizing" he was "the possessor" of another manner, merely a conduit for music that came to him inexplicably and unbidden, reinforces once again notions of the epiphany-like emergence of his most notorious compositional voice, which became the lynchpin of the Ornstein legend.

While in Vienna Ornstein saw *Der Rosenkavalier* and met a second time with Leschetizky, who "confess[ed] that he could not at first believe [that] the *Wild Men's Dance* had been seriously 'written out' as it stood."[85] From Vienna Ornstein went to Berlin, where he was introduced to Ferruccio Busoni, whom Ornstein characterized as "a great intellect in music." After Vienna he traveled to Norway, homeland of Mrs. Tapper, and made "his début in Christiania as a concert pianist with a group of Chopin pieces and the Liszt E-flat Major Concerto." He also, for the first time, played some of his own newer compositions: likely the "Two Impressions of Notre Dame" and perhaps even *Danse sauvage*. The confusion and incredulity of the Christiana critics foreshadowed the reactions he would face once back in America: "it was amazing that Mr. Ornstein should have decided to play a little joke on the public and transfer it from the concert hall to the dental parlor." They concluded that he was "a young man temporarily insane."[86] Having brought her prize student to her home country Mrs. Tapper headed back to the United States.

On his own, Ornstein went to Denmark "and in Copenhagen gave his more than conventionally attractive *Russian Suite* and *Cossack Impressions* for piano to the Danish publisher, Wm. Hansen," who brought them out in 1914. Having visited six countries in a matter of months, Ornstein returned to Paris where he met Harold Bauer, the internationally famous piano virtuoso. Although Bauer expressed confusion with Ornstein's original compositions, he acknowledged the younger pianist "as a composer with a new and important message to deliver, one which deserved hearing." Martens characterized this encounter as marking "an epoch in Ornstein's career."[87] Whether it was Bauer in particular, or Paris more generally, Ornstein's horizons suddenly broadened while he was there.

Bauer, whose path would cross with Ornstein's over the years, was indeed a seminal force in getting the visitor known in Europe; he introduced Ornstein to Walter Morse Rummel, who provided the young pianist-composer with an entrée into Parisian musical society. Rummel (1887–1953) was also a pianist-composer and a close friend and champion of Claude Debussy. Upon returning to the United States Ornstein became one of Debussy's most ardent proponents and programmed his works on dozens of concerts, but it was Rummel who premiered many of Debussy's piano works including some of the preludes, etudes, *Six épigraphes antiques*, and *En blanc et noir*.[88] Rummel, like Ornstein, also became

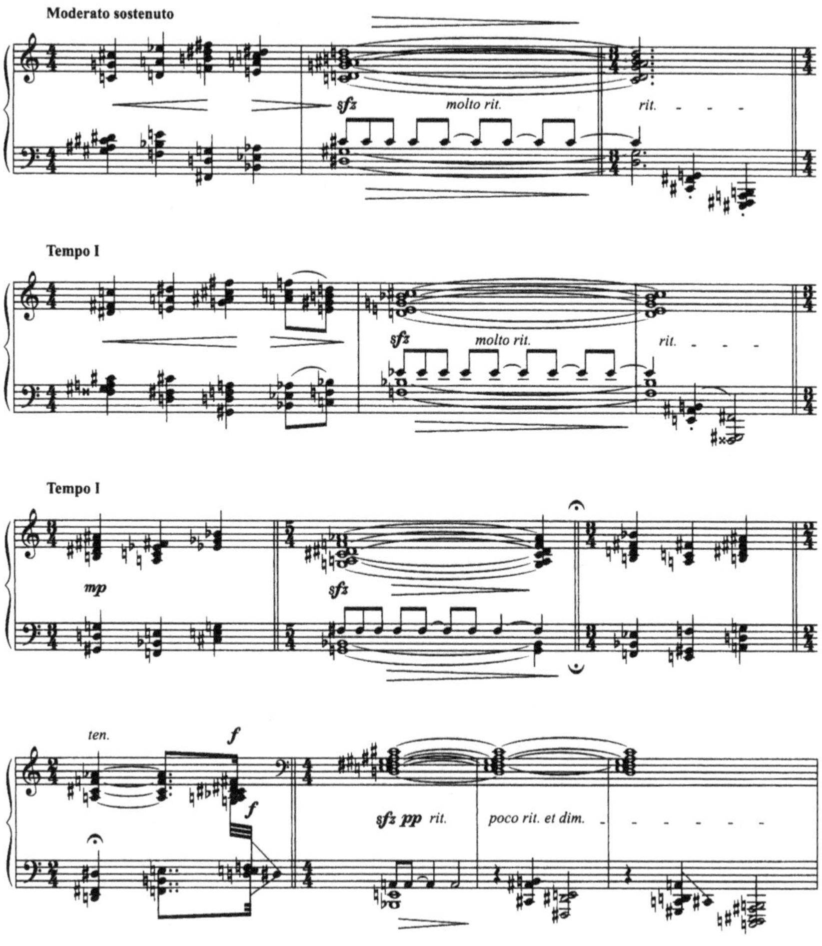

FIGURE 2.13. Leo Ornstein, *Impressions de Notre Dame.*

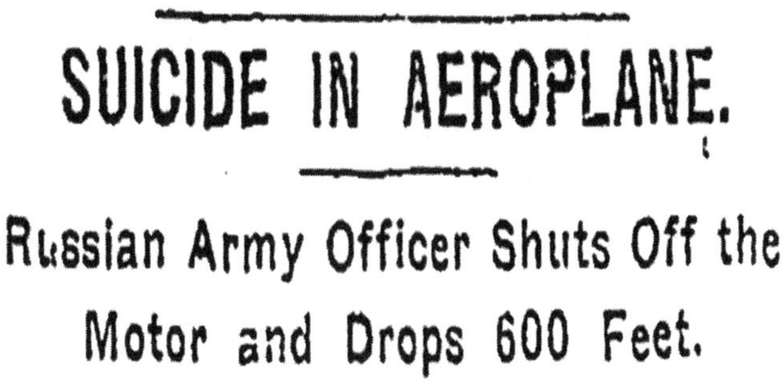
SUICIDE IN AEROPLANE.

Russian Army Officer Shuts Off the Motor and Drops 600 Feet.

FIGURE 2.14. *Suicide in an Aeroplane.*

famous for his interpretations of Bach, Chopin, and Liszt, three composers who formed a regular triumvirate in Ornstein's earliest recitals. The two men would have had much in common.

In addition, Rummel was a friend of American dancer Isadora Duncan (1878–1927), who had established a thriving dance school just six miles outside Paris. It is possible that Rummel (re)introduced Ornstein and Duncan, who three years earlier had given concerts within a couple of days of each other in New York. Legend surrounding this earlier encounter tells of Ornstein's bringing the infamous dancer home to meet his family. Given Duncan's penchant for younger men, she would have been thirty-three years old and he merely seventeen; it comes as no surprise to learn that she purportedly informed the family she intended to marry Leo. Whether the two enjoyed any kind of relationship at all is not known. Obviously, nothing came of her announcement, which was probably said in jest.

Rummel provided Ornstein with a letter of introduction to the poet, music critic, translator, and Ravel confidant Michel Dimitri Calvocoressi (1877–1944). Calvocoressi was a member of *Les Apaches*, a group of avant-garde artists, poets, and musicians in Paris who regularly met to discuss all matters pertaining to the arts.[89] Rubbing shoulders with such people would have been a stimulating and heady experience for Ornstein, who, with the help of his new acquaintances, devoted more and more of his energies to carving out a distinct niche for himself in contemporary musical culture.[90] Not coincidentally, Rummel's and Calvocoressi's favorite composers, Debussy and Ravel, would, upon Ornstein's return to the United States, become among his most oft-programmed composers.

Another important contact that Ornstein made while in Paris was the music writer, critic, and lecturer Paul Rodocanachi, who immediately took on the role of supporter and promoter. Depending upon the source consulted, different people were responsible for introducing Ornstein around town. In one telling Rodocanachi introduced Ornstein to Mrs. Landsberg, an amateur singer and recital hostess, who shared Rodocanachi's enthusiasm for Ornstein. It was through Rodocanachi and Mrs. Landsberg's son Bertie (who was Rodocanachi's partner) that Ornstein was invited by William Augustus Henry "Willie" King, a mutual composer friend, to play a concert at Oxford early in February 1914. According to this account, it was here that Ornstein met Roger Quilter (1877–1953), a man who came to play a significant role in his European success.[91]

Interleaved within his narrative of Ornstein's 1913–1914 European trip, Martens included Ornstein's first-person account of his time in Paris. It is among Ornstein's very few personal statements from this period and so worth reproducing in its entirety. As will be seen, issues of chronology and provenance rear their heads once again:[92]

> I went with my letter to Calvocoressi's apartment; he had a suite of rooms some three flights up in the *Rue de Caroussel*, and a blind woman—his mother—opened the door in answer to my ring. I was ushered into his studio, a pleasant room, its walls covered with books and pictures, with a grand piano littered with manuscripts, and a tall dark man, with a slight stoop, rose from his desk to receive me. He had a gentle voice and sympathetic manner and, after reading my letter, asked me in Russian—and it was a great pleasure to hear the accents of my mother-tongue again—whether I composed or merely played modern music.[93] I told him that I took the liberty of doing both, and he at once had me sit down at the piano. I played my *Wild Men's Dance* and the two *Impressions* for him, and he seemed amazed and unwilling to believe that the former could have originated in New York City. He insisted that I return the next day and play it again for him and for some musicians whom he expected to invite.[94] And thenceforward his kindness and interest were unfailing. He secured various wealthy pupils for me—for I was stranded—to coach in song and opera, and thus I was able to make a living without giving over my composition.[95]

Calvocoressi's introductions went beyond his musician acquaintances. As Ornstein recalls, he was introduced to an even larger circle of society, one that sounds similar to the milieu he inhabited while coaching operatic singers as the darling of St. Petersburg:

> Though I was too busy with my lessons and work to meet many people, I made the acquaintance of the Roumanian Princess de Brancovan and the gifted music-lover and musician, Mme. Landsberg—she sang very well—wife of the Brazilian banker of the same name, to each of whom I ascribed one of my *Preludes*, and for both of whom I played; as well as the American-born Princess de Polignac, who has taken such an interest in Stravinsky's music, and at whose musicales I also appeared.

Although Ornstein isn't specific, it's likely he is referring to two works from a set of three preludes that he wrote while in Europe and played at public appearances in London and Paris in the spring of 1914. They were eventually published by Schott. The three works, "Andantino," "Moderato," and "Allegro," are written in a dissonant idiom similar to "Impressions of Notre Dame" and others of his modernist-style works. Ornstein's detailed account of his interactions with Calvocoressi continued:

During February and March of 1914 Calvocoressi gave a series of lecture-recitals, two of them devoted to the *Géographie Musicale de l'Europe*, with musical illustrations drawn entirely from works of modernist composers. In the first lecture were represented Richard Strauss songs, piano pieces by Béla Bartók, Zoltán Kodály, Vilmos-Geza Zagon, Serge Liapounov, and Cyril Scott's "Jungle Book" pieces, which last I played. At the second lecture-recital I played my own *Impressions de la Tamise* and *Danse Sauvage*, and piano pieces (Op. 11 and 19) by Arnold Schönberg. Stravinsky's interesting *Melodies Japonaises* were also sung at this recital.[96]

Ornstein's circle of acquaintances grew. As Martens explains, it was while Ornstein was living in Paris that he first met the group of British composers from Oxford who invited him to return with them. Ultimately this led to his introduction to Quilter, whom Ornstein described as "a quite wonderful personality."[97] While visiting Oxford, he played for Dr. Ernest Walker, director of music at Balliol College, who remarked: "I've heard something strange, strange—something that makes me feel as though all the composite particles of the world were crumbling!"[98] What Ornstein played that elicited such a picturesque description is unknown; by this time in his visit he would have had a number of ultramodern works to perform.

According to Valerie Langfield, Quilter's biographer, Roger came from a family "used to comforts, money and servants; a family that felt it had a reputation to maintain and develop."[99] Bawdsey Manor, the family mansion, unquestionably reflected Quilter's station in life. Although he enjoyed every material comfort, Roger had been a shy child and plagued throughout his life by ill health. While his siblings excelled in sports, he excelled in music.[100] As Langfield describes it, his homosexuality set him apart from everyone in his family but his mother, and they developed an extremely close bond.[101]

In the late 1890s Quilter, like many English-speaking music students, attended the Frankfurt Conservatory, where he pursued piano and composition. There he fell in with four other students who together became known as the Frankfurt Five or Frankfurt Group: Roger Quilter, Balfour Gardiner, Percy Grainger, Norman O'Neill, and Cyril Scott.[102] Through Quilter Ornstein met Cyril Scott. During the peak years of Ornstein's virtuoso touring career, 1915–1921, he regularly programmed works by Scott, including *Danse nègre*, *Irish Reel*, *Dance of the Elephants*, and *Impressions from the Jungle*, with the first two performed most often. As with his fondness for the works of Debussy, which he likely got from Rummel, and for those of Ravel, which he took from Calvocoressi, Ornstein's attraction to Scott's music came from yet another of his European contacts, Roger Quilter.

He enjoyed multiple circles of musician friends. Together their influence would resonate for years to come in Ornstein's piano repertoire.

The Frankfurt Group, or Frankfurt Five, shared little by way of a solid aesthetic agenda other than to maintain their individuality. As Langfield explains: "What common factor there was—and Grainger was vocal in talking and writing about this—was harmonic: he wrote of the importance to them of 'the chord' and their compositions tended to be 'vertical' rather than 'horizontal', and so the more telling on the rare occasions when contrapuntal techniques were used."[103] Stephen Lloyd, in an article entitled "Grainger and the 'Frankfurt Group,'" offers a somewhat longer discussion of the group's aesthetic bond; it is not necessarily more helpful:

> As Sir Thomas Armstrong has shown, the "chord" (which he defines as a version of a chromatic chord on the major sixth of the scale with its ninth and appoggiaturas) was neither invented by the Group nor did it become their exclusive property—one only has to look, for example, to the music of Delius. Yet their thinking was often essentially chordal, especially Scott's who, as his harmonic language crystallized, made increasing use of the 1–4–7 chord (which is in fact the "upper half" of Scriabin's "mystic" *Prometheus* chord), notably to much effect in his Third Piano Sonata of 1956.[104]

Much the same can be said of Ornstein's most dissonant, futurist music, which is noteworthy for its coloristic chords built on fourths, or dense, highly chromatic chords that span a seventh, and for its avoidance of extended counterpoint. When counterpoint is hinted at—usually some kind of distant, short-lived, echo-like passage—it assumes especial significance. Ornstein's tendencies toward verticality and away from polyphony, his preference for irregular barring, avoidance of key signatures, and focus on rhythmic energy would all have been reinforced rather than challenged by his association with the Frankfurt Five.[105]

Quilter, the "graceful and wealthy young man . . . welcome wherever he cared to go," performed a similar role for Ornstein in London to that of Calvocoressi in Paris, introducing him to a wide circle of interesting people in positions to help.[106] Martens lists "Robin Legge, of the *Daily Telegraph* . . . the great [painter, John Singer] Sargent, Arthur Shattuck, and Mr. Winthrop L. Rogers, the publisher, a fine violinist and a music-lover keenly interested in all new developments" as among them.[107] But it was Quilter who took the most active role, and whose friendship had the greatest impact on his work. It was while enjoying an evening at Quilter's home (with Roger and his mother)—that included dinner and music, the opportunity to play "on a fine Bechstein," and "a discussion with a young painter"—that Ornstein became acquainted with the writings and art of William Blake (1757–1827).[108] Blake made a powerful impression on Ornstein as Martens reports:

> What he heard excited his interest in the highest degree; he read everything there was to be had of Blake's, and pored over his designs, notably those for Robert Blair's *The Grave* and Blake's own *The Marriage of Heaven and Hell*, as well as the splendid series illustrating *The Book of Job*. His instant sympathy with the artist-poet's ability to seize "the pictorial element of ideas, simple or sublime, and translate them into the appropriate language of sense," has been reflected in the tremendous sonata for violin and piano, Op. 31, which, together with three songs, as yet unpublished, were its first fruits.[109]

Op. 31 will be discussed later.

Aside from Martens's biography, which was written three years after Ornstein returned from Europe, no other published accounts survive to shed light on his time there. Correspondence from Ornstein to Roger Quilter, and from Bertie Landsberg to Quilter, however, provides a valuable rare glimpse into Ornstein's activities and precise whereabouts during his time in Europe.

In a letter dated February 5, 1914, Bertie Landsberg writes from 161 Avenue Victor-Hugo in Paris to Roger Quilter and refers to Leo:

> My dear Roger,
>
> Ornstein is just back [to Paris]—of all who spoilt him in England he is bubbling over with praise and gratitude, but most of all you. I was sure you would appreciate each other and am delighted. . . . All joy to you, Bertie.

Nine days later Ornstein wrote his own letter to Quilter who, in the brief time since they met, had begun to organize a London debut concert for Ornstein. This was quite in keeping with Quilter's habits; he generously helped Percy Grainger and others advance their careers by finding performance opportunities and publishers.[110] As Ornstein's letter demonstrates, although he was groomed as a pianist, at this juncture he is most concerned with presenting himself as a composer. This first London concert would take place March 27, 1914, in Steinway Hall.

> 14 February 1914
>
> Dear Mr. Quilter,   7 Montagu St.
>
> You are certainly the kindest soul and I don't know how I can thank you for all the trouble you are taking.
> I shall certainly take your suggestion and place some Bach either first in the program or else in the middle.

The reason why I was going to play nothing but Schönberg and myself was that I did not intend to be criticized as a pianist just now but after reading your letter I think it much better that I should play something the public is familiar with.

I have written to Steinway, telling them, that any suggestion you should/make they are to take it as coming from me.

So please if there is anything you wish to suggest please do so and they will carry it out. The manager of Steinway Hall, Mr. Mackey is in charge of this concert.

I shall be very happy to see you a week before the concert and thank you awfully for all the trouble it must be for you to have me meet people.

Am very sorry that you are too nervous to play and that the piece is too difficult, but I will have to leave out something to make room for the Bach pieces so I will try to console myself.[111]

When you are through with the piece will you please send it back. I suggest playing Bach in the middle of the program—it will be an oasis for the public to rest in [splodge—a cross between ? and !]

Will I be allowed to hear your music when in England? I have heard so much about it from Bertie.

26 Rue Washington   Yours sincerely
Paris   Leo Ornstein

P.S. I'm also sending you the programme and will later send a little biography written by Bertie.

The Steinway Hall concert put Ornstein on the musical map. Taking Quilter's advice he played "Three Choral Preludes" by Bach as transcribed for piano by Busoni, then two numbers from Schoenberg's Op. 11, "Six Little Pieces," Op. 19, and his own "Impressions of Notre Dame," *Three Moods*, Sonata Op. 28, *Impressions de la Tamise*, and what would become his signature piece, *Danse sauvage*. Critics were alternately amused, offended, and confused. A few, striving to comment upon something they understood, separated his pianism from his composing. Whether it was because of Quilter's network of acquaintances, or simply because of the novelty of the performer and the promised program, no one interested at all in the London music scene ignored the recital.

The next day, March 28, Ornstein's concert was reviewed in the *London Times*, *Daily Mail*, and *Daily Telegraph* followed by a brief story in *Musical America* on April 4. The *Times*'s review, "A 'Futurist' at the Piano," is a potpourri of impressions rather than a systematic assessment of either the pianist or the music. Its use of the word "futurist" was the first time the appellation was publicly attached

FUTURIST MUSIC.

WILD OUTBREAK AT STEINWAY HALL.

PALE AND FRENZIED YOUTH

FIGURE 2.15. Headline, review of Ornstein's first Steinway Hall concert.

to the composer; it would stick for the near term and become a convenient way of describing his most dissonant style. According to the anonymous reviewer, Ornstein was "a trick pianist" whose "facility is amazing." While confessing that the pieces were beyond traditional analysis, he also admitted to having been "stirred by their crudity, their energy, and often by their absurdity." In a final paragraph the writer criticized Ornstein's performance of the Bach preludes but, in comparing the most futurist works to those of Schoenberg, found Ornstein's pieces to be "more exciting."[112]

Richard Capell of the *Daily Mail* wrote of the "Wild Outbreak at Steinway Hall." Ornstein was described as "a pale and frenzied youth, dressed in velvet, crouched over the instrument in an attitude all his own, and for all the apparent frailty of his form, dealt it the most ferocious punishment." The reviewer heard the "wild men" of Ornstein's *Danse sauvage* "somehow in Notre Dame and the Thames too" (references to his two sets of *Impressions*). "R.C." took a kind of perverse pleasure at "living in an age when such joyous extravagances are possible" even if "nothing so horrible as M. Ornstein's music has been heard so far." He referred to the "harsh brutality [of] these piano pieces," but one can't help but sense that the author harbored a certain fascination with the music. It may be that the reviewer planted the notion of Ornstein's concerts as musical circus acts with his half-humorous remark that "sufferers from complete deafness should attend the next recital in numbers, for the spectacle presented by this young man involved in one of his frenzied improvisations is engaging." His review, like that of the *Times* reporter, concluded with a comparison of Ornstein's and Schoenberg's pieces, and with a warning against what the reviewer construed as Ornstein's sensational, and perhaps self-serving, style: "The contrast [of the Schoenberg pieces] was great with the savagery of the music of Ornstein, from who, however, we are quite prepared for work of true interest and talent if he overcomes his present leaning towards ferociously egotistical rhetoric."[113] This would not be the first reviewer to question whether Ornstein was a real talent or a charlatan.

The final London review seems to reflect the most serious attempt to come to terms with the "pianoforte recital of Futurist music," as it was billed. The writer quotes from the program notes that Ornstein's "ambition is to convey emotions only in the sounds into which his unconscious or super-conscious reason has translated them, without allowing any conventional contrivances to come between him and his auditors."[114] The reviewer questions what "conventional contrivances" refers to but concedes that Ornstein's music and manner were uncompromisingly unconventional.

Both the *Times* and *Telegraph* reviewers criticized Ornstein's interpretations of Bach, the former taking him to task for his tone and rhythm, and the latter finding fault with the "ultrasentimentalized" readings. But as everyone agreed, audiences had not come to hear him play Bach.[115] While Schoenberg had been heard earlier in London, nothing compared, so the critic asserted, with the "extraordinary series of strange, incoherent, incomprehensible, and often uncanny sounds . . . produced from one instrument in a London concert-room." The writer appears to be genuinely curious to know what Ornstein's impressions of Notre Dame were to result in "such violent—one might almost say brutal—assaults as Mr. Ornstein made on the piano in the second of those works."

Demonstrating a generous willingness to give Ornstein the benefit of the doubt, the critic concluded with a positive assessment of the effects of *Danse sauvage*:

> It was, at least, possible, however, at the end of his programme, to appreciate the point, originality, and suggestiveness of his "Wild Men's Dance": for here, at any rate, with all its strangeness and daring, was something with the pulse of rhythm in it, and something, moreover that brought vividly to the mind a picture of primordial beings in all the savage abandonment of the wildest of corybantic revels. This piece apparently delighted the audience, who, completely baffled though they must have been by what had gone before, gave the newcomer a very cordial reception.[116]

Just ten days later, on April 7, Ornstein gave a second recital at Steinway Hall. The same three newspapers covered the event, but this time the writers were more willing to be critical, even hostile; perhaps they were simply mirroring the audience's reception. Richard Capell reported in the *Daily Mail*: "This time the programme was made up wholly of his own music, and, though he had Mr. Algernon Ashton smiling appreciatively at him from the stalls, the audience held a strong hostile element."[117] The gallery hissed, booed, groaned, and guffawed with derision, and someone felt impelled to supply the missing melodic element in M. Ornstein's music with more tuneful whistling. In fact no London concert-giver in recent years has had such harsh treatment. No one else, it is true, has offered a London audience such fare." Having reported on the audience's reaction, Capell interjected his own thoughts: "there is no denying some sort of talent in this young Futurist. His keyboard technique is remarkable, even allowing for the laxity of this new art, which generously allows the fingers any alternative for every note. . . . But beneath his hurricane of fortuitous notes one caught indications of a feeling for original rhythm and an inventiveness in novel timbres."[118]

The *Daily Telegraph* reporter commented upon "one young hooligan . . . that went the length of throwing, or trying to throw, something on to the platform while Mr. Ornstein was at the piano." The critic too recognized "the composer's . . . wonderful feat of pianoforte technique of an unaccustomed kind."[119]

The *London Times* critic also applauded "Mr. Ornstein's agility as a pianist." While grudgingly admitting to the pieces possessing definite rhythmic qualities, he regretted that "any one in the audience could really have made musical sense of the horrible rhythmical noise which Mr. Ornstein produced, whatever kind of sensation they may have derived from it."[120]

The *Musical Times* wondered aloud "whether this eccentric player is to be taken seriously" and questioned the source of inspiration for his compositions—was it "his peculiar command of the keyboard [more] than . . . any other source"?[121] *Musical Courier* applauded "London's 'cultivated' people" who "dared to hiss and groan at the performances of a Futurist composer. . . . we are glad that one audience has summoned up the courage to be rude."[122]

There was, however, a more positive review, one that appeared on April 18 in *The Musical Standard*. "C.N." devoted over nine hundred words to "some frank impressions" of Ornstein's music. He acknowledged Ornstein as "the most advanced musician the 'Futurists' have yet given us" and suggested "that the majority of the audience was inclined to treat the recital as a joke." He reflectively concluded, however, that although he had gone "half inclined to blame; I stayed to praise." Like other critics, C.N. couldn't deny Ornstein his pianistic prowess: "The technical brilliance of Mr. Ornstein's playing is remarkable, and it is easy to imagine that the average pianist confronted with one of his works would find considerable difficulty in mastering it."

He also found space to comment upon Ornstein's youth and presence: "The composer himself is very young, very earnest, slim and slightly bowed.[123] He undoubtedly plays as he feels without regard to any written methods of the past or the present." C.N. then commented on each of the pieces. Of the *Two Shadow*

Pieces, Op. 17, he yields that "Mr. Ornstein has taught me much." Of *Eleven Short Pieces*, Op. 29, he finds the second piece "in a rugged way . . . beautiful." *Three Moods*, Op. 22, "are immensely impressive." "'The Wild Men's Dance' (Op. 13) is the most marvelous thing I have ever heard: the rhythm is electric and compelling, the playing of it must be a tremendous tax upon the powers of the executant, and the conclusion is breathless in its rapidity." C.N. put himself on the line with the strongest endorsement Ornstein was to receive from the London press: "Personally I see in Leo Ornstein one of the most remarkable composers of the day: his point of view is startling in its vehemence and uncontrolled daring—it seems almost terrible that this boy should set at defiance all the laws and principles of harmony, and yet give us music which has in it that germ of realism and humanity which is indicative of genius on the part of its composer."[124]

While it's questionable that any composer could have been completely pleased with broad incomprehension and such a lopsided reception, just two years later, in 1916, the twenty-two-year-old composer put the whole experience in perspective. Recalling the second London concert to Carl Van Vechten, Ornstein explained: "I couldn't hear the piano myself. The crowd whistled and howled and even threw handy missiles on the stage . . . but that concert made me famous." Van Vechten noted "Ornstein wound up with a smile."[125]

Soon after his second London recital, Ornstein sailed back to the United States, eager to prepare for his return to Europe in the fall of 1914. He was full of plans for another successful trip. During the summer of 1914 Ornstein corresponded with those who had made his stay there so enjoyable; the letters reveal a deepening friendship.

A note from Ornstein to Quilter dated May 18, 1914, reflects a more informal relationship than had existed between them in February. Ornstein addresses "Dear Roger" from Blue Hill, Maine, where he is "very hard at work on my Quartette which I hope will be ready to go to the printers in a few weeks." He enquires "How are your piano pieces getting on?" Ornstein signs "With love, Yours, Leo" and asks Quilter to "Please give my kindest/regards to your mother."[126]

Another letter from Blue Hill just eleven days later tells something of Ornstein's summer work habits, his musical preferences, and his plans for a return trip to Europe in the fall. The outbreak of World War I in the summer of 1914, however, interrupted those plans and forever altered Ornstein's career path. We can only wonder what tack it would have taken had he returned, fresh after his attention-grabbing London and Paris debuts, for an extended concert tour, and perhaps to live there. In *Les Apaches* and the Oxford group he had found a large coterie of friends who were equally committed to the modernist idiom; he enjoyed their camaraderie. He had also established a circle of supporters among patronesses and the society set who had taken him in; he could anticipate more opportunities to build upon his newly won fame:

29 May 1914

Dear Roger,

I am delighted to hear that you are going to have a vacation.

I am sure you need it and it will undoubtedly do you lots of good. I am very anxious indeed to see the pieces you have written. If they come in time I may be able to learn them and play them in Norway this Fall. I am working very hard over a Violin and Piano sonata and practicing at a great rate. Did you hear many of the "Russian Ballet" performances? How did you like the "Nightingale["] of Stravinsky what about "[The Legend of] Joseph" of Strauss. I have just gotten through with playing Mendelssohn and Liszt, it's an awful bore. Aren't you glad you don't have to play in public? I am studying some wonderful pieces by Debussy, which I'll play for you when I get back to London. I shall write to Strecker about it. I wish I could have been with you in Oxford when you saw the boys it must have been lots of fun. Please remember me to your kind Mother,

With love
Yours Leo.[127]

By August the war was in full swing in Europe, and conscription was underway. Quilter, at age thirty-seven, would not have been called up at this point in the conflict, but in a letter to Quilter dated August 25, 1914, Ornstein appears seriously concerned about the possibility.[128] Or perhaps he was more upset with the inexplicable results of "progress":

Dear Roger,

I have been wondering about you many days, and am terribly anxious to know what is happening to you just now. You will surely not have to go into service I hope because that would certainly be too dreadful. Now what do you think of our so called modern civilization, on the slightest pretence human beings are being butchered by the thousands and all because of what?, that's what I should like to know? Certainly savages were more justified in butchering each other, where they at least had the satisfaction of meeting their enemies face to face, and for the moment either realizing or imagining a grievance. But thanks to our great mechanical contrivances all one need do is just to drop a bomb in cold blood and have the satisfaction of having killed a thousand men. Progressing, aren't we? Do excuse this outbreak, but I just feel terribly about it. With love to you

Yours
Leo[129]

The eruption of war and the resulting cancellation of his plans meant that Ornstein was left in the United States with no immediate likelihood of his getting back to Europe, and no recital or concert engagements for the upcoming season. Interrupting the momentum he had recently established in London and Paris and losing contact with the friends he had just made could not have happened at a more inauspicious time for the eager composer-pianist, whose career seemed poised to take off. It became clear very quickly that, to have any prospects at all, Ornstein would have to give up the idea of a European career and devote his energies to building one elsewhere, primarily in the United States.

Compared to the London concerts his single performance at a monthly meeting of "The Bohemians" at Luchow's restaurant in New York on November 2, 1914, must have seemed a poor substitute and a decided turn downwards. A. Walter Kramer, Ornstein's champion from his earliest days, wrote a brief review for Musical America: "Mr. Ornstein, whose fine piano performances in New York will be remembered from four years ago, has developed in the time he has been abroad. He is an ultra-modernist." After enumerating the original pieces he played, Kramer asserted, "These works aroused great interest." A final paragraph of the brief remarks commented upon a talk entitled "The Song Singer's Art," which was given by a Mr. Max Heinrich at the same meeting. This was a far cry from Steinway Hall.

According to Martens, 1914 closed with a series of recitals in the South, likely a stopgap measure to make up for a concert season in New York that had already been booked.[130] No record of these concerts has been found at this time, however.

At least one of the Oxford crowd, Lucian Swift Kirtland, a writer of travel books, came to the United States, first for a visit to New York in early 1915, and then to take up residence in Poland, Ohio, arriving in late summer 1916.[131] In a letter he wrote to Roger Quilter on January 30, 1915, Kirtland reported that he had recently talked with Ornstein on the phone and would see him Friday night: "Some day we are getting into the country together."[132] But such a jaunt would have had to wait both until the weather cleared up and Ornstein's professional obligations took a hiatus. Kirtland's presence in New York at this particular time in 1915 meant that he was there to hear Ornstein's Bandbox concerts, the series of four recitals that put the young futurist on the musical map in this country.[133] A second letter from Kirtland to Quilter dated April 29, 1915, however, makes no reference to those recitals, nor the stir they created. Instead Kirtland relays that Ornstein "is going to South America until September to give concerts in Rio and to be the guest of the Landsberg's."[134] It would appear that Ornstein, though deprived for close to a year of personal contact with his London and Paris friends, still enjoyed their support. Like many European families of means, at least part of the Landsberg family would temporarily retreat from a continent in conflict and ride out the war years in another, calmer clime. Ornstein, shut off from Europe, permanently turned his gaze westward and worked at building a career in the United States.

3 ||| Circles and Triangles and Networks and Nets

As soon as he returned to America Ornstein began fine-tuning plans for another European trip. It is no wonder. He had the opportunity to perform an original symphonic work to be conducted by Sir Henry J. Wood in London, he had endeared himself to some of the most powerful musicians both there and in Paris, and he had gained entrée to important circles of patronage. A forty-concert trip to Norway was set for the fall of 1914, probably through the efforts of Bertha Feiring Tapper, and further concerts in England, France, and elsewhere were either planned or being discussed. The outbreak of war, however, dashed any hope of going back to Europe: all professional engagements were canceled; the momentum he had established on the continent was lost.

In very real ways, the war also cost Ornstein proximity to his first circle of friends, which he'd just found. His years as a student at the Institute dedicated to practicing and repertoire building, his voracious reading habits, his youthful discomfort in social situations, his large family, and his close ties with Mrs. Tapper and her established New York and Blue Hill circles meant he had little opportunity or need and few skills to cultivate friendships of his own. But that had changed in 1913 when Mrs. Tapper left him in Paris. Through M. D. Calvocoressi and Harold Bauer, and then Roger Quilter and Cyril Scott, Ornstein found similarly interested, ambitious, dedicated, and talented musicians and supporters who encouraged his development in both human and professional ways. For perhaps the first time in his twenty years he felt one of "the boys."[1] For perhaps the first time as well, Ornstein recognized the benefits of belonging to a group of his own peers. Although a few letters written by his English acquaintances suggest attempts on their part to maintain contact with Ornstein, after the spring of 1915 he assessed the situation, cut his losses, and focused his energies on what was more likely to produce results. His career became exclusively American; he never again went to Europe as a performing artist. With no ready-made group to embrace and nurture him on this side of the Atlantic, Ornstein had to create one of his own. The situation became even more urgent when in September 1915 Bertha Feiring Tapper unexpectedly died. Her efforts to get her favorite pupil before the public eye, however, were not forgotten.

In a letter written in the early 1970s to her nephew Peter Ornstein, Pauline Mallet-Prevost Ornstein offered her perspective on what had become Ornstein's isolation: "Leo never made friends in the profession. Most of them are self-inflated and uneducated due to the very nature of their occupations which demanded too much time devoted to practice at school age and then publicizing of their personalities. This is anathema to Leo and one reason for his problems. When his managers did all the promotion he could come across with the goods, but he shrinks as you know from raising a finger himself."[2] Pauline's assessment of Leo's lack of initiative on his own behalf suggests a lifelong pattern. And in his old age, Leo often described himself as lazy. But having learned much about Pauline Mallet-Prevost's own social development and interpersonal skills, it is not unreasonable to speculate that in offering such an explanation of her husband's "problems" she, in fact, projected her own discomfort in social situations upon him.

Numerous family stories refer to her being extraordinarily sheltered throughout her life right up to 1918 when she married Leo. In one case the new Mrs. Ornstein was described as afraid to cross a city street by herself, having never done so before.[3] Although she had grown up the daughter of privilege, she disdained the social obligations and rituals that went with her family's position; she actively sought to distance herself from that life and parents she perceived as less than affectionate. In assessing Leo, what Pauline didn't comment upon was her own complicity in Leo's situation, her active role in cutting him off from most of his family, almost all of his friends, and the places that had been familiar to him prior to their marriage. She cultivated his dependence upon her. While too often the wife of a famous figure is unfairly demonized, blamed for anything undesirable that happens to her victim-like husband (but seldom credited with his successes), in the case of Pauline Mallet-Prevost Ornstein too much evidence exists to ignore the role she played in extracting Leo from the people and milieu that had nurtured him before their marriage. As their children Edith Ornstein Valentine and Severo Ornstein have asserted on numerous occasions: "Mother wanted him all to herself." Extended family members concur. Over the years she succeeded in getting her wish. One is left to speculate on Pauline's motivations, both conscious and unconscious, and Leo's acquiescence, troubled as it often was.[4]

But Leo's interactions with his musician friends in Europe and letters found in numerous collections of his American associates paint quite a different picture from Pauline's of the modernist musician's personal initiative, especially during his early years as a touring pianist-composer. While Leo Ornstein might not have sought out or enjoyed close associations with many musicians in the United States after his marriage, before marrying Pauline he had worked hard to cultivate a roster of friends within and across the larger cultural and artistic milieu. His efforts paid off handsomely. Ornstein's circle became an intimate, vital society of its own, supporting his efforts and theirs—in many ways a subset of other powerful artistic groups. It also placed Ornstein at the heart of the burgeoning modernist movement in the United States.

FIGURE 3.1. Bertha Feiring Tapper's class. Seated center, Bertha Feiring Tapper; Leo Ornstein, Claire Reis seated to her left; Kay Swift, Pauline Mallet-Prevost seated to her right. *Photo Courtesy Vivian Perlis.*

Prior to Tapper's death, Claire Raphael Reis, a former student in Mrs. Tapper's studio, had already begun her own campaign to champion her classmate Leo Ornstein: first, because, like her teacher, she believed in his music and his pianistic talents, but, second, because she saw him as a potential lightening rod for the modernist cause to which she was committed and with which she would later become identified.[5] Years later she acknowledged that Ornstein's "dynamic personality and fiery enthusiasm as an artist made him very attractive."[6] He was a good front man for the cause.

Claire Raphael was born in 1888 in Brownsville, Texas, and then broadly educated in New York City, France, and Germany. She returned to the United States "convinced that [she] should keep up [her] interests in the arts and also find a wider circle of enlightened friends."[7] While in Europe Raphael had studied piano, attended the theater, and taken advantage of opportunities to hear Felix Weingartner's Berlin Philharmonic Orchestra. It was likely there that she first encountered musical modernism, although the precise form it took is unknown.[8] Much to the advantage of America's modernist musical culture, once Raphael returned, she put her "luminous, nourishing energy" to work and succeeded in creating the wider network she sought.[9]

In the fall of 1914 Raphael invited her good friend Waldo Frank (1889–1967) and a new acquaintance, Paul Rosenfeld (1890–1946), to accompany her to an informal recital given by Ornstein at Tapper's 362 Riverside Drive home.[10]

The exact date of this event is unknown, though given the summering habits of Tapper and her teaching calendar, it is likely not to have occurred before the beginning of October at the very earliest. Raphael on piano, Frank on cello, and A. Walter Kramer on violin had formed their own informal chamber ensemble; they played sonatas and trios together one evening a week. In the pianist's words, "we made up an *avant-garde*, exploring a new world in the universe of music." Rosenfeld was "the only 'outsider' allowed to listen to our trio-evenings."[11] But Rosenfeld's outsider status would not remain for long. Upon attending the recital Frank and Rosenfeld, who knew each other from their Yale days, became instant believers in Ornstein. Frank's reaction to hearing Leo's music for the first time has been recounted earlier. Whether Rosenfeld was aware of Ornstein's infamous concerts in London during the spring of 1914 while he too was visiting Europe he never revealed.[12] It is known that he attended a concert given by Alexander Scriabin at Bechstein Hall in London, in March of that year, and was transported by the experience.[13] Like Raphael, who returned from Europe determined to keep her artistic interests alive, Rosenfeld sailed back determined "to awaken . . . the

FIGURE 3.3.
Paul Rosenfeld.
© 2006 The Georgia
O'Keeffe Foundation
/ Artists Rights
Society (ARS),
New York.

slumbering consciousness of the American people."[14] His interest in Scriabin continued well into the 1930s, during which time he wrote four articles on the man and his music.

After the fall 1914 Ornstein recital Rosenfeld must have immediately imagined multiple possibilities for the futurist virtuoso. Within a year, he wrote to Raphael from Blue Hill, Maine, where he too had taken to summering, and where he and Leo were strategizing ways Ornstein could be promoted and employed to further the cause of modern music.[15] Excerpts from his August 6, 1915, letter to "Dear Claire" explain:

> I've been discussing with Leo his plans for the winter and we've decided to consult you. The project under consideration is a series of six Sunday night recitals—at $10 the series, to be given during the months of December [1915], January, and February [1916]. Leo thinks he can get Steinway Hall for very little. I suggested giving a comprehensive course in modern piano music, semi-private, the audience limited to sixty or seventy.[16] After each recital, a general discussion. Will you give us your general idea Claire? Do

you think they'll be any difficulty in getting the audience? The point is that in the back of my mind there is a desire to help organize a Modern Music Club,—an association which will here perform for it each year the new chamber music, and I wonder whether an audience gotten together for Leo's recital wouldn't help form a nucleus for such a society? There's really a crying need for such an organization to make headway against the sluggish conservatism in musical circles. The idea was forcibly presented to me when Leo went over the d'Indy violin Sonata for me; during the ten years since its publication, no one had seen fit to make the world familiar with one of the finest works of this genre (N.Y. excess provincialism it seems to me).

Of course it's rather late in the year to talk of forming a club of that sort for this winter season, but the Leo-audience would be a step in the same direction, which gives us something to think with you for next year—don't you agree? You remember speaking of a similar matter, don't you, during one of our talks last Spring?[17]

Although Rosenfeld and Ornstein were only getting around to talking about the series in the summer, clearly Rosenfeld and Raphael had had their own conversations about modernist matters months earlier. For the next few years, Raphael, Kramer, Frank, Rosenfeld, and Ornstein formed the nucleus of a modernist booster club, and Ornstein was the focal point. The degree to which their efforts put Ornstein *and* musical modernism in the spotlight cannot be overestimated. As his fame grew, the cachet his name provided their mutual cause was real; the benefits were reciprocal. Ornstein worked with and for his friends. He was an active participant in the larger modernist artistic initiative. From early on A. Walter Kramer, a close friend of both Bertha Feiring Tapper and Raphael, wrote lengthy, musically insightful articles that were placed in periodicals with large readerships.[18] Kramer did his best to stir up interest in his friend and in new music. In retrospect these articles were of seminal importance to Ornstein's career. The first of these extended pieces appeared in the December 12, 1914, issue of *Musical America*. In a story entitled "Has Leo Ornstein Discovered a New Musical Style?" Kramer pulled out all the stops and presented what would quickly become the essentials of the Ornstein legend.

Ornstein's physical appearance became an important component. Describing Ornstein when he had first met him in 1910 Kramer recalled: "To me there was something ascetic in his face, the face of a dreamer, who had in him that which distinguishes genius from the rank and file." Gradually bringing us up to date, by the end of the article the dreamer has become "a prophet." From then on, much would be made of Ornstein's artistic demeanor, his physical presence at the piano; photographs would capitalize on his Lisztian mane of hair.

Quoting directly from the composer, Kramer made reference to Ornstein's inexplicable stylistic epiphany, the second and most oft-repeated component of the legend. He reviewed the sudden appearance of new sounds unprepared by any experience Leo had had with similar music. Kramer then devotes a significant amount of text to reviewing the London and Paris debuts and speaks of Ornstein's plans to return, had the war not intervened.[19]

Perhaps what is most noteworthy in this particular article is Kramer's discussion of Ornstein's compositional process and aesthetic goals; Kramer, a musician and composer himself, wants his readers to understand that Ornstein eschews formalism of any kind. Taking on a pedagogical tone, Kramer explains: "Let us understand that Mr. Ornstein's purpose is not to discover harmonies that are new, or that are altered in the manner of the modern Frenchmen. The opening group of notes in his 'First Impression of Notre-Dame' . . . does not claim to be an altered 13th or anything of the kind." A few bars of the introductory measure of this work and of his third prelude from *Three Preludes*, Op. 20, adorn the top of the article for readers to consult.[20] He goes on: "His music is color—for that is the basis on which he builds. He hears his compositions complete long before he sets down even a note of them. At times he carries them around with him for months before he puts ink to paper." Indeed Ornstein possessed an extraordinary aural memory. Once a piece was set in his head, he could perform it over the course of many years without writing it down or forgetting it. Of course, this only held for his shorter, solo piano works.[21] He was also an accomplished improviser, a skill that not only enabled but likely reinforced his championing an intuitive approach to composition.[22]

Anticipating those who might find Ornstein's music "ugly" Kramer asserted: "He deals with elemental matters, not with ideas of the *salon*. Color and atmosphere —the latter far removed from the hot-house type, which the lesser contemporary French-men give us—mean everything to him. Nor does melody akin to our accepted interpretation of it appear in his music."[23] Heading off charges of Ornstein being merely sensational Kramer suggests: "Speak to Leo Ornstein: hear him defend his aesthetic principles and he will convince you of the sincerity of his art."

Not content to simply champion the man or his aesthetic, Kramer offers a primer on how pianists might accommodate the various combinations of notes "which cannot be fingered according to the adopted method of piano-fingering." He launches into a discussion of the technical requirements needed to play certain pieces. He refers to Ornstein's "bewitching effect in arpeggios" achieved by "pressing down the damper pedal and releasing it immediately after striking the keys." Quoting Vincent d'Indy's assessment "that rhythm was the least explored of all those things which go to make music," Kramer finds "Anger," the third of Ornstein's *Three Moods*, to be a study of just that. "Leo Ornstein has worked out remarkable rhythm in this piece. It is vivid, thrilling, and it leaves you gasping as he strikes the last note with an intensity that is overpowering."

Finally, lest readers are left thinking that Ornstein is merely interested in things musical, Kramer assures them that Ornstein is "well posted on all contemporary developments in the art world" and then speaks of Igor Stravinsky, "the man of the hour," as well as modern painting and literature. The author finishes his testimonial-like article with a prediction of Ornstein's place in music history: "Leo Ornstein may be ahead of his time. I am inclined to think that he is ushering in a new epoch; that he is employing his genius toward the attainment of a new musical expression, an expression, which perhaps not permanent in itself, must play an important role in the development of the music of years to come. And I am certain that he is a prophet of this development, that he will lead us to the music of the future."[24]

Given that Kramer was a close associate and championed Ornstein throughout his public career, the piece must be considered a sincere tribute, but it must also be recognized as a bit of advertising, an effort to separate Ornstein from the pack, to stir up interest in a forthcoming event. The opening sentence says as much: "What Paris and London heard last Winter of Leo Ornstein's daring musical innovations New York will have an opportunity to evaluate for itself in the near future." He later refers directly to "the four recital-programs of modern music which Mr. Ornstein will give in New York beginning late in January." Kramer shares that Bertha Tapper, the previous month, had invited him to her home to listen to Ornstein and to interview him.

Whether Kramer had a hand in the actual arrangements for the upcoming so-called Bandbox concerts, which would put Ornstein on the modernist musical map, or whether he was recruited to provide important and necessary publicity in response to a request from Bertha Feiring Tapper will probably never be known. The size of the article, occupying a full page and spilling over to another, with a photograph of Ornstein as well as examples of scores, and the references to the forthcoming recitals suggest a carefully orchestrated effort by an experienced hand. Whether Raphael Reis, Frank, and Rosenfeld had roles in what immediately transpired is unknown, but also not unlikely. Raphael Reis was committed to Tapper, and Tapper was committed to Ornstein. Frank and Rosenfeld were committed to seeing modernism prosper.

Beyond his cooperative efforts with Kramer and Tapper, a letter of December 7, 1914, shows Ornstein agreeing to meet with one of his newest fans, the writer Waldo Frank, "to play some more of my music to you."[25] It is likely that

Frank took advantage of the audience with Leo to gather material for an article of his own. His very first published story was a fifteen-hundred-word piece titled "Leo Ornstein" that appeared in April 1915 in *The Onlooker*.[26] On February 25, 1915, just three days before the third of Ornstein's series of Bandbox concerts, Ornstein requested the article Frank had finished in December: "A magazine in Pittsburgh wants an article on me. Can you send over the one you have written? I may be able to place it there."[27] Whether *The Onlooker* was the periodical Ornstein had in mind is unknown. But what is clear is that far from sitting back and watching others work on his behalf, Ornstein was in the middle of the effort.

Starting in 1916, Paul Rosenfeld began a thirty-year career of arts criticism that resulted in 196 articles and four books devoted exclusively to music, as well as others that touched upon the subject: four of his articles focused on Ornstein, three of the books had lengthy passages on the composer, and another was dedicated to him.[28] Advancing Ornstein's and musical modernism's causes were one and the same. What Rosenfeld and Ornstein had imagined as a series of six concerts at Steinway Hall taking place in the early months of 1916 became four intimate Sunday recitals at Arthur and Claire Raphael Reis's home, two in March and two in April that fitted around Ornstein's increasingly busy schedule.[29]

As Rosenfeld and Ornstein had first planned, the recitals featured predominantly modern music for the piano: numerous pieces by Scriabin and Debussy, a d'Indy sonata, works by Ravel, Bartók, Busoni, Schmitt, and Casella, and of course Ornstein's own "futurist" music. Rosenfeld and Frank, just starting out their literary careers, developed important connections that they would enlist to market Ornstein and their own cultural agendas.[30] As will be shown, over the years the three men developed a complex triangle of relationships colored in part by the petty jealousies that attend many group friendships, and Rosenfeld's tendency to ignore personal feelings or notions of loyalty when it came to his published criticisms.[31] Both Ornstein and Frank, along with most others in the arts world, suffered at some point as a result of Rosenfeld's pen, although the critic treated Ornstein more gently than most.[32] While Ornstein's estrangement from the arts scene in the mid-1920s left him less vulnerable to Rosenfeld's published opinions, Frank's ongoing public career meant the widely read negative assessments had the potential to do real damage. Given Paul Rosenfeld's importance to Leo Ornstein's early career, we will return to him.

|||

New York in the late teens had no established modernist musical circles into which Ornstein could slip; it would take until the early twenties for them to coalesce in America. When they did, with the creation of the International

Composers' Guild and the League of Composers,[33] it was with more formal and focused intentions than the loosely configured *Les Apaches*, or the Oxford group, or the Frankfurt Five, or the Raphael Reis-Frank-Rosenfeld-Tapper-Kramer efforts of 1914–1916. By then, however, much had changed in Ornstein's life, and he was less free to benefit from their support. In hindsight, despite Ornstein's remarkable rise to prominence, it would appear that he suffered from poor tim- ing: the outbreak of war had denied him a newly budding career in Europe, and then the emergence of modern music societies in America came too late to sup- port him at the peak of his energies and popularity. Given the price exacted by the war for millions of others, perhaps its cost to Ornstein was minimal.

The informal recital at Tapper's house and the spark it ignited aside, the fall of 1914 was the slowest of Ornstein's years as a performer. As noted earlier, according to Martens 1914 closed with a series of recitals in the South that were likely a stopgap measure to make up for a concert season in New York that had already been booked months earlier.[34] The only public performance on record for fall 1914 was one Ornstein gave at the Bohemian Club in New York on November 2. Compared to the London concerts, this single performance at Luchow's restau- rant must have seemed a poor substitute and a decided turn downwards. Kramer covered it in a brief review: its purpose seems more an excuse to get Ornstein's name before the public than to critique the performance. "Mr. Ornstein, whose fine piano performances in New York will be remembered from four years ago, has developed in the time he has been abroad. He is an ultra-modernist." After enumerating the original pieces he played, Kramer asserted, "these works aroused great interest."[35] But while Ornstein's career and musical modernism appeared to be stalled in the closing months of 1914, much else was happening in the city that would have a direct impact on him.

By 1914 photographer Alfred Stieglitz and those who surrounded him at "291" were already deeply involved in shaping the visual arts scene, and they had been at it for close to ten years.[36] The "Stieglitz Group," as they became known, included photographer and cofounder Eduard Steichen and a roster of artists and writers whose names would soon become synonymous with American mod- ernism: Arthur Dove, Marsden Hartley, John Marin, Alfred Maurer, Georgia O'Keeffe, Abraham Walkowitz, and Max Weber, to name a few. Participants of a more literary bent included Hart Crane, Edmund Wilson, and Raphael Reis's friends Waldo Frank and Paul Rosenfeld. By the close of 1923 Wilson would become yet another important associate of Ornstein's.

The 291 Fifth Avenue meeting place became the regular site of thoughtful discussions and artistic nourishment for all who partook, with Stieglitz presiding. Though often unyielding in his opinions, Stieglitz was also committed to those who shared his beliefs. He found buyers for the works of his coterie, and when none could be found, he supported them himself with stipends that freed them to do their work.

When Tapper died, Kramer and Reis, along with Frank and Rosenfeld of the Stieglitz circle, became Ornstein's best-placed advocates: initially at least they equaled his manager in securing the public's attention. Raphael Reis, Frank, and Rosenfeld also represented the nexus between the Bertha Feiring Tapper circle and the Stieglitz Group. With feet in both camps they were perfectly poised to bring music into the modernist mainstream. Broadly interested in art and literature himself, and comfortable interacting with artists and writers, Ornstein flourished in this company, his creativity thrived on the nourishing presence of interested and interesting others throughout his life. His most fecund creative periods are testament to the power of outside attention, stimulation, and involvement.

When Ornstein married Pauline Mallet-Prevost on December 13, 1918, he was at the height of his fame, and his close friends Frank and Rosenfeld were making their own names. As a gift for the occasion Rosenfeld presented Ornstein with a painting by John Marin, an important Stieglitz acolyte, and an increasingly close friend of Rosenfeld's; the summer landscape scene stayed in the family until 2003, an enduring reminder of Ornstein's interactions with this important group, and perhaps of summers spent in the country.[37] The extent of Ornstein's relationship with Marin or the precise circumstances of their first meeting is undocumented, although members of both Ornstein's and Marin's surviving families agree the two men knew each other. They would have had much in common in both temperament and experience.

Both had made important contacts in Paris—Marin first met Steichen and Stieglitz there; Ornstein had found his first set of friends while visiting the city. In Europe, both had visited the Tyrol and been completely taken with the region; Marin's visit resulted in a number of watercolors, which, Ruth E. Fine observed, reveal him "embarking upon his first serious exploration of the mountain landscape, a subject that was to be of great importance to his work."[38] Ornstein had climbed there, and after his marriage, he built a home in North Conway, New Hampshire, on land given him by his father-in-law deep within the White Mountains and not far from the state's highest peak, Mt. Washington. He would retreat to the extended family compound, "The Crags," between concert engagements and during the summer.[39] Both Marin and Ornstein enjoyed hiking in the out-of-doors and kept at it well into old age: Maine and New Hampshire provided excellent opportunities for lengthy expeditions.[40]

In addition, both men had been inspired to creativity by Notre Dame Cathedral: Marin in 1907, 1908, and 1909 with a watercolor and etchings, and

Ornstein in 1913 with his *Two Impressions*. As far as conforming to artistic conventions, both eschewed traditional, formalist thinking, whether in painting or music, and both relied heavily on their instincts, in which they had great confidence. But perhaps what would have drawn them closest was their mutual love of Maine. It had been Ornstein's regular refuge since shortly after he arrived in the country, for as many as perhaps twelve years. Beginning in 1914, Marin summered at Small Point, Maine, and then starting in 1919 and continuing with few breaks through 1928 made a summer home in a place that was intimately familiar to Ornstein: Stonington on the southern tip of Deer Isle. In 1933 Marin purchased a house near Addison, Maine, at Cape Split and spent large parts of every year there until his death in 1953. Believing that one had to know something well before painting it, Marin spent decades learning Maine's lessons. Both men found the inspiration and solitude they needed there. In 1915 Rosenfeld summered in Maine as well, spending significant parts of each day during the months of July and August with Ornstein. Through the Marin painting, Rosenfeld expressed his own connection with both Marin and Ornstein.[41]

Starting in 1919 Ornstein left Maine for New Hampshire. In addition to building a home there, he ultimately built a separate studio building as well. Severo Ornstein described "The Crags," the Mallet-Prevost estate: "The total land was over 500 acres of woodland and encompassed several hundred feet of relief. Grandpa initially started to build his place on top of one of the two crags that gave the place the name. But it would have involved a mile and a half long driveway being built up a mountainside and proved impossibly expensive. As it was the driveway was probably about ⅓ of a mile up to our house (which was somewhat beyond Grandpa's house) from the public road." In addition to the Mallet-Prevost farmhouse and numerous farm buildings was a house for a cousin, Grayson McCouch, the house that Leo and Pauline built, which grew successively larger as two additions were built and eventually overtook the senior Mallet-Prevost's house in size, a chauffeur's cottage, where Pauline and Leo spent their last years in New Hampshire after selling their own house, garages for each of the dwellings, a gas pump, tennis courts, and enormous lawns. As Severo recalls, "it was quite a place to grow up."[42]

Even with all that New Hampshire offered, throughout the 1930s and early 1940s, Ornstein took his family on "occasional summer trips to the Maine coast every summer."[43] Severo remembers, "favorite spots were Old Orchard Beach, Orrs Island, and Deer Isle." Leo's daughter Edith recollects visiting Maine as well, but also sees those trips tinged with no small amount of nostalgia for her father. She perceived Leo as attempting to restoke his creative fires, which had burned so productively when he'd summered in Maine as a young man, but which

FIGURE 3.4. William Zorach, *Leo Ornstein, Piano Concert*, 1918.
Reprinted with permission of the Zorach Collection, L. L. C.

FIGURE 3.5. Leon Kroll, American, 1884–1974, *The Musician—Leo Ornstein*, oil on canvas, 86.5 × 101.9 cm. *Friends of American Art Collection, 1919, 874. Reprinted with permission of The Art Institute of Chicago.*

had cooled noticeably over the years away from the spotlight and teaching. She concluded, "he couldn't capture what he'd had."[44]

It was possibly Marin who introduced Ornstein to his close friends the artists William (1887–1966) and Marguerite (1887–1968) Zorach. Or perhaps it was Frank or Rosenfeld, both of whom were regulars in the group. Marin had exhibited at a number of shows with the Zorachs. They were successful and well known in New York modern art circles and friends with not just Marin, but also Abraham Walkowitz and Max Weber of the Stieglitz group. Both Zorachs had exhibited at the Armory Show in 1913. Like so many New Yorkers trying to escape the heat and congestion of the city, they left their West 10th Street house to spend spring through late fall in the country. Between 1915 and 1918 they went to the White Mountains of New Hampshire, where they created dozens of oils and watercolors that captured their deep feelings for the landscape as it changed over the seasons. Like Ornstein and Marin, William and Marguerite Zorach were inspired by the mountains.

Just before William turned from painting to devote himself almost exclusively to sculpture he created one of the most striking portraits of Ornstein that exists: *Leo Ornstein, Piano Concert, 1918*. The futurist painting, with its overlapping, vivid colors, and clearly delineated vertical planes, is much indebted to Eadweard Muybridge's photographic motion studies of the 1870s and Marcel Duchamp's *Nude Descending a Staircase* (1912). The painting vibrates with the energy and excitement regularly ascribed to Ornstein's concerts. One can feel the momentum of Ornstein's hammering hands. Zorach was taken with the raw power of the young pianist, and according to one account later regularly bemoaned the disappearance from the arts scene of one so promising. According to John Marin's daughter-in-law, Norma Marin, who knew the Zorach family well, "Bill Zorach told of Leo Ornstein all the time. How very gifted he was, how he led an unfortunate life. So much talent and then he disappeared."[45] Precisely which aspect of Ornstein's life Zorach considered unfortunate is unclear beyond his disappearance from the public scene. Certainly Ornstein's material needs were well taken care of throughout his life. Zorach would likely have empathized with at least part of Ornstein's story: both were Russian Jews who had arrived in the country as poor immigrants, both were devoted readers of poetry, and both achieved fame in their fields, although Zorach's was slower coming and longer lasting.[46]

In 1919, in response to an ad in the *New York Times*, the Zorachs rented a cottage in Stonington, Maine, where they too worked and spent time with John Marin, who lived in town.[47] After traveling to Cleveland and then around California and to Provincetown, Massachusetts, in 1923, William and Marguerite bought property on Robinhood Cove in Georgetown, Maine, west of Boothbay

Harbor on the southern coast, close by Orrs Island. Thereafter, like Marin, the Zorachs regarded Maine as their real home and spent at least half of each year there. Similar to the Tappers and their musician friends the Parkers and Kneisels, Ornstein's painter friends found the coastal climes restorative. Quite aside from any artistic bonds, Ornstein, Marin, Zorach, and Rosenfeld would have been bound by Maine, and specifically by Deer Isle. Perhaps Ornstein's "occasional trips" to the coast were his attempt to stay in touch with these people as well as the place.

While Zorach's portrait might be the most famous, Ornstein became the subject of many other renderings. Had no written artifacts detailing Ornstein's importance to America's early modernist culture survived, the number of paintings that were made would prove his centrality to the movement. His youth, his notoriety, his aesthetic mien made him an ideal object for artists. Leon Kroll, one-time president of the Society of Painters, Sculptors and Graveurs, chairman of the art committee of the Academy of Arts and Letters, winner of numerous awards at major art shows, and cousin of William Kroll, violinist in the Kroll Quartet, painted his own Ornstein portrait in 1917: *The Musician—Leo Ornstein*.[48] It projects a different Ornstein. As Kroll explained in his memoirs, his father had played both the cello and bass viol: "I was brought up knowing something about music." Kroll's comfort around musicians informs the work. The dramatically simple portrait in shades of blue and brown captured the twenty-four year old from the perspective of the artist seated close by looking through the raised lid of the grand piano as the musician played. The lack of distracting detail conveys an architectural clarity and modernity to the work. Ornstein's open-collared shirt and loose-fitting jacket suggest an intimate, private moment. His eyes are closed, his head is tilted just slightly downward; his graceful left hand is raised and hovers over the keyboard as if he is divining the sounds. Kroll has caught the artist in a moment of mystic communion with his music.[49]

If Ornstein's relationships with Marin, Kroll, and the Zorachs were occasional, his associations with Rosenfeld and Frank became central. Beginning in 1917, Rosenfeld served in the army, and so he was removed from the center of his artistic activities and friendships including his with Ornstein. Numerous letters from Rosenfeld to Frank during his stint in the service, however, show him trying to stay on top of developments. Ornstein's personal interactions with Rosenfeld reached their peak prior to his marriage in 1918, with the two men summering in Maine in 1915 and 1916. While for many years they lived close by each other in Manhattan, and visited each other as late as 1920, the relationship clearly took on a different cast after 1918.

A letter that Rosenfeld wrote to Claire Raphael dated July 25, 1915, expressed the many reasons Rosenfeld was drawn to Ornstein. After reporting on "how very sick and feeble Mrs. Tapper had been feeling all summer," Rosenfeld launches into what became a homily on the conjoined relationship of art and life and Ornstein's embodiment of their unity:

> I needn't protest to you that I love art, I consider it one of Life's greatest privileges to serve her. But—how does art that [is] warm-hearted, impure, behave? How does the art that comes from fear and cowardice and self-intoxication react to life? Quite in the manner of Tristan and Isolde in offering a substitute for some of the grand emotions. . . . And I contend that it is important to give their emotion back to life and to draw them away. For we want fuel to heighten that imagery that seeks to transform matter into spirit, and that fuel can only be given the world by artists of grand and lofty impulse, free and brave and glorious. Don't you agree.

Rosenfeld's aspirations for a transcendent art are already evident, as is his tendency toward emotional prose.

At this point in the letter, Rosenfeld refers back to earlier conversations with Waldo Frank when the two men had discussed similar ideas: "And that is why I feel that life and art go hand in hand. For both aspire alike . . . Waldo explains my attitude is a realization that I will never be a first-rate artist and his own is a realization that we have to give up life in order to be a first-rate artist. And there it stands. The question that only time can decide."

As the letter draws to a close Rosenfeld imagines his hopes for the fully integrated art-life realized in Leo Ornstein:

> I think Leo is on the same track. For he's thrown "art" over, and gives back to life, and to nature, and the song of the winds and the birds and the beating of his own heart, as the only truth. Energy, energy, is his continual cry. And so his hatred of concerts and so much art, and his own desire to awake the spirit of individual expression, and to seeing the world through his own eyes. I think for Leo the creation of beauty is far less important than the sensing of that beauty, and that his art aspires not to the making of fine music but to the making of fine people. Only in that sense does "all service rank the same with God" if I have love at heart. And that love casts itself in the artist, too.[50]

Rosenfeld does not question whether Ornstein had any such lofty aspirations for himself or his music. He pins his hopes on Ornstein as a musical artist capable of real transcendence, and in the process he transports himself with his own prose. Catching himself, Rosenfeld apologizes to Reis: "Pray forgive me if I've preached, I've been priggish. I know you'll understand."[51] By investing Ornstein with near-spiritual powers, Rosenfeld placed the young composer-pianist on a pedestal, elevating him beyond the reality of his accomplishments or perhaps his aspirations. When, just a few years later, Ornstein changed aesthetic directions and pursued a more expressive rather than experimental course of composition, one that didn't support the modernist agenda to which Rosenfeld was committed, the critic was at a loss. Over the next few years his disappointment would show. The two, however, remained cordial friends at least.

In a letter to Sherwood Anderson dated June 24 [1920], Rosenfeld spoke of the ennui that had settled over New York the past spring: "It seems to have been a miserable springtides for everyone." Among his comments upon Ernst Bloch's poor health and passing references to Stieglitz, O'Keeffe, Marin, and Dove, he remarks upon Ornstein: "Ornstein I believe has done nothing at all. He worked for a month with the laborers on his place in the White Mountains and found that didn't satisfy him; now he talks of going into business."[52] A few weeks later, in mid-July Rosenfeld visited Leo and Pauline in the White Mountains "for a couple of weeks."[53]

While Rosenfeld and Ornstein never collaborated on an artistic project, beyond the critic taking some piano lessons with Leo during the summer of 1915, starting in 1916 Rosenfeld wrote numerous articles championing his music; Rosenfeld's work appeared in *Seven Arts*, *The Dial*, *The New Republic*, *Vanity Fair*, and *Modern Music* among other publications.[54] In addition he devoted an entire chapter of his 1920 book *Musical Portraits: Interpretations of Twenty Modern Composers* to "Ornstein," and another titled "The Ornstein Double Sonata" in his book *Musical Chronicle 1917–1923*.[55] In 1924 he dedicated *Port of New York* to Leo Ornstein, although he does not discuss either Frank or Ornstein anywhere in his text. Given Ornstein's retreat from the public in the early years of the 1920s, his absence from the body of the text was understandable. Slighting Frank, however, was remarkable given the critic's stature at the time.

An Hour with American Music, a survey of fifteen composers published in 1929, contained an extended discussion of Ornstein's role in America's musical coming of age. Rosenfeld recalled Ornstein's original aesthetic of "spontaneous, uncalculated, virginal response; of indifference to systems and habits; and shrewdest attention to the rhythmic processes." He described him as "one of the first American composers with a strong musical background" and explained: "as none before him in the country, he gives the sense that music is his native language, and that he inherited facility with it as naturally as he inherited facility with human speech."[56] But in 1929 Rosenfeld questioned "the intensity of the native direction" and concluded that "Ornstein too has his limits."[57] Mentioning only one specific piece in the entire chapter, a collaborative project between Ornstein and Frank, Rosenfeld singled out the *Poems of 1917* for criticism: "But maturity has been slow in developing. Ornstein's intensity has not materially increased since those exciting hours of début. . . . No doubt Ornstein's recent quartets and sonatas and quintets are better put together than the *Poems of 1917*, say."[58] Rosenfeld's acknowledgment that Ornstein wrote "magnificently for the piano" and possessed an "extraordinary harmonic sense" didn't prevent him from also assessing his more recent compositions as formulaic, lacking in freshness, and "more conventional and second-hand." Such critical remarks were not, perhaps, what Ornstein wanted to hear, but they were not unreasonable observations.[59] In the same passage he criticized Frank's style and its "revolutionary formula" full of "'energizing' and violent and clangorous words that have been preferred merely for their 'strength' and without regard for their fitness."[60] Given Frank's small contribution to Ornstein's *Poems*, including him in a book that surveys America's *musical* history merely to make a disparaging remark appears gratuitous. Rosenfeld would, no doubt, defend his critique on aesthetic grounds. The *Poems of 1917* will be discussed at greater length later in this chapter.

Rosenfeld's 1929 criticisms of Frank were the second he published; the first, which appeared in *The Dial* in January 1921, took Frank to task for his novels, his most recent one, *The Dark Mother*, especially. He called the writing "tangled and uneducated" and the results "clumsy and irritating." The review went on for ten pages. Perhaps feeling as if he'd come down too hard, he ultimately conceded that Frank did possess "immense narrative power" even if his present efforts left them hidden.[61] The review clearly had caused Rosenfeld a great deal of anxiety. Writing to Sherwood Anderson in November 1920, Rosenfeld referred to "revenge," only to discount it as a motivation, although he does not spell out the nature of Frank's offensive action: "I do not think the element of revenge entered even into the first [version]. There was exasperation in it, hate of a certain thing in him, bad taste even (the family in 79th Street crept in because I was deadly sick of hearing Waldo trying to prove that he was a Spanish Jew, and that El Greco was also a Spanish Jew, and that there was something *mysterious* in the fact that no painter appealed to Waldo more than did the latter), but not malice, no ill-will." Lines later Rosenfeld explained why he felt compelled to publish his thoughts; as one comes to understand, there was more behind the two men than aesthetic disagreement:

> Sherwood, don't you see, I have got to publish that thing on Waldo
> even if it is going to mean hell. I have got to break that false circle which
> Waldo has drawn about himself, and which Margy has helped strengthen,
> the circle that forbids anyone to be frank with him about his work, and
> that threatens everyone who dissents with excommunication. I can't have

any subject on which I have to keep silent out of policy—that is dishonest and is unfair to myself as well as to others. I will not keep silent because a man is my friend, and if to-morrow I should feel myself cooking with some resentment against you or Van Wyck, I would go ahead, so help me God. Perhaps I ought not to have friends. I'm certainly in a way, "heartless." But if I have been violent and even cruel to Waldo, it is because I have a tendency to evade for the sake of comfort, and this time I am going to burn my bridges behind me.[62]

Like modern highway drivers who position themselves in the far left lane going exactly at the speed limit, Rosenfeld attempted to police Waldo's fame. He failed. Over the next decade Rosenfeld's criticism would be less sought after and Frank's influence and reputation would grow. By the late 1960s, however, all the members of the Frank-Rosenfeld-Ornstein triangle would suffer at history's hands.

It is not known whether Rosenfeld was aware of the effusive letters that Leo had written to Frank regarding precisely the novels that the critic had castigated. Did he intend to rebuke Ornstein, as well, for being part of Frank's forbidding "circle"? Regarding Frank's novel *Our America*, of 1919, Ornstein had written to Frank: "I cannot recollect anything in criticism which has moved me so. . . . I doubt whether you yourself can possibly realize what a beautiful book it is."[63] In response to *City Block*, published in 1922, Ornstein enthused: "I have read the first two chapters and it is simply glorious—I haven't read anything as vibrant for a long time."[64]

Rosenfeld's criticisms were strong, and in the case of Frank, they were tinged with no small amount of malice. In light of the fact that Rosenfeld and Frank appear to have at one time enjoyed an extremely intimate relationship, his criticism of Frank is all the more stinging. The only clue to a rift between the two men appears in one of Frank's many notebooks. In volume VIII, which covers the years 1922–1924, Frank has an entry titled "Stock-Taking." It reads: "Aged 35 years: In sound body and sound mind. I have not had syphilis, I have not had gonorrhea. But I have had Paul Rosenfeld. I remember Pascal's prayer of Thanksgiving to the Lord for his *maladies*. There is a good deal to this."[65] Whether the entry refers to a sexual liaison or Frank's feeling as if he'd contracted and suffered Rosenfeld, much like a disease, is unclear. However one interprets it, the remark is not positive.

A third critical review written by Rosenfeld that appeared in *The Nation* in 1939 regarding Frank's novel *The Bridegroom* seemed almost tired of the battle. Perhaps Rosenfeld's much reduced stature in the critical world clipped his wings and made him more reflective. While he assessed Frank's newest novel as "his most objective, mature, and interesting one so far," and conceded that he was "a gifted, vigorous, and immensely thoughtful writer," the praise seems grudging. As

Charles Silet has observed, "it still is obvious that [Rosenfeld believes] Frank is not a natural writer like D. H. Lawrence, Sherwood Anderson, or William Carlos Williams."[66]

Just as Rosenfeld's sympathy with and use for Ornstein and Frank waned over the years, letters addressed to Frank from Ornstein reveal a relationship that only deepened over time. Early letters written from Ornstein to Frank in 1914 that were signed "With kind regards" morphed into "Yours," and then "Love." An undated but early letter suggests how far the relationship had traversed: "Dear Waldo. Your letter came. I know how disgusted you are with me. Nevertheless I was more than happy to hear from you. Won't you please remember that Leo is an incorrigible rascal, but he loves you always. Maybe you will find it easier to forgive me then. I am going to call you up to-night so I hope you will be home." It was signed "Leo."[67] We don't know what Leo's rascally behavior entailed.

Frank's marriage to Margaret Naumberg in December 1916 did not get in the way of Leo's and Waldo's friendship either, or their habit of spending time alone together.[68] In the summer of 1917 Leo gave precise instructions to Waldo for getting to Stonington, Maine, on the southern tip of Deer Isle where he was summering:

> Dear Waldo: Forgive me for not answering your letter before. I have been very busy. I have just written to the Fischers so you will be sure to see proofs of the Prelude to the Poems of 1917. I am expecting you here at any time. Do come soon. You do not know how I am looking forward to spending a little while alone together with you. So don't you dare to disappoint me. The best rout [sic] for you to come here is: Take the eight o'clock train from N.Y. to Boston. You arrive at two. At five a boat leaves India Wharf on Atlantic Avenue for Rockland Maine. It is a night's journey so get a state room. See that you are awakened early enough to catch the Morse that leaves from the same landing. *The Morse leaves at 5:15 a. m.* You have to land at Stonington where if you let me know the date of your departure I will meet you. From then on all your troubles will cease. Much love. In haste.[69]

The precise nature of Frank's troubles are not spelled out, although they likely had to do with Frank's numerous infidelities, which he shared with his wife, and the toll they were taking on the marriage.

The Ornstein-Frank relationship was creative, personal, intense, emotional, inspiring, cajoling, teasing, forgiving, and most important long-lasting; the two stayed in contact through the 1950s and on more than one occasion addressed each other as "brother."[70] Jealousy of their closeness and the mutual admiration they felt for each other may well have colored Rosenfeld's critical judgment as much as his high artistic standards, although Rosenfeld would protest his objectivity. A letter Rosenfeld wrote to Sherwood Anderson in July 1923 reveals additional tensions in the Rosenfeld-Frank friendship: "There was a while early in the spring when I thought I might drop writing on music, as I was getting stale on it; and Waldo when I saw him volunteered the advice that I should do so. That made me reconsider (I have become morbidly suspicious, I am afraid) and it seems to me that everyone has to keep hammering steadily at one little spot, whatever else he does." A line later Rosenfeld writes: "What do you think? I shall not suspect you, Sherwood. You are a really great friend."[71] As the Frank-Ornstein friendship strengthened, Rosenfeld needed his own close confidant, and Anderson became that person.

Aspects of Ornstein's life found their way into Frank's notebooks from as early as 1918–1922 where he noted possible themes for stories and plays: one he titled "Leo's Tale." The writing is cryptic, as hastily jotted ideas for creative works often are. The entry reveals, however, Waldo's familiarity not only with Leo, but also with the more intimate realities of the extended Ornstein family. The "Tale" is not the story of Leo, but of Jacob Titiev; it could only have come from Leo, however. A comparison with Titiev's personal journal attests that Frank understood some troubling aspects of Leo's brother-in-law's marriage and family situation. The story idea reads:

> A Russian Jew who gives up factory and face to bring Family to America. Starts in again in absolute poverty in New York—insurance agent. Two sons and daughter. Wife forces him to study at night—Pharmacy—the children must have chance. At last succeeds once more: boy at Harvard, girl studies music= he broken with effort,—Feels how his wife has always driven him *for them*—feels that he is a creature and a slave *for them*. Adam his son assumes Americanism and is enraged by it. . . . son and wife who he leaves—inferiority, madness: The wealthy house is a Hell. Children come to hate him He has given them *all*—he is mad rage and despair.[72]

Ideas for a play that follow pages later may or may not speak specifically of Ornstein's situation, but they do reveal what some thought were Ornstein's motivations for marrying Pauline Mallet-Prevost, and the initial relationship between Leo and Pauline. The brief entry is titled simply "Play": "A man marries a girl for her money. She knows this. Lady reserved fine 'unheroic' demeanor. He comes to see her truly . . . and to love her. She, all along has loved him. Now he must really win her. The tracing of the 'failure' or 'success' of this."[73] If Frank had Leo and Pauline in mind, he would not have been alone reading their marriage this way, at least initially. A letter from Florence Koehler, an Ornstein acquaintance from England, to Roger Quilter dated March 27, 1921, explains that although she hasn't seen Ornstein, she hears of him: "I fancy he has married someone not very attractive or sympathetic but she is rich. Ornstein has provided for himself materially at least." It goes on to explain that while she has tried to visit, the new wife put her off on a conventional excuse.[74]

The nature of Leo's and Pauline's pre-marriage relationship is difficult to document. They knew each other for two years as students of Tapper and jointly participated in a scholarship committee, along with Pauline's parents, that was formed to honor Mrs. Tapper's memory a year after her death. Leo played at a benefit recital to raise money for the scholarship. Other evidence of their interactions is less concrete. A story that Pauline recalls in her *Reminiscences*, and that the children repeat, tells of Leo being invited to the Mallet-Prevost's Park Avenue home for dinner when he was still quite young, likely sometime between 1908 and 1910. According to the tale, the shy young man walked back and forth passing the house numerous times before mustering the courage to ring the bell, which he eventually did. Family references to Leo and Pauline as childhood sweethearts, or as being "engaged" in any official way, may be exaggerations, however. There is not a single mention of Pauline Mallet-Prevost in any extant letter to, from, or about Leo prior to 1919 in the Frank, Reis, or Rosenfeld collections, and many names are mentioned. If she had been an important presence in Leo's life one assumes that even the briefest of references would appear.

It's possible that a letter from Rosenfeld to Frank obliquely suggests Pauline's presence on the scene. In a brief note dated August 6, 1916, Rosenfeld first mentions his fears of being perceived as "favored for the musical job on the *Seven Arts*," something he clearly wants to avoid given his closeness, at the time, to Frank, one of the editors. He then confesses, "The news of Leo is news indeed, for I've heard nothing from him or about him since I saw you. I hope he's not too bilious by now, damn his dear little heart."[75] It is possible that because of his teacher's death, Ornstein no longer had access to the Tappers' summer home, thus making him "bilious." He may also have visited the Mallet-Prevost's New Hampshire retreat in part because it gave him a place to stay. His removal from Maine to New Hampshire, even only temporarily, would have surprised both Frank and Rosenfeld, who likely knew nothing of Pauline Mallet-Prevost.

Or it could be that word of an informal engagement got out to Ornstein's two friends, and he feared their spilling the beans, thus making him "bilious," although the term seems a bit strong. Ornstein wasn't in New Hampshire for long that summer, if he were there at all, but spent the majority of July and August in Maine. It is possible that Ornstein's very public career was reason enough to keep an "engagement" secret. (Given the chatty, and at times petty, quality of Frank and Rosenfeld, it is hard to imagine Leo's secret surviving as such.) Regardless, it's agreed by all the family that Pauline had set her sights on Leo early on, perhaps when they were both pupils in Tapper's studio. This may have become the source of the notion of a years-long engagement. It's possible too that in her mind she was engaged, and he was oblivious.[76]

Based upon all available evidence, including stories in *Musical Courier* and *Musical America* that express complete surprise at the swiftness of the marriage, at least as far as the public was concerned, the engagement lasted no longer than the single day between its announcement and the ceremony.[77] Immediately after the noontime wedding at her parents' home, conducted by a justice on his lunch break, Leo and Pauline headed west, where Ornstein performed a series of concerts. All newspaper stories referring to their engagement and marriage refer to her family's established social station and prominence both in this country and abroad. Given Leo's humble background and public persona as an artistic anarchist, theirs was a most unexpected union.

Neither of the ideas Frank jotted in his notebook morphed directly into any of his published novels, stories, plays, or poems, although they may very well have become parts of composite characters or informed the plots of other works. Their existence, however, suggests the degree of insight and intimacy enjoyed by Frank and Ornstein regarding each other's situations. Like Ornstein and Marin, Ornstein and Frank were well matched. They shared an abiding, mystical faith in intuition and instinct and rejected the confines of traditional institutionalized religion. Ornstein, the son of a cantor, expressed rabid atheistic views as an adult.[78] In 1920, after a mystical experience, Frank converted to Judaism. While God appears often in Frank's writing, it is not the God of modern churches or synagogues or devoted religious belief. As Paul J. Carter explained, "Frank's career is an attempt to make man aware of his bond with the cosmos and at the same time to create a culture in which spiritual values can survive and flourish through art. . . . Waldo Frank is a modern projection of the mystic tradition in American culture."[79]

Frank enjoyed a more traditionally privileged background than Ornstein, at least by American standards. Born August 25, 1889, he grew up on the west side of New York City, attended a private preparatory school in Switzerland, and in 1907 enrolled at Yale. In 1911 he graduated with bachelor's and master's degrees and was elected to Phi Beta Kappa. For the next two years he worked as a reporter for the New York *Evening Post* and then the *New York Times*. In 1913 he spent eight months in Paris, returning just about the time Ornstein arrived. Beginning in 1914, Frank lived in and around Greenwich Village and over the next six years traveled in the United States. Starting in 1921 Frank began what would become a practice of world travel, visiting Portugal, Spain, France, Algeria, and Morocco.

FIGURE 3.6. Leo and Pauline. *Photo courtesy the Ornstein family.*

In 1926 he spent the month of May in Cuba before returning to Bailey Island, Maine, for the summer. By the latter half of the 1920s Frank became increasingly identified with Latin American issues and causes. Herein may lay another explanation for Ornstein's unique, continuing relationship with this early friend long after he married in 1918.[80]

Pauline's father, Severo Mallet-Prevost, was a prominent attorney in New York. He had been born in Mexico, had a home in Paris, was fluent in French and Spanish, and founded the Pan American Society in 1912. Between 1921 and 1927 he served as president of the Society and thereafter held the office in an honorary capacity. At one point he acted as U.S. Counsel for the government of Venezuela and was named a "special assistant to the Attorney General of the United States in the Peralta-Reavis case, involving title to New Mexico and Arizona." According to his obituary, he "specialized in foreign law, especially in the Latin-American field . . . and was decorated by Spain, Greece and Venezuela for his professional work in foreign matters."[81] Among Frank's papers are many letters from Severo Mallet-Prevost to him on the "Mallet-Prevost, Colt & Mosle" letterhead expressing interest in arranging dinners with the writer and some of the attorney's friends "who are deeply interested in Latin America."[82] Different as their political positions were, Mallet-Prevost and Frank would have had their own friendship based upon shared interests in Latin and South American affairs, similar fluencies in French and Spanish, and mutual connections with Leo Ornstein.

That Frank remained an intimate of Ornstein's after the latter's contact with all other friends had broken off may have been the result of an even more complex set of relationships than known to have existed heretofore. Through Leo, Frank met the senior Mallet-Prevost. The Frank–Mallet-Prevost relationship may have put Pauline in a box. She dared not extract Leo from their friendship, and perhaps didn't want to; she had no choice but to team with Frank herself, a situation that Frank mirrored. Over the years Pauline corresponded with Waldo, reading his books and offering her own laudatory remarks about their effect, and Frank became a cordial and supportive friend of hers as well.

In his 1926 book *Time Exposures*, by Search-Light, Waldo Frank dedicated his chapter XVI, "Rare as Music," to a discussion of Leo Ornstein and the ways "the Machine of the virtuosi" and the "sterilizing world of the American Concert" had run him dry. Regarding Ornstein's disappearance from the public arena Frank observed: "He had had the wisdom to marry a true musician (*read:* naught of the virtuoso)—Pauline Mallet-Prevost, like himself a former pupil of Mrs. Tapper who had died not too early to see Ornstein's struggle but too soon to see if he emerged." Not content to stop at painting the concert world as machine-like and unfeeling, Frank makes Ornstein a martyr to his art: "And the rite began in which was sacrificed the circus-performer, the Pullman-jumper, the darling of thrilled ladies—in which was produced the scarce known Ornstein of to-day." Given Ornstein's continuing presence in the New York and Philadelphia music scenes throughout the 1920s and 1930s, Frank's remarks are dramatically over-stated. Ornstein certainly pulled back from the near maniacal schedule he had kept between 1916 and 1920, but he did not disappear from the scene altogether. He continued to concertize, and his name was still known and used to endorse many musical projects. As with much of Frank's writing, the author appears to get caught up in his own emotional creations without letting facts check his prose.[83] With only occasional breaks, Waldo Frank and Leo Ornstein kept up a correspondence and a friendship and saw each other during summer visits.

Ornstein collaborated in two artistic projects with Frank. In December 1916 Frank married Margaret Naumberg, a close friend of Claire Raphael Reis and along with her cofounder of the Walden School. When the United States joined the war effort the following year, Frank was a twenty-seven-year-old married man; he registered for the draft as a conscientious objector to the war "and not because of pacifist or religious views."[84] Ornstein attempted to enlist but was refused because of his diminutive size and weight. He decided to try again, only this time as an ambulance driver. Numerous driving lessons using his brother's car were unsuccessful, and he ended up never serving. Ornstein's brother Manus, with whom he was close, had successfully enlisted as an army doctor; whether this was the impetus for Leo's own attempts is unknown. Throughout 1917, Ornstein was still regularly billed as the "Russian" pianist and composer. He was unaware at the time, as was discovered decades later, that a series of errors made at the time of his immigration to the United States meant he was not yet a citizen; he truly was a Russian pianist. Whether this would have prevented him from enlisting had he met all other requirements is unknown.

Frank's and Ornstein's physical distance from the war theater did not prevent them from working together on an artistic project inspired by the conflict: the *Poems of 1917*. With a prose poem "Prelude" by Frank and ten programmatically titled solo piano pieces by Ornstein, the two men crafted a joint artistic response. Ornstein's piano poems appeared as musical analogues of the works of the World War I soldier poets—Wilfred Owen, Ivor Gurney, Isaac Rosenberg, and Siegfried Sassoon—whose heartrending verses brought the inhumanity of war home on both sides of the Atlantic.

While Frank and Ornstein worked toward a common end, the relationship between Frank's "Prelude" and Ornstein's music is not direct, perhaps intentionally. It may also, however, reflect their distance from one another, the result of Ornstein's relentless concertizing schedule, which took him far away from Frank's New York base. Over the course of 1917 Frank remained in the city editing at *Seven Arts* while Ornstein toured extensively across the North American continent. A note in Frank's papers also reveals that he endured a "serious operation and illness: August 1917 to September 1918."[85] There would have been little time to work together. Letters from Ornstein to Frank document the composer's attempts to move the project along as he prods Frank to get his "Prelude" to Fischer, the publisher.

The Carl Fischer edition of *Poems of 1917*, which appeared in 1918, included an introduction and lengthy descriptive notes by Frederick H. Martens. This is the first time that Martens's name appears in connection with Ornstein or Frank, and it is unclear how he became involved in their project. Later in 1918 Ornstein wrote *Two Oriental Songs* to poems by Martens, "Gazal (Arab Love Song)" and "Tartar Lament," and then Martens published a biography of the twenty-five year old composer, which until recently has remained the most complete published source of biographical information.

In 1930 the Brooks-Bright Foundation with the sponsorship of Mrs. Florence Brooks-Aten sponsored a national anthem competition, not to replace the "Star Spangled Banner," but to provide an alternative song for patriotic occasions. "America: A Patriotic Song" was Martens's and Ornstein's entry. Upon winning the first prize, which brought with it a $3,000 cash award, it was arranged for SA, SSA, SAB, SATB, and TTBB. Ornstein's piece was a wholly tonal, traditionally conceived choral work. In keeping with its sentimentally patriotic message, replete with a heavy dose of "thys" and "thous," the piece bears no traces of the futurist anarchic composer of the teens but stays solidly in F major and 4/4. Appropriate to its intended purpose and likely performers, the melody makes no demands whatever on vocalists and stays within a comfortable range for all parts; it avoids challenging leaps or intervals. For a brief period, Martens became another, if tangential, member of Ornstein's modernist circle and a valued advocate. His collaborative efforts with Ornstein, however, ceased with the anthem, while Frank's continued.

Frank's rhapsodizing, inward-turning "Prelude," at least that which made it to publication, wanders and rambles. One is uncertain how the opening lines relate to the world of 1917 at all. Like his wife, Margaret Naumberg, Waldo Frank was taken with self-study and deeply interested in Freudian ideas; he often made himself the subject of his most searching journal and notebook entries. The "Prelude" reflects that same predisposition: "All the years of my life have been the years of my anguish. I was a child and I wept as the great laughing world spun against my will. And there came upon my little soul swift storms of despair when the world laughed no more but was black, and was a blow against me." Six stanzas later the focus becomes somewhat clearer: "I stood high upon the agony of the living and looked upon men, upon the pity of men who had love and who cast love away. This year, I was a man and looked about me. And I saw my brothers and my sisters, they who in all the common blackness of their lot had only love, and who hated each other. And the laughter of our Prison was clear to me. So the years of all my life shall be years of my sorrow."[86]

Ornstein's titles are more direct in their suggestiveness of the war: I. No Man's Land; II. The Sower of Despair; III. The Orient in Flanders; IV. The Wrath of the Despoiled; V. Night Brooding over the Battlefield; VI. A Dirge of the Trenches; VII. Song behind the Lines; VIII. The Battle; IX. Army at Prayer; X. Dance of the Dead. The music is, like Frank's "Prelude," intensely personal and introspective. None of his ten titles relates directly to Frank's text, although the degree to which any are related to the music itself is questionable as well. Martens suggests that "the ten numbers may be considered variants of the thought voiced by [Frank]: 'The men and women were angry together and rended one another,'"[87] although this may be an attempt by Martens to find connections where none really exist. Indeed, the pieces sound like brief meditations on vaguely weighty ideas. We learn from correspondence that not all of Frank's lines were published; Ornstein apologizes for their having to be cut. So it is possible that a more direct link between the poetry and the music or at least with Ornstein's descriptive titles had existed than remains. Correspondence from the time shows both men attempting to meet deadlines and space demands of the publishers.[88]

As A. Walter Kramer had done in his December 1914 article, Martens's six pages of descriptive comments, complete with musical examples and instructions for how to achieve the desired effects, revealed a partisan of the first order. Regarding VIII., "The Battle," Martens explained: "This evocation of the battles in a war whose shock of myriads of guns and millions of men outdoes everything from Marathon to Muckden, could only have been written by Leo Ornstein. It has remained for him to express with an eloquence and fervor all his own, the shock of embattled nations in physical and moral clash." And as Martens points out, Ornstein sanctioned his remarks: "It is in order to help the many who will wish to penetrate their meaning . . . that the following notes have been written with the composer's approval."[89]

The seventeen-minute, ten-piece work, *Poems of 1917*, resembles Schumann's *Scenes from Childhood* in its single-minded focus upon a subject, although Schumann's collection contains much greater variety of mood and contrast between pieces than does Ornstein's. Knowing what we do of Ornstein's composing habits, and recognizing that his touring schedule at the time allowed for no long periods of time to write, it is probable that the *Poems* originated as brief improvisations that he programmed individually as the need arose or the spirit moved him. With both his brother Manus and his friend Paul Rosenfeld serving in the armed forces, Ornstein likely had very strong feelings about the war. There is no record, however, of the entire set ever having been performed straight through.[90]

The ten solo works range in duration from three that are under a minute in length—III., "The Orient in Flanders," IX., "Army at Prayer," and X., "Dance of the Dead"—to VIII., "The Battle," which comes in at three minutes and twenty seconds. The remaining six fall between a minute-and-a half and two-and-a-half minutes in length. For all their modernist dissonance, their forms are quite traditional: themes and variations, and ternary forms dominate. Years earlier a ternary form had conveyed the ear-splitting sounds of *Wild Men's Dance*.

As in Schumann's *Scenes*, Ornstein's *Poems* focus upon small melodic motives and brief rhythmic gestures. Similar to his earliest futurist pieces, Ornstein doesn't develop any ideas, and there are no transitional passages. Even the simplest expression of imitation or counterpoint is absent. Dissonance levels are high most of the time, although there are distinct periods of relative rest. Drama results from sudden juxtapositions of ideas, dynamics or registers, or particularly clangorous chords at structurally important moments. Schumann, however, is not the only possible influence. Like Debussy in his early works, Ornstein frequently repeats immediately what he has said, causing the music to circle back and slow down in its unfolding. This allows Ornstein, as it did Debussy, to wring maximal music from a minimum of musical ideas.

The first and second pieces, "No Man's Land" and "The Sower of Despair," recall the impressionist master also in their harmonically ambiguous tonal language. The first piece begins with the left hand reiterating a pattern that emphasizes fourths while the right hand outlines a whole-tone melodic fragment. In the second half of the two-minute piece, left-hand tritones undergird the repeated and decorated melody and reinforce a sense of ambiguity. To assume, however, that Ornstein's harmonies consciously served a programmatic purpose or that the larger work contained some kind of spiritual component would be, in Ornstein's words, "pretentious." While the names of his pieces suggested extramusical associations, Ornstein insisted "the notes have to stand on their own."[91]

The embedded melody of "The Sower of Despair" features tritones as well, this time over a repeating cycle of left-hand chords that outline minor ninths and major sevenths. But more important to the overall mood of the work is the right-hand, thirty-second-note, five-finger filigree that murmurs unabated the entire 2'35" of the "poem." The piece would have been a showcase piece for Ornstein's oft-noted speed and agility and extremely sensitive touch at the keyboard.

"The Orient in Flanders," the third of the pieces, features a very brief pentatonic melody in the left hand while the right repeats an unchanging rhythmic pattern. Both hands play in the treble clef, perhaps suggesting a thinner, more transparent sound often associated with music of "the Orient." It is noteworthy that Ornstein's piece A la chinoise (Impressions from Chinatown), Op. 39, written just one year earlier in 1916, spends most of its five minutes in the treble register as well and focuses upon a similarly brief, although not pentatonic, tune. The two pieces bear great resemblance to each other. Perhaps given the size of the Asian presence in Flanders during World War I, the forty-four-second duration of "The Orient in Flanders" is appropriately minimal. One wonders which "Orient in Flanders" Ornstein had in mind when imagining this piece.

Whether the individual pieces of Ornstein's Poems of 1917 were consciously composed, specific musical responses to the war or instinctive improvisations and variations on earlier works that were loosely configured and collected to go with Frank's "Prelude" is impossible to determine. There are no sketches for these works, although none exist for his most famous, earliest pieces either. Martens begins his introduction to the Poems by referring to their being composed in

Montreal. Since Ornstein never lived in Canada, but only toured there, these pieces likely emerged while he was on the road.

The paths of Frank and Ornstein crossed multiple times in the twenties. In January 1923 the *New York Times Book Review*, in its "Books and Authors" column, advertised a series of Sunday afternoon recitals and readings to take place at the Greenwich Village Theatre.[92] Carl Sandburg, Alfred Kreymborg, Eva Gauthier, Louis Untermeyer, Robert Frost, Vachel Lindsay, D. H. Lawrence, Alfredo Casella, Waldo Frank, and Leo Ornstein were all listed as presenters. Kreymborg, Untermeyer, and Frank would have known each other from their *Seven Arts* days. Ornstein often accompanied Gauthier and would have known Casella from the International Composers' Guild, which Raphael Reis had helped organize the previous year. Circles and networks continued to overlap and interweave.

Waldo Frank and Leo Ornstein collaborated once more. In 1927–1928 they joined forces to create a set of five songs that became Ornstein's Op. 17.[93] Given Ornstein's dislike of any constraints being placed upon musical conception, songs must have posed particular challenges for him. Words have a way of making demands, either by their sonic qualities—accents, number of syllables, vowel and consonant combinations—or by their meaning. It is not surprising then that Ornstein's songs are seldom considered among his most convincing creations. With the exception of his song "The Corpse," for which Ornstein wrote both words and music, none of Frank's texts reads like something Ornstein would himself utter. Frank's lines are often overripe: "Is that my soul ablaze beyond/Drawing me to my own self splendor?"[94] At other times they are self-consciously picturesque: "Shades of tremulous color garment the single hued sun-light of my joy."[95] Ornstein's own "The Corpse" begins: "In silence he lies upon the black waves,/His eyes hidden in the moving waters and the sea crying over his body." Writing both words and music, Ornstein had complete control over the artistic product.

Ornstein's music isn't particularly well- or ill-suited to Frank's words; on the contrary, it provides what might be construed as an additional voice. The expected arsenal of Ornstein gestures and effects is present: numerous arpeggiated passages, regularly varying meters, much repetition, asymmetrical phrase groupings, high levels of dissonance, and dramatic glissandi. While the accompaniments provide a showcase for Ornstein's particular technical gifts, the music does not necessarily upstage the lyrics. More like a Merce Cunningham–John Cage ballet, the two parts occur simultaneously. The songs were performed by Marian Anderson and the Philadelphia Orchestra during the 1929–1930 season.[96]

Ornstein's lingering friendship with Frank may have endured, in part, because of their shared artistic projects, or their shared artistic projects may have been the result of their enduring relationship. Regardless of which is cause and which is effect, Frank remained Ornstein's one living connection with those days when the futurist pianist-composer was the most notorious musician in America. Ornstein's many beautiful cello pieces, written throughout his life, may reflect the continuing presence of Frank, a talented amateur cellist, in the composer's consciousness.

When Ornstein was at the peak of his fame, numerous writers wrote articles, reviews, and chapters on the pianist-composer including some of the most famous names in modernist literary and artistic circles: Lawrence Gilman, Carl Van Vechten, Charles L. Buchanan, Winthrop Parkhurst, William J. Henderson, Gdal Saleski, and Henry Cowell. Ornstein became both a cause célèbre and a whipping boy.

Over the years, as Ornstein's inner circle became wider and better placed, opportunities presented themselves to collaborate with still more and different people across the arts. It is likely through his friendship with Waldo Frank that Leo Ornstein's name was mentioned to the up-and-coming writer and critic Edmund Wilson, who needed a composer-collaborator on a new project he was imagining. While nothing ultimately came of their efforts, the story of the projected ballet-pantomime entitled *Cronkhite's Clocks: A Pantomime with Captions* and the web of personal relationships it reveals illustrates how deeply Ornstein was embedded in multiple modernist circles.

Edmund Wilson was born in Red Bank, New Jersey, in 1895, attended the private preparatory Hill School in Pottstown, Pennsylvania, and in 1912 enrolled at Princeton. There he met and befriended the future editor John Peale Bishop and writer F. Scott Fitzgerald. After a stint in the army during World War I, he settled in New York and by 1919 began a series of jobs with *Vanity Fair, The Dial,* and *The New Republic*, eventually staying with the last named. At a time of great financial insecurity Gilbert Seldes, managing editor of *The Dial*, got Wilson a job as the American press agent for Ballets Suedois, the experimental Swedish dance company. As will be seen, Wilson did an exceptional job getting the word out.

In November 1923, the Ballets Suedois arrived in New York for its first American tour. The company, the brainchild of art collector Rolf de Maré, had been formed in 1920 in Paris, and had by 1923 established itself as a worthy alternative to the more famous and entrenched Ballets Russes, which had been founded in 1909. Its multidisciplinary approach, which often relegated dance to a status secondary to drama, painting, film, or acrobatics, caused the company to be viewed by many as even more adventurous than the Russian troupe. As Nancy Van Norman Baer has observed, "the Ballets Suedois would come to be identified as much with the dynamic interpretation of visual arts as it was with dance. . . . [I]t willingly ceded control of production aspects to the visual arts it employed."[97] The new art form it proffered caused no small trouble for newspaper editors, who were unsure which critic to send to review a performance.[98] One can imagine that this same categorical confusion would have been an attractive quality for Ornstein, who had spent much of his early performing and composing career railing against formalism and traditional modes of aesthetic thought.

The Ballets Suedois made its U.S. debut with a custom-made American "ballet-sketch," a work called *Within the Quota*, in November 1923. As Robert M. Murdoch has described it, *Within the Quota* "was a playful spoof satirizing America, especially Hollywood, stereotypes, and poking fun at Prohibition, immigration quotas, and tabloid journalism . . . conceived as a 'ballet-cine-sketch' it included a cameraman 'filming' the action on stage."[99] Prior to this transparently American story, de Maré had engaged Darius Milhaud, Georges Auric, Arthur Honegger, Francis Poulenc, Germaine Tailleferre, Alfredo Casella, and Erik Satie to write music for his daring productions. For *Within the Quota* he hired Cole Porter. One reporter characterized the score as "almost beyond description. It is futuristic in every sense of the word; instead of the ballet interpreting the music, the music appears to interpret the ballet."[100]

Given our current understanding of Porter's style, interpreting any of his works as "futuristic" requires an imaginative leap of the first order, but as the reporter continues, one is left to concur that perhaps the descriptor is not misplaced. "Before the curtain goes up . . . [it] suggests a ship entering the harbor: You hear the whistles blowing in the distance. Gradually they come nearer. There is a roar of traffic, a hurdy-gurdy playing a few strains—in fact the music is New York. It is not beautiful harmony, but vivid musical description. . . . The only word that describes it perfectly is Truth. It is truthful music, for it is not merely beauty, but a truly marvelous blending of discord and harmony."[101]

The eighteen-minute work was performed sixty-nine times in cities across the United States, including New York, Philadelphia, Washington, and dozens of smaller cities in Pennsylvania, upstate New York, and Ohio. Wilson's early marketing achievement meant that he got to meet the most important artistic movers and shakers. As Gail Levin described the invitation-only dress rehearsal at the Century Theater on November 25, 1923, it "attracted critics as influential as [Waldo] Frank; society patrons of the arts such as Gertrude Vanderbilt Whitney (the sculptor and future founder of the Whitney Museum), Otto Kahn, and the Damrosch sisters; writers Edna Ferber, Carl Van Vechten, and John Dos Passos; and noted artists George Bellows, William Glackens, Childe Hassam, and Boris Grigorieff, a Russian émigré painter."[102] Of those listed, both Frank and Van Vechten had been early partisans of Ornstein's and written on his behalf. In addition, the Damrosch sisters would have known of Ornstein from his days at the Institute of Musical Art. Ornstein would have been well represented at the 1923 reception with friends and early fans.

The whiff of impending success of *Within the Quota* and the company's novel approach to dance inspired Wilson almost immediately to create his own Ballets Suedois story-scene; by December 1923 he had started writing *Cronkhite's Clocks*. Like many of his contemporaries, Wilson was a fan of Charlie Chaplin. As early as 1919, Waldo Frank had spoken enthusiastically of Chaplin as the nation's "most significant and most authentic dramatic figure." Frank explained why he felt so strongly: "Within the cultural limitations imposed upon him by his public, he is a perfect artist. Inimitably graceful, mobile of body and feature, capable of a kaleidoscopic scale of feeling from tears to laughter, from 'rough-house' to the most delicate mimic dance, where is his equal in our dramatic world?"[103] Wilson determined that Chaplin was the perfect conduit for his dramatic ballet-pantomime and within a month of the company's arrival in the country persuaded Rolf de Maré to finance a trip to California so that Wilson could entreat Chaplin to participate in his project. He spent the month of February on the West Coast.

In a letter dated January 15, 1924, Wilson wrote to his Princeton friend and editor colleague John Peale Bishop describing his dramatic project as "a great super-ballet of New York." He enthusiastically explained "that it would include a section of movie film in the middle, for which Ornstein is composing the music and in which we hope to get Chaplin to act. It is positively the most titanic thing of the kind ever projected and will make the productions of Milhaud and Cocteau sound like folk-song recitals." Wilson described the dramatis persona and sounds: "It is written for Chaplin, a Negro comedian, and seventeen other characters, full orchestra, movie machine, typewriters, radio, phonograph, riveter; electromagnet, alarm clocks, telephone bells and jazz band."[104] If, in fact, the list of office equipment, appliances, and tools describe parts of Ornstein's score, it would be the single instance of his using such resources in a musical composition. Although Ornstein was often described as a "futurist" he never employed nontraditional instruments or used extended techniques in any of his works.[105]

Chaplin did not consent to the Wilson-Ornstein project, preferring instead to appear only "in shows that he himself created."[106] In addition, performances by the Ballets Suedois that had originally been scheduled for the West Coast in spring 1924 never took place. Plans to have the company spend six months of each year in the United States and six months in Paris were canceled. By the end of 1924 the Ballets Suedois was in serious financial straits and in March 1925 disbanded. Additional opportunities that had opened up for Ornstein meant he could not devote his full energies to the project, although Wilson attempted to keep it alive through 1925.

Among a catalog of Ornstein's works housed at Yale are listed two pieces for which no scores exist: "Ballet Pantomime" and "Lima Beans." A hand-scribbled note by Pauline clarifies that they are one and the same piece; they remained unfinished. Whether this was because of Chaplin's refusal, the company's dissolution, or Ornstein's own choice to leave the work undone is not known. He never returned to the project and never collaborated with Wilson again. But his admiration for Wilson's writing remained unchanged, and his awareness of the author and critic's activities continued for decades mostly by word of mouth. Wilson's friendships with Waldo Frank, and then later with Paul Rosenfeld, remained intact. Over the years Wilson's admiration for Rosenfeld's musical criticism grew at the same time Rosenfeld's clout as an artistic tastemaker and his personal fortunes diminished. As late as September 1945, Wilson campaigned on behalf of Rosenfeld, encouraging his editor friends to engage the nearly forgotten critic. When Rosenfeld died in 1946, Wilson felt a tremendous sense of loss.

As late as 1952, Wilson was still an ardent fan of Chaplin. In a letter he wrote to Waldo Frank in November of that year, he referred to the Chaplin film *Limelight*: "The Charlie Chaplin film is wonderful (sentimental, but it doesn't matter)—and his greatest piece of acting."[107] One wonders whether Frank had had a hand in the Wilson-Ornstein efforts of 1924 beyond perhaps recommending his friend Ornstein as a possible collaborator. In January 1962, Wilson wrote to Van Wyck Brooks commending Frank's book on Cuba: "Waldo Frank has been here for Christmas. He has written—rather to my surprise, since I expected something pontifical and perfunctory like his books on Russia and Israel—a very fine full-length book about Cuba. I am astonished at his continued vitality."[108] Frank and Wilson had kept up their friendship, much as Frank had with Ornstein.

Through much of the twenties Leo Ornstein attempted to maintain fragile ties with his friends and acquaintances from his broadly configured network. But it became increasingly difficult as he moved away from Maine, and then from New York City, and then into a teaching studio in Philadelphia. They continued to seek him out, however, and he responded as he could. As late as the mid-thirties, Claire Raphael Reis and the League of Composers recruited Ornstein as a composer and a pianist. He traveled to New York and performed in their concerts. But teaching duties and family responsibilities worked against his regular involvement, although, as will be seen, he made multiple attempts to return to the concert world.

Pauline's letter from the early 1970s that portrays her husband as "shrinking from raising a finger himself" may speak of the eighty-year-old composer, but hardly of the youthful or even the middle-aged musician. Ornstein was not self-promoting, that is true. But he did work to near exhaustion concertizing across the continent and promoting the cause of modern music, his own and others, people he called his "friends." Ornstein trusted that if his own compositions had any worth, they would eventually take their rightful place in the repertoire. With the current spate of recordings of his music, his belief may be proving correct.

4 ▦ The Bandbox and After

Forced by the war to abandon his planned European tour for 1914, Ornstein's life soon unfolded in a series of dramatic turns: He quickly catapulted to fame as the *enfant terrible* of modern music in a career that would be exclusively American, by 1918 his mentor Bertha Feiring Tapper would be dead, Ornstein would marry a wealthy New York debutante, and he would identify himself as an American, rather than a Russian, pianist.

During the slow autumn following his return from Europe in 1914, Ornstein and his circle were laying plans for by far the most significant event in his American concert career: a series of four concerts of modern music that he gave at the Bandbox Theatre in New York in January, February, and March 1915. Consisting entirely of modern music, they allowed Americans to hear for the first time radical pieces of Schoenberg, Ravel, and Scriabin, as well as a host of other "futurist" composers, including, of course, Ornstein himself. The concerts created a sensation. They mark the beginning of musical modernism in the United States and may be considered the musical equivalent of the 1913 Armory Show in art.[1]

The Bandbox Theatre was not a typical concert venue. It had opened in 1912 as the Adolph Phillipe Theatre, and in 1914 management had changed the name to Bandbox. It survived only until 1917, when a cinema replaced it. At the time of Ornstein's concerts it had just been rented by the Washington Square Players, an experimental theatrical group comprised of young people from the Washington Square area of Greenwich Village. Led by Edward Goodman, they were not professional actors, but emulating a new trend in Europe, they sought to create original theater in small venues. They performed only on Friday and Saturday nights, leaving the theater dark the other nights—Ornstein's recitals occurred on Sunday and Tuesday nights—and because the Players believed in minimal set designs as a rebellion against the elaborate productions typical of Broadway, Ornstein did not have to cope with problems of scenery and staging.[2] Compared to the larger concert halls of New York, the Bandbox Theatre was small, seating 299.

The first concert occurred on January 26, 1915. On that recital Ornstein played Erich Korngold's Sonata in D Minor, Maurice Ravel's Sonatina, Arnold Schoenberg's *Three Piano Pieces*, Op. 11, Isaac Albéniz's *Iberia*, Launy Grøndahl's *Impromptu on a Negro Motive*, Cyril Scott's *Danse negre*, and three of his own pieces, *Improvisata*, *Impressions de la Tamise*, and *Wild Men's Dance*. *Musical Courier* reported that he also played some Debussy on the program; perhaps he did so as an encore.[3] Ornstein programmed the Grøndahl and the Scott because he "wished to show a Norwegian's and an Englishman's treatment of what they call a negro theme."[4] Perhaps he had prepared them with Norway and England in mind.[5]

On the second concert, February 13, 1915, Ornstein performed César Franck's *Prélude, chorale et fugue*, Scott's *Impressions from the Jungle*, Schoenberg's *Six Short Piano Pieces*, Op. 19, Vítezslav Novák's *Pan*, Op. 42, Debussy's second series of *Images*, and Ornstein's own *Dwarf Suite*. For a third concert, on February 28, Ornstein programmed Scriabin's *Four Preludes* and Sonata in F-sharp Minor, Op. 23, Albéniz's *El Albaicin*, Debussy's *Children's Corner* and *L'Isle joyeuse*, Ravel's *Gaspard de la nuit*, and of his own works, *Seven Sketches* and *Two Shadow Pieces*. Identification of the Ornstein pieces is problematic. The *Two Shadow Pieces* have the same opus number as *Five Piano Pieces*, Op. 17, and may be part of that set. David Joel Metzer believes the *Seven Sketches* to be the same as *Seven Fantasy Pieces*, which may be the same as the *Seven Fantastic Pieces* mentioned in *Musical Courier*.[6] The final concert, on March 16, consisted of Vincent d'Indy's Sonata in E, Op. 63, Debussy's *Estampes*, Albéniz's *Iberia*, Gabriel Grovlez's *Trois improvisations sur Londres*, and his own *Three Moods* and *Three Burlesques*. At the request of the audience he concluded with *Wild Men's Dance*.

With these concerts, Ornstein was squarely in the public eye for a period of eight weeks. He was featured on the cover of the March 24 issue of *Musical Courier*. Reviewers for *Musical America*, *Musical Courier*, the *New York Herald*, and the *New York Times* regularly commented upon the size of the crowds with "audience[s] so large that parts of it had to find seats on the stage."[7] They noted Ornstein's pianistic abilities, describing his tone as lovely and expressive, and his technique as formidable. Special mention was made of his sensitive pedaling.[8] He knew "the colors of the keyboard palette as do few contemporary exponents of the pianistic art."[9] Regarding the music that Ornstein played, opinions were, as might be expected, mixed. The *New York Times* found that "the pieces by Schoenberg have no discernible relation to the art of music as it has hitherto been known, either in melodic outline, rhythm, or in harmonic structure."[10] To another critic, however, "Schoenberg at least shows method in his 'madness.'"[11] Yet compared to Ornstein's own compositions Schoenberg sounded "modest and almost anaemic."[12] Critics were particularly impressed with Ravel's *Gaspard de la nuit*, possibly for its sheer virtuosity.

Brief descriptions of Ornstein's own compositions reveal a respectful curiosity on the critics' parts. Although his works seem to defy traditional analysis, they are regarded as "full of interest." One critic in particular found something entirely new in Ornstein's *Improvisata*, *Impressions de la Tamise*, and *Wild Men's Dance*: "They express something which has never before been expressed by music, sentiments allied to the ugly, weird, grotesque, rather than to beauty."[13] Another reviewer hearing the same music found "an undeniable significance" in Ornstein's

FIGURE 4.1. Ornstein on cover of *Musical Courier*.

"pungent and at times acrid" harmonies.[14] Whether reviewers were confounded or persuaded by the music that Ornstein programmed, they concurred that these concerts "evoked genuine interest with the audience"[15] but more importantly they "aroused much interest in musical circles" in general.[16] By the fourth recital the audience had been at least partly won over; they specifically requested a repetition of *Wild Men's Dance*.[17]

The Bandbox concerts were Ornstein's declaration of artistic intention, and few people have had more successful debuts. For Ornstein they meant new management and the chance for a solid concert career. They also gave him a venue for his own music to be heard. With the Bandbox Ornstein became the *enfant terrible* of new music, and if few other performers were willing to play his music, that mattered less. Ornstein himself could do it. In the eyes of the public Ornstein the composer and Ornstein the pianist were for the next ten years one and the same.

Almost immediately after the last Bandbox concert Ornstein signed on with Martin H. Hanson, one of the more prominent concert managers in New York. A native of Hamburg, Germany, Hanson had come to the United States and established his agency in 1905, after spending time in Australia as representative of the London concert manager F. Vert. A formal announcement of Ornstein's new relationship with Hanson appeared at the end of an article in *Musical Courier* on April 14, 1915, stating that the pianist's "next tour" will be under the management for M. H. Hanson.[18] Soon Hanson began placing large advertisements in the major musical journals.

By the time Ornstein and Hanson came to terms the 1915 concert season was for all practical purposes over. Ornstein wasted no time in the spring of 1915, however, appearing in two recitals. The first occurred on March 19, just three days after the final Bandbox performance. It was a strange event, possibly suggesting to Ornstein just how much he needed someone like Hanson. In a shared recital at the Plaza Hotel Ornstein appeared with the tenor Paul Draper and dancers Bertha Knight and Spalding Hall. Stage decoration lent a surreal quality to the affair. The stage was bedecked with artificial trees holding golden apples (possibly oranges, the reviewer was not certain) and with green urns, which stood out even more against a plush curtain. The reviewer who described this backdrop lamented that it was a shame a normal grand piano should be so placed in this "futurist" atmosphere but did acknowledge that Ornstein needed it (he was a pianist after all). Ornstein opened the concert. He performed Debussy's *Cloches à travers les feuilles* and *Pagodes*; Grøndahl's *Impromptu upon a Negro Motive*, "Schoenberg's 'Two Pieces,' Op. 2, no. 2, *Mässig*" (probably referring to the *Three Piano Pieces*, Op. 11, no. 2, performed on the January 26th concert), Scott's *Dance of the Elephants*, and Ornstein's *Impression of the Thames*, Prelude, Op. 20, no. 2, and "Anger" and "Joy" from *Three Moods*.[19]

In the second part of the concert Paul Draper sang songs of Karol Szymanowski, failing to impress with either the pieces or the performance. The third event on the program, the "futuristic" dancing of Bertha Knight and Spalding Hall, probably prompted the scenery. Precisely what they did is not clear, but they were in period costume (which period is not specified), they made the audience laugh, and

FIGURE 4.2. Ornstein ad in *Musical Courier*.

for once at a futurist concert that was the artists' intention. They danced to music (unspecified) of Debussy.[20]

In spite of the incongruous props, Ornstein could hardly afford to pass up this performing opportunity. When he agreed to appear he probably had no manager, and the list of sponsors was too enticing to ignore. They included Mrs. Charles H. Ditson, whose family owned the music publishing firm Charles Ditson, and Mrs. Otto H. Kahn, wife of the most powerful impresario in New York. For a young man just gaining a foothold, an opportunity to play for such influential people was important. One can also imagine that Ornstein had no idea of the particular stage setting until he walked through the door of the Plaza, and then all he could do was make the best of it.

Ornstein's second post-Bandbox recital was in Toronto on May 1. The newspapers suggested that he was brought there by a Jewish organization.[21] The concert was eagerly anticipated, and Ornstein did not disappoint, both exciting and perplexing those who heard him. Critics debated whether he was mad, but none doubted that he was a fine pianist. They were less sure about his compositions—he played "Funeral March" and *Wild Men's Dance*—and while they acknowledged the pieces' power and originality, they were not entirely convinced of their musical value, or even if they were music.[22] This was a theme Ornstein had heard before, and would hear again. Even when reviewers conceded that what Ornstein did somehow fell within the definition of music, their comments would often be laced with disdain and sarcasm: "All this music was, however, so unutterably stupid that its curtailment would have passed as an act of mercy."[23]

Ornstein toured for the next seven years under Hanson's management. With Hanson Ornstein's performing career, until then defined by personal contacts in Norway, Paris, London, and New York, expanded all over North America. Only World War I and then his own popularity in the United States forestalled a European career. By late spring of 1915, Hanson's publicity machine had swung into high gear. Articles about Ornstein, about his summer doings, about his compositional activities, about his programs for the next year began to appear in musical journals, no doubt evidence of Hanson's work, as well as Raphael Reis's, Frank's and Rosenfeld's. Interviews and more extended articles also appeared, not always flattering. Ornstein thus became a prime subject in Frederick Corder's article "On the Cult of the Wrong Notes," and a heated debate about whether Ornstein's music represented a new school of writing or "noisy nonsense" broke out in *Musical America*. Literary journals began to take notice. Lawrence Gilman mentioned him briefly in the *North American Review*, and James Huneker treated him extensively in his column "Seven Arts" in *Puck*, although the latter was likely the result of Frank's efforts rather than Hanson's.[24]

American music publishers also became interested in Ornstein. In May Carl Fischer announced that it would publish his latest futurist work, the Violin Sonata, Op. 31, which "in many ways surpasses his previous works in audacity," an assessment that we will see was not purely advertising rhetoric. At the time of this announcement, however, Ornstein had not yet composed Op. 31—that was to be a summer project—but either he hinted to Fischer at its content, or when he finally did compose it felt pressured to live up to its billing. Fischer also announced that it would publish a set of nine piano pieces, his *Nine Miniatures*, Op. 7, and two songs, "Mother o' Mine" and "There Was a Jolly Miller." It was truly an eclectic catalog.[25]

Carl Fischer and Hanson both apparently had great expectations for the Violin Sonata. *Musical Observer* reported that it would be given several performances in important venues the next year, and in September *Musical Courier* reported that Ornstein had completed it in Blue Hill, Maine. According to *Musical Courier* it "promises to be a greatly vital composition, rich in new colors and devices, gripping in its message and offering many novel and interesting problems to both violinist and pianist. It is undoubtedly destined to deepen the impression made by his creations heard last season."[26] After all this hype it was never performed during the next season, probably because of its difficulty. Ornstein made several appearances with the violinist Vera Barstow, but instead of Op. 31, they performed his more traditional violin sonata, Op. 26.[27]

Op. 31 is dense, dissonant, and thoroughly atonal. The opening measures are typical of the entire work. The first chord in the piano, A-A♯-B-C-C♯-E-F♯-G♯ is followed by a chord that contains E-D-D♯-A♭-B♭-C♯, and by the third beat of the first measure all twelve pitches of the chromatic scale are heard. The violin part, which begins with two tritones, A-E♭, followed by F-B, contains eleven different pitches in the first measure. Meter is irregular throughout, changing thirteen times in the first fourteen measures alone. The tempo likewise changes frequently, and when the music builds toward a climactic point it tends to drop off suddenly into contrasting material, never quite allowing the climax to resonate. As a consequence Ornstein maintains a constant level of tension throughout not only the movement but the entire twenty-six minutes of the piece; the listener is accorded virtually no letup or points of relaxation. The combination of what appears to be a focus on chords, the irregular and changing meter, and the feeling of continuous unfolding without stops suggests the musical values of the Frankfurt Group. Op. 31 also rings of the same expressionistic angst that characterized Schoenberg's works of this period, such as *Erwartung* or *Pierrot lunaire*. Even though Ornstein knew Schoenberg's music by this time, it was still a remarkable piece for someone in the United States to write in 1915.

One interview reminded Ornstein just how fast it had all happened. Ornstein was taken aback when in 1915 Harriete Brower remembered that she had heard him play five years ago. "Ah, how long ago it seems!" he responded. "A lifetime appears to lie between that time and to-day, so much has happened to me—I am another person."[28] She also quotes Ornstein as saying, "it must have been in the Mendelssohn, g minor," which he had played on the Institute commencement exercises on June 6, 1910. It was a different world for Ornstein then: In early 1910 he was still studying with Mrs. Tapper, had not appeared in public, had not made the Columbia recordings, had not even made his first trip to Europe, and no strange new sounds had rattled his brain. Now, in 1915, he had turned the musical world topsy-turvy, and he was, suddenly, a celebrity.

The summer of 1915 was a fateful summer for Ornstein personally, although he had no way of knowing it would be at the time. As had become his custom he went to Blue Hill, Maine, with the Tappers. It would be the last summer that he would spend with Mrs. Tapper. In August she took ill and went to Boston, where her daughter lived, for medical treatment. She expected to return to Maine, but her illness took an acute turn and she died on September 2. Ornstein went to Boston but appears not to have been at the funeral. The service, held at Tapper's married daughter's house, was private, and other than family there were few

FIGURE 4.3. Ornstein, Violin Sonata, Op. 31, mm. 4–8.

people present. According to *Musical America* the only nonfamily members in attendance were Franz Kneisel and Horatio Parker, intimate musician friends with homes close by Tapper's Blue Hill retreat.[29]

It is possible that *Musical America* got it wrong, that Ornstein was mistaken for a member of the family, which he practically was, but after the Bandbox concerts Ornstein was no longer an unidentifiable, anonymous figure; he would have been noticed. Given his closeness to the Tappers, Ornstein's absence is surprising. Yet Paul Rosenfeld reported in 1915 that not all was well between Ornstein and the Tappers. In July Ornstein planned to leave Blue Hill, where Rosenfeld had also come, and go to Boston to confer with publishers and managers; he confided to Rosenfeld that he might not be back. The news clearly upset Rosenfeld, who had little reason to be there without Ornstein. A week later, however, these plans changed, and Ornstein conducted his Boston business by correspondence. Rosenfeld sensed tension between teacher and student: "Mrs. Tapper adores the boy, but she has a fearful desire to mother him, which takes the stupid forms of lectures before strangers, and a hen-like solicitude for his personal welfare. Good God, is there any relationship in which tact isn't trumped? How terrible that failings in tact and common sense can destroy so utterly all we try with years of devotion to upbuild!" Mrs. Tapper had not only taken Ornstein into their home in Blue Hill, but had actually had a cabin built for him, which Rosenfeld described as "just a room with three little windows, adrift on a rock in the pines, and as Leo sits at the keyboard of his miniature seminary, and looks out of the door, he sees the Blue Hill through a cut in the trees."[30]

The principal hostilities, however, may have come from Mr. Tapper. It is not unlikely that he resented the near decade of attention lavished on Ornstein and considered him a wedge driven between him and his wife. As Rosenfeld reports, things were not smooth between them: "The Tapper couple hasn't been getting on well." Mrs. Tapper had been ill much of the summer, which probably served to exacerbate the situation. Similarly given her single-minded focus upon her prodigy one wonders if there were hostilities, or at least ill-feelings, between Tapper's biological children and her prized pupil. At Mrs. Tapper's funeral Ornstein may not have been welcome by Mr. Tapper or by her children.

Ornstein's concertizing began in earnest in December 1915, with a program at the Cort Theater in New York and then a series of five recitals at Steinert Hall in Boston.[31] They consisted entirely of modern music, including Debussy, Schoenberg, Albéniz, Korngold, and his own compositions, which he presented under his own name (*Improvisata*, *Impression of the Thames*, and *Wild Men's Dance*) and under the pseudonym "Vannin" (*The Night* and *The Waltzers*). Vannin was Ornstein's more diatonic, sentimental alter ego, and this was his first public appearance. Critics were fooled, scrambling for more information about Vannin: "No one in the house could tell who the enigmatic individual was, and desperate inquiries accomplished nothing."[32]

How and why Ornstein chose "Vannin" or any pseudonym remains a mystery. He did not figure prominently in Ornstein's compositional career, appearing for only a few years, and with only a handful of pieces. As might be expected, the press figured out his identity, and that may have prompted Ornstein to give up the charade.[33]

With fame and Hanson came a new image. When Ornstein appeared at the Cort Theater, he had let his hair grow long, long enough to fall in his eyes and cover his face when he bent over the keyboard, which was his usual stance. He wore a velvet artist's coat that to one reviewer created an "almost exact likeness of Arnold Daly as the poet in 'Candida,'" and reminded another reviewer of the poet Marchbanks in the same play.[34] The coat itself was not new, as Ornstein had worn something like it as early as 1913, but the hair and the image were.

The Cort Theater, which seated 1,085, was full, and the audience was disturbed, amused, and astonished with his wild music and vigorous performance, but they cheered enthusiastically when he was finished. Response was so positive that Hanson added another New York recital in January. Critics remained as puzzled as ever. The *New York Times*, acknowledging that "what he did in many ways was remarkable," and that his enthusiasm, zeal, and conviction were matched by his technical skill, nevertheless wondered if the effect of *Danse sauvage* would be the same "to most ears if fistfulls of notes were recklessly pounded upon the instrument by any unskilled person in the same rhythms." The *New York Sun* called him an "extraordinary virtuoso," and at the same time "an agent for the spread of evil doctrines in musical art." A full plate of modernism was more than many listeners could take, however, and the hall was noticeably less filled by the end of the second concert. Later Ornstein would leaven his doses of modernism with more works from the traditional repertoire.[35]

Yet all was not well. Ornstein was not happy with Hanson. In late 1915 when he was in Boston, Ornstein visited Jacob Titiev, who by this time had become a successful pharmacist there. Titiev, who had not seen Ornstein since the New Amsterdam concert in 1911, was surprised one day to find him in his drug store, "sitting near one of my tables. With his hands dug in into his disheveled hair. All black and thin."[36]

Ornstein then explained to his brother-in-law how he had been engaged to concertize in Europe, how that had been canceled because of the war, how Hanson had taken the few thousand dollars that he had for advertising and expenses, but during the entire eight months that Hanson had managed him, he had secured a total of three concerts for one hundred dollars each. But his concern went beyond the money. "When it comes night, and he sees that all the other artists, as Padarewsky [Paderewski], Joseph Hoffman [Josef Hofmann], Yasha Cheifetz [Heifetz] and the rest, are playing. He is the only one to stay home in the dark. He is actually fading away!"[37]

"Is there no other manager?"

"No! I come to you. You are the only man that can help me!!"

"How? In the first place I am torn away from the musical world for years. If I ever knew any person connected with music, he must be dead by now!

"Besides, I have three children in college. Three college tuitions, piano lessons. Vocal lessons. Maintenance of the family, it means really a mint of money! I make all that with my ten fingers! I can't even afford to keep a clerk!!"

FIGURE 4.4. Ornstein as the young Liszt. MSS 10, *The Leo Ornstein Papers,*
Irving S. Gilmore Music Library, Yale University.

These arguments mattered little. According to Titiev Ornstein sat in
the shop, crying. When Titiev took Ornstein home with him, his wife, Rosa,
Ornstein's sister, sided with Leo and joined in the lamentation. Titiev felt the
family pressure; he had to help Ornstein.

"I had not a minute's rest. Between the two of them I had neither day, nor
night."

Titiev then hatched a plan. He hired a druggist to cover in his absence, and
set out to promote Ornstein. Beginning with smaller cities around New York,
he visited music stores, found out what the best concert venues were, and who
were the important musicians and critics, those in the musical community whose
opinions mattered. He then invited them to an afternoon concert of modern

music, including Ornstein's compositions, to be followed by an evening concert of more traditional repertoire. At the same time he diligently worked the newspapers for advance notices about the concerts.

Did that actually happen? We don't know how often this formula was repeated, as Titiev is not specific about either places or dates. Yet one concert fits precisely this scenario. It occurred on December 21, 1915, in Providence, Rhode Island. That would have been approximately one month after Ornstein appeared in Boston. The afternoon concert drew a small audience of mostly professionals, but the evening recital was packed.[38] This fact did not escape Ornstein. The afternoon recital, on a cold, gloomy day at Churchill House in Providence was the last public concert of all modern music that Ornstein gave.

Ornstein's early concerts, consisting entirely of new music, were advertised specifically as futurist. This may have been one reason he was not an easy sell for Hanson, and in that case Hanson may have miscalculated. Titiev's suggestion that Ornstein separate the futurist from the standard repertoire may have started as an experiment, but could not have produced more telling results. Ornstein learned quickly from it, and after that a winning formula was found. Ornstein's *enfant terrible* image could be exploited, and Ornstein would play just enough of his shocking works to titillate the audience, but not so much to overwhelm them and turn them away. As Varèse discovered with his disastrous attempt to present all-contemporary symphonic music in 1919, the American musical scene was not ready for a steady diet of ultramodernism. Only when the new music organizations of the 1920s found a better, more all-encompassing formula were the futurists, or ultramoderns as they were then called, able to break through the conservative bulwark that enclosed American classical music.[39]

But Ornstein was not happy with the compromise. According to Claire Raphael Reis Ornstein wanted to play modern music—Bartók, Ravel, Milhaud, and Albéniz—but Hanson insisted that he play a more traditional repertoire, one that would showcase his pianistic ability and, not incidentally, sell more tickets. Was it only Hanson, or did Titiev suggest the same thing? Leo acquiesced, but he also protested, "I am not a virtuoso. I am a maker of music; these moderns are my comrades in the new adventure. Let me help my new friends by helping the public to know them."[40]

When Claire and her husband, Arthur Reis, offered to host a series of private concerts for Ornstein in their home, she allowed Leo to choose the program, all contemporary music, and to explain "about these new comrades-in-music."[41] A. Walter Kramer, discussing these concerts, noted Ornstein's affinity to contemporary composers: "They are not simply matters of novelty to him, they are personal, they mean progress in art, an advance toward the liberation of musical art from the shackles of tradition."[42]

The public forum was more restrictive about programming. On returning to New York, in late January 1916, Ornstein not only played a more traditional recital of classics, limiting his shockers to Cyril Scott's *Dance of the Elephants* and his own *Three Moods*, "Funeral March," and *Wild Men's Dance*, but resurrected an early Sonatina he wrote in 1909. The Sonatina has traces of Ravel and Debussy, a slight Russian sound, but is traditional in melody, harmony, and form. Whether Ornstein programmed it to make a point or because he liked it is not clear, but he did include it on a number of concerts in 1916.

Beginning in February 1916, Ornstein's touring accelerated. In the fall he had surrounded his Boston concert with two others in Fall River and Lowell, Massachusetts, and he had played a concert in Glen Falls, New York. In February and March 1916 he began to crisscross across New England, the mid-Atlantic, and the Midwest. From a third recital in Boston, he went to Montreal, then back to Boston for his fourth recital, out to Chelsea, Massachusetts, before his fifth and last Boston concert. This was followed by two recitals in Aeolian Hall in New York, one with the violinist Francis MacMillan, the other solo. He then went to Chicago and Grand Rapids, Michigan, and in April he returned to New York for one of the private performances at Claire Raphael Reis's home that had been planned the summer before, then again back to Chicago for another recital, only to return to New York for one more concert. He remained in New York throughout May, where he gave four recitals, two with the violinist Vera Barstow.[43] This schedule would only get busier during the next five years.

The new formula worked. His notoriety as a futurist provided a draw that few pianists could match, and his ability as a virtuoso on the traditional repertoire won over even the most conservative of critics. Reviewers heaped on accolades: "a brilliant player," "unusual genius, thorough musicianship and a brilliant virtuosity," "splendid technique and is both poetic and charming in his interpretations," "splendid pianist."[44] As far as his own compositions went, both audiences and critics loved, and loved to hate them: "Audiences everywhere have taken him to their bosoms, albeit some of them may register apprehension."[45] "The audience was confused or enlightened, annoyed or amused, enthusiastic or condemnatory according to its separate individualities, but no one was left unmoved."[46] H.F.P. dismissed Ornstein's "March of the Dwarves" as a "vaudeville trick," another critic referred to the "noise that poured forth in tremendous volume (some people call it music)," while a third suggested that Ornstein turn to orchestral music, for its wider tonal palette, and compared him favorably to Stravinsky: "Parts of the Ornstein numbers heard last Saturday are as intensely gripping and mystically vapory as some of the Stravinsky measures in "l'Oiseau de feu."[47]

How many of the concerts of the 1915–1916 season were due to Hanson and how many to Titiev will never be known. In his journal Titiev claims that he worked with Ornstein at least four months. His efforts did lead to a dramatic encounter with Hanson:

> One morning I heard the door of my Drug Store open. I stept out from my back room and saw a gentleman above the average height. Dressed as an actor. With a high hat. A silver handkerchief protruding out of his upper pocket. With kid gloves and a kane.[48] A big cigar in his mouth. Birds of such feather do not belong to Leverett Street. I thought that stray bird may be looking for somebody's address.
>
> I went over to him and asked him, if I can be of any use to him. He told me he wants to see Mr. Taitieff. I kind of smiled:
>
> "You can tell me what you would like to see him about?"
>
> "I must see him myself."
>
> "I am Mr. Titiev."
>
> "I want to see the old man."
>
> Suppressing a laugh, "I happen to be the oldest one in this here establishment."
>
> Taking off his hat and bowing, "I bow before you. You are a greater man than I am! I could not sell Leo, for love or money. Tell me how you did it."
>
> All the time he kept his hand outstretched. I was afraid to give him my hand. I could not understand what he is driving at. At last he said to me,
>
> "My name is Hanson, I am managing Leo Ornstein."
>
> On hearing that I at once shook hands with him. I asked him to sit down. He took out some portfolio and showed to me all the clippings that I obtained for Leo.

Titiev then described to Hanson how he would go to a city where a concert was scheduled, look through all the local papers for articles about Ornstein. If there were some, that was well. If one paper had little about Ornstein, he would take columns from the other papers to the editor and insist that they write about him. He personally invited all the critics to the concert. Titiev was obviously a forceful and persuasive man, but he accomplished much that an ordinary manager could not simply because he was on site and diligent in pursuing a single goal. He did not have an agency and dozens of artists to look after.

According to Titiev, Hanson then offered to take him on as a partner, but Titiev refused. He knew that this was not his milieu, and that he still had his family to support. In the concert business he explained, "I could never be home."

After 1916 Ornstein and Titiev drifted apart. In spite of all his work Titiev did not hear from Ornstein for sixteen years. In the meantime Ornstein was busy. He again spent the summer in Maine, although he did not remain there entirely as *Musical America* said he would. Now that Bertha Feiring Tapper was no longer alive, he had to find another place to stay. To the press he was circumspect, *Musical America* reporting that he had left New York to spend the summer in "a secluded part of Maine," and *Musical Courier* describing it as "in the Maine woods."[49]

Ornstein had moved to an island, Deer Isle, just beyond Blue Hill off the Maine coast. Ornstein did leave Deer Isle long enough to make two appearances that summer. On June 21 he performed before the New York State Music Teacher's Association, in Syracuse, New York. The program is not identified, except to indicate that it was typical Ornstein fare, "a varied program of classical and modern music." That it was well received is confirmed by a later article announcing a concert for the following March in Syracuse, "made in consequence of the extraordinary success which he achieved when he played for the New York State Teachers' Convention."[50]

On August 1 Ornstein traveled to Beverly, Massachusetts, to meet Vera Barstow for a concert at Dawson Hall, the summer home of Mrs. Robert Evans. Ornstein played some of his traditional repertoire, Chopin, Schumann, and Liszt, and with Barstow played two of the *Russian Impressions*, works that he had dedicated to her.[51]

Ornstein opened the 1916–1917 season on September 10 at another unusual venue, the Manhattan Opera House, in New York. The opera house, built by Oscar Hammerstein, father of the well-known lyricist of American musicals, sold popular-priced tickets but had fallen on hard times. The manager Morris Gest had remodeled it, launched a Sunday night series, and hoped to return it "to its former standard of music and art," making "a strong bid . . . to retain the high-class patronage it once enjoyed." Tickets were priced so that many who could not afford classical concerts could attend. In his first outing with orchestra since the Bandbox concerts, Ornstein played none of his own music, but rather the D Minor Concerto of Anton Rubinstein.

Ornstein's touring in the 1916–1917 season took him across the American continent. He first made a large swing through the Midwest, with stops in western New York and Chicago, then headed south, stopping to play in St. Louis and other "intermediate places" on the way. He gave three concerts in the South, in New Orleans, Houston, and Atlanta. Some recitals in New York, Massachusetts, and Montreal were followed by a tour of the Canadian West, where he performed in Winnipeg, once solo and once with Vera Barstow, and then in Saskatoon. In between concerts in Toronto and Montreal was another New York recital. A list of known concerts for October, November, and early December 1916 indicates the extent of his activity. There were almost certainly others as Hanson tended to mention only the bigger stops.

Significant about this schedule is not the number of times that Ornstein played, but the number of miles that he logged on the train. Not counting

October 1, Montreal	November 15, Winnipeg
October 3, Buffalo (recital with Vera Barstow)	November 16, Saskatoon (with Vera Barstow)
October 18, Chicago	November 17, Winnipeg (with Vera Barstow)
October 21, St. Louis	
October 26, New Orleans	November 25, New York City
October 29, Houston	December 3, Montreal
November 2, Atlanta	December 7, Toronto
November 12, Brooklyn (with Emily Gresser)	

TABLE 4.1. Ornstein concerts, October–December, 1916.

possible intermediate stops, altogether he logged an estimated 11,207 miles in sixty-seven days.[52] Touring picked up again in January and February, Ornstein crisscrossing the country more than once. In January he performed in New York City; Columbus, Ohio; Fall River, Massachusetts; and Ft. Worth, Texas, the last two concerts with Vera Barstow. This was followed by a California tour, where he played in Sacramento, San Francisco, Los Angeles, and San Diego. He began his trek to the West in Baltimore, where he appeared with the Duchesse de Richelieu (daughter-in-law of the Prince of Monaco), a soprano who "sings only for charity," followed by stops in Cincinnati and Minneapolis before arriving in California.[53]

In early March Ornstein was back in the East, with a benefit concert for the Tapper Scholarship fund at the Princess Theatre in New York, followed by a repeat of the same program, which consisted entirely of Chopin and Ravel, including *Gaspard de la nuit*, at Steinert Hall in Boston. *Gaspard* was radical enough that reviewers were not sure what to make of a "tone-poet's conception of a hanging," but others found that Ornstein's dedication to the piece, his willingness to link it with Chopin, and his masterly performance of it, in which "every phrase has a shading in some part of its curve, like the flowing graces of Spencerian penmanship," was convincing evidence that it must have merit. For a Boston reviewer Ravel could only be considered "mad as a March hare."[54]

Ornstein then appeared at a Morning Musical in Onondaga, then in Baltimore in an unusual recital with the Duchesse de Richelieu. They did not perform together, but even though sharing the same evening Ornstein played a full program. It included *Danse negre* by Cyril Scott, Rachmaninoff's C-sharp Prelude, nocturnes and waltzes by Chopin, the Gounod-Liszt "*Faust* Fantasy," Liszt's *Liebestraum*, parts of Schumann's *Kreisleriana*, and his own Sonatina and *Three Moods*. J.O.J., reviewing the concert for the *Baltimore Sun*, noted particularly the dissonance between Ornstein and the mostly society audience that came to hear the Duchess, who were anything but courteous. Nevertheless J.O.J. was impressed and observed "that Ornstein is an artist there is no gainsaying."[55] On March 12, Ornstein returned to Montreal where he gave a lecture on modernism in music, followed by a recital the next evening that "aroused the usual amount of discussion."[56]

Although Ornstein received either rave or overtly hostile reviews wherever he went, the tours of December 1915–February 1916 elicited a level of enthusiasm from critics and audiences alike that not even Ornstein could have imagined. His concerts prompted at least two futurist cartoons in local newspapers. In Buffalo Ornstein and Barstow not only won over audiences, but led two critics, who had been waiting impatiently for a breeze of modernism, into paeans of ecstasy over the full blast they got. The *Buffalo Courier* praised Ornstein for his courage to break from tradition, and the "fascination and sensuous beauty" of the first movement of the Violin Sonata, Op. 26.[57] In a longer article the *Canadian Journal of Music* confronted the question of Ornstein's futurism and in a swirl of impressionistic rhapsodizing referred to the "singing of distant countries, Eastern sunsets, Arabian flowers" in the first movement, the "petulant mockery" in the Scherzo, and the "serene dignity" of the finale. The reviewer then bore down on the issue of futurism: urging the listener to abandon himself "to the magic impressions of this 'new music'" and leave behind the "prejudice of 'orthodox' constructive formulas and of obsolete theoretical text books," the reviewer stressed, "it is the PRESENT age, . . . that finds itself mirrored in the works of the new school." Thus "why persist in calling this natural product, this unfettered outpouring, this true and genuine self-reflection of our *present* environment, 'futurism,' as if it were something apart and disconnected from traditional Art?"[58]

In St. Louis, Richard L. Stokes began by quoting Schumann's comment about Chopin, "Hats off, gentlemen, a genius." Stokes was clearly moved: Three times he referred to the concert as "amazing," and as for "Anger" from *Three Moods*, "it was stark, towering rage; it was blind and terrible fury. The piano roared like a menagerie of chafing lions, and bellowed like a herd of infuriated bulls. It was not beautiful and was not meant to be; it was an impressionistic painting, with sounds used for pigments, of the most violent of the emotions."[59]

But nowhere in the country did Ornstein receive a more tumultuous ovation than in Atlanta on November 2, 1916, and nowhere did it mean more to a city.[60] Atlanta had been at best lukewarm toward the arts, and the organizer of the concert, Annie May Bell Carroll, had taken considerable risk when she arranged this one. Citizens warned her that it could not succeed; others had tried and failed. She persisted with her small amateur organization, the Music Study Club, and signed a contract with Hanson. She was prepared for the same fate that had

FIGURE 4.5A AND 4.5B. Cartoons about Ornstein.

A FUTURIST VIEW OF FUTURIST MUSIC

awaited others the past seven years: no one would come, especially for as radical and controversial a figure as Leo Ornstein.

To her surprise and delight, however, every seat was taken well before the concert, and the back of the hall was packed with those who could not find seats. They filled the aisles, spilled out onto the platform, stood ten deep at the rear, young society women perched precariously on steps. Then the concert began. To a certain "Treble Clef," it was not a concert but a Revival Meeting. A miracle.

Age of Miracles' Still Here
For Atlanta Actually Crowds
To Ornstein Piano Recital

FIGURE 4.6. Headline, review by Treble Clef.

The audience was as enthusiastic as they were many. The mood was more like a revival, or possibly a football game, than a concert. Dead silence drifted through the room while he played, even from those standing on weary feet, as the audience hung on every note. Then at the conclusion of each piece the crowd, "rose to him as a unit," with sustained applause. To one veteran reviewer, "No such spontaneity of applause has been heard in a concert room in this city for years."[61]

When it was over "suddenly a young woman arose from her seat near the platform and faced the audience. She was blond and pretty, and her cheeks were flushed. In her eyes was the light that never shone on land and sea." For five minutes Annie May Bell Carroll spoke. She spoke of her discouragement, of the skeptics who did not believe, her persistence, and now she saw the beginning of the musical Renaissance, in which Atlanta would become the musical leader of the South. She then sat down and began to cry.

With her speech, greeted even more wildly than Ornstein himself, the revival meeting ended.

Although most critics do not describe Ornstein's concerts as a foot-stomping religious experience, Atlanta's event was not unique. Not all his concerts may have been revivals, but conversions were common. He regularly encountered many who came as skeptics, yet stayed to cheer. He seldom failed to win over even those members of the audience who had come, like spectators at a gladiator show, to witness an atrocity. Responses like Atlanta's were typical: the audience "frantically applauded his every effort, recalling him many times," they "stood on their feet at conclusion, shouted bravo."[62] Spontaneous, enthusiastic ovations greeted him again and again.

Atlanta also provided Ornstein an opportunity to hear another kind of music. On October 31, Britt Craig, columnist for the *Atlanta Constitution*, decided to give Ornstein a tour of musical venues that a classical pianist would not be expected to frequent. The experience became the basis for a Craig's column the next day, in which he described Ornstein's reaction in detail.

Craig's first stop was a jail in Atlanta, where for a small bribe some of the black prisoners provided a brief blues performance. Ornstein indicated that he had never heard such music: "To think, that such as this existed and I never heard it until now." Following that Craig took Ornstein to the 81 Theater on Decatur Street, a vaudeville club that featured African American performers. When Ornstein heard a ragtime piano player and a "buck and wing dancer," he could not contain his excitement: "Before I knew it, Mr. Ornstein was swaying his shoulders and rolling his eyes toward the ceiling." And then when a "big, fat high-yellow," came on stage and sang a blues song, "Mr. Ornstein shouted with glee. He was like a boy seeing his first circus. Pretty soon he got to be as big a show to the negroes as they were to him. But he didn't care. He was having the time of his life." Craig believed his sojourn had a corrupting influence on Ornstein: his article concludes, "I hope I didn't do anything wrong carrying him down along Decatur street. Reckon I did?"[63]

The surprising element in all of this is less Ornstein's reaction than his willingness to accompany Craig on his tour. Why was Ornstein going along with Craig's plan of exposé? Although he may not have adduced Craig's motives, when approached by Craig, Ornstein was likely eager to be shown these places because he was not, in truth, unfamiliar with this type of music. Two days before arriving in Atlanta Ornstein had given an interview to the *Houston Chronicle*, extolling the music of the southern blacks.[64] Given that the *Chronicle* interview followed closely Ornstein's visit to New Orleans, one can assume that during his visit there he had encountered some sort of blues or jazz. Craig's remarks provide direct confirmation of Ornstein's enthusiasm for such music, but by the time he arrived in Atlanta Ornstein may not have been the naïf that Craig believed.

Craig, however, had no choice but to follow through with his intended plan to present Ornstein as such, or the column would lose its punch. After all, the drama of Craig's column comes from him introducing earthy emotional music to this effete classical musician who is locked up in a transcendent world, not to mention modernism, which Craig probably had no clue about anyway. Craig also could not have known that Ornstein, the poster boy of the avant-garde, the classical Russian pianist and champion of Chopin and Liszt, was thoroughly aligned with and attuned to spontaneous, raw emotional musical experience, and that he had already been exposed to and excited about southern African American music. As Goodson observes, Craig, "the cocksure, streetwise reporter, fills his article with the reigning stereotypes of the day."[65] The last laugh is on Craig, as Ornstein, it turns out, is hardly the stereotype that Craig needs in order to make his column work, even though Craig does his best to make him out as such.

Ornstein spent the summer of 1918 at Sylvester's Cove, Deer Isle, Maine, apparently to the dismay of other vacationers. He had rented a large house there—whether all or only part of it is not clear—just below The Firs, a popular and fashionable resort in the early part of the century (see fig. 2.4). According to *Musical*

Courier Ornstein "not satisfied with eight to twelve hours' work in his Forty-second Street studio in New York City, has transferred his almost incredible activity to the place where he went to rest." The result was "those seeking rest from city noises are fleeing from the proverbial quiet of the Cove to other parts of the Island."[66]

Ornstein's practice schedule may have been prompted in part by two concerts he had scheduled that summer, an unusual occurrence. On June 4, he appeared at Carnegie Hall with the Metropolitan Orchestra in an Ampico piano demonstration, playing the Rubenstein Concerto (the Ampico will be discussed in chapter 6). Then in late June Ornstein made a special appearance before the New York State Teachers' Association. He had originally planned to play the MacDowell *Keltic Sonata*, but because of compositional pressures from publishers he was unable to give it the kind of time he felt necessary to have a piece ready for performance, and consequently he substituted a group of his more recent works, including *Impression of the Thames*, "Funeral March," *A la chinoise*, Prelude, C-sharp Minor, *Three Moods*, and two poems from *Poems of 1917*.[67]

The year 1918 proved an important one for Ornstein for personal as well as professional reasons. He continued to concertize, the 1917–1918 season beginning with a lengthy West Coast tour. Stopping by Detroit on the way, Ornstein played in San Francisco, Berkeley, Oakland, San Jose, Sacramento, Los Angeles, and Seattle. Response was typical: audiences loved him, "frantically applaud[ing] his every effort, recalling him many times, and many of his hearers holding the firm conviction that here was a man who was serious of purpose."[68] His receptions in San Francisco and Los Angeles were noteworthy, in both cases among the largest crowds of the season, with typical Ornstein results: "Leo Ornstein's Los Angeles recital was a sensational success. A capacity audience, including all the prominent musicians of the city, was present and expressed its admiration for the pianist in no uncertain manner. His playing of the modern group and especially of his own compositions, caused astonishment and delight and he was accorded a veritable ovation."[69] He received a similar reception in San Francisco.[70]

Ornstein, however, could still offend the conservative critics. The writer for the *Sacramento Bee* questioned whether the concert should have been allowed in the first place, curiously not because of Ornstein's compositions but because of the liberties that he took with the traditional repertoire. As for Ornstein's music: "It was not music as we understand it. It was weird, horrible."[71] In Seattle, Cyril Arthur Player resorted to sarcasm: after observing that Ornstein's "Funeral March" was for someone whose "death was a painful one," and then providing a scenario for *A la chinoise*, which involved the drinking of too much rice wine and mayhem committed with a cutlass in a joss house, he renamed *Wild Men's Dance* "Impressions of a Hail Storm on a Zinc Roof," "instructive for those interested in being reminded what a Hail Storm sounds like on a Zinc Roof."[72]

Following his fall 1917 West Coast tour Ornstein stayed in New York at the beginning of 1918. He played two concerts in New York, one at Aeolian Hall and one at the Brownsville Labor Lyceum in Brooklyn, but between his December 7th concert in Seattle, and a February 27th concert with Hans Kindler in Philadelphia, there is no record of other Ornstein activity. By 1917 Ornstein had already become an institution, "the most discussed figure on the concert stage today," "the most spectacular pianist before the public," and his visits were eagerly anticipated.[73]

The 1918–1919 season, one of the most fateful for Ornstein, began inauspiciously and in some confusion. America was still at war, although it would soon be over.[74] Closer to home, however, the flu pandemic raged, causing concerts throughout the country to be either canceled or postponed. It hit hard in Philadelphia, which placed a ban on all entertainment until the end of October. Ornstein was scheduled to begin his season with the Philadelphia Orchestra on November 1 and 2, but because of the situation there the concerts were postponed to November 29 and 30.[75] In the meantime Ornstein was asked at the last minute to substitute for Ossip Gabrilowitsch, who had taken ill, for the opening concert of the New York Symphony Society with Walter Damrosch. In place of the Tchaikovsky Concerto Gabrilowitsch had programmed Ornstein performed the MacDowell Concerto, to both critical and public acclaim.[76]

Although Ornstein had played the MacDowell Concerto as early as 1912, he suddenly developed a renewed interest in MacDowell beginning in 1918. This concerto became his principal orchestral vehicle for the next two years, Ornstein performing it at least nine times. The choice of the MacDowell itself in the fall of 1918 seems to have been a late decision of Ornstein's. As recently as June 1918, it was stated that on his November concerts with the Philadelphia Orchestra he would play the Schumann Concerto.[77] As noted above, he originally had planned to play the *Keltic* Sonata on a recital that summer. Because of compositional demands, however, particularly the need to orchestrate *A la chinoise* and "Funeral March" for performances by both the New York and Philadelphia orchestras, Ornstein, at the suggestion of Walter Bogert of the Teachers' Association, "reluctantly" agreed to substitute a recital of his own works. Since the recital included his Sonata for Cello and Piano, Op. 52, Hans Kindler likely accompanied Ornstein there, although the announcement of the concert does not mention Kindler.[78]

Ornstein's reluctance to program his own music is reflected in many of the recitals during the 1918–1919 year. His standard recital in the fall of 1918 included some modern works, by Ravel, Scriabin, and Debussy, folk music elaborations by Scott, and more traditional pieces such as Beethoven's *Appassionata* Sonata, Op. 57, Schumann's *Kreisleriana*, Rachmaninoff's popular Prelude in G Minor, pieces by Chopin, and as his finale Liszt's *Rigoletto* Fantasy. The only work of his own that he performed with any regularity was his Prelude in C-sharp Minor, one of his more traditional compositions. Although most critics responded positively to Ornstein's programming, not all audiences were happy with the turn of events. "Leo Ornstein Fails to Play His Own Music," chided the *Milwaukee Journal,* which noted that Ornstein did not give in even though the audience in calling for encores made its wishes known.[79]

Ornstein had a heavy schedule planned for the fall: the Academy of Music in Brooklyn on November 6, the Genevese Valley Club in Rochester on November 8, two recitals at Aeolian Hall in New York City on November 12 and 16, Montreal November 17, Rochester November 19, St. Louis November 22, Chicago November 23 or 24, Milwaukee November 25, and Philadelphia with the Philadelphia Orchestra November 29 and 30.[80] He may not have made all of these concerts, however. A report on his November 12 recital indicated that he was playing "under the handicap of an approaching attack of influenza," which forced him to cancel the November 16th concert.[81]

Whether it was nerves or influenza, however, is not clear. Two weeks later *Musical Courier* reported that Ornstein had "entirely recovered from the nervous breakdown from which he suffered recently."[82] In any case Ornstein's recovery was remarkably rapid; he apparently missed only one concert, the second New York recital, which was postponed to December 7.

Ornstein's schedule for the first half of December was only slightly less busy. On December 1 he performed at the New York Hippidrome, followed by an engagement on December 2 in Johnstown, Pennsylvania, the postponed Aeolian Hall Concert on December 7, and in Philadelphia on December 12 in a concert with Greta Torpadie featuring a group of Ornstein's songs. He was scheduled to leave that same evening for concerts in Akron and Canton, Ohio, and Keokuk, Iowa.[83]

Personal matters delayed the trip, however, but only briefly. The same night as the Philadelphia concert, the New York papers carried the announcement that Leo Ornstein would wed Pauline Mallet-Prevost, daughter of wealthy attorney Severo Mallet-Prevost and a fellow student in Bertha Feiring Tapper's piano class. The couple were wed the next day, Friday, December 13, in a private noontime ceremony at the Mallet-Prevosts' home. They then left immediately for the concerts in the Midwest.[84]

The end of December brought a brief respite. Ornstein played only one concert, at the Selwyn Theatre in New York, which was a joint appearance with Greta Torpadie, who substituted at the last minute for Vera Barstow. Barstow had gone to France to entertain the troops and would not arrive back in time.

January found Ornstein in the Midwest, with concerts in Detroit on January 6, the University of Wisconsin in Madison on January 14, and Saginaw, Michigan, on January 23. In February his schedule became more intense. He began in Tulsa,

Oklahoma, followed by "several cities in the Southwest," whose names and dates are unidentified.[85] On February 7 he then played the MacDowell Concerto with the St. Louis Symphony, followed by concerts in Utica, New York, February 11, Trenton, New Jersey, February 13, Altoona, Pennsylvania, February 17, Johnstown, Pennsylvania, February 18, and Philadelphia, February 19.

On March 7 and 8 Ornstein played the MacDowell Concerto with the Philadelphia Orchestra under Stokowski. He also heard his orchestrated versions of the "Funeral March" and A la chinoise. They were neither a critical nor a popular success. The audience laughed out loud during A la chinoise, and the critics had a field day. The Philadelphia Inquirer observed, "It may serve some good and useful purpose to produce such cacophonies as these at a symphony concert, but what that purpose can be the ordinary person must be at a loss to imagine," while F.L.W. referred to the "pillow fight of the march funebre," with "Scriabin left at the post by the twittering violins, the crying flutes, the unbelievable horns." The same reviewer also voiced concern that "The rent is likely to be raised on buildings where such music as 'A La Chinoise' is rehearsed."[86] Musical Courier made a valiant effort to defend Ornstein: "However, it was Ornstein's 'A la Chinoise' that put the O in Omega. As a humorous and grotesque work of art, it was a tremendous success, and we cannot believe but that the composer meant it to be a humorous tone poem."[87] Ornstein himself agreed that the orchestrated version of these pieces was not entirely successful. Years later he stated, "It may still be that the piano version is the best. That was true of Chinatown which Stokowski did for the Phila Orchestra but it never was as good as the piano version."[88]

Ornstein rounded out the 1918–1919 season beginning with a performance of the MacDowell Concerto with the New York Philharmonic Orchestra, Josef Stransky conducting, at Carnegie Hall, on March 12, for a "Save a Home Fund Concert." This was followed by a joint recital in Philadelphia with Sophie Braslau, contralto, and Efrem Zimbalist, violin, although Ornstein played only solo pieces and did not accompany either. He then gave a solo recital in Cleveland, on March 23, made an Ampico appearance at Carnegie Hall on May 3, a joint concert in Montreal with the soprano Frances Alda on May 26, and a final appearance with the violinist Max Rosen at the Manhattan Opera House on May 31.[89] Musical Courier noted that his Montreal concert was Ornstein's seventh appearance there in the past two years. The article also observed that he had to refuse several June dates so he could spend his time composing.[90]

The 1918–1919 season had presented Ornstein more as a pianist than as a composer. While he still performed considerable amounts of modern music, especially works of Debussy and Ravel, he played less of his own, and critics focused more on his pianistic skills than his compositional abilities. Critics liked what they heard and found Ornstein had matured as a performer. E.W.B. observed, "The Ornstein of two years ago, that sensational giant of tone and technic, has, in the most amazing way, become the instrument through which beauty, the purest abstract beauty of music, is being poured out in unstinted generosity. One wondered at the balance of mentality and emotion that has come to Ornstein in these two years—development by such leaps and bounds is almost uncanny."[91] A. Walter Kramer echoed a similar sentiment: "Mr. Ornstein has grown during the last year; his playing has taken on a greater authority, and he builds more surely and with a clearer outline in the music of the masters. . . . Adjectives are unnecessary in describing his tone, and speeds have nothing to do with him technically. We had forgotten for a moment that we were writing about a genius."[92]

Audiences reacted even more enthusiastically than the critics. By 1919 Ornstein was at the peak of his popularity, his draw immense. He constantly performed before packed halls, often more than two thousand, in many places the "largest audience of the season."[93] At the Hippodrome in New York a $6,000 house was guaranteed, an extraordinary sum for 1919. On his tours most of the professional musicians of a city turned out to hear him, and at least one reviewer noted a disproportionate number of men in the audience.[94] Ornstein not only played to packed audiences, but sometimes found himself mobbed by fans, a term at least two reviewers used. He was the 1910s rock star. James Huneker, with some exaggeration, described how at Ornstein's Aeolian Hall recital on December 7, 1918, the audience "early mobbed the lobbies, marched at intervals to the stage, and long clung there to walls, to organ pipes, pedal base, stairs, or any niche offering a view."[95] At another concert the audience was more polite, but would let him go only after he came back on stage with his coat and hat on.[96] An even more dramatic encounter occurred at Ornstein's Philadelphia concert with Sophie Breslau and Efrem Zimbalist. *Musical Courier*, in an article entitled "Ornstein Mobbed in Philadelphia," described the event:

> He had shortened his part of the program because of the lateness of the hour. After the concert the crowd would not let him go. As usual Ornstein had a car waiting for him to take him to the station for the last train to NY, but the crowd blocked all passages and the stage entrance. He began to shake hands and was kissed by an elderly lady who then made a lengthy speech. Another member of the crowd shouted, "Why should he not go back to the stage and play some more, even if the lights in the theater have been turned out." Ornstein was finally rescued by his friend Philadelphia's Assistant District Attorney, who called in six burly policemen to create a phalanx through which Ornstein and his entourage could escape.

Ornstein observed that it was an event never to be forgotten.[97]

One announcement for the 1919–1920 season stated that Ornstein's bookings for the year were "unusually heavy," another that he would appear in seventy concerts, and a third that for the season he would average four concerts a week.[98] The season was to feature a second swing through the Northwest and Pacific Coast, and another through the South, playing in seventeen different cities in Texas, Oklahoma, and several southern states.[99] He also received offers of a European tour, but because of the demand in North America turned it down, believing that he could "conquer Europe later."[100]

To what extent Ornstein actually followed the projected schedule is impossible to verify.[101] He did postpone his start of the 1919–1920 season, canceling some engagements in September and early October because he wanted more time to compose. Sources do not indicate precisely what was eliminated, however, although reference to three concerts, in Columbus, Ohio, on October 7, Erie, Pennsylvania, on October 12, and Dayton, Ohio, on October 14, suggest that Ornstein had scheduled an early season tour of the eastern Midwest.[102]

Ornstein's 1919–1920 season began with a solo recital at Aeolian Hall in New York on October 18. The first half consisted of contemporary compositions, including some of Ornstein's own, and the second half nineteenth-century pieces. After opening with a piano transcription of César Franck's *Prélude, fugue et variation* Ornstein then performed Scriabin's Sonata No. 3, Op. 23, selections from Debussy's first series of *Images*, and his own *Three Moods* and *Poems of 1917*. The second half consisted of Schumann's *Symphonic Studies* and several pieces by Liszt. Reviews were mixed; Ornstein's pianism was praised, but befitting the critics' generally conservative positions relative to modern music, they had difficulty accepting the musical worth of the modernist half in general. H. F. P. went so far to call the Scriabin sonata "rubbish." The audience too apparently still had a difficult time understanding Ornstein, some holding their ears when they heard the dissonances, others laughing out loud.[103]

In November Ornstein played the MacDowell Concerto twice, on November 21 and 22, with the Chicago Symphony Orchestra, to both critical acclaim and audience enthusiasm. Critics noted his virtuosic power, his "suavity of tone," and his singing style, all requirements for the demanding work.[104] He then returned to a second concert at Aeolian Hall in New York, on November 29, which consisted of all modern music, including works by Debussy, Satie, Ravel, Scriabin, d'Indy, and of, course, Ornstein himself. The major works on the program were Scriabin's Ninth Sonata, one of his late works, known as the "Black Mass," and d'Indy's Sonata, Op. 63, a lengthy piece that is seldom heard today. Ornstein closed with his own "Funeral March," *A la chinoise*, and *Wild Men's Dance*, which brought repeated calls from the audience to hear them again. This time the critics were enthusiastic about Ornstein's playing, if not his music. As one noted, his status as a composer may not be settled, but "as to his rank as a pianist there can be no question." "As a pianist he is of the great."[105]

Various reports from December suggest Ornstein had a complicated schedule, particularly given travel requirements in that pre-jet age. According to *Musical Courier* Ornstein was to appear with the Cincinnati Orchestra in Huntington, West Virginia, on December 8, and then give a solo recital in the same city shortly after that (perhaps December 9). *The Philadelphia Inquirer* placed Ornstein in New York on December 10, where he was scheduled to play the Rubinstein Concerto with the Cincinnati Orchestra when they appeared in New York at the Metropolitan Orchestra, but according to reviews Ornstein was suddenly taken ill at the last minute while returning from an engagement in Indianapolis, and at the time of the concert "was lying critically ill." Neither the nature of Ornstein's illness nor details about what he was doing in the Midwest is known, although the reporter could have confused Ornstein's Cincinnati appearance with Indianapolis. In any event, Ornstein's illness was short lived. He managed to recover quickly enough that he was able to play the MacDowell Concerto with the Boston Symphony Orchestra on December 19, to ecstatic reviews, even from H. T. Parker, who compared him favorably to Josef Hofmann.[106] Obviously the Boston Symphony Orchestra liked what they heard, as they engaged him to appear with them in a five-city tour, which included Hartford, Connecticut, Philadelphia, Baltimore, Washington, D.C., and Brooklyn.[107]

As the 1919–1920 season demonstrates, Ornstein was evolving as a concert artist. He played less modern music and more traditional repertoire, in some cases avoiding his own compositions entirely. Whether Ornstein had sensed that the novelty of his ultramodern compositions was wearing thin, or had simply grown tired of performing them, their absence did not damage his reputation. Critics noticed that with a new focus on the classical repertoire came a new mastery and an artistic maturity: "He has grown and broadened tremendously in his art, and now is one of the most interesting and important pianists in the top ranks."[108] Ornstein seemed to have settled down: "The exuberance and fire, the dramatic and erratic characteristics have faded away, and their place has been usurped by a lyricism as exquisite as it is rare. Ornstein has become a lyric poet in tones."[109]

Yet Ornstein could not escape his reputation entirely. He had always demonstrated extraordinary talent as a pianist, but his fame was built upon the performance of ultramodern music, and the crowds still eagerly awaited *Wild Men's Dance* or *Three Moods*. Ornstein's compositions enhanced his own performances. They made him more than just another Russian pianist, an easily marketable but all too common figure on the American concert scene. People came to hear not just any futurist avant-garde music, but specific pieces. Ornstein quickly recognized that *Wild Men's Dance* was an anticipated event on any concert, and it

A Cartoonist's Impression of What Ornstein's Wild Men's Dance Does to Heaven's Finest Harpists of the "Old School"

FIGURE 4.7. Cartoon of Ornstein and Old School.

became the grand finale, the piece that everyone waited for. If not always pro-grammed, it was often the encore. *Wild Men's Dance* was Ornstein's anthem.

Thus by 1920 Ornstein had established himself as an unqualified superstar in the concert world. He had broken out of the niche he had created as the most visible symbol of modern music, to be recognized as a mature artist of the piano, although the public would never let him entirely forget his futurist past. In great demand, he had reached the pinnacle of his profession and could look forward to years of full and active concertizing. In retrospect, however, the 1919–1920 season was the apex of his career. Although he did not fully depart the world of the tour-ing artist for several years, he never again had such a busy season, and we see from that point a gradual decrease in the number of performances, until in 1926 writers could speculate, "Whatever happened to Leo Ornstein?" The next five years were a time of transition for Ornstein, as he grappled with pressures and concerns, some of which from our vantage point today are not entirely clear. If there ever was a turning point in Ornstein's life, however, it was then, as he chose to do what few artists of his caliber and reputation do, walk away from a lucrative and, in every respect, highly successful career. The next chapters focus on this critical time and explore the reasons for Ornstein's puzzling and extraordinary choices.

5 ||| Identity

As Leo Ornstein catapulted to prominence by introducing and then abandoning his most jarring futuristic compositional style, Western society underwent its own tumultuous revolutions and reassessments. In retrospect the dissonant, rhythmic pounding that characterized so much of Ornstein's music of the time was an apt response to a world that to many seemed out of control. The early years of the twentieth century and especially those surrounding World War I were as dangerous, dynamic, disappointing, and unsettling as any in modern history. But the century hadn't started out that way. America's star and the national mood appeared to be ascendant. A new emphasis on urban and industrial culture and the results of the Spanish-American War (1898–1902) had moved the United States from the wings to the center of the world stage. Progress seemed inevitable.

The assassination of Archduke Francis Ferdinand, first in line to the Austro-Hungarian throne, in Sarajevo in June 1914 and the worldwide catastrophe that followed, however, touched every corner of American life. While Ferdinand's death is often cited as igniting the "war to end all wars," in reality the Great War was the culmination of years of political unrest in Europe. Although the United States initially pursued an isolationist course, the sinking of the *Lusitania* on May 7, 1915, with 128 Americans among its 1,200 dead spurred a reassessment of that policy. As other nations took sides, the conflict spread until most of Europe and much of the Middle East were enmeshed; within two years the United States officially joined the conflict. In the four years between 1914 and 1918, nine million combatants would lose their lives to war. But war was not solely responsible for the slaughter of a generation.

The influenza pandemic that took hold in late winter 1918 compounded and continued the carnage the war had begun; this time, however, it was more than soldiers who died. The flu brought the reality of death, which had for the most part been confined to numerous battle theaters in Europe, into the homes of every American. The nation's late entry into the war, in April 1917, just nineteen months before the armistice, might have portended fewer casualties for the United States than for those countries who had been involved since the earliest conflicts. But the coincidence of the peak of the flu epidemic with the last months of the war meant that the disease joined with the enemy and accomplished what only weapons had done previously. The flu continued killing long after the last bullets had been fired and the last whiffs of mustard gas had evaporated, and America was not spared. U.S. soldiers returning to the waiting arms of their loved ones in the fall of 1918 unknowingly infected entire families. The uncommonly fast incubation period of the air-borne virus left health agencies and governments unprepared. Fear of contamination caused cities across the nation to enact laws prohibiting public assemblies of any kind. From New York to Pennsylvania to Wisconsin to Colorado to Georgia, mayors closed theaters, churches, lodges, dance halls, and saloons; closures lasted up to six weeks. A brief story by H. T. Craven that appeared in the October 26, 1918, issue of *Musical America* suggests what happened in numerous cities across America. Titled "Philadelphia Concerts Again Postponed," and dated October 21, the story begins: "Musical events in this city still await the decline of the influenza epidemic. The embargo on amusements, which was to have been lifted this week, will continue, it is now announced until October 28; thus the opening of the Philadelphia Orchestra's season undergoes another postponement. Friday afternoon, Nov. 1, is now set as the date for the first concert in Mr. Stowkowski's series."[1] Influenza hit Boston, Philadelphia, New York, and Chicago especially hard in October, which ultimately turned out to be the deadliest month for the nation. According to one source, 195,000 Americans died in October alone.[2] The start of Ornstein's own 1918–1919 concert season was postponed because of the public assembly ban, and it would be interrupted very briefly by what might have been a mild case of the illness that he contracted in November 1918.[3]

While the disease did not discriminate by class, it often took its greatest toll in the poorer neighborhoods of cities, where sanitation and health care were lacking. The high proportion of immigrants within these poorer enclaves meant that in many cases they suffered disproportionately. The virulence of the 1918 influenza pandemic is borne out by statistics: more U.S. service members died of illness (63,114) than of enemy fire (53,402).[4] In eighteen months the disease infected a quarter of all Americans and killed more than 675,000. Somewhere between 20 and 40 million people worldwide succumbed to the disease.[5] The century that had started out so hopeful with its promises of scientific breakthroughs and technological and medical advances seemed headed irrevocably toward self-destruction. Progress had turned on itself.

Among the most profound and insidious results of the events of the time was a growing fear and distrust of immigrants, who beyond being seen as competitors for jobs and bearers of disease, were often cast as diluters of "American" culture, as it had been imagined and promoted in the nineteenth century. Given the republic's history as a nation founded by immigrants, acknowledging the problem was especially vexing since it suggested a kind of elitism and class consciousness that the early colonists had themselves sought to escape. The first large group of immigrants to experience wide-scale discrimination was the Irish. In a series of exoduses starting in the 1820s, the Irish had come to America to escape political oppression and then, in the 1840s, famine. Once in America, they formed strong communities rooted in close family relations and shared religious beliefs. Their ability to speak English, their fair skin tone, and shared British cultural heritage made the transition smoother than it might have been. The ritualistic practices and hierarchical structure of Roman Catholicism, however, were foreign to a dominantly Protestant population, and that, along with the threat they posed to employment opportunities for those Americans already established and seeking work, contributed to widespread discrimination. "No Irish Need Apply" was a sign familiar to many living in Boston and New York. Attitudes toward the Irish exposed an unattractive vein in national thought and behavior. Between 1880 and 1900, Italian immigrants underwent similar experiences. The darker complexions, especially of southern Italians, provided another reason to fear and ostracize the newcomers.

When, starting in the early years of the twentieth century, large waves of Eastern European Jewish immigrants flooded American cities, the cumulative effect of their poverty, language, dress, appearance, customs, and religious practices stressed to the breaking point what had been at best grudging accommodation of foreigners. There was little obvious common ground, and little interest, among many first-generation immigrants to assimilate into American culture, something large numbers of Irish had eagerly sought and accomplished with great efficiency. At the beginning of the twentieth century it was not newcomers per se who were problematic, but the particular newcomers who posed the problem. Ornstein arrived in 1906 as one of these: Jewish by religion and ethnicity; Russian by nationality; one of thousands who made their first home in the Lower East Side of New York, a place set aside for the Other.

Throughout his public years Ornstein's religious, ethnic, and national identities were malleable constructs, as much imagined and imposed by others as consciously crafted by the composer himself. Their strategic usefulness dictated their choice. Ornstein's public identity reacted to and changed with the protean political, cultural, and artistic milieu in which he moved. Early on he was billed as a Russian pianist, with no mention of his Jewish heritage, although the first major piece on Ornstein, an article by W. W. Kramer that appeared in *Musical America* in 1911, says little about his ethnic origins, other than to mention briefly his background. Kramer was more interested in Ornstein's love of literature, especially Shakespeare, Burns, Browning, and Ibsen; he noted in particular that Ornstein had composed some twenty songs, all on Burns's poetry.[6] But the Russian adjective was useful, suggesting associations with a number of popular, proven virtuosi. Being Russian conveyed authority to the young pianist. As will be seen,

FIGURE 5.1. Ornstein, Russian pianist.

Ornstein's identification as an American composer or as a Jewish musician later served specific purposes as well.

After the success of his 1911 debut, Ornstein pursued a concert career. His first manager, Kuester & Richardson, not only billed him as "The Russian Pianist," but implied that he had just arrived in the United States, a full six years after the fact: "First Season in America."[7] Soon, his youthful appearance was seized upon and turned to advantage, and Ornstein was hailed as "the young Russian pianist," a phrase repeated by the *Boston Globe* three years later, in December 1915.[8] In a review of his stunning London debut in 1914, the *Daily Mail* called him a "pale Russian youth," although *Musical America* referred to him as "Russian-American."[9] At this point, American writers on the arts wanted some credit for the successful young musician. With one exception his manager, M. H. Hanson, regularly used the phrase "Russian Pianist" when promoting him. The exception was the concert season of 1915–1916 in which Hanson, capitalizing on the notoriety Ornstein had gained from the Bandbox concerts, billed him as "The Ultra Modern Composer-Pianist."[10] When the *New York Times* announced Ornstein's engagement to Pauline Mallet-Prevost in 1918, below the main headline "Leo Ornstein to Wed Society Girl" ran the subheading "Russian Pianist and Composer Engaged to Miss Pauline C. Mallet-Prevost, Also Musician."[11]

Promoting Ornstein's Russian ethnicity/nationality made sense to many people. To identify Ornstein as Russian was to align him with a national musical tradition that had produced a number of famous pianists. While his youthful study at the St. Petersburg Conservatory gave him a legitimate claim to the identity, the adjective offered a cachet that was more advantageous than informational. For many, the label also helped explain Ornstein's radicalism. Not only had Russian musicians become the de facto standard for concert pianism, but for some Russia was the logical birthplace for the new movements in the arts. According to Mrs. John Herrington, an art critic, this was because "her people have absolutely no use for or fear of public opinion; whereas America is bound hand and foot by that very fear from which the Russians are so free." She then singled out two Russian artists who pointed to the future, the dancer Anna Pavlova and Ornstein.[12] The same article also labeled Ornstein a "futurist," a term that had originated in 1909 with a specific movement in Italy, led by Filippo Tommaso Marinetti, but had at least in the United States become a generic term for anyone who espoused what was considered extremely radical ideas in the arts. The immediate embrace of futurism by a number of Russian painters, Vladimir Tatlin and Antoine Pevsner among them, and the publication of Marinetti's futurist manifesto in *Le Figaro* in Paris lent international momentum to the movement. Ornstein himself, aware of the label applied to him, disavowed any connection with the movement proper, and all evidence suggests that such was the case.[13] But his minimization of the lyrical elements in his early, infamous compositions, which simultaneously emphasized percussive dissonances, and his break with aesthetic traditions made such a disavowal appear semantic, not substantive. This music was nothing like that of the past: it had to be futurist. At the same time Ornstein was also called a cubist, although it is hard to discern any connection with the artistic movement, beyond Ornstein's personal ties to members of the Stieglitz circle.[14]

A number of Ornstein's own compositions reinforced his Russian billing, as many referred to Russia, at least in their titles. Sometime before 1911 he had composed a *Russian Suite* (*Suite russe*, Op. 12), a collection of seven short character pieces for piano.[15] These were written before he discovered his modernist style, although they are one of the few sets of early pieces he continued to perform after he had achieved ultramodern notoriety. While each piece has a title, only the first, "Doumka," refers in any overt way to Russia. Doumka, alternately spelled dumka, is a Ukrainian word denoting a song or instrumental work that is modeled on rustic folk melodies. Ornstein's two-page "Doumka" is characterized by numerous quick, passing triplets that energize the larger *andante espressivo* tempo. These recall similar passages in Tchaikovsky's 1886 andantino cantabile, solo piano work "Dumka," Op. 59. This piece is nearly four times the length of Ornstein's. Both works feature circumscribed melancholy melodies and similar dotted rhythms that many associate with Eastern Europe, but otherwise they are more Romantic than Russian sounding. It is likely that Ornstein knew Tchaikovsky's "Dumka" and used the elder composer's subtitle "Russian rustic scene" as a source of inspiration for the title of his own work. The rest of Ornstein's set, however, is without any direct reference to Russia. Other early works that do have Russian ties were *Cossack Impressions*, Op. 14, a two-volume set of piano works written in 1914, and *Suite Ukraine*, Op. 17, written sometime around 1913.[16]

Through 1917 Ornstein continued to explore his Russian heritage in his music. In 1916 he composed *Three Russian Impressions* for Violin and Piano, which were entitled "Olga," "Natascha," and "Sonja." Curiously he dedicated the first of these to the American violinist Vera Barstow, with whom he was touring at the time. In 1917–1918 he composed *Six Russian Songs* and *Three Russian Choruses*. The latter pieces were heavily publicized and survived several transcriptions: Arthur Hartman arranged the last chorus of the group, *Russian Festival*, for violin and piano; Ornstein's good friend Hans Kindler performed *Russian Lament*, the first number in the set, in a cello arrangement. There were also some *Russian Sketches* for piano solo, composed prior to 1918 by "one Vladimirsky, who, according to rumor, is as much Ornstein as was a certain enigmatic Vannin." That many of Ornstein's works cited in Marten's biography are no longer extant makes crosschecking possible relationships between pieces impossible.

Ornstein's Russian identification came to an abrupt end in 1918. Gone are the original Russian compositions, and Ornstein seems to have launched a campaign to convince the musical world not only that America had a rich musical culture, but that he himself was at heart an American. Press notices began to refer to him as "the young American composer and pianist."[17] He programmed Edward MacDowell's Second Piano Concerto, a big, virtuosic Romantic work written in 1884–1886, as his principal vehicle for appearances with orchestras for the next two years. MacDowell, who had died in 1908, was considered America's greatest composer at the beginning of the twentieth century. In 1900 Rupert Hughes asserted such opinion to be unanimous.[18] A pianist as well as composer, MacDowell was named the first professor of music at Columbia University in 1896, and his many short piano pieces made him a household name in parlors throughout the country. Although MacDowell's music was grounded in a European Romanticism that transcended national boundaries, he was acutely aware that national musical sources could inspire a work, something he attempted to demonstrate repeatedly. He also vigorously championed the cause of American music, particularly the American composer, seeking to imbue his own compositions with an American spirit, often through programmatic titles, or in some instances, such as his *Indian Suite*, through indigenous borrowing.

The *Indian Suite* (the programmatic subtitle given to his Orchestral Suite, No. 2), one of his most performed compositions, incorporated transcribed Native American melodies taken from Theodore Baker's *Über die Musik der nordamerikanischen Wilden*, a collection that gained considerable renown in musical circles in the late nineteenth century.[19] Some of the music of the *Indian Suite* is quite compelling, particularly the fourth movement "Dirge," which MacDowell considered among his finest movements. But in spite of the ethnic origins of the thematic material, the work is essentially an example of European Romanticism. Romantic practices, from the use of harmony and orchestral color to structural approaches, completely overwhelm the work's professed unifying Native American elements, which musicologist and conductor Charles Anthony Johnson has reduced to an "Indian rhythmic figure consisting of two short repeated notes."[20] MacDowell's 1903 reference to "Dirge" as expressing "a world-sorrow rather than a particularized grief" might have made the work especially potent in 1918 as large portions of a globe wrestled with the tragedies of the preceding years.[21] Regardless of the authenticity of the work, however, in the second decade of the twentieth century, there was no composer more heralded as American than MacDowell; associating himself with this concerto could only have enhanced Ornstein's stock in the particular political environment.

Ornstein, who had played the MacDowell Concerto as early as 1913, first performed it in 1918 on October 31, with the New York Symphony Society, Walter

---

MacDowell Honored by Leo Ornstein

That turbulent spirit and so called futurist composer, Leo Ornstein, has shown a great diversity of character by playing recently wherever possible the music of our great American composer, MacDowell. Ornstein has now played the MacDowell concerto in D minor with every orchestra in America, except the Minneapolis Symphony, for whom he could not play, as the date offered was impossible. He has now played the Mac-Dowell concerto with the Boston Symphony six times, twice in Boston and once each in Washington, D. C., Baltimore, Philadelphia and Hartford. Rumor has it that Ornstein will play a great deal of MacDowell in the near future.

In private conversation, Ornstein recently stated that any one, no matter where born, but brought to this country as a mere child, and growing up here; any one educated as he himself was at a school like the New York Academy of Friends, and securing his musical education from an American woman, the late Mrs. Thomas Tapper, must naturally be imbued with a true American spirit; must naturally feel that he is an American, first, last and all the time; and if a true artist, no matter to what branch of art devoted, must be filled with a fervent desire to see American art and American reproducing artists appreciated by the American public.

FIGURE 5.2. Ornstein discusses being an American in *Musical Courier*.

Damrosch conducting. Ornstein and the concerto were last-minute substitutions, as Ossip Gabrilowitsch had been scheduled to appear.[22] Nevertheless Ornstein proved a huge success, playing the work "with dramatic effect," "in superb command of tone, technic, rhythm and interpretative appeal."[23] Ornstein continued to perform the MacDowell Concerto throughout the 1918–1919 season, with the St. Louis Symphony Orchestra, February 7 and 8, the Philadelphia Orchestra, March 7 and 8, and the New York Philharmonic Orchestra, March 12. In the 1919–1920 season he performed it with the Chicago Symphony Orchestra on November 29, and the Boston Symphony Orchestra on December 19, a performance that sent the Boston critic H. T. Parker into paeans of praise, as he compared Ornstein favorably to Josef Hofmann. After the performance Ornstein was engaged to perform the concerto with the Boston Symphony Orchestra on a tour that included Hartford, Philadelphia, Baltimore, and Washington, D.C. By 1920 *Music Courier* could claim that "Ornstein has now played the MacDowell concerto in D minor with every orchestra in America, except the Minneapolis Symphony," and the only reason he missed that one was because they could not find a mutually satisfactory date.[24]

Lest there were any doubts about motivations for programming the MacDowell so frequently, Ornstein dispelled them in an interview that appeared in *Musical Courier* in January 1920: "In private conversation, Ornstein recently stated that anyone, no matter where born, but brought to this country as a mere child, and growing up here . . . must naturally feel that he is an American, first, last and all the time; and if a true artist, no matter to what branch of art devoted, must be filled with a fervent desire to see American art and American reproducing artists appreciated by the American public." Ornstein stressed that in spite of his convictions that art was international, he believed "that the artists of each country must help to develop art with all their own national characteristics." According to the writer, Ornstein saw his performances of MacDowell as his contribution to this effort: "in playing MacDowell, admittedly the greatest of all American composers, he is but giving vent to his opinions on the subject, and is but trying to do his share toward advancing American aims and duties."[25]

Ornstein's concern about American music had surfaced as early as 1916. In an article that appeared in the *Houston Chronicle* that spoke of a tour of the southern and southwestern states, which included stops in Houston, New Orleans, and Atlanta, he stated that American music did not yet exist, but that he expected to find it in the South. Asked about ragtime, he conceded that it was "distinctively American," but being based on artificialities, it was ephemeral, soon to die out. He believed that a true American music could come from southern blacks, because their music "is the utterance of emotion, pure and simple,—as music must be. Because it is sincere, natural, and elemental, and therefore beautiful. And because it comes from the soil." Ornstein's association of emotional simplicity and naturalness with black Americans might easily be read as a manifestation of patronizing, racist attitudes held by many whites at the time. But it was never that alone. It is first of all entirely consistent with Ornstein's overall musical aesthetic. Beyond that, connection to the soil was important for Ornstein: "From the soil come all things. Only there can the musician, the painter, the poet, get the fundamentals that will alone make his work live." According to the composer, connection to the soil was precisely what had given Walt Whitman his power as a poet. Ornstein believed that America did not yet understand this relationship, which was why Whitman was not more revered, but he saw that changing: "The time will come when Whitman will be placed with Shakespeare, among the immortals. Only to Shakespeare can I compare him."[26] Regarding "Negro" music Ornstein did not specify what he had in mind, but he had just come from New Orleans and likely heard jazz there.

With the exception of a few isolated recordings that had limited circulation, such as those of James Reese Europe and his "Society Orchestra" in 1914 and 1915, in 1916 jazz was virtually unknown to the majority of the American public.

Practically no jazz had been recorded until 1917, when Victor Records released "Livery Stable Blues" and "The Original Dixie Jass One-Step" by the Original Dixie Land Jazz Band, ironically but not surprisingly a group of white musicians. The great migrations of jazz musicians to Kansas City, Chicago, and New York had barely begun; jazz was still a local art. For Ornstein, as for most people at the time, it would have been an entirely new experience. Ornstein's comments do make clear that in 1916 he was speaking as an outsider, both to the South as a region, but also to the larger nation. He found himself drawn to the more emotional temperament of southerners, which he considered the foundation of art, and which he related to his own background, growing up in the largely rural Ukraine in the southwestern corner of Russia.[27] In 1916 Ornstein still saw himself as Russian.

Why then the change in identity in 1918, the apparently sudden interest in being seen as American? At twenty-five years of age, after twelve years in the United States, did Ornstein have a change of heart, or was it all a matter of marketing? More important, does it evince Ornstein's own indigenous patriotism, or were there other forces shaping and possibly changing his point of view? Who or what was behind it? Given the public nature of Ornstein's life, and the thoroughness of his identification with Russia and Russian musical traditions, at least in the press, such reimagining was not insignificant.

With no explanation from the composer, we are left to speculate regarding the reasons behind his identity change from Russian to American. There were, however, numerous events occurring in the larger political arena that would have been known to Ornstein, and would have encouraged him to rethink his ties to Russia whether they were political, cultural, or artistic.

The war itself undoubtedly had some effect. After the sinking of the *Lusitania*, an outpouring of patriotism and a revulsion against Germany grew to fever pitch in the United States. Once conscription was announced, young men rushed to join the armed forces. Wilsonian idealism fueled the hope that this was "the war to end all wars." Ornstein himself was caught up in the war fervor. According to a report in *Musical Courier*, Ornstein attempted to join the army but was rejected by the examining board because he was two and a half pounds too light. He then decided to volunteer to drive an ambulance in France or Russia "wherever his services could be used by the Red Cross," but this was a problem because Ornstein did not know how to drive. He borrowed his brother Manus's touring car and spent part of 1917 assiduously practicing his driving two hours per day, as if preparing for a concert.[28] For reasons unknown nothing came of his efforts, but while in Deer Isle, Maine, during the summer of 1917 Ornstein decided to contribute in another, more personal way. Many were worried about a possible food shortage at the time, and Ornstein did what he considered to be his part by planting a vegetable garden. He devoted an hour a day to it and christened his radishes and cabbages the "Wild Men" of the species.[29]

After the war Ornstein's place of birth, his numerous pieces referring to aspects of Russian culture, his years of billing as a Russian composer-pianist, and his association with anarchism, even if only of a musical type, became liabilities in the political environment that was just beginning to breed the national hysteria known as the Red Scare. The media kept the conflation of Russian-Jewish immigrants with radical, subversive behavior in the forefronts of the public's thinking.

In 1917 and 1918, the government passed three acts that would have caused anyone with Ornstein's religious and ethnic background to reassess his situation, particularly someone who had been described as a revolutionary and an anarchical musician numerous times in the press, and who had played concerts for such radical causes as women's suffrage or for union workers.[30] The Espionage Act of 1917 and the Sedition and Alien Acts of 1918 were emotional responses to what many at the time believed were well-founded worries about the security of capitalism in the face of growing socialist movements, especially those originating in Russia. According to Julian F. Jaffe, the nation enjoyed great unity during the war, but that cohesiveness "tended to disappear once peace was established." As he assessed the situation, "the public cast about for a new scapegoat; this it found in the 'radical agitator' who served as a replacement for the hated 'Hun.'" In addition to posing an economic threat, which the Irish and Italians had done years earlier, Russian-Jewish immigrants were now cast as harborers of radical ideas who, as a group, challenged the very foundations of America.[31] And in the paranoia of the time, radicals got deported.

The Espionage Act of 1917 threatened anyone suspected of interfering with the recruiting of troops, with disclosing information related to national defense, or with undermining the war effort in a myriad of ways with a $10,000 fine and twenty years' imprisonment. The language of the act was vague enough to provide the government with significant latitude to interpret any criticism of national policy, including antiwar speeches, as suspect. The Sedition Act of 1918, an amendment to the earlier Espionage Act, broadened its powers and targeted anyone who publicly criticized the actions of the government. Conscientious objectors were arrested and imprisoned; fear was rampant. Ornstein's attendance at a Quaker School when he first came to the country might have prompted him to be concerned, even though he was never a member of the Society of Friends. Since their founding in the late 1600s, the Quakers had been one of a group of peace churches that believed in pacifism, and in postwar America, pacifists were collectively suspect.[32] According to Todd J. Pfannestiel, churches, schools, and universities were especially dangerous because of the "presence of intelligentsia among them . . . who confined their operations to brain storms rather than physical force."[33]

Section 3 of the 1918 Sedition Act enumerated punishable offenses:

> Whoever . . . shall willfully utter, print, write, or publish any disloyal, pro-fane, scurrilous, or abusive language about the form of government of the United States, or the Constitution of the United States, or the military or naval forces of the United States . . . or shall willfully display the flag of any foreign enemy, or shall willfully . . . urge, incite, or advocate any curtailment of production . . . or advocate, teach, defend, or suggest the doing of any of the acts or things in this section enumerated and whoever shall by word or act support or favor the cause of any country with which the United States is at war or by word or act oppose the cause of the United States therein, shall be punished.[34]

In October 1918, Congress passed yet one more act aimed at suppressing ide-ological opposition. The Alien Act empowered the government to deport any alien who was a member of an anarchist organization. The purposely broad language eventually resulted in the infamous Palmer raids of January 1920 when union offices and headquarters of socialist and communist organizations across the nation were ransacked and destroyed by zealous government agents intent on ferreting out sub-versives. A. Mitchell Palmer, Attorney General at the time, defended his actions in a brief paper entitled "The Case against the 'Reds.'"[35] But, according to Robert K. Murray, before he did, "between February 1917 and November 1919 more than 600 aliens had been arrested and detained," of these, "only sixty had actually been deported." Naturalized citizens could also have their citizenship papers revoked if they were suspected of espousing radical philosophies. In December 1919, 249 deportees were shipped from New York to Finland and then sent on trains to the Soviet Union, even though, according to Murray, "the majority of these . . . hadn't ever participated in anarchist activities and had no criminal records." It was "their belief in theoretical anarchism, rather than their actions, [that] had made them subject to expulsion."[36] Critics had already branded Ornstein a musical anarchist.[37] In the highly charged atmosphere of the time, Ornstein could only wonder if gov-ernment agents would forget the word musical.

Ornstein's own concert schedule suggested, if not a radical orientation, at least an affinity for the working class, as he frequently sought venues to reach them. Ornstein appeared in Brownsville at least twice and a third time elsewhere in Brooklyn, at a concert at the Brooklyn Academy of Music sponsored jointly by the East Side Recreation Center and the Brownsville Recreation Association. Brownsville was an area in Brooklyn of approximately 2.2 square miles. Between

1880 and 1900 it had grown from a rural outpost of New York City to a densely populated area of mainly Russian Jews. By 1907, 96 percent of the residents of Brownsville lived in tenements, small buildings of three of four stories, with four or five families per building. The first floor usually housed a commercial enterprise. Poverty abounded. In 1910 two-thirds of the residents had been in the United States less than ten years, and 85 percent were from Russia.[38]

On the first Brownsville concert, which took place on May 20, 1916, Ornstein shared the stage with the Russian Balalaika Orchestra. His second Brownsville appearance was on June 7, 1917, at Brooklyn High School P. S. 84, under sponsorship of the People's Institute of Brooklyn, Brownsville Civic Forum. Ornstein cared enough about the concert that he was willing to journey back from Deer Isle, where he was spending the summer, specifically for this event.

Ornstein knew his Brooklyn audience. He began the recital with his *Russian Suite*, for which the large crowd sat in absolute silence, only to erupt with sustained applause when it was over. He followed that with a long, varied program that included Debussy, Albéniz, Scott, Liszt, Mendelssohn, a group of Chopin pieces, two Rachmaninoff preludes, and according to one reviewer, the first New York performance of his *A la chinoise*. The entire program was received enthusiastically.

On February 18, 1918, Ornstein returned again, this time to the Brownsville Labor Lyceum. In 1900 the Lyceum had become a meeting place for many labor groups and soon thereafter became the Socialist Party Headquarters. By the early 1900s it had also become the cultural center of Brownsville, and among those responsible for presenting concerts there was Sol Hurok, who almost certainly arranged Ornstein's.[39] According to Hurok, "music thrived in Brownsville," and unlike New York, "there was never any lack of audience."[40] While the residents of Brownsville might view Ornstein's appearance as a cultural event, to the world outside he was flirting dangerously with socialism.

There was no lack of audience for Ornstein's concert. The Great Hall in the Labor Lyceum, which held two thousand, was packed, two hundred extra chairs were added, and there were still people standing in the aisles and the doors. Ornstein's program is not reported, but his success was sufficient that management sought a return engagement in March, something that did not occur only because Ornstein had already arranged a tour to the Midwest and western Canada.

Brownsville was not the only place where Ornstein played for working-class audiences. In February 1916, Ornstein performed in Chelsea, Massachusetts, for a crowd of almost two thousand, which according to newspaper reports was comprised of "almost entirely working people." For this concert ticket prices were set at fifty cents. In March 1916 Ornstein joined the violinist Francis MacMillen for a concert at Aeolian Hall in New York, which was sponsored by the East Side

Wage Earners' League. The Wage Earners' League had been formed in 1911 by the Woman Suffrage Party and the Women's Trade Union League to promote the cause of women suffrage. And in what must be one of the strangest events of his career, in January 1917 Ornstein attended a luncheon with police officers who were experimenting with eating on 25 cents a day. Ornstein was interested in the movement and ate with them something called "peanut hash." He then played for them a piece he had composed especially for the occasion entitled *Calory Rag*. Unfortunately the piece is lost; it may have been improvised.[41]

All of this does not add up to a political philosophy but hints that he may have held left-wing and possibly even socialist political beliefs. Socialist leanings would not have been unusual for a Jew coming out of the Lower East Side in the early twentieth century, or for an artist or intellectual in modernist circles, but there is no record of Ornstein's ever having participated in a political party or engaged in political activity beyond his performing venues. According to Ornstein's son, Severo, Ornstein was extremely interested in politics and later in life would discuss it at length. He was always for the underdog and apparently held highly divergent opinions from his very conservative father-in-law, Severo Mallet-Prevost. Regardless of his personal political views, however, his public appearances would have been sufficient to raise suspicion about him in the minds of many.

Later in life Ornstein's leftist tendencies had moderated, although he remained committed to social justice. By this time he had seen fascism in Europe, Stalinism in Russia, and McCarthyism in the United States and had become more cynical about people's motivations.

Ornstein's interest in working-class venues, which seems dichotomous with his musical elitism and his strong opinions about what music was good and what was not, is rooted in his idealism. Ornstein's musical idealism was so intense that he had virtually no sympathy for anyone who was either second-rate or insincere. And Ornstein's standards in both regards were extreme. When it came to music there was no compromise. At the same time Ornstein loathed what he considered the pretense and artificiality of elite society. According to Pauline, he and she led a hermit life precisely to escape that culture. He abhorred the social ritual concomitant with a concert career and went to great lengths to avoid it. Except for the cellist Hans Kindler, with whom he had a strong musical bond, Ornstein later had few friends in the classical musical world, although as we have seen in the previous chapter he had a number of close ties both to avant-garde musicians and to the literary and artistic world of modernism in the 1910s.

When Ornstein summered in Deer Isle, Maine, he got up early each morning to spend time talking to the lobster fishermen. After he and Pauline moved to New Hampshire, Ornstein became closer to some of the native woodsmen and workers on his place than to most in the concert world. He joined them in outdoor tasks, such as using a crosscut saw, and when his house was being built in 1919–1920, he worked alongside the laborers in the actual construction. According to Pauline, however, the workers ironically did find him "a bit WASPish."[42] Ornstein enjoyed the company of workers because they did not talk music, and they were, in his eyes, free of pretense. With them "he did not have to tolerate half baked and stuffy thinking that could not be ignored but that was still not worth combatting."[43]

Even though Ornstein probably never had real connections to any of the suspected radical political groups or openly espoused socialist or Bolshevik ideas beyond his interest in connecting with workers, his religious, ethnic, and national identities and his willingness to play in venues associated with socialism, coupled with his flaunting of traditional musical aesthetics for revolutionary, even anarchical, ones, to the extent that critics affixed the label "anarchist" to him, placed the pianist-composer in a vulnerable position. When merely having a foreign name or speaking with an accent made one suspect, Ornstein might have felt like an easy target. So the Russian pianist-composer became an American one.

Yet throughout his life Ornstein had to negotiate not just two but three cultures: Jewish, Russian, and American. He experienced them serially, but each time he acquired the next, some aspect of the earlier remained and was modified. As with many Eastern European immigrants, by the end of his life the three had melded together, but the process took time. Ornstein was not one to whom life evolved gradually, one year blending into another, but for whom life unfolded in a series of sudden, traumatic, major changes. Some breaks were the result of circumstance, Ornstein being almost a passive observer. Others were his own choosing. His admittance to the St. Petersburg Conservatory, his immigration to the United States, his sudden new compositional direction—each dictated an entirely new trajectory for his life. The Bandbox series of concerts were another, for after their success, Ornstein was a celebrity, ready to capitalize on his new status.

Ornstein's youthful trip from Kremenchug to St. Petersburg to attend the conservatory was more than a wrenching from home and family; it was a venture into an alien culture: The child of the shtetl was thrust into the salon. At the time Jews in Russia were isolated in a world of their own within the official confines of the Pale, an area just north and west of the Black Sea that had been created by a decree of Czar Nicholas I in 1835. Most Jewish children attended Jewish schools, and many Jews did not even speak Russian. Over a sixty-year period Jews from both urban and rural parts of Russia were uprooted and herded into the Pale, until by the 1897 census, close to five million Jews lived in an area about 400 miles by 800 miles. This was home to the extended Ornstein family.

St. Petersburg lay far outside the Pale and in 1891 had seen the deportation of two thousand Jews, many in chains.[44] And regardless of where they lived, Jews were either barred from most universities and most professions or had their entry severely restricted.

Music, however, was one of the few professions open to Jews, and the St. Petersburg Conservatory, the most prestigious conservatory in Russia, had actually been founded by a Jewish composer-pianist, Anton Rubinstein. Rubinstein's success as a child prodigy, the impression he made on Queen Victoria, and his triumphant tour through Norway, Sweden, Prussia, Saxony, and Austria attracted him to the sister-in-law of Nicholas I, Grand Duchess Yelena Pavlovna, who had formerly been Princess of Saxe-Altenburg. Rubinstein's own urbane charm did not hurt matters, and his virtuosity at her soirees enhanced both of their positions. As a consequence a significant number of students at the Conservatory were Jewish, which may have lessened somewhat Ornstein's sense of being displaced. By all accounts, however, the suddenness and degree of change were a great shock to the young boy.[45]

Ornstein underwent a similar cultural shift when he came to the United States. Once again he was uprooted, but this time it was from the opulent circles of the Russian salons to the immigrant haven of the Lower East Side of Manhattan. If this new American home reminded him of his younger days in the Pale, Ornstein would not stay there long. His father, who became a cantor at one of the more prestigious synagogues in the area, remained totally immersed in the Old World; young Leo did not.[46] Quickly securing a scholarship to the newly founded Institute of Musical Art in New York City, Ornstein broke with his family's traditions and attended a Quaker school.[47] Although twelve years old when he arrived in the United States, Ornstein rejected completely his parents' Old World ways, an act later symbolized by his marriage to a wealthy New York debutante of French background. Ornstein was even more vehement about the Jewish religion. According to his son, Severo, "His rational/anti-religious streak ran very deep. As an intellectual he always scoffed at the 'mumbo-jumbo' of religion—and not just organized religion—at all religious ideas. You rarely met a more ardent atheist."[48]

Ornstein's trajectory followed that of many second-generation Jewish immigrants who wished to identify thoroughly with the new culture and to assimilate as much as possible. Ornstein may have arrived at his American identity through a somewhat more circumscribed route than most Ashkenazi Jews, through the upper echelons of Russian society in St. Petersburg, and he may have felt stronger about the evils of religion, but nevertheless the ethnic pattern of his life was typical and, as we will see, symbolic.

Nevertheless, to some Ornstein's Jewish background was cause for concern. Daniel Gregory Mason, staunch upholder of Anglo-Saxon values against the "Jewish menace," sounded the alarm, focusing his rhetoric specifically on Leo Ornstein. In an article written in 1920, "Is American Music Growing Up?" Mason called for an emancipation from "alien influences" and contrasted the Anglo-Saxon qualities of moderation, restraint and sobriety against the "Oriental, especially, the Jewish, infection," characterized by speciousness, superficial charm, persuasiveness, "violently juxtaposed extremes of passion," and "poignant eroticism and pessimism." In Mason's view no one had caught the disease more than Leo Ornstein; Ornstein personified all that was wrong with contemporary American musical culture. He did credit Ornstein with throwing it off, to an extent, but only at a price, which left him "devoid of energy and, as it were, permanently anemic."[49]

Mason, calling moderation not the absence of passion but a passion itself, recognized that it would in the short run be artistic suicide to adopt such a position, where in New York at least, "only the sensational, the excessive, the exaggerated can be heard." But moderation to Mason defined artistic integrity. At the same time Mason argued, "if he (the artist) is not himself he will never, despite momentary popularity, be anything." It is hard to unpack the levels of irony here, as no musician in America before the public prior to the 1920s stuck to his guns more than Leo Ornstein. Of course, Ornstein's message was so opposed to Mason's that Mason could not, as many writers did, recognize that Ornstein spoke not just for his ethnicity, but for his time as well.

Daniel Gregory Mason conflated many categories, ethnic, racial, geographic and religious. To him Jewish equaled "Oriental," a terminology common at the time, and passion was a quality of race, not of social norm or individual temperament. Aesthetic issues became not only ethnic issues but class ones as well. Mason's particular musical distinction between Anglo-Saxon and alien, that is, Jewish, musical values is in one sense an elaboration of a theme that goes back more than two thousand years, that of a style of restraint versus a style of unbridled emotionalism. Millennia earlier the Greeks characterized it as a battle between Apollo and Bacchus. Mason himself was direct heir to a lineage that went back to early-nineteenth-century America, where Mason's grandfather, Lowell Mason, had identified a clash in religious music in geographic terms: the civilized East versus the untamed West.[50] Lowell Mason, who considered the extreme emotionalism of frontier hymnody a direct threat not only to established religion, but to Eastern values of decorum and civilized behavior as well, transformed the difference into an aesthetic one. In the twentieth century Daniel Gregory Mason made the distinction racial. He considered it his mission to uphold the view, still prevalent in many circles, that the art of music was a sacred trust and must remain abstract, pure, and morally correct.

Why, then, did Mason focus on Judaism? He came from a segment of society in which anti-Semitic sentiments flourished. In the late nineteenth century, anti-Semitism was particularly strong among three groups: rural populists, lower-class workers, and patrician New Englanders, who shared some of the same concerns as populists about the impact Jews were having on the world of finance, and who blamed the panic of 1893 at least in part on Jewish machinations.[51] The Boston Brahmin Henry Adams, in particular, held a deep prejudice against Jews, and his writings, more than any other's, represented the sentiment of late-nineteenth-century New England elites.[52]

Although Mason himself lived in New York, where he was Professor of Music at Columbia University, his background was Boston patrician. Born in Brookline, Massachusetts, to the most prominent and wealthiest musical family in the country, his father, Henry Mason, founder of the Mason & Hamlin Piano Company, was a very successful businessman, and his grandfather Lowell Mason had been the first American to make a fortune in music, through his hymns, many publications of music collections, and his work as the founder of music education in the public schools.

Mason's emphasis on Anglo-Saxon values was itself left over from the nineteenth century, when strong sentiment existed to preserve the Anglo-Saxon and Christian heritage as part of American identity. The influx of Irish Catholics earlier in the century had challenged the Protestant homogeneity that underlay America's sense of self, even though regional variation within Protestantism was itself intense and in some instances disruptive. The influx of Jews in the 1870s and 1880s had galvanized American Christianity even further and tended to create a sense of crisis about American identity. The most popular voice of this fear was that of the Reverend Josiah Strong, who published *Our Country: Its Possible Future and Its Present Crisis* in 1885. By 1910 this book had sold over 175,000 copies, an extraordinarily large number for a polemical, nonfiction work.

Strong advocated in no uncertain terms that the Anglo-Saxon race was God's chosen people, destined "to outnumber all the other civilized races of the world," people who would in his ominous metaphor serve as both the model for the rest of humanity and the force to make it happen: "Does it not look as if God were not only preparing in our Anglo-Saxon civilizations the die with which to stamp the peoples of the earth, but as if He were also massing behind that die the mighty power with which to press it?" Envisioning an imminent Armageddon, he called upon Anglo-Saxons to close ranks "for the final competition, for which the Anglo-Saxon is being schooled."[53]

The Hebraic qualities Mason heard in Ornstein's music thrust Ornstein into the center of a major controversy in American society, as anti-Semitism peaked in the early 1920s. By this time the German Jewish population that had arrived mostly in the late nineteenth century had established a strong economic foothold and been absorbed into mainstream American culture. The new wave of immigrants that began arriving in the twentieth century, however, Ashkenazi Jews from Eastern Europe, particularly Poland and Russia, tended to be less artisan and middle class and more rural and working class; they concentrated in a few areas, particularly the Lower East Side of New York and Brooklyn; they maintained many Old World social units, and their customs seemed even more foreign than those of the other recent immigrants, the Irish and Italians. By 1920 Ashkenazi Jews were moving out of the ghetto into more established positions, thus getting closer to the upper echelons of society, which considered them threatening not only because of their different religion and culture but also their politics. Political agitation on the Lower East Side had coalesced into a brand of socialism that many in the Anglo-Saxon establishment found alarming regardless of the ethnic or religious origins of its proponents. For a conservative America, still uneasy with industrialization, immigration, and the twentieth century itself, socialism, frequently equated with the Red Scare and Bolshevism, was just more trouble caused by these "alien" people populating the large cities. For Mason it was too easy to associate the musical revolution that so concerned him with the rabble on the Lower East Side.

Mason was not alone in his prejudices. Several books published after World War I raised the specter of a serious ethnic threat to Western society. Lothrap Stoddard, in *The Rising Tide of Color against White World-Supremacy*, saw the war itself as disruptive of the deserved Anglo-Saxon domination of the world, which had nearly been achieved in the nineteenth century. His stance is blatantly racist, his tone apocalyptic: "Ours is a solemn moment. We stand at a crisis—the supreme crisis of the ages." As the title indicates, he feared the press and expansion of "fast-breeding" people of color, particularly into the United States, and he believed that they would swamp "the whole white world."[54] His is only one of the most shrill of many statements on this subject, and Mason himself was not the only musician to succumb to such prejudice. Composer Carl Ruggles was openly anti-Semitic, and Edgard Varèse more discreetly so. Several scholars have traced the tensions between the League of Composers and the International Composers' Guild to anti-Semitism.[55]

Ethnic fears came fully out into the open when given concrete and forceful expression by one of the most powerful men in the United States, Henry Ford. Ford's automotive empire had made him, according to some, the wealthiest man in

America, and his fundamental idea, to create an automobile that most Americans could afford while paying workers a decent living, had made him a folk hero. Eccentric and strong-willed, Ford often went to extraordinary lengths to promote social causes. In 1915 he sponsored a "peace ship," a chartered steamer that sailed to Europe "to respond to the call of humanity . . . to establish an international conference dedicated to negotiations leading to a just settlement of the war."[56] Ridiculed in the press, the effort was a total flop and made Ford look like a fool.

Ford's next major social effort was not as benign or idealistic. Following his abortive venture with the peace trip, Henry Ford decided that, rather than struggling for headlines, he would create his own outlet. To that end he bought the *Dearborn Independent*, a small country weekly that had been in existence for about twenty years. Beginning on January 11, 1919, the *Independent* reserved one page for "Mr. Ford's Own Page," which usually contained an editorial written by Ford or passed on by him. On February 22, 1919, Ford lashed out against the Bolsheviks in an article titled "What of the Melting Pot?" The (unbylined) writer answered his own question with a disturbing euphemism:

> The problem is not . . . with the pot so much as it is with the base metal. Some metals cannot be assimilated, refuse to mix with the molten mass of the citizenship, but remain in ugly, indissoluble lumps. How did this base metal get in? . . . What *about* those aliens who have given us so much trouble, these Bolsheviki messing up our industries and disturbing our civil life?[57]

To Ford and many others in the world, fear of the Bolsheviks transferred into hatred of the Jews, as political labeling soon gave way to racial stereotyping. Ford became convinced that it was the Jews who posed the biggest threat to society. Aiding and abetting Ford's anti-Semitism was Boris Brasol, a shadowy former member of the Imperial Russian Guard infantry, who had also been an attorney and one of the foremost drama critics in Russia.[58]

A staunch monarchist, Brasol had come to the United States as the czar's representative to the Inter-Allied Conference, but resigned following the Bolshevik victory and decided to remain in the United States. In 1918 he worked for U.S. Army Military Intelligence, and after the war for the United States War Trade Board. He was also vice chairman of the Russian Officers' Union in America.[59] Handsome and personable, he quickly ingratiated himself into conservative circles and was contracted for a speaking tour of the Midwest by the American Constitutional League, where Ford or Ernest Liebold, Ford's secretary and general alter ego, may well have heard him.

At the urging of Liebold, the *Independent* published an article by Brasol on April 12, 1919, "The Bolshevik Menace to Russia." It was essentially an anti-

Bolshevik statement, not unusual, given the tenor of the time, but it did establish a connection between the *Independent* and Brasol. Whether Liebold was acting directly on Ford's orders is not clear, although Brasol's ideas were entirely consistent with Ford's own views.

Brasol's anti-Semitism was as strong as his anticommunism, and like many czarists the two were strongly linked in his mind. For decades radicalism and revolution had been blamed on the Jews in Russia. The Black Hundred, an extremist group that had created much of the havoc following the 1905 revolt that had forced the Ornsteins to leave Russia, espoused a virulent anti-Semitism. Brasol was a member of the Black Hundred and in the United States bragged openly about a case in which they had attempted to frame a Jewish merchant for the murder of a prostitute. The trial went on for eighteen months and made headlines across Russia. The merchant, Mendal Beylis, was finally acquitted in a complex verdict, which Brasol would rue to his American friends even though he himself admitted that Beylis was innocent.[60]

Brasol had bigger designs than an occasional article in a relatively obscure newspaper, however. He had brought with him a book published in Russia in 1917, *The Protocols of the Learned Elders of Zion*.[61] The *Protocols* purportedly documented a secret meeting held during the First Zionist Congress in Basel, Switzerland, in 1897. Led by the "Grand Rabbi," this meeting set forth a plan to gain world domination for the Jews through the leadership of a single Jewish Sanhedrin, or World Council, which would control the financial markets of the world and undermine the stability of capitalist society. Brasol, together with Natalie de Borgy, a young woman of Russian descent who worked in the War Department's Eastern Department, translated the *Protocols* into English.

Brasol then began to seek someone to publish them. De Borgy's boss at the War Department, Harris Ayres Houghton, who was in agreement with Brasol's views, showed the translation to various members of the government, including members of the Cabinet and chief justice of the Supreme Court, Charles Evan Hughes, who promptly forwarded it to Louis Marshall, president of the American Jewish Committee.[62] Houghton also contacted Frederick Ohl, publisher of the *New York Herald*, who turned the book over to Herman Bernstein, a foreign correspondent at the *Herald*, to evaluate for possible publication. Bernstein pronounced them a "clumsy forgery," and the *Herald* chose not to publish them. Nevertheless they continued to circulate in Washington, and at the same time began to appear in London and Paris in various other translations.

Through Liebold, Brasol finally found his publisher in Henry Ford. On May 22, 1920, the *Dearborn Independent* ran an article, "The International Jew: The World's Problem," the first of a series of ninety-one articles on "the Jewish question." Much of the material was taken directly from the *Protocols*, although the articles were more a commentary on than a reprint of them. Ford's campaign reached an even wider audience in October when Liebold issued an anthology of articles that had appeared in the *Independent*, with the inflammatory title *The International Jew: The World's Foremost Problem*. This volume sold between 200,000 and 500,000 copies and was followed by three more anthologies within the next eighteen months.[63]

The Jewish community fought back, rallying considerable support among Americans who were tolerant of Jewish culture and appreciative of the contributions Jews had made. Then on August 16, 1921, the *London Times* dealt a fatal blow to the entire argument that a coordinated plot existed for the Jews to create a Zionist world domination by exposing the *Protocols* for what they were: a total and complete forgery.[64] The *Protocols* had originally been written by Maurice Joly, under the title *Dialogues in Hell between Machiavelli and Montesquieu*, published in 1864. The pamphlet was intended as an attack on Napoleon III, and there is no mention of Jews in it. In 1872 Hermann Goedsche, writing under the name of Sir John Retcliffe, converted the *Protocols* into an anti-Semitic tract by substituting the word Zion where the word France originally appeared and "We the Jews" for the word "Emperor." Goedsche's work was translated into Russian in 1872 but achieved little circulation until Sergius Nilus's first edition of 1905. The Black Hundred quickly adopted Nilus's work as justification for their anti-Semitism, making it, of course, known to its members.

Later Ford, under pressure, recanted the anti-Semitism of the *Dearborn Independent*, but it is not clear how sincere that about face was. He was confronted with lawsuits and threatened boycotts of his products, and he waited until 1927 to issue an apology. In any event the damage was done, and what had been a whispered stealth campaign thanks to Henry Ford moved into the American mainstream.

The *Protocols* tracked Ornstein like a mysterious cloud. As they first had become public in Russia in 1905 and were used as one of the principal justifications for the anti-Semitic backlash against the Jews, indirectly they were at least partly responsible for Ornstein's emigration. In the 1920s, when Ornstein was at the peak of his fame and beginning to have doubts about his public career, the *Protocols*, mainly through the pen of Mason, once again began to haunt him.[65]

Throughout the 1910s Ornstein, Schoenberg, and Stravinsky had been to American musicians and music lovers the three names associated with radical modernism or futurism in music. They were also all associated with Judaism.[66] And while Stravinsky's Jewish background is itself controversial, and Schoenberg did not tout his, at least at that time, it would not have escaped someone like Mason.

THE
INTERNATIONAL
JEW

THE WORLD'S FOREMOST PROBLEM

Being a Reprint of a Series of Articles
Appearing in The Dearborn Independent
from May 22 to October 2, 1920

NOVEMBER, 1920

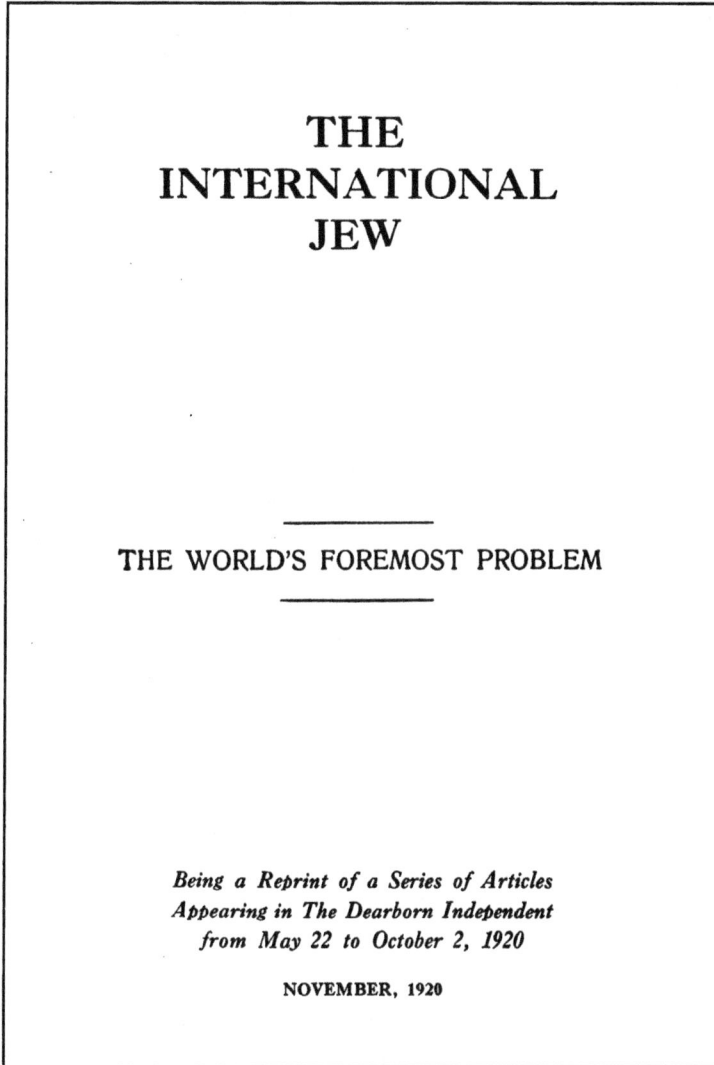

FIGURE 5.3. Title page of *The International Jew.*

With Ornstein his Jewish background was apparent to most, but he did not stress it overtly as Ernst Bloch did. To many it sounded clearly and unequivocally in his music, although critics had trouble distinguishing what was Hebraic, what was Russian, and what was "Oriental," a term used in this context to designate a vague Eastern European, Middle Eastern sound; it was all exotic. Unlike his Russian and American identities, which Ornstein had a hand in shaping and then promoting, his Jewishness was something he would leave to others to emphasize. And emphasize they did. No one did so more strongly, consistently, and over a longer period of time than Paul Rosenfeld, who as early as 1916 heard in Ornstein, particularly in the "Funeral March" in the *Dwarf Suite*, a strong Russian-Jewish element. In a single paragraph, Rosenfeld conflated the Jew, the modern city, and the Old Testament:

> Ornstein began making music out of what he himself had felt, it was the voice of the city proletariat that pierced, raucous and dissonant but with a primeval starkness that left no suspicion of the sentimentally sordid, into European music. The "Dwarfs" of the six musical moods that comprise his first wholly individual utterance are scarcely the gnomes of Grimm's Fairy Tales. They are the stunted and subterranean lives of those ground by want and ignorance. It is precisely the fact that Ornstein offered the world, not what one could wish the unfortunate and despairing to feel, but what in their sunless existence they do feel, that to-day makes the concert audience turn in revulsion from the grim hatred that speaks in the pitiless "Dawn," from the naked grief of the "Funeral March" that better perhaps than any other music, voices the tragedy of the Russian Jew. One wonders whether in any other composition, even in his setting for chorus of the Thirteenth Psalm, the composer has again succeeded in recapturing the accents that recall, across all the culture of Europe, the savage and solemn utterances of the Old Testament.[67]

When just four years later Rosenfeld discussed Ornstein in his 1920 book, *Musical Portraits: Interpretations of Twenty Modern Composers*, his ardor for the young composer had cooled because Ornstein, in his view, had moved away from his radical new approach to embrace a more conservative compositional style. But still Rosenfeld heard the sound of the Jew: "He is the resurrection of the most entombed of spirits, that of the outlaw European Jew. . . . He is Lazarus emerging in his grave clothes into the new world. . . . [T]he 'Poems of 1917' are full of the wailing and rockings of little old Ghetto mothers. Again and again Ornstein speaks in accents that resemble nothing quite so much as the savage and woeful language of the Old Testament." Because of the massive Jewish immigration to the modern city, and especially to New York City, Ornstein was in Rosenfeld's mind "a mirror held up to the world of the modern city."[68] Rosenfeld also saw fit to frame his displeasure with Ornstein's change of style with imagery associated with the Jewish synagogue: "Something not entirely reassuring has happened to the man. . . . The racial element is softened, become gentler and duskier and more romantic. The Jew in it no longer wears his gabardine. If he wears a prayer-shawl at all, it is one made of silk."[69]

In his 1923 references to Ornstein's Double Sonata, Op. 89, Rosenfeld stressed the Jewish element strongly: "Themes recall the arias and recitatives of synagogue cantors that must have come into the child with the first light of the world, and echo the subtle elaborate cadences, the Oriental monotony, of the ritual chants. Themes recall the street-songs, part Slavic, part Jewish, of the towns of the Pale; vulgar tunes of the working people and the nurse-girls, scraps of the tavern and the road."[70] Rosenfeld also continued to hear in Ornstein's music the Lower East Side: "Themes speak violent sensuality drowned in black, violent passion submerged and become fear, become hideous weariness and depression, become the lurid blue and black of the East Side of New York. Certain appear which seems like the raucous cries of suddenly felt steely power, the stamps, the gestures, the whistles of one who would represent with his own person the might of machinery" and "there is something in him that has the crude black power of the engines and the piles of industrialism."[71]

If Rosenfeld was disappointed with the more expressive Ornstein, he nevertheless continued to recognize the importance of what he had done. In his 1929 book *An Hour with American Music*, Rosenfeld distinguished Ornstein's earlier radical musical style from Schoenberg's, Stravinsky's, and Bartók's by characterizing it as "extremely violent and dissonant," as opposed to the "merely atonic" of the other composers. He found Ornstein's music compatible with both the city of the "age of steel" and Ornstein's own background, being planted on the Lower East Side "in sensitive youth." Yet he continued to hear a strong Jewish voice as well: "The vehement Preludes, Moods, Poems, and Dances of Ornstein's first creative period, Debussian in the thickness and richness of their steely harmonies, but Oriental and Yiddish in their wailing melodies, their abruptness and dismalness, were heavy with unrelieved tension."[72]

Rosenfeld was far from the only critic to hear a Jewish element in Ornstein's music, and the others too had trouble sorting Hebraic qualities from those of Eastern Europe. An anonymous review in *Musical Courier* of a concert by Ornstein and Hans Kindler in 1920 entitled "Impressions of Ornstein Music" describes at length Ornstein's First Cello Sonata (Op. 52) and the first movement of the Third Sonata, which were given in a private performance. He refers several times to the Hebraic character of certain passages, each time, with one exception, hedging on whether it is Hebraic, Eastern European, or Slavic: "Slavonic or the Hebraic," "Eastern European, possibly leaning toward the Hebraic," "Hebraic or East European manner." At one point he is certain: "Again one is feeling the Hebraic phrase manner decidedly."[73]

Deems Taylor likewise commented on both a Russian and a Hebrew character in Ornstein's Piano Concerto: "His themes are strongly racial in character. Their rhythms, frequently immensely complex, could have been devised by none but a Russian, and the melodies themselves are of the wailing, undulatory Orientalism that characterizes so much Hebrew folk-music."[74] It would seem that for Taylor, Russian, Hebraic, and Oriental musical styles are closely related, perhaps indistinguishable. H. T. Craven heard something similar in the Piano Concerto, but found it to be more precisely Slavic, with Tartar elements, and hints of Borodin and Stravinsky.[75] Henry Cowell reacted to the concerto quite similarly to Craven, complimenting it for being "what Stravinsky's should have been but was not," and noting in it "a Jewish wail that puts Ernest Bloch to shame."[76] W. J. Henderson, in the *New York Sun*, was less precise. He singled out the second movement of the concerto as not only having a "strongly Oriental flavor," but containing "some of the most original and significant music of the score."[77]

A. W. Kramer did attempt to separate Jewish from the Russian elements in Ornstein's Piano Sonata (probably Op. 54). Kramer, like Taylor, uses the terms Oriental and Hebrew synonymously, but he does note a deep Semitic tone sounded through all the four movements, in a wailing theme, a theme common to Oriental and Hebrew music, and views it, like Ornstein's earlier "Funeral March" from the *Dwarf Suite*, as "the woe of our generation, not the personal sorrow of a man."[78]

When Ornstein's Piano *Quintette* premiered three years later, in 1928, critics had similar, almost identical reactions to the ethnic element. One of the clearest examples of a passage that many critics as well as Ornstein himself heard as Jewish or Russian occurs at the beginning of the second movement of the *Quintette*, which opens with a haunting melody played two octaves apart by the first violin and cello. This is followed by another theme played by the viola. The first, predominantly diatonic and conjunct, is a single flowing long line. The second, dominated by thirds, stresses short motivic cells, the most prominent appearing in double augmentation (first in thirty-second, then in eighth notes). There is a clear Eastern European sound in this passage. Other exotic elements are easy to identify: the (wailing) octave melody, the appoggiatura and arabesque figurations, the turn of the motive around thirds, and prominent augmented seconds.

In an investigation of Ernst Bloch's music Alexander Knapp attempted to characterize those elements that are particularly Jewish. He noted exotic scales that use the augmented second and augmented fourth intervals, rhapsodic melodies that consist more of expansive motivic cells than long lines, frequent changes of meter and tempo with beats divided into unequal groupings, complex cross-accents, and an overall highly subjective tone, confirmed in the score by the use of expression marks such as *misterioso*, *intenso*, and *frenetico*.[79] Beyond the passage discussed, Ornstein's *Quintette* displays all of the above characteristics. Ornstein himself admitted that it might be "embarrassingly overcharged," and that he was less interested in unity than expressive power.[80] The two outer movements espe-

FIGURE 5.4. Leo Ornstein, *Quintette* for Piano and Strings, second movement, beginning.

cially contain many metrical and tempo changes with highly unusual rhythmic divisions, and the score is peppered with expression marks such as *con fuoco, agitato feroce, calmato,* and *tranquillo e languido.* Many critics actually heard Ornstein's *Quintette* as a derivative of Bloch's own Piano Quintet, written five years earlier.

To label these musical characteristics as specifically Jewish, however, would be questionable, and Knapp acknowledges such. As Abraham Idelsohn has observed, most of these features are typical of any music that has been labeled Oriental, exotic, or associated in any way with the Middle East or Eastern Europe. It is most famously apparent in the *style hongrois,* of Liszt's Hungarian Rhapsodies, but may be found even earlier in eighteenth-century opera and instrumental

FIGURE 5.5. Leo Ornstein, *Quintette* for Piano and Strings, second movement.

music. Derek B. Scott has cataloged an entire "bag of tricks" that a composer could pull out whenever he wanted to portray the exotic or the Other. More often music with such stylistic features was an artificial construct, valid less for its ethnic authenticity than for the perception of ethnicity it generated in the minds of the listener.[81] Rather than reflecting roots, the stylistic features formed a well-known code to signify the Other. It is a sort of nineteenth- and twentieth-century *Affektenlehre*, to be applied consciously and for a specific purpose when the composer wished.

According to Scott, of all ethnic groups, "the construction of Jewishness in Western music is most fraught with contradictions," in part because the Jew is depicted in so many ways, sometimes as hero as in Handel and Verdi (*Judas Maccabaeus* and *Nabucco*) or MGM movies (*The Ten Commandments* with Charlton

Heston), sometimes as arch-villain as in the *Protocols* or Shakespeare (*The Merchant of Venice*), and sometimes as Other, as in Sullivan's *Ivanhoe* or Jerry Bock's *Fiddler on the Roof.*[82] Reviewers of Ornstein's *Quintette* quickly caught that it portrayed the Other, but were hard pressed to identify who that was. M. S. Moses-Smith guessed that a "racial sentiment" was present, but ventured no further than that, although it should be noted that in the 1920s the term "racial" often appeared to be a stand-in for Jewish. H. T. Craven believed he detected a "Slavic, though perhaps Tarter" accent,[83] a sentiment echoed by the anonymous critic for *Musical America*, who described it as "Tartary and the Russian East, the land in particular of Borodin."[84] Was Craven simply recycling his comments of 1925, or is Ornstein that consistent? Idelsohn voices the same sentiment as Scott: In reference to composers who attempt to write consciously Jewish music, "On examination of their creations we discover not a single element that bears Jewish features that might be reckoned a distinctly Jewish contribution."[85]

This same issue may be found if we return to the "Funeral March" of the *Dwarf Suite*. This work is of some importance to Ornstein, as it was almost certainly the first composition in his modernist style. Carl Van Vechten heard the same message in the piece as Rosenfeld: "In the *Dwarf Suite* he gives to us a picture of the lives of the struggling Russian Jews."[86] Frederic Martens hedges on its ethnic composition; to him the *Dwarf Suite* represented "the life of man, for man is a dwarf, a pigmy, helpless in the grip of cosmic forces," and he found the "Funeral March" to be "the tonal embodiment of encompassing grief, an Oriental chant with the wail of hired mourners."[87] Yet one could read the "Funeral March" as more Russian than Jewish. In its melodic shape and tone one can hear echoes of Tchaikovsky's *March Slav*.

Ornstein own's description of the "Funeral March" is similar in symbolic content to Rosenfeld's, Van Vechten's, and Martens's, but Ornstein avoids any ethnic suggestions at all:

> In this I tried to describe a funeral in the East Side, New York. I had lived there for several years. I saw the awful poverty, the squalor, the sorrow of the stricken family, the sympathy of friends, the indifference and harshness of others in the streets, the solemnity and impressiveness of the funeral, and yet, over all, there was an angle of beauty in the realization of the eternal principle that this was really an insignificant thing and meant nothing. I am trying always to project the thing into space and to comprehend its lack of significance unbound by worldly prejudices. That is why I am a futurist.[88]

While one could extrapolate Jewish qualities in this piece, those qualities that could be so labeled, its motivic content and lyricism, the moaning wail of the melody, and a general overall melancholy tone, these are precisely the qualities that Idelsohn disavows as being too ubiquitous throughout Western music to warrant a specifically ethnic label. The same could be said for the Russian connection. Other than its triple meter, unusual for any kind of march, in its motion, with its deliberate pace and dotted rhythms, in melodic shape, circling as it does in seconds and thirds, and in its timbral contrast, beginning in the tenor region and expanding into the upper octave, the "Funeral March" evokes some of the more famous funeral marches of Western composers, its most salient feature being the overweening dissonance and chromaticism. In tone, structure and deployment of register, it is more Chopin on chromatic steroids than an ethnic statement.

Ornstein himself was much aware of the importance of his Eastern European, although not always specifically his Jewish, roots. In 1918 at the latest he told Martens, "There is hardly a composition of mine which fails to offer proof of what a lasting and thorough impression Greek ritual music and the Asiatic chant have made upon me, though I have never exploited traditional 'themes' or 'material.'" Martens himself observed that Ornstein had absorbed "Oriental chant" as a child, the "ritual music of the Greek and Armenian Churches, semi-Oriental in character," in Petrograd, where he "regularly attended the services in the great Russian cathedrals, so fascinated was he with these ritual chants."[89] From this latter statement, which Martens almost certainly got directly from Ornstein, it is clear that Ornstein heard Russian (non-Jewish) chant in his youth, which helps explain some of the sounds of his music and some of the confusion of critics. This statement also suggests that even as a child he was moving away from Judaism.[90]

Four years later Ornstein reiterated the Eastern qualities of his music and was more specific about the Jewish element. He acknowledged as perfectly natural a resemblance in the trio of his Cello Sonata to Tchaikovsky's *1812 Overture*, pointing out to Frank Patterson, the interviewer, that "it has its basis in the Russian and the Jewish hymn." He also called Patterson's attention to its similarity to Ernst Bloch's *Schelomo*, a work that is consciously Hebraic in style.[91]

Anti-Semitic intensity abated during the 1920s, but it did not go away. The stereotypical Shylock, the mercenary, mendacious Jew, continued his run in American literature, most famously in the form of Meyer Wolfsheim in Fitzgerald's *The Great Gatsby*, a dark-side counterpoint to the very real success of many East Side Jews in business. Jews were also reaching the pinnacles of some professions, notably law, where Louis Brandeis had been appointed Justice of the Supreme Count in 1916, and Felix Frankfurter Professor of Law at Harvard, later to take his own place on the Supreme Court bench in 1919.

Pressure was mounting on Henry Ford to recant his prejudicial position regarding the Jews. It came to a head when the *Dearborn Independent* attacked Aaron Sapiro, a former rabbinical student and the founder of the National Council of

Farmers' Cooperative Marketing Association, in 1924, claiming Sapiro's efforts to organize farmers was part of the Jewish plot to gain control of American farmers. Sapiro fired back, suing Ford for defamation of character, to "vindicate myself and my race."[92] Two years later a mistrial was declared, but the publicity did Ford little good, and in 1927, under further pressure, Ford was forced to issue an apology for his entire crusade. Skeptics doubted the sincerity of Ford's recantation, but it did reflect a reality he could not ignore, that Jews were making significant positive contributions to American society.

Ornstein stayed out of the argument, at least directly, but his success and the strong Hebraic quality perceived in his music combined to make him something of a hero in the Jewish community, or at least to several Jewish writers who interpreted Ornstein's life and music as symbolic of feelings and struggles of the Jewish people. We have already seen this in Paul Rosenfeld's writings. In 1926 and 1927, just as this issue was culminating, a number of lectures, books, and articles appeared in which Ornstein was featured prominently. In 1926 an unidentified writer was invited to give a talk "What the Jew Has Done for Music" to the National Council of Jewish Women. He acknowledged what he believed everyone knew, that in the field of popular music, Jews held "almost a monopoly." He then singled out four twentieth-century composers, Schoenberg, Stravinsky, Ornstein, and Bloch, as evidence of Jewish accomplishments, although *Musical Courier* does not report what he said about each, only that they "occupy an especially prominent position" in modern music.[93]

That same year Waldo Frank, under the pseudonym "Search-Light," published *Time Exposures*, brief biographical sketches of twenty famous individuals. Leo Ornstein joined Alfred Stieglitz, Ignace Paderewsky, John Dewey, Georgia O'Keeffe, Sinclair Lewis, Carl Sandburg, Charles Chaplin, and others as subjects of Frank's sketches. Frank did not stress Ornstein's ethnicity, but in describing, with some journalistic license, Ornstein's family history, made a claim for Ornstein as the everyman of Jewish immigration: He refers to a time, "when his family, implicated in the Russian revolution of 1905, fled house and fortune in the Ukraine. They found the customary gray rooms and black bread in our East Side ghetto and Leo's father became the Cantor of some cellar synagogue."[94] Frank then describes Ornstein's career in mythical terms: "He was a flame, a bright flame, barely sheathed in the frail scabbard of his body." He was not "the Machine of virtuosi," but in Frank's words, "you're the Music yourself." Ornstein fought the world of the virtuoso, but was ground up by the Machine of "Statler hotels, press agents, interviews, society ladies of 'forty' with a thirst for 'twenty,' flappers sipping thrills and programs full of rhapsodies, gimcrack and gymnastics. . . . So the boy died in the Machine, and the man was born," someone who retired to

New Hampshire to "compose dark, heady, restrained and integrated works which he left in the dust on the piano."[95]

In 1927 Lazare Saminsky published an article in *Modern Music* that specifically elaborated on Jewish contributions to modernism. Entitled "East Meets West," Saminsky singled out Ernst Bloch, Louis Gruenberg, and Ornstein as three "outstanding" composers in the idiom. He traced their strength to their "dual spiritual allegiance," but found that Ornstein had "lost the most through his adoption," that "his music create[d] the definite impression that he has been artificially torn from his true spiritual fatherland, Russia." He also heard in Ornstein's music echoes of Rachmaninoff, Borodin, and Scriabin."[96] Saminsky's assessment, not an entirely favorable one, reached a wider audience when it was reprinted in his book *Music of Our Day, Essentials and Prophecies* in 1930,[97] a time when other writers were dismayed with Ornstein because his music did not fulfill its original promise, or because Ornstein did not follow the modernist trajectory through the 1920s.[98]

Gdal Saleski published an even more extended discussion of Ornstein in the same year as Saminsky's, 1927. In its title, *Famous Musicians of a Wandering Race*, and its heft, 463 pages, Saleski's book was designed to showcase the importance of Jewish contributions to Western musical culture. It contains brief sketches of composers, conductors, instrumentalists, and singers, most of them famous, going back to the eighteenth century. In the Preface Saleski confirmed that the book was written as a response to the anti-Semitism around him; after observing that three-quarters of a century had elapsed since Wagner published his infamous *Judaism in Music*, Saleski expressed concern about "the same Aryan (rather Nordic) myth that has since come to the front in America."

Of the three hundred musicians Saleski included, Ornstein, with ten pages devoted to him, had by a wide margin the longest entry. Most of Saleski's account is drawn from other sources, particularly Martens's, Frank's, and Kramer's, and Saleski stresses the radical nature of Ornstein's compositions, observing how to many he "represents an evil musical genius wandering without the utmost pale of tonal orthodoxy, in a weird No-Man's land haunted by tortured souls, wails of futuristic despair, cubist shrieks and post-impressionistic cries and utterances." He does, however, quote Frank, that Ornstein's sounds represent the cry and wail of the young Jew in the new world.[99]

Ornstein was also featured in an article in *B'nai Brith Magazine* in 1927. Heyman Zimel viewed Ornstein as the product of three elements, or opposing forces, that shape his work: "the sombre mysticism of Russia," "the throbbing, pulsating spirit of American life," and "the challenge of the rejuvenescent Hebrew spirit." He then quotes Rosenfeld to emphasize the importance of the last element, although the article goes on the stress mostly the revolutionary nature of

Famous Musicians
of a
Wandering Race

BIOGRAPHICAL SKETCHES
OF OUTSTANDING FIGURES
OF JEWISH ORIGIN IN
THE MUSICAL WORLD

By

GDAL SALESKI

ARS LONGA

VITA BREVIS

NEW YORK
BLOCH PUBLISHING COMPANY
1927

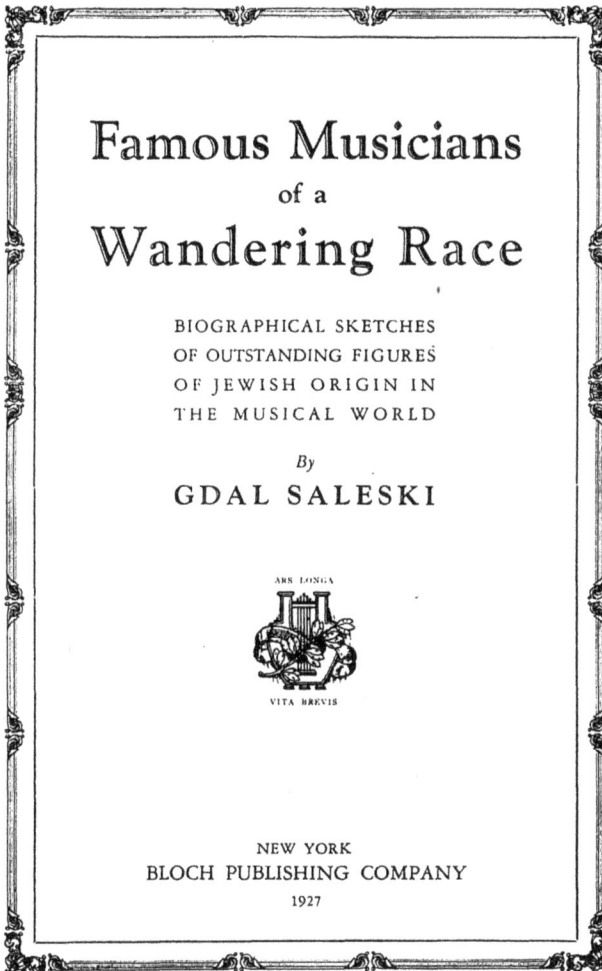

FIGURE 5.6.
Gdal Saleski,
*Famous Musicians
of a Wandering
Race.*

Ornstein's musical compositions.[100] Ironically most of the discussion is of his early avant-garde works, with little mention of his more recent compositions.

By 1927 Ornstein had become a concrete example of Jewish accomplishment, a prime exhibit in the anti-Semitic backlash, but he was also more than that. The Hebraic wail so frequently heard in his music elevated Ornstein to an allegorical status, as representative of the Jewish journey so many immigrants' sons took. Unlike Bloch, or later Schoenberg, who returned to their Jewish musical roots consciously, Ornstein's use of Jewish-related material was not an exercise in nostalgia or a deliberate exploration of his past. The "Oriental" melodies that burst through in Ornstein's music were themselves flickers of what existed in the mind's recesses of many Eastern European Jewish immigrants, but which for most had been buried.

This point can best be understood by considering the 1917 novel *The Rise of David Levinsky* by Abraham Cahan. Cahan (1850–1951) was a Lithuanian Jew who came to America in 1882. An avowed socialist, he founded the Yiddish newspaper *Forwerts* (*Forward*), named after a German socialist paper, and quickly made it into the most important Yiddish newspaper in the world. He also wrote many articles and three novels, of which *Levinsky* is considered his masterpiece, and probably the most well-known work of fiction about the Jewish immigrant experience. Levinsky comes to the United States as a young man, an immigrant with a deep love of learning, determined to get an education, to go to college. He ends up going into the garment business and succeeds, spectacularly, becoming very wealthy. Yet he is unsatisfied. He is unable to make a marriage, he feels lust and yearning for a romantic love, but at the same time he looks back wistfully on a traditional marriage. By this time, however, he has shed his religion, and he goes into old age lonely and isolated, with only memories.

According to Maury Klein, "Levinsky is a classic example of an immigrant spiritually trapped in mid-passage. Outwardly he has become completely Americanized; inwardly he cannot shake free of his old identity which has been stifled and warped in the new world." "He belongs to neither world, but occupies a painful social and spiritual vacuum between them. This is the poignance of his lament that business success has brought no solace to his spirit, has left him hungry and yearning."[101]

Ornstein is that man with a twist. Ornstein's life was music, and as his phenomenal talent pushed him into the new, he acquired education, fame, immense success, and wealth. He shed his religion quickly and easily, and had no trouble marrying outside his ethnicity. He seems to have turned his back completely on his religion and his heritage. Possibly Ornstein accomplished this precisely because of his music, which not only gave him entrée into the new world but had already, in Russia, distanced him from the old.

Yet his music suggests that, like Levinsky, he could not escape his heritage. No matter how buried, it was there, and when Ornstein turned to composition, working intuitively from the depths of his subconscious as he often stated, that heritage surfaced. It is precisely that which gives Ornstein allegorical status as the embodiment of the Jewish-American journey. In describing "The Jew in Our Day," Waldo Frank could have been describing Ornstein:

> The modern Jew may be indifferent, even hostile, to the enormous fact of his tradition; he shares it, nevertheless. . . . If a man lies down on the deck of a fast steamer, he is still moving; if a man runs against its direction, he is still moving with it. Any Jew who knows he is a Jew and has, however vaguely

or antagonistically, some sense of Jewish tradition and some experience of the state of the Jews in the modern world, is deeply affected.[102]

Levinsky may have been torn between two worlds, but the old was buried. He, like many Jews, particularly of the second generation, not only wished to assimilate into the new world as thoroughly as possible but also to forget the Old World part of them. Hence that past is seldom given voice. Few rejected that past as completely as Ornstein, yet because he dug so deeply into his subconscious when composing, Ornstein's works are dramatic confirmation of just how important that past was. In that sense his music, which had been an escape from his first world, also bridged old and new. Through their surfacing in music he could exorcise the demons haunting him from the old. Ornstein voiced in sound the deepest recesses of the mind of the Eastern European New York Jewish immigrant, and in doing he also suggested that the voice of the past does not always speak in a single, easily identifiable accent. In Ornstein's case it was a dual past, both Jewish and Russian.

It is significant that with the exception of Frederic Martens Ornstein's greatest champions, A. W. Kramer, Paul Rosenfeld, and Waldo Frank, were all Jewish.[103] Frank, who was personally close to Ornstein, saw with particular acuity Ornstein not only as Jewish allegory, but Jewish-American: "Ornstein's music is the full-throated cry of the young Jew in the young world, background of the old passion of storm and repression. But upon it breaks of fire, interstices of flight, America's release. . . . New hope, new dream, new life. An answer to the lamentation of the Jewish fate is in Ornstein's music; a sort of angry joy, lust of a new conquest, Hebrew the seed, American the fruit."[104]

It is no wonder that in the charged atmosphere after World War I Ornstein's music and career could be the focus of so much discussion. From the Red Scare through the anti-Semitic campaigns of the 1920s Ornstein had had attached many labels: radical, anarchist, futurist, prophet, Russian, Jewish, American, destroyer of all tradition, and later to some in the avant-garde, turncoat. Ornstein himself tried to escape his pasts in many ways, ranging from his marriage to a wealthy debutante, to a home deep in the New Hampshire mountains, and finally to his complete abandonment of a public career. Yet until he was forgotten he symbolized many things to many people, eliciting intense debate, musical, political, and ethnic. The question of Ornstein's own identity was at the heart of much of that debate.

6 ‖‖ The Turning Point

By 1920 Ornstein began to question the direction his life was taking, and he became increasingly uncomfortable with touring and the world of the virtuoso. Was he a composer or a performer? He was unhappy with his manager, Hanson, with whom he never had a close relationship. He had become disillusioned with the radical phases of musical modernism and had turned to a more traditional expressiveness in his own compositions, a move that distanced him from ultramodern musical circles just as they were finally taking root in the United States. Ornstein, who had led the fight for new music, found himself scorned by many who had championed him just a few years earlier.

According to some, touring had not been easy for the young Ornstein. Nervous, high-strung, at first he appeared awkward and ill at ease on the concert stage, "a young man of a rather distraught, disheveled appearance and a sort of cowed, hang-dog manner," "a pale and frenzied youth." He "slouched" upon the stage, or "crept crouching to the piano stool like one oppressed by some fear." Jacob Titiev claimed that he had to literally shove him onto the stage for his 1911 debut. Even in private gatherings his body language suggested someone who would rather be somewhere else, at least until he started playing. Waldo Frank describes one of the recitals at Claire Raphael Reis's house: "Now a youth, not much over five foot, in his late teens, sidled past the rows of seats; and as he came close to the piano his head seemed to sink into his shoulders. He crouched rather than sat on the piano stool."

Yet how much of that was real fear, and how much was a carefully—and brilliantly—constructed stage persona? For a time he modeled himself on Liszt. With long black hair and a velvet coat, Ornstein appears very much the Romantic virtuoso of old. To many his look was in keeping with a futurist artist, an impression that only deepened when he tore into the piano as if a wild beast that had not eaten for weeks. The critic of the *St. Louis Post-Dispatch* likened him to a Picasso—not to Picasso himself, but to a cubist painting: "'A Picasso!' Yes, a Picasso he was, of the same period as the Guitar Player at the Carroll Galleries. His neck depressed, his countenance—what I could see of it in the dim irreligious light—sullen, his long flaillike arms depending [sic] limply from high, narrow shoulders, his constrained bearing, that of a human about to be delivered of a painful message, his hair mussed up unbecomingly, his coat collar a study in cubism—altogether not precisely a prepossessing portrait."

Ultra-Modern Cartoonist Depicts an Ultra-Modern Composer—Leo Ornstein.

His small build, long hair, pale demeanor, his eyes, "soulful," "wildly flashing," his "listless" manner before he played served only to heighten the drama of what happened when he did begin. Ornstein crouched over the piano, his head almost on the keyboard, then "dealt it the most ferocious punishment." Waldo Frank's vivid description, quoted earlier, of Ornstein drooped over the keys when he finished "like a spent male after coitus" captures the intensity with which he performed.

Two years of constant touring and concertizing, and the fear had been converted to nonchalance. Many of the theatrical flourishes were gone—the long hair, the velvet coat, the crouching over the keyboard—and he "darted" rather than slouched to the keyboard.

The drama was not gone, however, and Ornstein's trademark mannerisms, the "familiar shrug of the shoulders, nod of the head, and completely exhausted look at the finish of each number," remained, as well as a seeming indifference to the audience, as if Ornstein himself were in some sort of trance.

Once Ornstein sat down at the piano he was absorbed. He was neither afraid nor nonchalant. He was both lost in the world of sounds, many sounds that he himself had created, and aware of where he was, in the midst of a maelstrom of his own making, a cacophonous wave that he himself had set in motion. Ornstein knew what to expect: there would be cheers, hoots, laughter, at times so much commotion that he could hardly hear himself. He had experienced that first in London in 1914, and even there, one hears a note of smugness in his own description: "'At my second concert, devoted to my own compositions, I might have played anything. I couldn't hear the piano myself. The crowd whistled and howled and even threw handy missiles on the stage . . . but that concert made me famous,' Ornstein wound up with a smile."[1]

In 1920 Ornstein's friend and champion Paul Rosenfeld wrote to Sherwood Anderson about a mood of ennui that hung over the avant-garde scene in New York. "It seems to have been a miserable springtides for everyone . . . Everywhere there appears to be a sort of palsy. . . . I can readily comprehend that the general rottenness should have touched you, too. For it is a general rottenness in which we all are involved. . . . Why it is so hard for us to hold together I don't know." Ornstein, Rosenfeld noted, had tried to escape to New Hampshire, and Rosenfeld hints that he was considering abandoning his career: "Ornstein I believe has done nothing at all. He worked for a month with the laborers on his place in the White Mountains and found that didn't satisfy him; now he talks of going into business."[2]

Ornstein would not abandon the concert world for another five years, but his disillusionment is apparent in Rosenfeld's account, and while major changes in his life lay in the future, Rosenfeld's letter does suggest that Ornstein was beginning to have doubts about his career. The complex of factors that would finally result in Ornstein's complete disappearance from public view first surface, or at least enter the record, in 1920. In the next chapters we will trace these and attempt to elucidate the various pressures and enticements that led Ornstein away from the life of a virtuoso and celebrity to virtual seclusion, from the most notorious modernist musician in the country to an almost completely forgotten and abandoned figure. But first we must address another more specific question that Rosenfeld's letter raises: Just what was Ornstein doing in the mountains of New Hampshire in the first place?

As we have seen, almost since he began studying with Bertha Feiring Tapper Ornstein had vacationed on the Maine coast. As a student, he spent the summers with Tapper and her husband at their summer home at Seal Cove, in Blue Hill, Maine. After Mrs. Tapper died, Ornstein moved further down Blue Hill Bay toward the ocean, to Sylvester's Cove, Deer Isle. Little is known of those years, other than he liked to rise early, spend time with the lobster and clam fishermen, and practice. *Musical America* reported that in the summer of 1916 he was "in the secluded part of Maine."[3] Yet the area was a favorite of musicians, with the Kneisel Chamber Music Festival in Blue Hill, and when Ornstein was with the Tappers he often engaged in informal music making with major artists who summered there. That continued after he moved to Deer Isle.

Ornstein's marriage to Pauline changed his summer habits. Pauline's family had a cottage on five hundred acres near North Conway, New Hampshire, and she convinced him to try summering there as an experiment. The land faced the Presidential Range and bordered on nearly seventy-five miles of government-owned wilderness. The cottage itself was a mile back from the road, and no one else lived on their land. In those days before snowmobiles, paved roads, or many cars, it was truly isolated.

Pauline has left a detailed account of the early years in New Hampshire in her *Reminiscences*, a collection of memoirs that she penned after some fifty years. Like the Titiev story, *Reminiscences* contains a wealth of information, and little corroboration. Thus while there is hardly specific reason to doubt many of the anecdotes that Pauline relates, one must keep in mind that this is Pauline's interpretation of not only events, but of motivations and feelings as well. Leo's voice is silent in this manuscript, and while Pauline may at times speak for him, one cannot assume that she necessarily does. For instance, according to Pauline, retreat to the woods of New Hampshire suited both her and Leo, as they were both recluses. While this may describe Pauline's proclivities, and Leo apparently enjoyed time away to work,[4] we know that he also thrived in stimulating company. Pauline herself had rebelled against the ceremony of her wealthy New York upbringing, which demanded that she dress formally for dinner, even while on vacation; now that she had a young genius on her hands, she wanted him to herself. Whether it was the coast or the presence of so many high-powered musicians, artists, and literati, she seemed uneasy with the idea of summering in Deer Isle. Leo himself seemed willing to participate in the New Hampshire experiment.

Once settled into the cottage, Pauline relates, they threw themselves into country life with all the enthusiasm of the two neophytes that they were. They started a garden and argued about technique. Leo, who according to Pauline had never planted a seed in his life, noted that the instructions on the package called for the seeds to be planted ¼ inch below ground. He then chastised Pauline for her lack of precision in this regard and was convinced that nothing would grow. When seeds finally sprouted he was amazed and took a tape measure out each day to chart the plants' progress. Actually Leo's connection with the soil was greater than Pauline thought. It had begun in Deer Isle, where the year before Leo had planted a "Victory Garden," giving one hour a day to the project. According to *Musical Courier*, he dubbed his cabbages and radishes the "Wild Men" of the species.

For the couple in New Hampshire obsessive weeding, a good growing season, and many wild berries and fruit trees nearby provided an abundance of fruit and vegetables that led them to discover canning and preserving. Two city people, Pauline saw them as enthralled with their new world, and later they would repeat this experiment on a grander scale with a farm in Pennsylvania. But by the end of this summer they had decided to build a house on the Mallet-Prevost land.

FIGURE 6.2. View from the Ornstein cottage, North Conway, N.H. *Photo courtesy the Ornstein family.*

Construction started immediately, and by the following spring the structure and much of the interior was up. For many years this was their home, although by necessity they spent much of their time elsewhere. They relinquished the New Hampshire house only after they were in their eighties and felt that they could no longer deal with the difficulties of winters in rural New England.

Compared to later in the century, conditions were primitive: no electricity, no phone, no refrigeration other than an ice box for which they had to haul ice, no paved roads, no automobile, only horse-drawn sleighs and wagons. The house was lit with kerosene lamps, and they cooked on a wood stove. Yet they were determined to live there for as much of the year as possible and to the extent that their schedule allowed. Even while on tour they would travel back whenever there was a break in the concerts. Once they came back from Chicago, only to return forty-eight hours later, to have two days of quiet in the woods. Staying in their house proved difficult during the winter: they had to walk a mile to the road on snow shoes, then travel several miles in a horse-drawn sleigh to reach the railroad. Once the snow was so deep they nearly lost the horse as he wandered off the road, only "head, ears and back could be seen struggling above the snow," and he nearly turned the sleigh over.

Gradually conditions improved, with electricity, automobiles, and paved roads, and the Ornsteins became fascinated with other facets of New England rural life. They attempted to harvest syrup from the many maple trees on their property. For them it seemed a moving and surreal experience. After hauling buckets of sap the necessary boiling began: "We took turns at stoking the fire and its glow, at night, over the snow made a picture one could never forget. The terrific volume of steam from the boiling sap reflected the fire's color and we found ourselves pressured by forces that were entirely new to us."

After the main house was built, Ornstein needed still further seclusion to work. Possibly remembering the cabin Mrs. Tapper had built for him in Maine, he had built a studio, a small one-room shingle structure with a porch across the front, about a quarter-mile up the hill from the house. No phone was allowed in the studio, and there were to be no visitors. Ornstein could work in undisturbed isolation. It would be like Blue Hill all over again. The principal challenge was to get a piano into the cottage, which meant a path had to be cut through the woods. "By a miracle the piano arrived unbroken, as the cart had to go over rocks and tree stumps and many holes. The path is now nearly grown up and another will have to be cut to get the piano out."[5]

Beginning in the fall of 1921 we see evidence of the ennui that Rosenfeld described in his letter. For the 1921–1922 season Ornstein's concert appearances dropped markedly from the hectic pace of 1920–1921, resulting in the slowest season for him since 1915. Changes began in April 1921, when Ornstein decided to leave Hanson, his manager of the last five years, and signed on with Arthur Judson, who was just establishing his business. What prompted the move is not clear. Possibly there was still lingering resentment from Ornstein over his early treatment by Hanson, possibly disagreement over his schedule or programming persisted. Whether Pauline played a role in this decision is not known. The complete absence of correspondence from any of the principals leaves us only guessing.

Later Arthur Judson became "the most powerful figure in the music business," but his career took off only in 1926 with his involvement in the creation of the Columbia Broadcasting System: at one point he held controlling interest. Although he sold control of CBS, his connections allowed the founding of Columbia Artists Management, which he headed for many years.[6] In 1921,

FIGURE 6.3. Ornstein's studio. *MSS 10,
The Leo Ornstein Papers, Irving S. Gilmore
Music Library, Yale University.*

however, Ornstein's move would not have been a step up. Judson was a new, relatively unknown figure in the business. He had begun his career in music as a violinist, and at age nineteen was made Dean of the Music Conservatory at Denison University. While there he gave the U.S. premiere of Richard Strauss's Violin Sonata. In 1915 he was appointed Manager of the Philadelphia Orchestra and from that base attempted to build an artists' management business. Since most touring musicians were already under contract, he had few opportunities to add established stars like Ornstein.

Ornstein began the 1921–1922 season later than usual, with an appearance in Harrisburg, Pennsylvania, on December 8, where he performed the Rubinstein Concerto with the Philadelphia Orchestra. This was followed by two joint recitals in December, the first with the Dutch cellist Hans Kindler, the second with the pianist Ethel Leginska. Hans Kindler was one of a few musicians with whom Ornstein developed a close friendship in the United States. From 1914 to 1931 Kindler was Principal Cellist with the Philadelphia Orchestra, and from 1927 he appeared on the podium as conductor. In 1931 he went to Washington, D.C., to found the National Symphony Orchestra. Ornstein had played with him on several occasions in 1918 and 1920 and had dedicated his Second Cello Sonata, Op. 52, to Kindler. Kindler and Leginska also performed Op. 52 together several times. Ornstein's 1922 performance with Kindler was at a venue important in the early twentieth century. They appeared at the Ballroom Bellevue-Stratford, on Monday morning, December 19, under the auspices of the Monday Morning Musicales. There is no record, however, of what they played, but it was probably Op. 52. Such clubs were more than a women's social gathering. Originating in the nineteenth century, by the early twentieth they had become the core around which musical activities in many municipalities revolved, as the leaders of the club took on the role of organizing a variety of concerts, with all the details such implies. One agent, who well knew tough negotiators when he saw them, referred to the clubs as "the most potent force in music today."[7]

Ethel Leginska, called the "Paderewsky of woman pianists," was one of the most extraordinary women in twentieth-century American music. Born Ethel Liggins in Hull, England, she studied extensively in Europe, in Frankfurt and Berlin and in Vienna with Leschetizky. She changed her name to Leginska and began concertizing at age sixteen, first in Europe and then from 1913 in the United States. She was noted for demanding programs and fiery, passionate performances. She also began to compose and was able to see many of her larger works, including two operas, performed, a rarity for a woman at that time. She quit concertizing in 1926, which made her American concert career, 1913–1926, almost exactly contemporary with Ornstein's, 1915–1925. But whereas Ornstein retired from public view, Legniska moved into an area that placed her even more

FIGURE 6.4. Ethel Leginska. *Photo Courtesy Music Division, The New York Public Library for the Performing Arts, Astor, Lenor and Tilden Foundations.*

before the public, conducting. In a field even more difficult for a woman to break into than composing, she had notable success, conducting major orchestras in both the United States and Europe.

The Ornstein-Leginska recital began with works by Mozart and Schubert and closed with Mozart's Sonata for Four Hands in D Major. Between them was the premiere of the principal work on the program, Ornstein's Sonata for Two Pianos. Four years later Ornstein reworked the sonata to create his Piano Concerto, one of his most important compositions. The revisions were extensive, in spite of Ornstein's claim that he never altered a note once he originally set the piece down. Part of the revisions had to do with the different media, but the changes go well beyond that.

Musical Courier had reported in August 1921 that Ornstein was completing the sonata, and that it would be "written in a new vein."[8] *Musical Courier* never defined what the new vein was, but reviews of the concert suggested that the piece was enthusiastically accepted and "ran true to type." According to one reviewer the first movement, "Introduzione e Fantasia," was "fantastic, weird and trembling," consisting harmonically of "a few consonances, many dissonances and many tones that seemed to be neither." The second movement, "Andante mysterioso," recalled Schoenberg's *Five Pieces for Orchestra*, and the finale, which alternated between duple and triple time, had a distinct dance quality and "was the nearest approach to normal of the three movements." To A. W. Kramer, "There is a thrilling beauty in this music, a beauty that stuns and amazes you; and sometimes annoys. But it is there."[9]

Kramer also noted how far modernism had traveled since Ornstein shook up the American musical world in 1915: "When Leo Ornstein played here in 1915 in his famous series of recitals at the Bandbox Theater, he was called an iconoclast. Today our audiences understand his music. We have progressed."

The sonata may have had something to do with the hesitancy about his career that seemed to be gripping Ornstein. Probably begun in 1920, it was the most complex work that he had written to date. It was more than an expanded improvisation; it demanded a level of development and control that Ornstein had not yet experienced or perhaps mastered. Only the Violin Sonata, Op. 31, was of comparable scope, and Ornstein had for all practical purposes lost control of that piece. As he acknowledged, he had at the least approached the edge of chaos and wished to go no further. His words about Op. 31 can rightly be read as a desire to pull back, to create something more expressive, which he confirmed himself, but Ornstein may not have been talking in only a stylistic sense. With Op. 31 the problem was more than chromaticism and dissonance. Ornstein needed to rethink how to handle large multimovement structures.

Ornstein had responded to Op. 31 brilliantly with Op. 52, but Op. 52, for all of its lyricism, is episodic and derivative. It is not a complex piece. The Double Sonata is, and its own history suggests that, while he believed the piece had potential, he was not satisfied with the results. As a consequence Ornstein was at a crossroads. For the first time doubt began to creep in. Should he continue, and if so how? Here was a man supremely self-confident in his own musical talent; hurdles that would daunt an ordinary musician, from technique to memory, were unknown to him. Compositions came in a flash and required little if any working out or revision. His own talent had, however, also worked as an albatross: At the Institute Ornstein had at best endured his music theory classes, and he showed no interest in learning counterpoint. His own compositions were almost entirely miniatures, at times striking and perceptive programmatic portraits, but works devoid of development or sustained structural logic. Most fit into simple traditional forms, such as ABA. With his keen musical intuition, however, Ornstein must have known that the Double Sonata demanded more. It was time to reconsider where he was and what he was doing.

As for the Ornstein-Leginska recital itself, Richard Aldrich observed that it seemed strange that the performers played the Mozart, which was written for one piano four hands, on two pianos. Aldrich speculates that possibly it was because each had a piano contract with a different manufacturer—Leginska was a Baldwin artist, Ornstein had long been with Knabe—but possibly too Pauline was watching from the wings. It is telling that Leginska and Ornstein were scheduled to tour with this program, but except for a single follow-up concert in Boston, that never materialized. Leginska did contract a "long continued illness" in early 1922,[10] but that did not prevent her from appearing in the Boston concert with Ornstein on February 5, and in a concert with Hans Kindler on February 23. For whatever reason, cancellation of the tour was not because of a lukewarm reception from the audience. Ornstein and Leginska were, however, two strong artistic personalities, which did not escape the notice of Harry Levine when they repeated the program in Boston: "If the distinctive personalities of both artists did not blend into that homogeneous whole which we are wont to associate with two-piano recitals, they nevertheless supplemented each other in a fascinating juxtaposition of temperaments that have much in common."[11]

Ornstein also made several unusual public appearances. Most had to do with his contract with Ampico, manufacturers of a type of reproducing piano, which will be discussed below. Another very different one was a massive benefit for the pianist Moritz Moszkowski, who was elderly, in bad health, and financially infirm. Fifteen pianists participated in the December 21st concert, including Wilhelm Bacchaus, Harold Bauer, Alfredo Casella, Ossip Gabrilowitsch, Percy Grainger, Josef Lhevinne, and Germaine Schnitzer. The curtain opened with all fifteen pianists on stage, each sitting at their own piano. They alternatively played solo and in various combinations of duets and trios, and for the finale, all joined for Schubert's Military March with Walter Damrosch conducting. Before the finale Damrosch explained that the last piece needed less a conductor than a traffic cop.[12]

Two other appearances, one in Harrisburg, Pennsylvania, the other with the Philharmonic Society of Philadelphia, rounded out Ornstein's year.[13] For the Harrisburg concert Ornstein opened his program with a piano transcription of the Prelude to Wagner's *Lohengrin*, an unusual selection for him, although he thought more highly of Wagner than much Italian opera. According to Ornstein's son Severo, Wagner's music did trouble him because it was "too German."

Ornstein's 1922–1923 concert schedule proved even sparser than that of 1921–1922. He appeared in Baltimore with the soprano Marie Sunderlis on October 12, gave three "intimate" recitals at the New Gallery on Madison Avenue in New York, and another program with Ethel Leginska at the Greenwich Village

Theatre. The New Gallery recitals were so named because Ornstein delivered a short talk about each work before he played it. The Ornstein-Leginska recital consisted of "ultramodern selections," including works of both pianists.

Possibly to compensate for Ornstein's abbreviated concert activity both he and Pauline moved aggressively to develop a teaching studio. On October 25 *Musical Courier* announced that Pauline had reopened her studio at 1349 Lexington Avenue, and that she stressed teaching children, encouraging their natural abilities through improvisation. That previous March, Arthur Judson placed a half-page advertisement in *Musical America* announcing that Leo would accept a limited number of pupils. Even for Ornstein's teaching schedule Judson acted as agent.[14] At the same time the *Musical Observer* published a ten-part course on piano playing by Ornstein, with the overall title "Modern Principles of Piano Technic."

Yet if the 1921 and 1922 seasons were confirmations of Ornstein's displeasure with the concert world and evidence of a new interest in pedagogy, he was once again ready to resume the circuit the following year. His reemergence began with a return to Hanson, in November 1923. Again, details about this switch are completely absent. Hanson immediately booked Ornstein for a short but intense West Coast tour—December 6, Anaheim; 7th, Los Angeles; 10th, San Francisco; 12th, Riverside; 13th, Alhambra; 14th, Long Beach[15]—and by February 1924 Hanson could boast in a full-page ad that Ornstein already had twenty-eight dates booked for the 1924–1925 year. By this time Ornstein's appearance had also changed. He now wore a modern, conservative suit or tuxedo and had short hair slicked down in 1920s fashion. There is still something of the matinee idol in his appearance.

Once again how much credit does Hanson deserve for reviving Ornstein's concert career, and how much of Ornstein's inactivity can be placed on Judson for not securing dates? Ornstein was apparently displeased with the concert world by 1921, and Pauline was doing all she could to encourage him to think of alternatives. But *Musical Courier* had reported in August 1921 that Judson was "booking an extensive tour for the pianist-composer for the coming autumn and winter," a tour that never materialized, at least to the extent the announcement implies.[16] Whether that reflected Ornstein's desires or Judson's shortcomings is difficult to know. That Judson would place a large advertisement for Ornstein the teacher rather than Ornstein the concert artist the next year suggests that Judson management was doing all it could to satisfy the wants of a major client. That Judson began running advertisements for bookings for the 1922–1923 season suggests that by March 1922 whatever misgivings Ornstein may have had about continuing the concert circuit they were insufficient to pull him off of it. That still leaves open the question: How much of the December 1923 tour was actually arranged by Hanson, and how much by Judson?

FIGURE 6.5. A more mature Ornstein. *MSS 10, The Leo Ornstein Papers, Irving S. Gilmore Music Library, Yale University.*

After opening the 1924–1925 season in October with the New York Symphony at the Worcester Hall in Worcester, Massachusetts, Ornstein then embarked on an extensive tour of the Midwest. Included were some major stops, such as an appearance with the Minneapolis Symphony Orchestra on December 7, but most were recitals in smaller venues, suggesting that the tour had been arranged hastily. That Ornstein could fill a schedule on relatively short notice, however, gives every indication of his continuing draw. He performed in Delaware, Ohio; Alliance, Ohio; Clinton, Iowa; Jacksonville, Illinois; Springfield, Illinois; at Bethany College, Lindsbourg, Kansas; Peoria, Illinois; and at Cornell College, Mt. Vernon, Iowa, in November, and in the first ten days of December gave recitals in Sioux City, Iowa; Des Moines, Iowa; Oshkosh, Wisconsin; Faribault, Minnesota; Moorhead, Minnesota; and Mankato, Wisconsin.

Audiences as usual loved Ornstein, but some in these Midwestern cities found his ultramodernism jarring. For many it was probably their first taste of such music. Commercial radio had barely begun, and few recordings were being made of ultramodern compositions. The *Jacksonville Courier* reported that after being shaken up by Ornstein's sounds equilibrium had to be restored: "But too much modernism might produce indigestion, so the following Chopin numbers came to heal and restore us to the beautiful in music." Chopin in this instance became a balm for modernism. Nevertheless the anonymous reviewer conceded that Ornstein's A la chinoise, referred to as the "Chinatown Jumble," was "distinctly characteristic" and was enthusiastically received.[17]

Yet the tour itself may have convinced Ornstein that it was not time to resume the concertizing life. He returned to Philadelphia exhausted, with no plans to appear in public until the premiere of his Piano Concerto with the Philadelphia Orchestra on February 13.

In general the concerto was received favorably even though critics were puzzled by it and groped to label it. In the program notes Ornstein stated that it is "not a concerto in the sense of being an exhibition piece for the piano with orchestral accompaniment. It is distinctly an ensemble composition," a point that may have something to do with its origins as a two-piano sonata. Following Ornstein's suggestion, H. T. Craven called it a symphonic rhapsody and S.L.L. labeled it an orchestral fantasy. Critics were mainly divided regarding its stylistic originality. Craven referred to its Slavic character, and S.L.L. and Lawrence Gilman both heard echoes of Scriabin and Stravinsky, among others. Critical evaluation depended largely on the stance of the critic: the extent that he expected originality and the avoidance of derivative influence. To Gilman, Ornstein was "advancing very rapidly backward," whereas to Craven it is "rich in individualistic instrumental devices, informed by imaginative virility and a wealth of savage and even brutal beauty." Gilman even found the Stravinsky influence troubling, pointing out that "Stravinsky, as he himself has insisted, is no modernist."[18]

Two other developments influenced and ultimately may have determined Ornstein's decision to curtail performance. The first was his recording contract to use the Ampico piano; the second was a teaching appointment. The Ampico was a reproducing mechanism that could be placed in pianos—it was in essence a higher-level player piano, the principal difference being that the Ampico could reproduce dynamics and nuance in a way that the regular player piano could not. Player pianos had developed in the late nineteenth century in response to the overwhelming popularity of the piano itself in nineteenth-century America.

In 1800 pianos were relatively rare in the United States. Because they had to be imported from Europe they were expensive, and only the wealthier could afford them. Beginning in 1823, when Jonas Chickering began manufacturing pianos in Boston, domestic piano makers found a ready market for their instruments. The large German immigration in the middle of the nineteenth century brought with it a number of other manufacturers, such as Wilhelm Steinweg, soon to become Steinway, and many craftsmen. By the late nineteenth century pianos could be found in all price ranges, and virtually every middle-class home had one. The piano had become an essential piece of furniture.

In keeping with the gender code of the time, girls were expected to learn to play the piano, and the piano in the parlor provided a principal source of entertainment. This was, of course, especially important for the daughters of the household, when they were entertaining young men in the parlor. It was all Victorianly proper. At the end of the nineteenth century, however, new developments threatened to unseat the piano's privileged position in the home. The phonograph provided a whole range of music, and it required no talent whatsoever. Piano manufacturers were quick to respond, and soon player mechanisms, which had existed for some time, became popular. The player piano had arrived on the American musical scene.

The player piano had one major advantage over the phonograph, or the Edison: tone quality. Since a player piano was just a means of activating the piano action itself, the sound was no different than what someone sitting at the instrument would produce. There was one major drawback, however. Piano rolls, the source controlling the player mechanism, could only indicate pitch and rhythm. Dynamic nuances and pedaling effects could be achieved only roughly by the operator of the foot bellows. As a consequence those details that rendered a performance musical or artistic, that is, those very interpretive qualities that set the virtuoso apart, were beyond the capacity of the technology to capture.

Around 1900 Edwin Welte, of the Welte Piano Company, which had pioneered player pianos in Germany, teamed with an associate, Karl Bockisch, to remedy this shortcoming. By 1904 they had developed the "Vorsetzer," a mechanism that sat in front of the piano and pressed the keys according to instructions on a perforated roll. Unlike player pianos this device, consisting essentially of wooden fingers that even mirrored the length of a man's hand and finger, could vary the strength with which the key was struck, thus reproducing dynamic nuances. They also developed a means of controlling the pedal. The device, began to be marketed in 1905 as the Welte-Mignon, with rolls of some of the most famous musicians of the time, including Debussy, Mahler, Ravel, and Paderewsky.[19]

Not only was the Welte-Mignon expensive, but it involved a massive box that was placed in front of the piano. Soon a means was found to place the mechanism inside the piano, and soon also there was competition. In the United States two companies developed separate mechanisms to achieve the same results. Both the Duo-Art Pianola Piano, developed by the Aeolian Company, and the Ampico, developed by the American Piano Company, appeared in 1913. Other, smaller companies appeared with mechanisms, but the big three—Welte-Mignon, Duo-Art, and Ampico—dominated the reproducing piano market throughout the teens and twenties, until for both technical and economic reasons their popularity plunged at the end of the 1920s. Because Ornstein was associated closely with the Ampico, we will concentrate on that particular type of reproducing piano.

The American Piano Company was founded in 1908, with the acquisition of three major piano manufacturers, Wm. Knabe & Co., Chickering & Sons, and Foster-Armstrong. It later added several other companies, the most important being Mason & Hamlin. The American Piano Company developed its Ampico in 1913, but the first Ampico did not go onto the market until 1916.

Throughout the teens and early twenties the company flourished and its outlook was bright. Over the years the company had purchased a significant number of piano manufacturers, making it the largest piano company in the United States. They divided their pianos into three tiers, based on quality, reputation, and, of course, price: at the top were those made by the three companies Knabe, Chickering, and Mason & Hamlin. Middle-tier pianos were made by Haines, Fischer and Marshall, and Wendell. Third-tier pianos were made by Foster, Brewster, and Armstrong. The Ampico mechanism proved popular, especially when placed in the company's first-tier grand pianos. Cost itself was a factor. Most people able to afford the reproducing mechanism could afford a better instrument.

When placed in a top-tier piano the result was potentially a literal reproduction of what would have been heard in the concert hall, only one could listen in one's living room or parlor. Pianists by this time could be heard on the phonograph (and on Edison cylinders, a reproducing mechanism virtually identical to the phonograph except for the shape of the storage mechanism), but the quality was nowhere near the real thing. Recordings were still acoustic, which meant that vibrations were captured physically with a horn, then reproduced physically, with no electronic amplification whatsoever. While some of the horns could produce considerable volume, the sound was decidedly tinny, and the frequency range limited. Electronic recording did not begin until the mid-1920s.

In theory at least the roll represented the performer's interpretive ideal of the composition. The way the rolls were created mitigated against that, however. The performer was recorded on a note recorder, which marked the notes on a role with a pencil rather than actually cutting stencil marks in the paper. This allowed for easy editing, and at this point all that was recorded were rhythm and pitches. Even these could be adjusted, including the elimination of any wrong notes, with a pencil and an eraser. At that stage what was recorded was not that different from other player-piano rolls, as the roll itself did not automatically reproduce all the nuances of the artist's performance. Only after the pencil roll was made did the work of adding interpretation began. This was not done, however, by the artist but by editors, staff, who were usually musicians. These persons would take notes during the recording session and then, based on the notes and a general familiarity with the style, would add expression, particularly dynamics and pedaling. Ampico pianos had two dynamic mechanisms, one a series of seven discreet levels, and the second a crescendo and decrescendo mechanism. This allowed a wide range of dynamic levels and shadings, although in practice it did not always work out that way. The mechanism was extremely complex, not reliable from one instrument to another, prone to go out of adjustment, and the rolls themselves subject to wear, tear, and stretching. As a consequence many reproduced performances were reduced to a homogenous ooze. If something went wrong with a mechanism, for instance, the roll often defaulted to a general *mezzo-forte*.[20]

In 1926 Clarence Hickman invented a process whereby dynamics could be recorded. Through a complicated setup Hickman was able to record onto a roll the time elapsed between a pair of contact points connected to the hammer, and by measuring the distance on the roll between two points the speed of the hammer, and hence the dynamic level, could be determined. Hickman realized that the speed of the hammer to produce a similar dynamic level varied between treble and bass, and he took that into account in his calculations, creating a sliding scale. It was both a complex and a labor-intensive process, as each distance needed to be converted into expression codes. In a virtuosic Liszt piece, for instance, there would be many notes.[21]

In the Ampico process the editor actually made the musical choices, and typically only after a roll was assembled did the performer actually hear it. He had veto power over its release, and in practice this meant a certain amount of negotiation between performer and editor. How much control the performer had depended partly on who the performer was and how much he cared. Ornstein was one of Ampico's "big four," their primary classical pianists, who also included Sergei Rachmaninoff, Josef Hofmann, and Leopold Godowsky.[22] Consequently the company took more time and care with his rolls than some of the lesser-known artists, and he had more leverage in demanding that the final product meet his artistic approval or not be released at all. Because of the time and complexity of recutting rolls and the company's own desire to have the rolls available to the public, there was considerable pressure on the performer to approve, with as little modification as possible, the editor's solutions.

We have found no evidence of the details of negotiations, so it is not clear how extended or difficult they were, or how insistent Ornstein was upon a perfect or at least acceptable performance. According to his public statements Ornstein was proud of his rolls, but we don't know whether this was his true feeling or only propaganda to help Ampico sell them. It is entirely possible that because his public performances were notorious for being unpredictable, that is, he did not stick to one consistent interpretation of any piece, it simply did not matter to him.

Ornstein's attitude toward even his own compositions was somewhat cavalier: once he had composed a piece, he was no longer interested in it. In some cases at Ampico the artist simply made the roll and left, never expressing concern about it. Whether Ornstein went that far is unlikely, particularly given the number of rolls that he made that were never released. Altogether Ornstein made sixty-five rolls, but only twenty-four were released.[23] We don't know, however, why they were not released, or whether that was Ornstein's or the company's decision.

Regardless of the degree of involvement of the artist, the result was not a live performance but a construction, carefully built by an editor, who worked in varying degrees of collaboration with the performer. In some ways it is comparable to a modern electronic recording, where tape or later digital slices are compiled to create the finished product. These are usually assembled from takes that the performer herself has made, and consequently do represent more than a general intention but are the performer's actual creation. There are exceptions to this, one of the most notorious occurring in the 1950s when two high C's by Elizabeth Schwarzkopf were inserted into a recording of *Tristan und Isolde* by Kirsten Flagstad, who had trouble reaching the note.[24] In the digital age such substitution is even easier, and it is possible to assemble an entire piece from minute samples. Yet even when the final product is an assemblage of the best of multiple takes of the performer, everything is filtered through a sound engineer, whose decisions from microphone placement to balance through equalizer choice to selection of room acoustics, which can be altered electronically, has a major impact on how the recording sounds. Few recordings today represent an actual unvarnished performance. Even when one is billed as recorded live at such and such place, the engineer still does a certain amount of doctoring.

Yet because of the limitations of the Ampico recording technique, in which only notes and rhythm were recorded directly, the role of the performer diminished and the role of the editor loomed even larger than in modern recordings, in which most of the editing consists of assembling various takes and smoothing out the rough edges of the splices. While certain aspects such as balance can be modified significantly, this is less a factor for solo piano music than large ensembles, and the raw material from which the final version emerges *is* that of the pianist. With modern electronic stereo equipment, the finest nuances of what was performed can be captured and reproduced.

We do not know exactly when Ornstein signed a contract with Ampico, but it was clearly before May 25, 1916. On that day Ornstein gave a demonstration concert of the Ampico in the Music Room of the Biltmore Hotel. Under the headline "Futurist Pianist Amazes Audience at the Biltmore Hotel," the *New York Times* described the event, in which Ornstein first performed several pieces live, and then sat while the audience heard the Knabe piano reproduce the same pieces with at least theoretically the same interpretation. For this Ornstein chose traditional repertoire: Liszt's *Liebestraum*, Debussy's *Reflets dans l'eau*, and Chopin's F-sharp Minor Nocturne, although he did include his own *Berceuse*.

Ornstein was the first pianist to give a live demonstration of the Ampico, which had just begun marketing in 1916. The "recital" was well attended; the audience included Ossip Gabrilowitsch and Leopold Godowsky, well-known pianists who would later become major Ampico artists themselves. According to *Musical Courier* the audience "was amazed and delighted at the artistic and sympathetic rendering of Ornstein's playing by the Knabe-Ampico."[25] Ornstein's recital preceded by four-and-a-half months the famous "Affair at the Biltmore," as the *New York Globe* dubbed it, a demonstration by Godowsky, which scholars have identified as the first public demonstration of the Ampico. According to Ampico's own assessment, "so perfect was the reproduction—so marvelous the fidelity of the replica to the performance of Mr. Godowsky, that the audience was first amazed—then moved to the most enthusiastic applause."[26]

Ornstein continued to give many demonstrations of the Ampico for the next ten years. His five-year contract with Ampico from 1920 states that he is to perform 100 concerts per year. While he probably did not perform that many, he did perform frequently, and in most cases most reviewers were amazed at the demonstration. Sometimes the demonstration would be with an orchestra. On April 23, 1919, Ornstein performed the Mendelssohn Piano Concerto in G Minor with the Philharmonic Orchestra at Carnegie Hall, with the Ampico performing the first movement, and Ornstein himself playing the second and third movements. At other times the Ampico substituted entirely for Ornstein. In the summer of 1919 a concert at the Rivoli Theater featured a performance of the first movement of the Rubinstein Concerto in which Ornstein was heard "through the medium of the Ampico reproducing piano."[27]

Part of Ampico's promotion technique was multipiano concerts featuring several artists, each sitting on stage at their own piano, first hearing the Ampico play a piece they had recorded, and then playing it a second time live. Not all the performers were as sanguine about doing them as Ornstein was. In 1920 Ornstein, Mischa Levitzki, Leopold Godowsky, and Arthur Rubinstein were scheduled for a multicity tour of this type. Arthur Rubinstein remembered what he called a "funny and a little shameful concert tour together."[28] In his autobiography he describes it in more detail:

> And now I must tell of a shameful episode in which I shared with three colleagues. Leopold Godowsky, Mischa Levitzki, Leo Ornstein, and I agreed

FIGURE 6.6. Knabe-Ampico advertisement.

to appear in six cities (not including New York or Boston) playing one piece each on a pianola, then treating the public to a repetition of the piece by the machine, over which we were forced to preside feeling not very proud of ourselves.[29]

Part of Rubinstein's embarrassment may have had to do with the Ampico recording process itself. As noted earlier, much of the interpretation was added later by an editor who attempted to capture what she heard. The interpretation itself was not the artist's but rather of some member of the Ampico staff. The result, and the secret of the success of the Ampico concerts, was that the artist listened to, memorized, and then played back what the roll had just played. Thus we have a convoluted and bizarre situation: The artist imitates the interpretation of the staff editor who was attempting to imitate the original performance. In this context it is no surprise that except for Ornstein's first concert, and Ampico's first venture into this type of presentation, the Ampico always played first in the concerts.

At that first concert the audience apparently did notice a difference between Ornstein's interpretation and the Ampico's, and Ornstein was forced to explain: "My public performances are influenced by my mood at the time. When I interpret for the Ampico, however, I never rest content until the final result is exactly as I would have it. In other words, the Ampico records of my playing represent the best I am capable of. It is here that I come nearest to perfection."[30] This statement is pure hogwash. Since it appeared in a display advertisement shortly after the concert, whether it is Ornstein's or a product of Ampico's own spin machine is not clear.

Unlike Rubinstein, however, Ornstein himself never seems to have been bothered by the Ampico events. Ornstein's indifference to a fixed interpretation may be one reason that he was willing to be the first performer to engage in the live-Ampico recitals. This may explain why Rubinstein was so embarrassed about the Ampico appearances. It wasn't his interpretation, it was that of the anonymous woman who added the expression marks to the rolls. Rubinstein's and Ornstein's role was to duplicate exactly what was on the roll. The artist was imitating a synthetic construction, not vice versa.

Another reason Ornstein may have been willing to submit to the Ampico experiments is that he already had experience with traditional recording, having made the two Columbia records in 1913. In the acoustic process the shellac disc recorded exactly what the performer played. There was no opportunity for adjustments of any kind, not even in volume. The sound quality was limited, and dynamics themselves were circumscribed. That the Ampico piano could reproduce the piece with full resonance—it *was* a Knabe grand playing it—and with a much wider dynamic and hence interpretative range must have been appealing. Listeners at the time, accustomed to acoustic recordings, would assume that the roll represented an actual performance. Only the most technically savvy would have any reason to believe that what they heard was an artificial construct.

By 1920, the year of the Ornstein-Rubinstein concert, a more serious threat to the reproducing piano appeared: the advent of commercial radio. To this time radio had been the province mostly of hobbyists and amateurs, although some were creating informal and irregular broadcasts, and some companies such as Westinghouse made broadcasts. On January 12, 1910, for instance, Lee De Forest, inventor of the vacuum tube and head of De Forest Radio Telephone Company, broadcast part of Puccini's *Tosca* live from the Metropolitan Opera. It was heard mainly by members of the press at special receivers set up for the demonstration, but as early as 1907 De Forest had predicted that "It will soon be possible to distribute grand opera music from transmitters placed on the stage of the Metropolitan Opera House by a Radio Telephone station on the roof to almost any dwelling in Greater New York and vicinity." Regular broadcasting by commercial stations was still a decade away, but by 1922 dozens of commercial stations had been established, and in 1923 the AM broadcast band with assigned frequencies was established.[31]

Radio electronics, especially the vacuum tube, brought significant advances in phonograph recording. The same microphone and the same amplification system found in radio could also be harnessed to create phonograph records of a fidelity and sound quality hitherto unknown. It also allowed reproduction of a much greater dynamic range, and through the placement of microphones successful recording of types of music, such as full symphony orchestras, that had before been difficult to capture. Although not yet the high fidelity that appeared in the 1950s, the difference in sound quality from acoustic recordings was noticeable.[32]

Ampico mistakenly saw the radio and the phonograph not as competition, but actually as a positive influence on the sale of reproducing pianos:

> The piano has in recent years come to be more fully appreciated by the general public, largely through the reputation of the reproducing mechanism. Last year sales reached the highest point in the history of the industry. The increasing use of pianos, especially those of high quality, and reproducing pianos is partly the result of the country's growing wealth and high standards of living, but has also been stimulated by the more general appreciation of good music fostered by the radio, the phonograph and the moving picture theatre. The piano industry, and especially the American Piano Company, has been particularly alert to the opportunities presented by these developments.[33]

It would not work out that way. By the end of the 1920s it had become clear that radio and the improved phonograph were seriously impacting not just Ampico's, but the sale of all types of mechanical pianos. From its beginnings around 1900 the player piano industry as a whole saw sales steadily increase, from approximately 40,000 in 1909 to a peak of 200,000 in 1923. After that they declined precipitously, dropping below 100,000 in 1927, and 50,000 in 1929. By 1931 fewer than 5,000 were sold. In a letter to Q. David Bowers, Otto Schutz, of the M. Schutz Co., maker of player pianos commented, "The business held up through 1926, but in 1927 fell by 50% due to the wide acceptance of the radio with built-in dynamic speakers. Grigsby-Grunow's Majestic swept the music industry and by the end of 1928 we were practically out of the player piano business and our sales had fallen by 80 per cent."[34]

Some bad business decisions at Ampico only hastened its demise, however. In 1927 its President, George O. Foster, along with other executives retired, and C. A. Wagner, a Vice President, was made President. Foster and others sold their stock, which was purchased by a syndicate of banking interests, in effect giving them control on the board. Sales continued strong in 1928, but profits were down, and Wagner was forced to resign. He was replaced by George Urquhart, who came from the bankers syndicate.

Urquhart then inaugurated a new policy that proved disastrous. The company at the time gave a dealer in each city exclusive rights to one top-tier, middle-tier, and third-tier piano line. Clearly the Knabe, Chickering, and Mason & Hamlin were what brought customers into the showrooms, and each dealer could concentrate on promoting one prestige line, often spending hundreds of thousands of dollars in advertising and building up a loyal clientele.

Urquhart decided to give the most successful dealer in each community exclusive rights to the entire line of pianos. If that dealer declined, then it was offered to the next. Dealers throughout the country balked at this new plan, with the greatest resistance coming from those dealers offered this apparent bonanza. Each dealer had worked hard to promote one particular instrument as their lead product and was identified with that line. The three-dealer arrangement had also meant that each top-tier piano would be featured in a community. As the *Music Trades* magazine reported in 1929, "This policy . . . did not serve to enhance the reputation or standing of any one of these three great names in the world of piano making." The same article commented on the effect that it had on the company as a whole:

It has taken, in some instances, generations to create and establish the prestige of great names which have adorned the pages of piano history. The piano business is one peculiarly based upon reputation, and as an art industry the reputations so hardly won could not be too carefully guarded. A seasoned piano man would hardly have fallen into some of the errors which have marked the maladministration of the affairs of the American Piano Company, under its most recent direction.

Partly as a result of this policy, partly because of larger market forces, Ampico's sales declined to $11,429,799 for the period ending March 31, 1929, resulting in a net loss of $235,235. Losses only increased after that. In 1929 Ampico stopped making reproducing pianos entirely and announced that it would begin to sell radios. Their publicity machine continued to maintain that radios in the home would encourage the sale of pianos, but by this time their rhetoric sounded a bit hollow:

> In the final analysis, however, the piano industry is not competitive with radio, but cooperative. Lower in price and requiring no skill for its operation, radio is a worthwhile line to carry. The instrument of the masses of the people, radio is doing much to make them musically-minded. Musically-minded people constitute the piano market. In this educational work, therefore, the two industries are working together. Properly coordinated, both should profit from it.

Such did not work out for the American Piano Company. They went into receivership on December 31, 1929, and although George Foster and some of the other former executives came out of retirement to rescue it, the damage had been done. They created a new company, the American Piano Corporation, and sold Mason & Hamlin to Aeolian. In 1932 Aeolian acquired, in a friendly take-over, what was left, to create the Aeolian-American Corporation.

Once the American Piano Company quit making reproducing pianos, it had no incentive to market the rolls. On April 19, 1920, Ornstein had signed a five-year contract to record with the Ampico, which was extended in 1925 to May 1, 1930. Ornstein was paid an average of $3,200 per year, the exact amount depending on royalties. He had already cut fifty-two of the sixty-five rolls he made using the Ampico before 1920, but as part of the contract he agreed to perform one hundred concerts per year, and to record with no other company. The former probably included a number of brief appearances, not full recitals. Because of the latter, however, we have no other record of Ornstein's playing when he was in his prime. As Ampico sales declined in the late 1920s, payments also ceased. Ornstein's last payment of record from the company was on May 12, 1928, for $3,250. It was listed in the company's books as "final payment."

Ornsein's contract was considerably less than that of Sergei Rachmaninoff, their most expensive artist, who received $10,000 per year against royalties, and Arthur Rubinstein, who received $6,000. Rubinstein's contract came only after some hard bargaining, however. He was originally offered a contract by Duo-Art, which he felt was insufficient, but was able to use that as leverage to get a better offer to record with the Ampico.[35]

During most of Ornstein's years with the company he was one of their most prominent poster boys, even though despite his notoriety he was not as well known a pianist as Leopold Godowsky nor a musical figure as Rachmaninoff. It was Ornstein, however, who gave the first public demonstration of the Ampico, and he was frequently featured in their advertisements. The purpose of the rolls was to sell pianos, and for that purpose Ornstein's youthful good looks were more important than his status in the musical world.[36] One picture of Ornstein from this time shows him sitting with his hands on the back of a chair, in a suit with hair combed neatly and a cigarette in one hand. He looks young, handsome, cool, and sophisticated, a perfect combination to entice women to bring their husbands or fathers into the Ampico store. Only film industry anachronism prevents us from calling this the Hollywood Leo.

The Ampico did provide Ornstein the opportunity to be a movie star, briefly. According to *Musical America*, "The role of motion-picture actor was recently assumed by Leo Ornstein, composer-pianist. A film entitled 'Immortalized,' in which the artist and certain of his colleagues of the musical world appeared, was exhibited at the Hias Bazaar in New York on Feb. 9. Mr. Ornstein appeared in person, playing piano numbers as well." The film itself is lost, and when asked about it late in life Ornstein had no memory of it. It was a promotional film for the Ampico, shown as a "special presentation" during "Music Week" at Carnegie Hall, May 4, 1922, "with the special assistance of Leo Ornstein." The first half of the event was an orchestral concert under the direction of Hugo Riesenfeld, consisting of Goldmark's Overture, *Sakuntala*, a Minuet by Franz Schubert, an "Irish Tune from County Derby" by Percy Grainger, and Franz Liszt's *Les Préludes*. After intermission the Ampico film was shown, followed by Ornstein's Ampico recording of the first movement of Anton Rubinstein's Concerto in D Minor, a piece that the company frequently showcased.

Little is known about the film itself beyond what is in the advertisement, which described it as "a picture Drama which tells how Science came to the rescue of Art and proved to be the realization of a dream." The only other clue is the extraordinary cast of characters listed:

The Persons in the Play

Character	Impersonated By
Leo Ornstein	Leo Ornstein
„Olga" Ornstein	Irma Harrison
Leopold Godowsky	Leopold Godowsky
Artur Bodanzy	Artur Bodanzy
Berthold Neuer	Berthold Neuer
Sergei Rachmaninoff	Sergei Rachmaninoff
Alma Gluck	Alma Gluck
Efrem Zimbalist	Efrem Zimbalist
William Thorner	William Thorner
Charles Fuller Stoddar	Charles Fuller Stoddar
National Symphony Orchestra	National Symphony Orchestra

Appearing in scenes incidental to the play

Eddy Brown	Rosa Ponselle
Anna Fitzie	Andreas de Sigurola
Alexander Lambert	Anne Swinburn
Alfred Mirovitch	Arnold Volpe
Mischel Piastro	Mana Zucca

And Others

Incidental Music Arranged by
Hugo Riesenfeld

Since Olga Ornstein, presumably Leo's mother in the film, was the only semi-fictional character portrayed by an actor, and since Ornstein was singled out by *Musical America*, some aspect of his life story must have provided at least a tenuous central narrative. How fictionalized it was remains unknown, but Ornstein may well have been the first musician to have his life story "immortalized" in a film. The other musicians probably had cameo appearances, their presence meant to demonstrate the breadth of the Ampico repertoire.

Since this was still the era of silent movies, a filming of Ornstein simply performing would seem a bit incomplete, but what he actually did is anyone's guess. At the very least one can assume that the Ampico piano played a significant role in the film, since promotion of it was the entire point of the whole endeavor.

With Ampico Ornstein seemed to have found a steady source of income. In 1922 as the Ampico and reproducing pianos were reaching their peak, this must have appeared as something secure and lucrative for far into the future. He was rapidly becoming the company's star. Little did Ornstein know that only one year after his "Immortalized" appearance sales of reproducing pianos would peak, followed by a quickly accelerating decline, and that in six years the entire Ampico episode would be over. Yet in Ornstein's decision to end his concert career the Ampico contract must be considered a major factor. According to his son Severo, it and his appointment to the Philadelphia Academy of Music were the two principal reasons he felt that he could leave the concert stage.

7 ‖‖ The Philadelphia Years

When we move from Ornstein's very public and successful career between 1914 and 1925, we are confronted with a very different challenge. Ornstein's years in the public eye gener-ated a plethora of information and sources. His closeness to the American modernists meant that much private correspondence was saved among their papers. After 1925 Ornstein, however, was less often before the public, and for a variety of reasons he further removed himself from contact with most of those with whom he had been close. Ornstein gradually, but inexorably, became a recluse and when he was rediscovered in the 1970s had all but been forgotten. For a number of years during that time he was active, primarily as a teacher, but both Leo and Pauline were notorious for not keeping any pieces of paper, be they let-ters, business transactions, or other materials. Thus we go from an abundance to a dearth of sources. The story by necessity becomes sketchy, and more reliant on inference. At the same time, the story itself slows. Months, years go by with few major developments, as the Ornsteins settled into a routine, first of teaching, then of retirement. And there are gaps, where the trail itself runs cold.

When a life stretches over 108 years, inevitably some will be more important than oth-ers. Significance is not parceled out equitably. Like a river, Ornstein's life reaches a major cataract in 1925, then slows and narrows for four decades until it broadens again in the 1970s. Those years in the interim are not in the least void of activity and interest, but the pulse of the current is different, as well as, in this case, the quantity of detail.

While Ornstein pondered the direction of his career, uncertain about the strains of touring that public performance demanded, and while Ampico still seemed a lucrative godsend, an unrelated event in Philadelphia ultimately proved decisive for his future. On August 7, 1924, Camille Zeckwer, who had served as President of the Zeckwer-Hahn Philadelphia Musical Academy since 1917, died suddenly at age forty-nine.[1] The Academy had been founded in 1870 by a group of three musicians from Leipzig, which included Camille's father Richard Zeckwer. In 1876 John Himmelsbach, who served as the first Director, returned to his native Germany, and Richard Zeckwer assumed that position, which he held until ill health forced his retirement in 1917. Camille succeeded him, and at the same time the Academy merged with the smaller conservatory founded by the violinist Frederick Hahn to become the Zeckwer-Hahn Philadelphia Musical Academy. Camille Zeckwer was both a pianist and composer, his works having been performed by major symphony orchestras in the United States, including those in Boston, Philadelphia, and Chicago. Following Zeckwer's death Frederick Hahn eventually assumed the positions of both President and Director.[2]

Zeckwer's unexpected death left a void in the Piano Department that needed to be filled immediately. In September Ornstein was asked to head the Piano Department, something he had not anticipated: "out of a clear sky came an offer to become head of the piano department in an important Academy here in Philadelphia." It was not a convenient decision; Ornstein had a full concert schedule for the fall of 1924, and he was in the middle of work on the ballet, *Cronkhite's Clocks*, in collaboration with Edmund Wilson. Yet in spite of the immediate hardships this caused Ornstein saw benefits: "It opens up a field of work which will ultimately leave me much more time for writing but just at present it is added to a full concert season and I hardly know which way to turn." More important the offer was good: "They made the proposition so attractive that I could not well refuse," although we don't know exactly what that offer was.[3] For Ornstein the combination of the Ampico recording contract and the position at the Philadelphia Academy seemed to guarantee financial security. Ornstein had made and saved a great deal of money as a performer, and even though he had married into a wealthy family, he, a young man from the Lower East Side, wanted to prove that he could provide. Little could he have known at the time that, with the advances in recording and radio technology, the days of the Ampico were numbered, and that in only four years, with the stock market crash of 1929, much of Ornstein's savings would be wiped out.[4]

But in 1924 Ornstein was clearly not yet ready to give up touring. When *Musical Courier* stated that Ornstein would devote his entire time to his duties at the Academy, it was forced to quickly correct that statement: "What the note should have said was that Mr. Ornstein would devote his entire teaching time to these duties." *Musical Courier* further explained that "Much of his time will still be devoted to concert playing as it has in the past. It was quite inadvertently that the *Musical Courier* gave the impression that this eminent pianist was withdrawing from the concert stage, which is, of course, not a fact. His admirers would not permit him to do so even if he desired it, which he most certainly does not."[5] As if to emphasize the point, Hanson, who was still his manager, inserted a quarter-page ad next to the correction, advertising Ornstein's activities for the 1924–1925 season, noting proudly, "November and December Fully Booked." This was followed by a full-page ad in the next issue of *Musical Courier*, which hailed his "triumphal opening of the 1924–25 concert season," with the New York Symphony Orchestra at the Worcester Festival on October 10.[6] What is not clear in this announcement is whether *Musical Courier* originally misrepresented Ornstein's intentions or whether Ornstein had at least briefly considered dropping his fall schedule. For several years he had vacillated about touring, pressured no doubt by both Hanson and Pauline, each of whom had their own agendas, but more importantly, by his own conflicting professional and personal desires and goals.

Reviews from the Worcester newspapers left no question that Ornstein could still excite an audience. The *Worcester Telegram*, observing that "Ornstein was one of the giants among the piano virtuosos," commented "it would be difficult to find a more vigorous and energetic musician than he; he fairly bubbles over with life and spirit. It is safe to say that more than one spinal column was affected by the way he carried the whole orchestra along in the second movement [of the MacDowell D Minor Concerto]," and the *Worcester Evening Gazette* stressed it was "the Ornstein who flashed before the public a few years ago as a pianist and futuristic composer and who has grown pianistically to admirable heights," and recounted the "spontaneous burst of applause at the close" (of the second movement), and the several curtain calls he was forced to take.

Thus in 1924 Ornstein's grip on the public had not lessened. Yet 1925 marked a major turning point for Ornstein. Whatever else he might have thought, whatever else Hanson may have planned, by the end of the 1924–1925 season Ornstein's days of touring had come to an end. The Ornsteins settled in Philadelphia, and for the next twenty-five years, his work would revolve around teaching, first at the Philadelphia Musical Academy and then at his own Ornstein School of Music. Philadelphia itself may have had a special appeal to Pauline, as the Mallet-Prevost family had lived there for several years before moving to New York. The call of the road remained, however. Several times over the next decade Leo attempted to revive a concert career, but all efforts came to naught. There would be other experiments, but of a different sort. At one time the Ornsteins would attempt farming, and finally in Philadelphia Leo and Pauline, eleven years after their marriage, began to raise a family.

As the Ampico company was rapidly disintegrating, the Ornsteins seemed to have found an ideal niche at the Philadelphia Musical Academy. A half-page ad in *Musical Courier* on March 12, 1925, heralded Ornstein's reappointment as Head of the Piano Department. By 1929 Ornstein had been made one of two Vice Presidents of the Academy, a position he held until he left in 1935. There is no indication of what his administrative duties included, however. This position as Vice President may have been more ambassadorial.[7]

Pauline found her own position at the Academy. By 1929 she and Leo were both listed on the piano faculty, and Pauline had a special role. The Academy had a Conservatory Department, a Preparatory Department, and a Normal Department. The Normal Department included a curriculum that offered teacher's certificates for violin and piano, public school music, and "The Pauline Mallet-Prevost Ornstein System for Children's Classes in Piano." The catalog described it as "A

The Philadelphia Musical Academy
(ZECKWER—HAHN)

Announces the

RE-ENGAGEMENT
of

LEO ORNSTEIN

as head of the Piano Department
for the Season 1925-26

(Mr. Ornstein Uses the Knabe Piano)

Philadelphia Musical Academy
Charlton Lewis Murphy, Director
1617 Spruce Street, Philadelphia, Pa.

FIGURE 7.1. Appointment to Philadelphia Musical Academy.

complete course in technical and teaching material for teachers. Lessons given privately." There is no further description of this, and it is curious that Pauline preserved no material related to this pedagogical effort, nor did she ever mention it in letters or interviews. This had clearly been an interest of hers for some time, as the advertisement for her studio placed in *Musical Courier* in 1923, mentioned in the previous chapter, stressed that she specialized in teaching children.

Another hint at Pauline's activities is to be found in the *Piano Sketch Books* of Leo Ornstein. This is a collection of eighty-three short piano pieces for children, divided into two books, with fifty-two pieces in Part I and thirty-one pieces in Part II. The pieces are progressive, beginning with extremely simple ones, and they have various children's titles, such as "My Little Boat is Sailing," "Sh! The Dollies are Going to Sleep," and "Birthday Party." The Preface, signed by Leo, states, "The present volumes are the result of a need I have long felt for original material that would meet the limitations of an immature hand and at the same time give the beginner a valid musical experience. An awareness of this need has been emphasized through contact with teachers in various parts of the country."[8]

The collection of pieces may have been modeled upon the more well-known six volumes of *Mikrokosmos* of Béla Bartók, which came out in 1926. Ornstein was well acquainted with Bartók's music. When the *Sketches* were actually composed is not known, but they were published in 1939. Given Pauline's interest in teaching beginners and children, one must wonder what sort of role she played in the creation of these pieces. That they are in Pauline's hand tells us little, since virtually all of Leo's manuscripts after their marriage and until her death are in her hand. While Leo took only advanced students in his own teaching, he did accept young children if they showed talent, and according to Severo he enjoyed making up bed-time songs for him and his sister when they were small. Severo remembers Leo playing at least one of the pieces for him on the piano. Severo also remembers the cover of the original published version of the *Sketch Books* "had a melange design of a piano and a masked cowboy—the latter was a specific sop to my interest in The Lone Ranger."[9]

Yet Pauline may have created some of the first pieces, which are little more than five-finger exercises. She may also have gotten some of the ideas from her studies at the Institute for Musical Arts, where Damrosch taught a pedagogy class.

Another class that Pauline taught was "Modern Music Study," which was described as "Intimate classes for the study and analysis of modern music for students and music lovers. The evolution of modern modes of expression will be traced and their relationship to classic music will be discussed and illustrated."[10] The catalog offers no further information about the course, how it was taught, or what was covered, even what was meant by modern music. Pauline is listed among some rarefied company in the catalog. The introduction mentions a number of "distinguished musicians" who have taught at the Academy; they include "Leopold Auer, Herbert Witherspoon, Leo Ornstein, Pauline Mallet-Prevost Ornstein, Leo Schulz, and Placido de Montoliu."[11]

Except for some minor changes in personnel, activities at the Academy remained quite stable through 1934. Pauline continued to teach the same courses, and Leo's activities remained a mystery, beyond his listings on the piano faculty and as Vice President. The 1934–1935 catalog, however, hints at some substantial changes in the Academy. A number of new faculty were added, including two in piano: Alexander Kelberine, "the distinguished Russian Pianist," and Josef Wisson, "well-known concert pianist and soloist with the Philadelphia Orchestra"; Pauline is dropped from the list of "distinguished musicians" in the Introduction. She still teaches the pedagogy class, but this time with Leo. Both are listed as teachers for the class, and the catalog explains: "Mrs. Ornstein, whose wide reputation as a child specialist qualifies her to give peculiarly valuable advice to teachers of beginners and young people, deals with every aspect of this problem during the first year. In the second half of the course advanced problems are dealt with by Mr. Ornstein, whose extensive experience as a teacher makes it possible for him to solve the most difficult and exceptional pedagogic problems and to lay down guiding principles of the greatest assistance to teachers of all grades."[12]

A new lecture course was added to the curriculum, "Critical Analysis of Past and Present Trends in Music, Musically Illustrated," taught by Leo Ornstein. Designed for the amateur as well as the professional musician, the catalog pumped it: "The evaluation of past accomplishment and present-day trends by one of the leading composers and pianists of the age is a clarifying experience to all who attend those lectures. In the chaotic confusion of contemporary tendencies, a clear analysis and vision is the only foundation for constructive creation and understanding." In light of Leo's disdain for musical formalism, one wonders at his commitment to a course focused upon analysis.

A separate flyer advertised a "Course in Language and Literature of Music," taught by Leo Ornstein. Designed for the nonmusician, it focused on how to listen and was meant to be interactive. Because of Ornstein's ability to play virtually anything on the piano, the student would have the opportunity to go back and rehear something, just as he could reread a paragraph in a book. More importantly, however, "Mr. Ornstein has developed an entirely original method which enables a group of listeners to experience through his technical equipment the creation of various musical forms." Ornstein would play a passage, and then improvise different alternatives; the class was asked to choose which one they preferred: "Through making such choices musical sensitivity will be developed and taste will be crystallized." Finally the course would survey the literature of music, through Ornstein's playing. Whether this was the same course mentioned in the catalog is not clear, as there is no date or further indication of the provenance of the flyer, other than the course was offered through the Philadelphia Musical Academy. It was probably after 1932, however, as William J. Charlton is listed as the contact person at the Academy; he was appointed Administrative Director in 1932.[13]

How well the new developments at the Academy sat with the Ornsteins is not clear, but between 1934 and the fall of 1935 something soured them on the place. As late as April, 1934 Ornstein is still listed as a Vice President of the Academy, and his students gave a recital on June 4,[14] but when the catalog came out for the 1935–1936 year, neither Leo's nor Pauline's name is anywhere to be found. For that year the only other substantive change is the addition of a Louis Travis, who taught banjo, guitar, and mandolin. It seems unlikely that that would be sufficient to cause them to leave the Academy, so their disillusionment must have resulted from developments in the previous year. The changes in Pauline's courses, the addition of at least one lecture course by Leo, and the dropping of her name from the Introduction suggest a level of tension between the Ornsteins and Hahn.

Dissatisfaction at the Academy it seems was not confined to the Ornsteins. In 1934 Joseph W. Clarke, who had been one of the directors of the Academy, left to form his own Clarke Conservatory of Music. According to the press release Clarke had been head of the Piano Department at the Academy for the past ten years, an erroneous statement. Probably Clarke assumed that position when Ornstein was elevated to Vice President. More germane, however, Clarke took with him seventeen faculty members of the Academy, which would explain the spate of hiring that occurred that year. Clarke's departure and the exodus he created do suggest that all was not well at the Academy, something Ornstein himself confirmed years later when he alluded to departures.[15]

The Ornsteins followed Clarke's model and founded their own Ornstein School of Music, beginning in the fall of 1935. For ten years they occupied the top floor of the Art Alliance Building, 251 S. 18th St., right off of Rittenhouse Square. The Ornsteins saved no business records from the school, and so we are forced to piece together information from fragments, scattered references, and interviews. What little evidence does exist suggests that the school grew rapidly.

By 1938 the school was thriving. Instruction was offered in piano, strings, and voice, along with music theory and, curiously, painting. The in-house newsletter "Passing Tones" announced that the Ornstein school had just enrolled their four hundredth student, and "students were busy," with recitals in several venues in and around Philadelphia, as well as compositional activity, including program music for a play and a one-act opera, both performed at Temple University.[16] In 1940 the Ornstein School could advertise a faculty of twenty-nine, not including Leo and Pauline, and a six-week summer school in addition to regular lessons, which began September 9, and classes and lectures which began October 14.[17] The Ornstein letterhead of 1941 boasted of "Instruction in Piano—Voice—Violin/All Orchestral Instruments/All Theoretic Subjects/for/Professional and Amateur."[18]

Two contractual letters have survived, the first to a Miss Mildred F. Smith, which states that the school receives 40 percent of any lesson charges for lessons given at the school. For lessons given outside the school to registered students, the school receives 20 percent. By the third year the school had broadened that agreement slightly. According to a second contractual letter, to Julia Shanaman in July 1938, the in-house arrangements remained the same, but the percentage the school took for outside lessons had risen to 25 percent, and there is no differentiating whether or not the students were registered in the school. There is no mention what the fees were in either letter.[19] Elizabeth Kessler remembers that in 1940, when she was a pupil of Ornstein, she paid nine dollars per lesson.[20]

In spite of the rapid growth of the school, according to Severo Ornstein they had difficulty making ends meet until after World War II, when the GI Bill,

FIGURE 7.2A. "Passing Tones," cover.

providing support for veterans to attend college, in conjunction with the millions of returning veterans, swelled the ranks of higher education. The Ornstein School qualified as an accredited institution, and by 1947 over 700 students were enrolled, and offerings had expanded to include an opera department.[21] Severo may be remembering the war years themselves, when the war drained the availability of young men to study and put an economic strain on most families. Records that do exist suggest the school was quite successful through at least 1941.

In 1945 the Ornstein School moved to 1906 Spruce Street, which was directly across the street from the Academy. This was, of course, too soon for the GI Bill to have any significant impact on enrollment. That the Ornsteins were able to buy the building suggests that they were at the least in a relatively strong

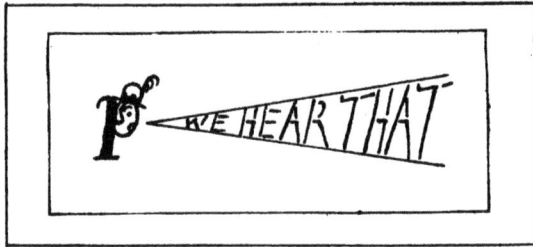
WE HEAR THAT

The four hundredth student has recently been registered. As we remember that our school is just in its third year we are quite proud of this large enrollment.

Eva Welch Voorhies made her Philadelphia debut February 2nd, playing compositions of Beethoven, Brahms, Franck, Chopin, Liszt and Debussy in the Academy of Music Foyer.

Pupils of David Sokoloff gave a most enjoyable Concerto Recital Sunday evening, March the sixth.

Among other appearances, Miss Helen Behre, violinist, and Mrs. Mabel W. Frazer, pianist, gave a joint recital at the Women's Wynnefield Hadassuh recently.

A monthly issue of Passing Tones will be part of next season's program.

An original number for violin, viola and piano by Andrew Welsh Imbrie was recently played at the Lawrenceville School with the composer at the piano.

Miss Muriel Hodge's trio gave a concert at the Miquon School, May first, and is booked for other engagements in the near future.

There have been some remarkable accomplishments in the painting class for five year old artists which is conducted each Thursday afternoon by Matthew Sharpe.

Blodwyn Wipplinger, 15 year old pupil of Leo Ornstein, played her first professional engagement Saturday evening, May seventh, when she gave a recital in the Presbyterian Church at Twenty-first St. and Fairmount Ave.

Waldemar Dabrowski recently completed program music for the play "Noah", several movements of which he played at Temple University Saturday evening, May fourteenth.

"The Dark Kingdom" an opera in one act by Charles Swier, had its first performance at the X group Parent Night at Temple University, May fourteenth

Miksa Merson of the piano faculty gave a recital Tuesday evening, May seventeenth at the residence of Mrs. Alexander Biddle in Bryn Mawr.

A recital by students in piano, vocal and violin departments was given Friday afternoon, May twentieth.

FIGURE 7.2B. "Passing Tones," p. 3.

and stable financial situation. We don't know how the purchase was financed, or whether Mallet-Provost provided any assistance in the form of a loan or gift. Neither would be unlikely.

At least two well-known musicians had training at the Ornstein School. Andrew Imbrie studied piano first with Pauline and then with Leo while in high school and college from 1937 to 1942. Interested primarily in composition, he went on to study at Princeton with Roger Sessions and then to France to study with Nadia Boulanger. His senior thesis, a string quartet, was recorded by the Juilliard Quartet. After World War II he received a master's degree in composition from the University of California, Berkeley, and remained for a distinguished academic career, spanning forty years as a professor. His many compositions, which include two operas, three symphonies, and five string quartets, garnered numerous awards, including the New York Music Critics' Award (1944), the Alice M. Ditson Award (1947), two Guggenheim fellowships (1953–1954, 1959–1960), and the Hinrichsen Award of the American Academy of Arts and Letters. He was elected to both the National Institute of Arts and Letters and the National Academy of Arts and Sciences.

The relationship between Ornstein and Imbrie was a close one. At first Imbrie looked up to Ornstein as something of a hero, "the first live composer that I had an intimate, personal friendship with, . . . a very romantic figure—a very excitable, Russian temperament."[22] Imbrie was the only student invited to visit the Ornsteins in New Hampshire, coming up there at least twice during the summer for lessons.

Imbrie recounts when he was about fifteen, "I was getting a little rebellious," and Ornstein suggested he study with someone else. Imbrie then worked with Olga Samaroff[23] and Rosalyn Tureck at the Philadelphia Conservatory for about a year but came back to Ornstein. Where Ornstein was reluctant to help was in teaching composition, although he did encourage Imbrie to compose. He was, according to Imbrie, "diffident about his own music," and resisted Imbrie's learning any of it. He sent Imbrie elsewhere to learn counterpoint, probably a wise move, given Ornstein's own aversion to employing this basic compositional technique. Yet Imbrie found that he received intangible compositional lessons from Ornstein: "I think he made a valuable contribution to me as a composer in just being himself, by being the kind of composer he is, completely in love with music—completely immersed in it and almost inarticulate about it—showing by example what a musician can be, without being able to analyze it."[24] This remark does make one wonder about Ornstein's analysis course at the Academy.

A second musician who studied at the Ornstein School was John Coltrane. Coltrane had moved to Philadelphia, where his mother was, after graduating from

High Point High School in North Carolina in 1943. By this time he was hooked on the saxophone, practicing constantly. In 1944 he enrolled in the Ornstein School of Music, to study saxophone with Mike Guerra, who had developed a considerable reputation as both a performer and a teacher. Rachmaninoff praised Guerra's performance in his *Symphonic Dances*, and Guerra also taught, for a time, Gerry Mulligan and Stan Getz.

Coltrane was at the Ornstein School only briefly, probably one year, and unlike Imbrie, would have had little if any contact with Ornstein himself. On the sax Guerra taught from standard method books, such as Klosé, and students played classical transcriptions, such as Schubert's famous *Serenade* (*Ständchen*). A friend of Coltrane's, David Young, remembers Coltrane's complete immersion in the relatively technically simple piece: "He worried me to death with that one [piece]. The first thing in the morning he'd get up and grab the horn—before he'd leave for work—and the first things when he'd come in that afternoon. The last thing at night he'd have that horn and the only thing I really remember is Schubert's 'Serenade.'" In addition to saxophone, Coltrane studied theory at the Ornstein School, which was also taught by Guerra. Guerra remembers Coltrane as quick and dedicated in theory also: "I wrote out complete chord progressions and special exercises in chromatic scales, and he was one of the few who brought his homework back practically the next day and played it on sight. . . . He was always asking for more."[25]

The school itself was administered by Pauline. Students remembered her as a large, formidable presence, with white hair that was pulled back tight, and always wearing a black dress. To them she was a perfect lady, "an Eleanor Roosevelt type," who spoke beautifully, but was a bit remote. They were in awe of her: "She was one tough lady." The atmosphere of the school was serious and focused, and it was Pauline who set the tone, often sitting at a desk near the front door, surveying everyone and everything that passed. She was always busy, however, given both her teaching and administrative duties.[26]

Ornstein himself seems to have remained in his second-floor studio and to have taught. He took pupils of all ages, if they were talented. In fact, he seems to have enjoyed teaching children, although there are conflicting reports of how enthusiastic he was about teaching at all. Lily Friedman felt that he was not particularly thrilled to be teaching and often appeared to be daydreaming.[27] Yet Ornstein had demonstrated a pedagogical interest as early as 1915, when he wrote what was intended to be a series of five articles for *Musical Observer* entitled "How My Music Should Be Played and Sung." These dealt more with the problems of performing his own, and by extension modernist music, and were not primarily broadly applicable piano pedagogical monographs. Much of his discussion involves how modern music must be approached with a different aesthetic than traditional pieces in the repertoire, a point applicable to all instruments. In fact, only the first two articles dealt with the piano; the third and fourth were to be about the violin and the fifth with Ornstein's vocal works. Ornstein seems to have completed only the first two, however; three, four, and five did not appear.[28]

In 1922 Ornstein once again addressed performance questions, this time in more detail. As we saw in the previous chapter, Ornstein's manager, Arthur Judson, announced that Ornstein was accepting pupils, at the very time that a ten-part series, "Modern Principles of Piano Technique," appeared in *Musical Observer*. The series was designed for the beginning student and consisted entirely of the physical principles of performance. It began with a detailed description of the position of the hand, the weight of the arm, and the relation of the fingers to the keyboard. Ornstein then progressed gradually through a detailed set of basic finger exercises, beginning with simple five-note exercises on C-G, and gradually introducing other patterns until in the tenth and final part the arpeggio was discussed. Each series contained photographs of Ornstein's hand showing the positions discussed.[29]

Everyone agrees that in lessons Ornstein was always a gentleman, and with his demeanor, energy, and foreign accent, he seemed like someone quite exotic. They remember him as being totally absorbed in music. Elizabeth Kessler recalls that he went over fingering and pedaling in great detail, although she allows that may have been because she was young.[30] Imbrie found Ornstein a strict disciplinarian when it came to piano technique and remembers how Ornstein taught technique from the piano repertoire, using matches which he moved from one side to the other to measure repetition, as he did with his own practicing. Technical problems were broken into small, about three-measure units, and Imbrie was expected to repeat those passages thirty or more times, moving a match each time. If a mistake was made then he had to start again at the beginning.[31] This story is repeated by Lily Friedman, whose score of the Mendelssohn G Minor Piano Concerto, which she studied with Ornstein, has different measures circled and the notation "75 times," "100 times," written next to them. Friedman remembers that Ornstein had a board with about a hundred yellow pegs in it, which was for the purpose of keeping track of repetitions. To Ornstein such work was purely mechanical. Ornstein told Friedman that she could read the paper while doing that, something she now disagrees with.

Another teaching technique Ornstein used was modeling, but only for the more advanced students. Imbrie and Kessler both report how Ornstein would play along with the student on a second piano, and the student would pick up the nuances, the phrasing, dynamics and ritards. According to Imbrie, "the communication was done on a musical level, not always at a verbal level at all." If there was a question Ornstein would explain, "but very often it wasn't necessary—all I had to do was to see what he was doing and then I would do the same thing and then it would hit me right—and we would go right on with the lesson."[32]

Ornstein assigned the repertoire for each student, and it was mostly traditional: Bach, Mozart, Chopin, Beethoven sonatas, Brahms. When Imbrie tried some of Liszt's music but was unenthusiastic Leo was not disappointed.[33] Asked whether Ornstein assigned any twentieth-century music, Friedman was emphatic, "Oh my God, no."[34] Ornstein did allow Imbrie to play Scriabin, and after much imploring, one of Ornstein's own pieces, the Tartar Dance.[35]

The same year that the Ornsteins founded their school, another event in Philadelphia was to have an impact on Leo's teaching career. Mr. and Mrs. George F. Tyler gave a million dollar gift to Temple University to found the Stella Elkins Tyler Fine Arts College. Along with a monetary gift to fund the school, Stella Tyler donated her fourteen-acre estate, which lay in a beautiful, natural setting some six miles north of the main campus. Influenced by the educational philosophy of John Dewey, the purpose of the new school was "to produce a real American art in a unique and progressive way."[36] The curriculum was innovative: during the first two years students would be instructed "in all media of artistic expression, such as painting, modeling, sketching, stone and wood carving, metal work, music and dancing," in addition to general courses in culture. Only in the last two years would they specialize in their own area of interest.[37] Ornstein's experience at Temple may have provided the idea and incentive for the Ornsteins to add painting lessons to their own school.

Tyler, who had studied sculpture, chose as dean of the new school her mentor, Boris Blai, who served in that position for twenty-five years. The *New York Times* reported that "The faculty, besides Mr. Blai, will include Franklin Watkins, painter, Earl Horter, etcher, and Leo Ornstein, pianist and composer."[38] Ornstein was thus a founding member of the school. It was small at the beginning, admitting twelve freshmen the first year, and until it was moved to the main campus in 2006 retained the feel of a rural small-arts school.[39] Music broke away on its own in 1962, when the Boyer School of Music was formed and located on the main campus. We do not know whether Ornstein taught anything at Temple other than piano, or how long he remained, although in 1947 Claire Raphael Reis referred to him as being at Temple University, and in 1949 the Thompson Cyclopedia indicated he was still there.[40] In 1955 Gilbert Chase also stated that Ornstein taught at Temple, but Chase's reference could have been historical.[41] Pauline briefly taught at Temple also, in the Oak Lane Country Day School, a laboratory school for children affiliated with Temple, which was founded on the same progressive ideas as the Tyler Fine Arts College.[42] Her stay was brief, however; an administrative "upheaval" caused Pauline to resign in 1937.[43]

Ornstein's personal life changed dramatically during his years in Philadelphia. On March 1, 1929, their daughter Edith was born; their son Severo was born October 13, 1930. As a consequence they began to reassess their living situation. Leo and Pauline had been married over ten years when Edith was born, and other than their New Hampshire house in the White Mountains, they had lived either in hotels or in townhouses. During the first two years in Philadelphia they had lived at the Sylvania Hotel. After that they moved into a town house on Locust Street, off Rittenhouse Square, and just a few blocks from the Academy. They were two self-contained people, "absolutely absorbed in each other."[44] By the late twenties they became aware that if they were to have children, this was the time; Pauline was thirty-eight years old when Edith was born.

In an interview with his grandniece, Holly Carter, when asked what kind of parent he was, Ornstein replied, "an indifferent one." Neither parent was negligent nor unconcerned about their children, but between their own heavy work schedule and their self-absorption, there remained a significant distance between parents and children. Both children remember being raised mainly by a nanny, Ida Hacket, who came to the family when Edith was six months old. She stayed with them until 1952–1953, long after Edith and Severo had graduated from college, and Edith had married. For Edith it was a positive experience; she bonded with the nanny, who became a surrogate mother. Severo did not bond as easily with her, and as a result he felt more acutely his parents' absence. Both children remember Leo practicing long hours when he was at home, and both remember one of the ways of having time with him was to move matches, his counting mechanism to determine how many times he had gone over a passage. This had the added benefit of both children absorbing a good bit of music. Edith described the experience: "As children my brother and I learned many of the pieces he was working on by sitting beside him and listening to him go over and over the pieces. If he wanted to repeat a passage many times, he would have us keep count for him by putting down little wooden matches each time he'd play the passage. We called it 'counting matches.' In this way we learned so much of the music by heart."[45]

Neither child went into music professionally, although Severo developed a deep love for the piano, which he still plays as a skilled amateur, and Edith studied ballet seriously as a young woman. Both Severo and Edith have had successful, although very different, careers. Severo went to Harvard when he was sixteen, and Edith graduated from Bryn Mawr in three years. Edith holds advanced degrees in anthropology and for a time was the head of Planned Parenthood in the state of Wisconsin. Severo went on to become a leading computer scientist, one of the

FIGURE 7.3. Edith and Severo with Severo Mallet-Prevost. *Photo courtesy the Ornstein family.*

few people who can claim, with literal truth, to have been one of the pioneers of the Internet.[46]

Soon after the births of Edith and Severo the Ornsteins moved from Philadelphia into the country. The move itself was prompted at least in part by the children. According to Leo, "I wanted the children to have some experience in a rural setting because I used to see them once in a while with their nursemaid. We had an apartment off the Rittenhouse Square, and I'd see them just going around like little animals in a cage."[47] The move also had to do with an affinity for country living that went back to their first experiment living on the Mallet-Prevost estate in North Conway, New Hampshire.

Whatever Leo originally thought of changing his summer residence from the Maine seacoast to the New Hampshire woods, according to Edith, Leo grew especially fond of the New Hampshire setting: "In the summertime we would leave Philadelphia, where we lived, and head for our summer home in the heart of New Hampshire's White Mountains. Of all the places in the world, this area is nearest and dearest to my father."[48] Thus the decision to move outside of Philadelphia in the 1930s was an easy one. They originally bought a large house with some land in Chalfont.[49] After about seven years they decided to try farming once again, but this time more seriously, and they bought a larger farm. Leo claims to have gotten the idea of farming from his father-in-law, but according to the family it was originally Leo's idea.

The farm was a major responsibility. At one point they had approximately sixty Guernsey cows. Given their schedule and their own urban background, they needed additional help, and they hired someone to run it. This worked until World War II, when help was difficult to find, and the work became difficult. Responsibility for milking the cows devolved onto Pauline and Severo, tasks they had to accomplish before Pauline had to leave to take the train into the city and Severo had to leave for school. The farm also caused tension within the family. Although it was apparently Leo's idea originally, he felt that it was draining them financially, and his frustration would surface in angry encounters at home. Screaming and crying scenes were not unusual in the household. Leo possessed an explosive temper and often threatened to walk out. The children would cry and plead, but as they remember such events, Pauline remained relatively calm, assuming their father would quiet down. Severo remembers Leo's threatening to leave more than once, although whether he ever intended to follow through with the threat was never determined. According to Severo, even though maintaining the farm was difficult, it did provide them with food and milk and a sense of self-sufficiency during the war when goods were scarce.

After around 1947 the Ornsteins sold the farm and moved to Merion, Pennsylvania, until the children were grown, and finally when they retired and sold the school, they retreated to New Hampshire year round. For a brief period they lived in Greenwich Village in Union Square.[50]

The new compositional trajectory that Ornstein displayed in the early 1920s, where he shifted from creating many shorter pieces to focus on a few more extended works for multiple instruments, continued through the late 1920s and into the 1930s. Virtually all of his 1920s–1930s pieces were the result of commissions or special opportunities; Ornstein was no longer his own vehicle for reaching the public, and, except for some small teaching pieces, he seems to have needed the motivation of a specific promise to undertake work on larger scores. Teaching and then the addition of family life undoubtedly took much of his time, but Ornstein had also discovered that the intuitive approach, whereby what were essentially improvisations could be remembered and recorded, where sounds simply entered his head in a sudden epiphany, was no longer sufficient for what he was being asked to do. Composition, in other words, became work.

The next major piece composed after the Concerto was his *Quintette* for Piano and Strings, written in 1927. It is by all accounts, including Ornstein's, his most important composition, and consequently will be examined in some detail. In contrast to an earlier piece like *Wild Men's Dance*, it is also an exemplar of the different approach that a more extended work demanded. The *Quintette* was commissioned by the prominent patron Elizabeth Sprague Coolidge, but no records of the transaction survive. This was not unusual for Coolidge's commissions, according to her biographer.[51] The commission was probably a personal one, not from the Elizabeth Sprague Coolidge Foundation established at the Library of Congress in 1925. Ornstein did recall later that he was paid $1,000 for the piece, the most he ever received for a composition. It bothered him that performers earned more than composers. That the Philadelphia Orchestra paid him $500 for composing his Piano Concerto and $1,500 for playing it, for example, seemed to him a serious distortion of values.[52]

The first performance of the *Quintette* took place in Philadelphia on January 1, 1928, in a concert sponsored by the Society for Contemporary Music. Ornstein shared the stage with Béla Bartók, then on a six-week tour of the United States. In addition to the *Quintette* the concert featured Bartók's Sonata No. 2 for Violin and Piano, his String Quartet No. 2, and Ravel's *Tzigane*.[53] The *Quintette* was repeated in New York on January 12 at a program sponsored by the League of Composers. The members of the Pro Arte Quartet were the featured performers in string quartets by Darius Milhaud, Louis Gruenberg, and Paul Hindemith, in addition to the Ornstein *Quintette*. That following November Elizabeth Sprague Coolidge programmed the *Quintette* in a concert in Paris, with Alfred Cortot as pianist.[54]

Critiques of the early performances were more polarized than mixed. Befitting its eclectic style, the *Quintette* was criticized both as being insufficiently modern—that is ultramodern—and too far outside the bounds of traditional structural principles. An anonymous writer for *Musical Courier* hailed it as "a work of genuine importance," which "combines beauty and modernism, though this combination is so rare that one had almost assumed its impossibility."[55] The French musicologist Henry Prunières dismissed it as "a work that smacks of the amateur," in which "impotence seeks to hide itself beneath useless complication."[56] An ardent supporter of 1920s ultramodernism, Prunières's comment is not surprising. Virtually all accounts, however, regardless of the critic's assessment of the work's musical worth indicate that the piece was enthusiastically received by the audience.

Years later Ornstein put his own thoughts regarding the *Quintette* into writing. "The *Quintette* is not a polite piece," he reflected, nor is it "Avant Garde." Granting that "it may even be embarrassingly overcharged," he pointed to the work's main virtue: "It is what I heard." And then he confessed how important it was to him to communicate a particular spirit to listeners: "Possibly it might have been less blunt and emotionally more reserved," he admitted, "but if one does not sense its almost brutal emotional directness, then I have indeed failed." To reach his goal of conveying raw emotional experience, certain principles had to be sacrificed, including "uniformity of style." But as Ornstein saw it, a more important principle was at stake: that "the music should be spontaneous and thoroughly uninhibited," and, apparently, that it should sound that way. Indeed, he went on: "I feel that so much of the music to-day deals with so many personal refinements that in the end musical implications are altogether erased." That brought him to an admission—though not in precisely these words—that the Quintette's lack of sophistication surprised even him, and that he had intended the work for a broad general audience: "While the rhetoric of the Quintette may be parochial I hope that whatever inner light there is will touch a universal chord in the listener. The untamed emotion of the piece at first annoyed and shocked my own ears, but any attempt to modify it destroyed whatever was genuine."[57]

Ironically the same unfiltered emotionalism that the ultramodernists applauded when it produced Wild Men's Dance and Suicide in an Airplane became the object of criticism when it resulted in the Quintette. While ultramodernism as a broad concept appeared to embrace a wide range of styles and impulses, it drew the line at compositional techniques that showcased lyrical expressivity.

Ornstein's later music—such pieces as the Second Cello Sonata, the Quintette, the Poem for Flute and Piano, and some of his later piano sonatas—reflects his Eastern European heritage, particularly in melodic content. Ornstein immersed himself in a completely different culture when he came to the United States, but he never forgot that earlier world; it permeates his music.

Between 1913, when Wild Men's Dance first trampled Mrs. Tapper's studio, and 1928 when Ornstein's Piano Quintette received its premiere, America's contemporary music scene had steadily stretched its collective modernist ears. In addition to Ornstein's own Band Box concerts in 1915, programs by newly founded new music organizations featured music by Antheil, Bartók, Berg, Bloch, Chavez, Copland, Cowell, Crawford, Debussy, De Falla, Gruenberg, Hindemith, Honegger, Ives, McPhee, Milhaud, Prokofiev, Ravel, Rudhyar, Ruggles, Salzedo, Satie, Schoenberg, Scriabin, Still, Stravinsky, Varèse, and Webern, to name only some of the more famous composers represented. This activity turned a nation once considered a musical-cultural backwater into ground zero for all that was new.[58] It is within the context of new music societies and their forward-thinking administrators and patrons that Ornstein's Quintette emerged.

Just as in the late teens when Ornstein had the mantle of futurist flagman thrust upon him by critics and taste-makers eager to find a champion for their aesthetic agenda, by the late twenties writers had recast him as a retrenching neo-romantic. In reviewing the Philadelphia premiere in January 1928, Linton Martin found the *Quintette* "almost sedately conventional beside the Bartók numbers [the Sonata No. 2 for Violin and Piano and the String Quartet No. 2, Op. 17]."[59] When it was performed days later in New York, F. D. Perkins observed that Ornstein showed himself "a composer no longer of the left wing."[60] The music of the *Quintette*, however, suggests another reading, one not so simple.

An overwhelming number of musical characteristics found in Ornstein's relatively short, "futuristic" piano works are also present in the larger, more formal *Quintette*. If, by composing a piano quintet, he consciously participated in the high-art tradition, he did so without feeling beholden to the conventions that had defined the genres of that tradition: large-scale functional harmonic structures, sharply defined, contrasting thematic materials, and broadly considered key schemes. Modal melodies only hinted at in the piano miniatures are expanded in the longer work. Driving rhythms that characterized an entire miniature piece are cast against more lyrical material. What were rapidly juxtaposed ideas enjoy more time between flashing changes. The thirty-four-year-old composer recognized the demands made by the enlarged size and scope of the genre and brought an enriched musical and emotional vocabulary to bear on the work, one gained over fifteen years of concertizing, composing, and thinking about music.[61] It is not so much that we are listening to a completely different voice as we are listening to a more mature, better read, and more experienced voice.

Ornstein's solo pieces were composed, first and foremost, for him to play on his concerts. That endeavor left him in full control of both their conception and their sounding outcome. By his own testimony, at least some of them arrived in his imagination whole and, rather than working them out on paper, he was known to perform them before ever writing them down.[62] It is also true that Ornstein's piano pieces of the time—the works that won him fame as an ultramodernist—were short works in the mode of nineteenth-century character pieces. As Ornstein's commitment to composition continued and deepened during the 1910s, however, he wrote more and more for the piano with other instruments. That led him beyond the character piece, or suite of such pieces, to multimovement works such as the Concerto, the Second String Quartet, and the *Quintette*. Not only did this trend cause him to depend more heavily on musical notation, but it tested his ability to create musical form.

"Every piece of music has to have a terrific inner logic," Ornstein told Vivian Perlis in 1977. "Music is not a random art." Yet, in almost the same breath, he also declared: "Music is something other than an intellectual concept."[63] In interpreting these remarks, one needs to take them as more mutually reinforcing than contradictory. It is well to remember that, while Ornstein had a lot to say over the years about his compositional philosophy, his comments fall into two main categories: things he said to journalists and critics during the time when he was helping modern music to blossom (1913–1920), and things he told scholars during the last three decades of his life, when he and his work had faded to a dim memory in the public mind. Each category provides its own insights. But neither was mediated by the intellectual discourses that grew up around modernism during the gap between Ornstein's earlier and later years. Composers participated actively in these discussions, from Schoenberg throughout the century. Indeed, the notion of the composer as an intellectual is now embedded in our view of music's twentieth-century development. Ornstein's comments about intuition, spontaneity, and a wariness of compositional theory proclaim his own distance from that practice.

Music composed in the Western classical tradition demands both intuition and intellect, and the line between the two is not always clear. Nevertheless, imagining a spectrum with intuitive sense experience at one end and analytical thought at the other, one could say that composers tend to rely on intuition ("inspiration") for their musical materials and more on intellect to direct the distribution of these materials over time. Melodies, for example, may come unbidden to the composer. At the spectrum's other end stand conventions and techniques that require intellectual working out: counterpoint, for example, or the "development" of material already stated, or even, perhaps, the shaping of a complete musical structure. In vocal music the text provides a formal starting point; in instrumental music form relies on statements and repetitions of material, and contrasts involving new material.

Certain formal patterns are fundamental to the Western tradition. In one simple pattern, material is stated, then repeated, often with some embellishment or change (AA'). In another, material is stated, then contrasted with new material, and then heard again: repetition, contrast, and return, yielding a three-part structure (ABA). Varied repetition of material can be expanded to large-scale variation forms. And since the 1700s, instrumental "sonatas" in several "movements"—that is, large-scale contrasting sections, each complete in itself, and with its own pattern of repetition and contrast—have come to be a near-universal formal structure. Formally speaking, for example, Ornstein's *Quintette* is a sonata for piano and string quartet.

Danse sauvage (*Wild Men's Dance*, 1913), an exemplar of Ornstein's dissonant, futuristic style, conveys the impression of an intense, spontaneous emotional outburst. Driving rhythm and high volume are the traits that first strike the listener's ear. Only twice does the dynamic level sink below the range between *forte* and quadruple *forte*: in measure 7 and again in measure 10, Ornstein indicates *mezzo piano*, but each is followed immediately by a *crescendo* that reaches *fortissimo* by the end of the measure. The hammering eighth notes, though incessant, never settle into regular patterns, for in the space of just under three minutes, Ornstein traverses no fewer than seventeen tempo markings and thirty-three meter changes. The harmony consists of dense, chromatic tone clusters that outline no tonality and never resolve into triads, although they develop a sense of centeredness by their repetition. *Danse sauvage* pushes the piano to the limit of its volume, speed, and range, ending with a final sonority that has the performer splayed out over the keyboard, from the lowest E♯ to the highest B♯.

Yet, if the sound of the piece and Ornstein's way of talking about his compositional approach suggest a makeshift form, *Danse sauvage* turns out to be a clear-cut example of single-movement sonata form—at least in its distribution of thematic material. It starts with a twelve-measure introduction, leading to the first theme (mm. 13ff.), essentially rhythmic and restated in different registers (m. 29; m. 45). At measure 69 a second theme arrives: a quick cascade of thirty-second notes leading to a quarter note, which is then modified and repeated. A highly unstable section follows (mm. 84–130), mixing supercharged intensity with calm, and sounding like musical development. After a measure of rest, a recapitulation begins (mm. 131ff.) with the first theme, followed by the second (mm. 147ff.). The work closes with a whirling series of trill-tremolo figures.

"I feel that every individual has to express himself as sincerely as possible," Ornstein told an interviewer in March 1915, "and that the moment that he conforms to set rules, he tries to mold his creation into a conventional form, then the music is not spontaneous as it ought to be in every respect. Music has no value when it is not spontaneous."[64] One might take this comment as a contradiction between Ornstein's ideas and his practice, for the form of *Danse sauvage* is certainly a conventional one. Yet the composer's account of the work's creation—its sudden, spontaneous appearance in his mind as a whole—testifies that the process of trying "to mold his creation" into any form at all was one that Ornstein skipped, at least with this work. By his account, he was spared the need to "conform to set rules," or any rules, in fact, because the piece was simply revealed to him: the product of an experienced, disciplined musical sensibility whose form happened to resemble that of other works that he had studied and played for years.

If *Danse sauvage* (1913) exemplifies Ornstein's "first," ultramodern style and the *Quintette* (1927) the second, the two works hold many musical traits in common, including modal melodies, hammering rhythms, blocklike construction, transitionless changes, and registral shifts for variety. Both also project high emotional intensity. Their rhetoric suggests a kind of romantic individualism overlaid with modern sounds. But the scale of the *Quintette*, whose three movements

FIGURE 7.4. Leo Ornstein, *Danse sauvage*, mm. 1–10.

together last almost forty minutes, and the forces for which it was written provide room for a side of Ornstein only hinted at in his earlier works: his gift for lyric expression.[65]

The spirit and energy of *Danse sauvage* lie behind the fourteen-minute first movement, "Allegro barbaro," of the *Quintette*. But here Ornstein alternates forceful, even violent expression with passages of quiet tenderness. The movement begins with seventy-four measures of various rhythmically charged motives.[66] Starting at the *Meno Mosso* (m. 75), however, Ornstein unveils his lyrical side. A modal melody winds its way through the string parts, and then is heard doubled and tripled while arpeggios undulate in the triple *piano* keyboard accompaniment.

At measure 83 Ornstein recasts a rhythmic *fortissimo* passage first introduced by the piano in measure 5 and then played at measure 29 by the strings in an *espressivo* line. As if to prove that the piano can sing too, he gives the newly lyricized theme to that instrument, soon followed by the viola, and then the cello. Four measures later, at *Andante con moto*, Ornstein shifts from 5/4 to 8/8 and then 4/4, and moves the same melody to the violins. Their *mezzo piano, lamentoso* octaves pull listeners through the interlude. As Ornstein builds intensity, he adds a viola to thicken the sound. Rounding out this section, at measure 120, *Andante*, the composer returns to the melody first heard at measure 75, now supercharged in a presentation by both violins and cello. Ornstein increases surface rhythm and the volume, and by measure 156, *Agitato feroce*, he has returned to the agitated drive of the beginning. But the large scale of this "Allegro barbaro" demands much more contrast, as well as more spacious and extended musical statements, and Ornstein convincingly provides both. The return at measure 378 of the idea first heard in measure 7, and at measure 388 of that heard at measure 27, modified rhythmically, recapitulates the movement's opening, suggesting that Ornstein was referring to the sonata-form design of a typical first movement. Indeed, much about the *Quintette* places it solidly in the Western classical tradition of chamber music, including its genre (the piano quintet is a standard grouping of instruments), its three-movement fast-slow-fast (*Allegro barbaro*,[67] *Andante lamentoso, Allegro agitato*) structure, and the emphasis on thematic development that pervades the work, demonstrating Ornstein's ability to write material that is flexible and mutable, yet distinctive. This latter trait allows him to achieve musical continuity in a work that is full of variety.

The single-movement sonata form's ability to balance unity and variety surely explains its use by many composers since the eighteenth century. And the similarities among Ornstein's first-movement motives and themes make them well suited to achieving continuity on a larger scale. Yet Ornstein's themes change continuously throughout the movement in a way that might be called developing variation. What is introduced beginning at measure 37 as a theme based upon an arpeggiated figure becomes an accompanimental figure at measure 128 in the viola and cello. This same arpeggio gesture forms the basis for other melodic adaptations throughout the movement. Melodies introduced in one meter reappear in a different meter, and the change sometimes affects their character.

All themes feature the interval of the second. The first theme in the entire work (m. 5), rhythmic in character, contains equal numbers of major and minor seconds; the first important lyrical theme at measure 75 stresses minor and major seconds with a descending minor third at the apex of the melodic arch; and a second lyrical theme at measure 193 is a chromatic descent balanced by a

FIGURE 7.5A. Leo Ornstein, *Quintette* for Piano and Strings, first movement, mm. 5–10, piano part.

FIGURE 7.5B. Leo Ornstein, *Quintette* for Piano and Strings, first movement, mm. 75–78, violin I part.

FIGURE 7.5C. Leo Ornstein, *Quintette* for Piano and Strings, first movement, mm. 193–199, violin II part.

chromatic ascent.[68] By casting themes in similar intervals but different gestures, Ornstein asserts their relatedness while reducing literal repetition.

Sonata form implies tonal hierarchy, however, as well as thematic contrast and development, and here Ornstein departs from tradition. The first movement of the *Quintette* shows some of the composer's ways of creating an integrated whole without depending on harmonic and tonal events. With their trilled A♭s and B♭s, the opening measures seem to introduce a composition in A-flat major. But the C octave pedal in the piano that joins in on the last beat of measure 4, and the polytonal chord that alternates with it (mm. 5ff.)—a combination of D-flat and C^7 chords, turning a measure later into a polytonal aggregate combining E-flat major and F minor triads—destroy any clear sense of tonality. Thus, from the very start, the sense of direction that music composed "in a key" provides is purposefully avoided. Other pedal tones, in fact, appear throughout the movement, but none carries the weight of lasting harmonic destination—in part because, surrounded by tritones and diminished chords—their power to create tonal hierarchy is undermined.[69]

Certain melodic progressions, as well as emphasized pitches, do make some local impact, but their effect tends to fade quickly. At measure 75, for example, the first violin plays an "espressivo" solo that draws its pitches from an F harmonic minor scale. Nine measures later the viola enters with a melody in B major that recalls the lyrical material first heard at measure 29. The appearance of these two melodies in F and B—keys a tritone apart—seems to promise more significance when, at measure 109, Ornstein starts a passage in which the violins and viola reiterate material also allied to F and B. Ten measures later, however, the cello and piano lines introduce unrelated diminished sonorities, then move on to other, equally ambiguous ones, and the emphasis on F and B turns out to be transitory. In sum, and generally speaking, by refusing to privilege any single key or pitch, except in passing, Ornstein's idiom foregoes the kind of eventfulness and power that harmonic modulation can bring. Contrast comes chiefly from restless, often violent tempo changes, as well as unexpected harmonic and rhythmic shifts. And unity is forged through closely related melodic motives and a continuously dissonant palette that, in the first movement, shows a preference for tritones and minor seconds.

If the first movement presents the extremes of Ornstein's emotional range, the second, *Andante lamentoso*, focuses more single-mindedly on quiet introspection; here is a ten-minute exploration of Ornstein's "expressive" voice.[70] He begins with *pianissimo* second violin and viola each playing a dissonant double stop *con sordino*.[71] As in the first movement, there are frequent tempo and mood changes, and the piece does, on three occasions, rise out of its quiet contemplation. But these are short-lived and contained and do not disturb the prevailing inward-turning mood. As an example, even a march section at measure 83 (a quarter note at 96 instead of the opening 76) is a *marcia funebre*. It begins *piano*, becomes more animated and louder, reaching *fff* at measure 107, but by measure 119 is back to *piano*. At measure 130 Ornstein writes *ppp Tranquillo*, and at measure 139, *Tempo Primo*. Throughout the march the metronome marking of a quarter at 96 keeps the tempo well within the *andante* range.

All is not, however, resigned melancholy. Ornstein achieves an impassioned moment beginning at measure 165, where the tempo increases noticeably and strings and piano explode triple *forte* with a modified reprise of the first theme heard at measure 5 in the piano of the "Allegro barbaro" movement.[72] The recollection of earlier material is an instance of Ornstein's nod toward traditional principles—in this case cyclic ones—that are typical of the genre. At measure 165, *Piu mosso*, a quarter note at 152 doubles the quarter note at 76 that begins and ends the movement. The melody that circles round and round in the piano and first violin, however, keeps even this momentary musical flare up in check. One never senses that the movement will take off on a more aggressive tack. By measure 171 Ornstein indicates *Poco meno mosso* and a *diminuendo* that disappears into *pianissimo* at the end of measure 172.

As in the first movement, thematic material in the second favors certain intervals: in this case seconds, rising minor thirds, and tritones. Ornstein's melodies fall away as they reach their ends or rise and stop before achieving a strong close. In measure 6, for example, as the first violin and cello rise from B♭ to linger indefinitely upon a C♯—there is a fermata—Ornstein introduces both a gesture (the rising augmented second, enharmonically a minor third), and the pitch C♯ that will ultimately prove significant in the movement.[73] But identifying one pitch as more important than others does not signal any embrace of a traditional harmonic plan, even though the movement ends with a C-sharp minor chord. For on the way Ornstein uses pedal tones on D, C, A, G, B, E, and F. He approaches the final long passage in C-sharp minor (starting at measure 173, *Languido*) with an A major seventh chord, and a descending melodic passage that moves from E to D to C♯. Like the first movement, the *Andante lamentoso* is constructed of a series of closely connected lyrical episodes, but with no clear-cut harmonic trajectory; tonal areas seem to change as Ornstein's mood directs. Themes are recalled by different instruments, and in different harmonic settings.[74] In doing so, Ornstein reveals unsuspected qualities of his materials.

The second movement differs from the first, however, in its use of counterpoint. In the first movement, Ornstein shuns the constraints imposed by systematic contrapuntal usage, as in the fugue.[75] But in the second movement, multiple melodic motives occasionally enrich the texture. Ornstein introduces the first such passage at measure 9. Here, the viola softly and tenderly (*con tenerezza*), plays a slow tune that opens on a minor third; it is joined at measure 11 by the first violin with a high, wailing figure that picks up on the same interval. At measure 13, the second violin adds a rhythmic double-stop motive. By measure 21 each of the strings has its own figuration.

Between measures 61 and 63 a different kind of counterpoint appears. Here Ornstein divides his strings into upper and lower voices and has them take turns with two different motives. The lyrical material is so similar that a listener might distinguish a greater difference between the instruments' tessituras than their melodic lines. A similar situation occurs at measures 175–188, where violins and viola alternate with cello to create the illusion of multiple strands occurring simultaneously, even as they take turns being heard. Ornstein uses these quasi-contrapuntal moments to great effect.[76]

Though different in mood, the *Allegro barbaro* and *Andante lamentoso* display the same musical vocabulary and passionate spirit that fired *Danse sauvage*. As with the earlier piece, Ornstein is still most comfortable in a dissonant harmonic idiom, and though aware of traditional structures, he is not confined by them. For Ornstein, however, unrelenting dissonance and ceaseless, hammered rhythms sufficed only so long; the exigencies of extended forms required a different approach.

After the calm of the *Andante's* conclusion, the opening of the third movement, *Allegro agitato*, reestablishes the vigor of the first. For thirteen measures, the piano hammers a *fortissimo*, dissonant arpeggiated figure in a duple meter. Although the second movement ended with a C-sharp minor chord, and the downbeat of the third movement's arpeggio contains a C♯ in a minor second dyad, C♯/D, the alternation between that dyad and B♭ octaves on the second beat and the intervening notes, which emphasize A and D, blurs tonal connection between the two movements.[77] When the strings enter with their unison melody at measure 4 in a triple meter (3/4), a melody that pulls toward A and D, Ornstein maximizes both pitch and rhythmic dissonance. The strings draw their melody from a hybrid scale: the lower tetrachord is built upon major mode, and the upper tetrachord includes an augmented second, suggesting Eastern European scales, but filled in with chromatic passing tones. Identifying this series is complicated further by the divergent spelling of the seventh scale degree as C♯ in the piano part, and D♭ in the strings (the D♭ is probably a notational convenience reflecting the immediate motive that pivots between A and D). Harmonic ambiguity is coupled with rhythmic ambiguity. What had been a straightforward duple meter in the first three measures of the movement is complicated when the string parts enter at measure 4 and are written in triple meter; the polymeter persists until measure 10.

Not willing to be confined by traditional formal requirements, Ornstein refuses to confine his melody within a single prevailing meter.[78] As with the other movements, constant changes in tempo and meter ensure that the music has momentum and contrast. Indications for *animato, marcato, barbaro, con fuoco e molto feroce, risoluto,* and *furioso* are answered by frequent *dolente, molto espressivo, tranquillo e languido, sostenuto,* and *tristamente* markings. Even as the movement rushes forward and pulls back, sometimes ceasing altogether—as it does at measure 211—it brims over with closely related melodic and rhythmic fragments that flow into and out of each other.

Contrapuntal textures are rare; only occasionally do voices overlap or offer different materials at the same time. And then, as earlier, the similarity of the themes is revealed: they sound more like variations or fragments of each other than discrete polyphonic lines. It is not unusual for Ornstein to create what appears a perfect setting for a fugal interlude, but then fail to follow through with the expected counterpoint. Such a moment occurs at measure 155. After a two-measure vamp, the viola enters with a solo line that has all the markings of a fugal subject. Two measures later the first violin and cello play the tune back to the viola. But in the absence of a viola, a countersubject, or a third "entry," the nascent fugue becomes a call-and-response—a moment of timbral contrast rather than a venture into textual density.

Ornstein's Eastern European roots show in modally inflected melodies that drop off as they close, and whose intervals of choice are, as in the first two movements, major and minor seconds and thirds. The overall unity of the *Quintette* is driven home by the prominent reappearance of the main theme from the first movement in the third movement. At measures 143–155 all strings join *fortissimo, Animato espressivo* to recall the defining lyrical theme of the *Allegro barbaro,* which began at measure 193. Indeed, its character is so similar to the themes of the third movement that it sounds comfortably at home there. Beyond similar pitch, harmony, and rhythm, all movements of the *Quintette* also share an approach to writing for the piano that can only be described as virtuosic. Blisteringly fast arpeggios, extended passages of octaves, technically demanding leaps and runs, dramatic crashing chords, and the involvement of the full range of the keyboard all reveal the talents and bravura of a concert pianist who once dazzled his audiences with Liszt.

The criticisms of F. D. Perkins of the *New York Herald Tribune* landed especially hard on Ornstein's third movement. Generally faulting the composer for "expressing what he had to say . . . [but] at too great a length," Perkins targeted the *Allegro agitato* for being "distinctly repetitious, relentlessly iterating an outstanding theme."[79] Ornstein's score shows that, in fact, he dwells in this movement on many closely related melodies and fragments that circle and intertwine, are interrupted and resume, creating together the impression of one constantly resurfacing melody. The *Quintette* is a three-movement sonata that, rather than emphasizing conflict among the different thematic and harmonic areas, makes its expressive mark by approaching redundancy. The similarity of materials within the movement—not to mention among all three movements—together with its length helps to explain Perkins's impatience.[80] It may also explain Ornstein's own admission, long after the fact, that the *Quintette* may be "embarrassingly overcharged" and "parochial" in its rhetoric.[81]

The *Quintette* has been compared to Ernst Bloch's Quintet for Piano and Strings written in 1923, and anyone listening to the two pieces will hear similarities.[82] While acknowledging few contemporary composers, Ornstein did respect both Bloch and Stravinsky and expressed appreciation for the former's *Schelomo*, a work for cello and orchestra written in 1916. Stravinsky's influence can be heard in the third movements of both quintets. At Ornstein's *Con fuoco e molto feroce* (mm. 165–175), hammered *fff* chord clusters in the left-hand piano part provide a forceful backdrop for a passage of octaves that doubles and fills in the second violin melody. The dense texture, circumscribed tune, and pulsing patterns recall Stravinsky's "Dance of the Youths and Maidens" and "Dance of Abduction" from *Le Sacre du printemps*. Bloch's third movement, *Allegro energico*, is replete with equally bounded melodic fragments and a similar rhythmic impulse. Starting at the *giocoso* marking, and especially where trills in the piano's left hand create a whirling background for the tune carried by violins, cello, and the pianist's right hand, the movement is infused with unrelenting Stravinskian energy and spirit. While showing the influence of the Russian master, however, both composers remain true to themselves. Ornstein is less committed to regular meters than is Bloch. Juxtaposing measures of 4/4, 5/4, and 6/4, Ornstein bends materials and swerves from one mood to another as he chooses. With extended passages in a single meter, and a preference for regularly placed accents, Bloch's music is squarer and more predictable in the way it creates momentum. In mood and tempo, Ornstein's three movements resemble Bloch's *Agitato*, *Andante mistico*, and *Allegro energico*: a standard scheme for a three-movement work in the tradition of the sonata. Modally inflected melodies in both suggest a shared experience of Eastern European sounds. That the two works were compared now seems inevitable.

Nevertheless, the differences between them should not be underestimated. Bloch's work is characterized by many disjunct melodies, straightforward rhythms, lengthy scalar passages in the piano, clear, dominant-tonic cadences, and assorted special effects in the strings: harmonics—both natural and artificial, *pizzicato, col legno, con sordino, sulla tastiera,* and *sul ponticello*. The strings are also asked to play quarter tones above and below the indicated notes. In contrast, Ornstein's piece calls for only one harmonic (the first violin's final note at the end of the third movement); the strings use mutes and play *pizzicato* in the *Quintette*, but there are no instances of what have come to be called "extended techniques." But Bloch is clearly after such effects; at one point as he instructs the pianist to sound "like an exotic bird."[83] Another difference is that Ornstein's piano writing is much more virtuosic. On many occasions Bloch's pianist is asked to play relatively simple accompanimental figures, long series of literally repeated chords, passages of block chords, and open octaves. Often the fast tempi make figurations challenging, but on the whole they fall well within the capacities of a pianist with a solid technique. Ornstein's *Quintette*, on the other hand, requires a pianist with the composer's own speed and facility at the keyboard: it is demanding in the extreme.

Whether Ornstein heard Bloch's Quintet, which was premiered in New York City at the Klaw Theatre in 1923, or knew the work through some other means is not known. Given his admiration for Bloch, it is likely that he did. It seems only natural that Ornstein wrote a quintet, given his close ties with string players and his own career as a performer. Elizabeth Sprague Coolidge's commission gave Ornstein an opportunity to ply his compositional skills, to keep his name in the public consciousness, and to showcase his extraordinary gifts as a pianist. In addition it produced a unique contribution by the once-infamous futurist to a traditional genre that had engaged a wide variety of composers in the early decades of the century: Max Reger, Béla Bartók, Gabriel Fauré, Anton Webern, Amy Beach, Ruth Crawford, Ernst von Dohnányi, and Bohuslav Martinů all wrote piano quintets. Holding its own among the various examples of the genre, the *Quintette* for Piano and Strings, Op. 92, proves the vitality of that chamber ensemble in the twentieth century and reflects Leo Ornstein's continuing development as a unique musical voice long after many champions of musical modernism thought he had no more to say.

Ornstein also had two opportunities to write orchestral music. On April 28, 1930, the Walnut Theater, one of the oldest and most venerable theaters in Philadelphia, premiered a new translation of Aristophanes' play *Lysistrata* by Gilbert Seldes. Although Seldes was not in Ornstein's immediate circle during his high modernist days, he was nevertheless at the center of the literary modernist movement. He had been managing editor of *The Dial*, the most important literary magazine of the time, and wrote an early and influential review of James Joyce's *Ulysses*. In contrast to most of his elite contemporaries, Seldes sought to bridge high and low culture in his many essays by championing the importance of figures such as Charlie Chaplin and Al Jolson and the Ziegfeld Follies. A new theatrical group, the Philadelphia Theatre Association, founded by Horace Howard Furness, Jr., chose Aristophanes' bawdy and challenging work as their first production. For incidental music they turned to Leo Ornstein, a local musical celebrity, who was happy to oblige. The play itself was a success, although the Philadelphia audience seemed "dubious about its propriety."[84] After more than forty performances in Philadelphia, it opened in New York, where it received at least 204 performances. Seldes, commenting on its success, observed that it had a longer run than any classic, or of any play of Shakespeare, and that it had been seen by 225,000 people, more than the entire city of Athens when it was written. Ornstein later made an orchestral suite from the incidental music, although the suite to our knowledge was never performed.

A second orchestral opportunity arose for Ornstein in 1937. The League of Composers, under a new plan begun the year before to spur interest in American music, commissioned six scores from different composers, each for a specific musical organization. Aaron Copland was to write a piece for the Minneapolis Symphony Orchestra, Colin McPhee for the Princeton University Glee Club, Quincy Porter for the Gordon String Quartet, William Grant Still for the Cincinnati Orchestra, and Leo Ornstein for the St. Louis Symphony Orchestra, under Vladimir Goldschmann. The names of Copland's and Still's pieces were announced as *Statement* and *Kaintuck*, respectively; the names of the others were not, presumably because they had not been composed.[85] For this event Ornstein wrote his *Nocturne and Dance*, which premiered with the St. Louis Symphony Orchestra on February 12, 1937. The piece was favorably received. The anonymous but obviously conservative critic for *Musical Courier* was relieved that Ornstein, the former "bad boy of American music," had mellowed and created a piece "notable for design, instrumentation and melodic interest," and that Ornstein had "apparently sensed the errors of his youthful musical pranks" and was "content to stay within the bounds of reason." As a result he expected Ornstein's future works to be important statements in the realm of musical modernism.[86] What the critic, of course, could not have anticipated was that after the *Nocturne and Dance* Ornstein would go silent for almost thirty-five years.

Ornstein also attempted to continue, sporadically and at different levels of commitment, some performing through the 1930s. The Piano *Quintette* proved especially valuable in this regard, as he performed it at least five more times after the premiere. We have already discussed the premiere on January 1, 1928. Two weeks later, January 12, he performed it in New York in Town Hall, in a concert sponsored by the League of Composers. In 1936 he performed it with the Stradivarius Quartet at Washington Irving High School in New York, and in 1937 returned again with the same group, for two performances in Philadelphia on March 30 and April 12, and in New York on March 31.[87]

Ornstein made a number of other appearances in the 1930s. On April 11, 1931, in another concert in New York sponsored by the League of Composers, he premiered his *Six Preludes* for Cello and Piano, with Alexandre Barjansky, the cellist for whom Bloch wrote *Schelomo*. He repeated this performance, again with Barjansky, on November 16 of the same year, in a concert in Town Hall sponsored by the Beethoven Association. Then in 1933 Ornstein appeared in Town

Hall, in a solo recital billed in the *New York Times* as "Leo Ornstein, Pianist, Appearing at Town Hall after an Absence of Four Years."[88] The critics observed a different Ornstein, "more the musing poet than the embattled warrior," and referred to his sensitive playing which "delighted the feminine element in his audience" with his "gorgeous tonal coloring and silken beauty of legato playing." The *Musical Courier* critic did feel that as a pianist he still deserved a following. It should be noted that except for Ravel's *Gaspard de la nuit*, which had by then become something of a proving ground for pianists, Ornstein played a traditional repertoire. None of his own works appeared.

Noting Ornstein's four-year absence, Olin Downes quoted an advance notice, presumably by an agent, in which the reason for Ornstein's absence was said to be because of health. Ornstein did go through a difficult bout of sciatica in 1929 or 1930, but other than that there is no record of health problems.[89] Neither was the claim of a four-year absence accurate. Even if we discount the appearances with Barjansky, Ornstein was scheduled to perform a solo recital at Washington Irving High School in New York on November 11, 1932.[90] When Ornstein appeared with the Stradivarius Quartet in 1937, much the same tack was taken; there a program note reads, "Leo Ornstein, Pianist-Composer, has returned to the concert stage after spending several years in composing."

Ornstein seems to have made a major attempt to revive a concert career in 1937. By 1936 he was restless, unable to remain within the harness that teaching demanded of him. Pauline confessed to Waldo Frank, "We have been submerged by teaching to such an extent that Leo has at last rebelled and decided that he actually wants to concertize next winter. No further comment is needed. . . . School and University schedules are not to be altered and one becomes a good deal of a prisoner."[91] Toward this end Ornstein acquired a New York agent, Joseph Mann, who placed a large advertisement in *Musical America* that Ornstein was accepting engagements: "Leo Ornstein, Pianist-Composer," "Now Booking—Season 1937–38."[92] If any concerts came of this effort, information about them has not surfaced.

At this point the trail ends. Ornstein to our knowledge never appeared again in public. What happened and why is a mystery. He composed little until the 1970s, and except for a few letters written to students of the Ornstein school, and a handful of other documents, no evidence of the Ornsteins between then and the 1960s exist. What we know about those years we know from the family, particularly their son and daughter, Severo and Edith. Their memories are important, but they were at first children and later observers, as they went their own ways to lead their own lives. Leo's and Pauline's professional world remains a box sealed as tight as the shell that they build around themselves. It reopened only when the world began to rediscover Leo Ornstein in the 1970s.

8 ||| Return from Oblivion

By the 1960s Ornstein's withdrawal from the American musical world was complete; he had been virtually forgotten. After Ornstein's own last performance playing his *Quintette* with the Stradivarius Quartet in 1937, Ornstein's music simply stopped being heard. Between 1937 and 1974 we have found only one performance of Ornstein's works, outside of a few by students at the Ornstein School of Music.[1] On January 23, 1949, the League of Composers sponsored a special tribute to Paul Rosenfeld, who had recently died. The program highlighted composers whom Rosenfeld had discovered and brought before the public in his writings, and for this concert Grant Johannesen played Ornstein's *Three Moods*, one of his early radical pieces. In spite of Henry Cowell's enthusiasm for the piece—"the more carefully wrought music of the other men sounded sometimes sleep-inducing, sometimes nervously insistent compared to the natural exuberance of the *Three Moods*"[2]—there was no ground swell of interest. Ornstein silently, stealthily slipped back into oblivion.

Ornstein's disappearance was gradual. As we have seen, his touring was on again, off again through the early 1920s, as he grappled with his career goals, until in 1925 J.F.P. in *Musical Courier* could wonder aloud, "Isn't it remarkable about Leo Ornstein? Where is he and what is he doing? So much talked about a few moons ago, and now apparently in the discard."[3] Ornstein was not entirely done at that point, with the Piano *Quintette* to follow in 1928 and the *Lysistrata* Suite in 1930, but when Henry Cowell assembled his major retrospective of American composers in 1932, *American Composers on American Music: A Symposium*, Ornstein was prominently and purposely missing. Yet Cowell could still feel his impact sufficiently that he was compelled to explain why he was not included: "His work is not treated in detail here because it has not influenced the general trend since 1920 at the latest, and because since about 1920 his style has become more and more conventional until it can no longer be considered original."[4] For someone like Cowell, as musically inclusive as he was, Ornstein no longer fit the modernist agenda. In his major history of American music, originally published in 1929, John Tasker Howard devoted two pages to Ornstein, although in the 1946 revision he observed that "in late years Ornstein has almost dropped completely from view." By the 1960s Ornstein had indeed dropped even from the historians' sights. Gilbert Chase had a brief paragraph on him in his 1955 history of American music, mainly observing that "his useful radicalism has acquired a sort of legendary remoteness," but in his 1966 edition Chase relegates him to a single footnote, an afterthought in a discussion of Henry Cowell's use of tone clusters. In H. Wiley Hitchcock's *Music in the United States*, the other important history of American music to appear in the 1960s, Ornstein's name does not even occur.[5]

Underground, however, Ornstein's memory was somehow being kept alive. When Frank Zappa issued his first album, *Freak Out*, in 1966, he listed people who had influenced him. The list is eclectic, ranging from Henry David Thoreau to Lawrence Ferlinghetti, from Muddy Waters to Charles Ives and Roger Sessions. Included on that list is Leo Ornstein. Zappa was a major fan of Edgard Varèse and Igor Stravinsky, but beyond that his knowledge of classical music was more than limited. Where he might have heard of Leo Ornstein in 1966 remains a puzzle.

Zappa was not alone, however. Vivian Perlis, who had founded the Oral History American Music project at Yale University in 1969, had people familiar with early American musical modernism ask her, "Whatever happened to Leo Ornstein?" "Whatever happened to Leo Ornstein?" had become a fifty-year mantra. Harold Schonberg repeated it again in the *New York Times* in 1976, although this time he put it in the pluperfect: "Whatever had happened to Leo Ornstein?"[6] In this article Schonberg acknowledged that Ornstein was once the great hope of American music.

In this atmosphere Pauline Ornstein began her own crusade to restore her husband to the public eye. She had made an earlier tentative attempt in 1950 when she sent a telegram to the Library of Congress asking for a copy of the score to the Piano *Quintette*, with an eye to publishing it, but nothing seems to have come of that effort.[7] Pauline fervently believed Ornstein to be a major composer, at one point comparing his fate to that of Bach. She did not want Ornstein to have to wait, however, until after his death to be rediscovered. By 1970, acutely aware that they were approaching eighty years of age, and certainly having no inkling that he would live another thirty years, she felt compelled to make a push to put Ornstein's name once again before the public. She explained, "I feel there is a great need for action before we vanish from this life."[8]

Pauline may have been motivated by her son Severo's attempt to interest the musical world in Ornstein. On January 5, 1967, he wrote to Elliott Carter asking for advice regarding the "status of my father's music which seems in considerable jeopardy of sinking into complete oblivion." Severo admitted that as an engineer the world of classical music promotion was essentially foreign to him, but he believed strongly in the quality of his father's music, particularly that recently composed, and recognized that someone dedicated to the task "of assembling and annotating" the oeuvre would be necessary. Severo felt he could perform that service, but beyond that was not sure where to begin, and hoped that Carter would "know avenues of which I am totally unaware."[9]

Severo has no memory of a reply and in the near term did little to follow up, although as we will see his efforts to assemble and annotate would prove decisive in the 1980s. His father's music had long been on his mind, however. Bonnie Hampton, who knew Severo when he was a graduate student at the University of California, Berkeley, and she was an up and coming high-school cellist active in chamber music circles remembers that Severo held his father's music almost in awe. Although Severo did not pursue the promotion of Ornstein's music at this time he may have planted a seed in Pauline's mind. In the letter Severo indicates that he had discussed the situation with his parents, and "if I can propose a scheme whereby something constructive can be done I think I could at least enlist cooperation in organizing the material, procuring names, approximate dates etc." Leo in this regard was useless: "my father himself exhibits utter indifference outwardly and has not raised a finger to help matters." Pauline, however, was motivated.

Pauline took a less direct and ultimately more fruitful approach. She engaged her nephew, Peter Ornstein, the son of Leo's older brother Manus and his wife Henrietta. Manus was the one member of the Ornstein family with whom Leo remained relatively close throughout his life. Peter was born in 1928, making him one year older than Edith and two years older than Severo; the cousins knew each other. After graduating from New York University with a degree in mathematics, Peter held several executive positions in media: in advertising at the Katz Agency and as operations manager of WNBC-TV, NBC's flagship station in New York. He then joined Merrill Lynch Inc., eventually becoming Vice President for Corporate Development. He lived in Greenwich, Connecticut, and his passion was sailing. He was a board member of the Indian Harbor Yacht Club, as well as a member of several other yacht clubs, and with his wife Barbara he frequently participated in races in the New York–Connecticut area.

Peter Ornstein was thus well positioned socially and through contacts in both media and finance to assist Pauline in bringing Leo's compositions back into the public eye. In addition Pauline had already been in contact with Peter regarding a book manuscript that she wished to publish. On June 26, 1968, she wrote to Peter asking him to read through several chapters of a monograph, "What Is Music," to get a lay opinion of its worth. She added that Leo was no help at all, thinking "that it is an absurdity for an old lady of 76 with no training or experience in writing to suddenly break out in a book." There were other advantages to interesting Peter in the book: Donald Hammonds, who was Vice President of the College Division of the publishing house Little, Brown and Company was the cousin of Peter's wife Barbara. So Peter had connections in the publishing as well as the media business.

Pauline's manuscript is likely derived from the lectures she gave at the Ornstein School of Music, as in the letter to Peter she refers to having lectured for

years on the subject. The manuscript itself is an abstract inquiry into the nature of music and why it creates an aesthetic effect. In it she attempts to buttress her argument with material from physics and music history. The thinking is naïve, in many cases mistaken, and suggests that at least in this area of intellectual investigation Pauline's hold on reality is at best tenuous, a point confirmed in 1981 when she admitted how she and Leo were "completely out of touch with things."[10] The manuscript was eventually sent to Hammonds and reviewed by Little, Brown. Hammonds rejected it, politely, on the grounds that he perceived little market for it as a textbook. What Hammonds did not send to Pauline was the expert review of the manuscript, which was scathing. The reviewer noted that it was "disorganized, repetitive and unfocused," and that "it would require heroic editing." Beyond such matters of editorial detail, however, the reviewer characterized the scientific material as not only well known, but as presented in the manuscript, "simply wrong." The historical material fared even worse. Calling it "hopeless," the reviewer elaborated "my notes on this begin with 'bunk' and end with 'intolerable.' The author knows nothing whatever of the history of music." The reviewer did give a glimmer of hope, however, suggesting that the "the author—perhaps with some skilled assistance" might embed her reflections on the nature of music into an autobiographical account."[11]

Hammonds picked up on the latter comment and suggested to Pauline that a "different rendering of the material," along the lines of a set of reminiscences, might be useful. This would by nature turn the subject more to Leo. Pauline took Hammonds's advice and began her *Reminiscences*, which although never completed, have helped at least these authors in filling in details of the Ornsteins' early life together.

Having more or less abandoned her effort to get the book published, she turned to promoting Leo's music. Her plan was to contact Roger Hall, Director of the Red Seal Division of RCA records. Red Seal was the name for their classical catalog. Remembering that Peter had at one time been at RCA, she him sent a draft of a letter to Hall, asking for his advice about its appropriateness. In the draft she predictably argues for Ornstein's importance, stressing his radicalism and atonal primacy in early-twentieth-century modernism. The letter is a curious blend of historically accurate argument and naiveté. Her strong and somewhat exaggerated sense of Ornstein's place in what she calls the "complacent post-Wagnerian" era of the early twentieth century is undermined by volunteering to send Hall old clippings confirming Ornstein's place in history and some student tapes of Ornstein compositions. There is a somewhat vague offer of a "monopoly in the form of some exclusive contract which should be of great value once publicity takes advantage of the life story inherent in this whole situation." She closes by offering to send copies of the scores for the Piano Concerto and the *Quintette*.

Pauline also mentions to Hall that "serious musicians all over the world still write asking where his works can be contacted." How much and how widely dispersed these queries were is not known, but at least one such letter has surfaced. On October 1, 1969, Jack Behrens wrote to Ornstein that he had come across Martens's biography, and this had spurred him to examine Ornstein's *Poems of 1917*, Sonata for Violin and Piano, Op. 31, "Two Impressions of Notre Dame," and *Three Preludes*. Behrens, who was then working on a degree in composition at Harvard University, lamented the absence of recordings and expressed interest and curiosity in what Ornstein had done recently and some of his ideas on recent musical developments.[12] Since this letter survived only because Pauline sent it to Peter Ornstein, how many similar ones Pauline and Leo disposed of will never be known.

Peter indicated that Roger Hall "indeed is your man." More than that, however, Peter contacted an old friend of his, Oliver Daniel, who would prove crucial to subsequent events. Daniel, a composer, was also head of the Composer's Division at Broadcast Music International (BMI) and on the board at Composers'

Recording, Inc. (CRI) a company founded in 1954 to produce recordings of contemporary composers, where, along with Otto Luening and Douglas Moore, he had been one of its founders.

As with Jacob Titiev in the 1900s and in 1915, once again a relative came to Ornstein's aid to rescue him from oblivion. In this case the rescue occurs in spite of Leo, as Pauline makes clear to Peter, "I can't discuss it with Leo because he starts from the premise that it is useless."[13] Leo's comment suggests that he had tried it before, and possibly he was remembering the 1930s, when he did at least make some effort to resuscitate a foundering concert career.

Pauline enlisted Severo at this point, to assemble the scores of the *Quintette* and the Piano Concerto and send them to Peter, which he did on October 1, 1969. But Pauline seems to have decided that Peter was her best shot at restoring Ornstein to the place in music history that she thought he deserved. Severo was going through a difficult period, involving both family- and job-related issues. Later Severo became the primary supporter of the Ornstein legacy, doing more than anyone, but at this point he was involved because Pauline had begun to leave manuscript copies with him in Boston, where he lived at the time.

Severo confirms that Leo "felt that the quintette contains some of his best writing although somewhat less radical in tone than the concerto. The [*Lysistrata*]suite is probably a middle ground." Significantly at this time none of the earlier radical pieces, which earned Leo his notoriety and "made me famous," are mentioned. Clearly Pauline with Severo's concurrence was looking at large multi-instrumental works. Severo mentioned that he would be copying tapes for Peter over one weekend, something of a puzzle, since there had been practically no performances of Leo's music since the advent of the tape recorder. Severo was probably referring to an old "home-brew" 78 two-piano recording of the Concerto that Pauline made with Helen Braun, another faculty member at the Ornstein School. Could Grant Johannesen's performance of *Three Moods* in 1949 have been taped? If so, the tape has disappeared; at least it does not appear in the later collection of Ornstein performances in Severo's possession.[14]

Having started the process Pauline had difficulty containing her anxiety. In January 1970 she wrote Peter asking for an update and stressed just how important she considered the initiative: "I cannot rest until these things are really under way and I can feel assured the world will not lose a priceless gift. It came far too near this in the case of Bach and although you may not fully realize it Leo is among the real giants and simply must be available to be heard."[15]

Whether or not Peter shared Pauline's assessment that Leo was another Bach, he had not been idle. In February Pauline finally heard from Peter with a complete rundown of what he had been doing. He had delivered the score of the *Quintette* to Thomas Frost of CBS Records, who showed no immediate interest in making a recording, but did suggest that it be given to the Juilliard Quartet, to "let them play with it." He also met with composer Jack Beeson, who wore several hats at the time. He was with the Ditson Foundation, and he was head of the Music Department at Columbia University. He was also one of three board members of CRI. Apparently Pauline had already been in contact with Beeson, as Peter refers to an earlier letter in which Beeson asked for some compositions of Ornstein's, because according to Peter, "as a teacher he had felt the lack of an Ornstein recording" for courses in twentieth-century music. That request occurred at a time CRI had a cash surplus, which unfortunately "was gone before he could do anything about this." Nevertheless Beeson indicated that if the Juilliard Quartet was not interested in the *Quintette*, he was.

In December 1969 Peter had lunch with Oliver Daniel. Peter had left with him scores for all three pieces, the Concerto, the *Quintette*, and the *Lysistrata* Suite. According to Peter, Daniel indicated he was "VERY interested" (Peter's capitalization), but had to leave for Europe for two months before he had time to examine Ornstein's works.[16] When Peter had first called Daniel in November, Daniel indicated that he had always been interested in Leo and informed Peter that "one of the major foundations is [sic] just set up a fund for the specific purpose of recording historically significant American music," and that he (Daniel) was one of three people on the committee to choose compositions. This sounds like CRI, but the reference to a major foundation may refer to further funding from another source.

Possibly for reasons of caution and not wanting to raise Pauline's hopes too high, Peter did not divulge everything. A hand-written draft of the letter contains further details and reveals a somewhat different picture from the version he finally sent. Frost at CBS Records found the project attractive, but stressed to Peter that he could not commit to anything. Beeson, who was interested in making a recording, was more specific about costs: a 12-inch LP would cost about $1,000 per side, most of the cost being rehearsal time for the musicians. If the Juilliard Quartet could be persuaded to record it, the cost would be reduced because less paid rehearsal time would be necessary since they had already been looking at the piece. Finally, Oliver Daniel, whom Peter refers to as "my friend" in the draft, strongly suggested that it would be to Leo's advantage if he were to affiliate with BMI.

In the meantime Pauline was pursuing other angles. She inquired of Peter whether the Ford Foundation announcement of a large grant for the recording of American composers, which she read about in the *New York Times*, might be an avenue of approach. The grant would provide $7,500 directly to a publisher for an LP of compositions by living composers who were either American citizens or residing permanently in the United States.[17]

At this point chronology becomes fuzzy. With a few exceptions, the only documents that exist are the letters that Pauline wrote to Peter, and these are frequently not dated. CBS Records did show interest in the *Quintette* and wrote directly to Pauline (or Leo) requesting a copy. Pauline "did not want to disturb your people (persons that Peter had contacted, presumably Daniel)," but suggested to Peter that if these people were not going to use the *Quintette* they return the score.[18] All of this makes perfect sense except the Juilliard Quartet supposedly had the *Quintette*, and Frost at CBS (the author of the letter to Pauline?) knew that and was counting on using them in a recording if they were interested. Perhaps Pauline was unaware of the connections. She knew that the Juilliard Quartet had the score, but had concerns about how they might be examining it. They did not have the parts, which would make readings by the ensemble difficult. Eventually the parts were sent, but more importantly Pauline feared that the Quartet would rehearse them without the piano, which would give a very limited sense of the piece, as "the piano is over 50% of the picture and without it only a false impression can be gotten." She also realized that because of the difficulty of the piano part, "no one on earth could read it completely at sight." She then recommended Grant Johannesen as someone capable of tackling the piano part.[19]

Pauline was also looking for other openings. In 1971 Pierre Boulez had just been appointed conductor of the New York Philharmonic, and he came to that position brimming with new ideas, many of which he outlined to the *New York Times* reporter Raymond Ericson on January 28. Pauline saw the article and one paragraph caught her eye:

> During the three seasons he has been engaged by the Philharmonic, the conductor intends to offer a "Perspective" series, stressing one of the great, durable forms in music. This will be the concerto. Next season he will begin with the baroque period, expecting to explore the Mozart concertos the following year.[20]

That was all she needed to hear. Pauline drew a heavy box around that paragraph, and then drafted a lengthy letter to Boulez. The very first sentence of the letter indicates that she did not read the paragraph carefully: "I understand that you plan to have your orchestra present something of a history of the concerto next season." She continues: "There is a piano concerto by Leo Ornstein which has never been published and the existence of which could not possibly be known to you. It has however an important place in the history of this country."[21] To demonstrate her point Pauline includes a copy of Olin Downes's 1925 review from the *New York Times*, in which he called it "so organic, so powerful, and in many places so beautiful," "very intensive music, stark and stripped to its essentials." As if a cue for Pauline, Downes writes, "This concerto should be heard soon again."[22]

Pauline then provides a lengthy account of Ornstein's career, stressing his importance to modernism in the early twentieth century, and curiously placing the date of Ornstein's withdrawal from the concert circuit at "around 1935," and she offers to send Boulez a copy of the full score of the concerto as well as a two-piano reduction.

Pauline received a brief, perfunctory acknowledgement of her letter from Boulez. It reads in its entirety: "Dear Mrs. Ornstein, Thank you for your letter of March 1st, 71. I have read with interest of your husband's career. All the best. Yours sincerely, Pierre Boulez."[23]

Rather than being discouraged by the brevity of the letter or the complete lack of mention of the concerto, Pauline took the reply as a positive sign. On March 13 she wrote to Peter: "The enclosed just came from Boulez. I am writing telling him that you have the score and that he will hear from you."[24] Neither Pauline's second letter to Boulez nor Peter's response survives, but Peter must have realized that this effort was going nowhere. A subsequent undated letter from Pauline to Peter refers to the cost of duplicating the Concerto, a problem Peter may have raised, possibly to discourage her. But this letter also confirms Leo's skepticism of the endeavor—"Leo is so pessimistic in general that he refuses to spend the money on what he feels is a hopeless cause"—as well as Pauline's utter conviction that Boulez would be interested in the Concerto: "I cannot see how Boulez with that Times review can refuse to have the score studied and given serious attention."[25] For the record the New York Philharmonic never did program the concerto; whether Boulez even received the score, much less examined it, is not certain.

Peter's efforts did reach Vivian Perlis, however, who would prove instrumental in the Ornstein revival. In 1968 she was working with the Charles Ives papers at Yale and realized not only the value of interviewing people who had been associated with Ives, but that time was running out, as many were elderly and not in good health. She and her colleague at the time Martha Maas sought out everyone they could find who had an association with Ives, and armed with a tape recorder preserved the thoughts and opinions of many that would otherwise have been lost. These interviews became the basis for the book edited by Perlis, *Charles Ives Remembered, an Oral History.*[26] Perlis admits that at first they did not call it oral history, thinking such involved more the political than the artistic arena, but the Ives experience made her realize that such indeed extended to the arts, and that many other composers merited similar treatment. In 1969 the project, now officially known as Oral History American Music, was founded, with Perlis as Director.

In the past thirty years Perlis has interviewed hundreds of people about dozens of composers, as she has compiled an impressive oral history of American music. When Perlis was asked about her original interest in Ornstein, she indicated that various people had asked, "Whatever happened to Ornstein? And wherever he is maybe you could find him. And you should find him, because he was very important at one time." Perlis goes on to say, "I wanted to find someone who was a piece of history and someone people mentioned and wondered about. That was my motivation in trying to find him and once you get started on something I get really obsessive."[27]

Perlis mentions two people who asked about Ornstein: Goddard Lieberson at Columbia Records, who had been an early supporter of the Oral History American Music project, and Oliver Daniel, who was working with Perlis on the Ives project, helping her locate people who had known Ives.[28] Where Lieberson's interest in Ornstein came from is unclear, but there is no mystery about Daniel, as we have seen. Peter Ornstein's connection with Daniel thus proved serendipitous, as Daniel knew the nature of Perlis's project and could impress upon her the importance of Ornstein as a follow-up possibility after Ives. Daniel could also provide Perlis with a direct contact to the Ornstein family, Peter.

Peter Ornstein was the conduit between Vivian Perlis and Leo and Pauline Ornstein. An undated letter from Pauline to Peter states "just had a call from your friend Mrs. Perlis." A later letter, written in 1975, refers to "your introduction to Mrs. Perlis." Perlis herself later confirmed this connection: "It was Peter who put me in touch with Severo who talked to Pauline and gave me a phone number."[29]

Perlis's contacts with Leo and Pauline began no later than 1971, probably in early 1971. A letter from Pauline to Peter, dated June 19, 1971, states, "we just heard from Mrs. Perlis," and the context suggests that it was not the first contact. This letter thus probably postdates the earlier letter discussed in the preceding paragraph where Pauline refers to a phone call.

From this we can piece together a chain of events: In 1969 Pauline writes to Peter soliciting his help in getting Leo's name back into the public eye. In late 1969 Peter contacts his old friend Oliver Daniel, who subsequently mentions Leo to Vivian Perlis, probably in 1970. Perlis, her interest piqued, is put in contact with Peter, who through Severo supplies an introduction to Leo and Pauline in 1970 or early 1971. Perlis then contacts Leo and Pauline, which inaugurates a long waltz through New Hampshire, Massachusetts, Kansas, and Texas, as she attempts to catch up with the peripatetic Ornsteins. The search was not easy.

Although the Ornsteins still had their home in North Conway, New Hampshire, they were constantly on the go, visiting their son Severo in Boston, their daughter Edith in Kansas, and spending winters on the Gulf Coast. They remained elusive. Perlis made appointments with the Ornsteins in Texas, New Hampshire, and Kansas, but Ornstein canceled them before she could arrive. According to Severo, Leo feared meeting Perlis, at one time in Kansas fleeing out the back door just as Perlis arrived at the front door. Finally in February 1972, it appeared the chase would end. Perlis had an appointment with Ornstein at Severo's home in Boston. Perlis describes the event:

> I arrived at the home of the Ornsteins' son, Severo, in Boston one dark February day with a definite date to interview this mystery man of American music. But once again, Leo Ornstein eluded me. Only a granddaughter was home, and my heart sank as she handed me a note: "Sorry, snow coming. Must return to New Hampshire while we can. Left some things in the dining room."[30]

Perlis had been talking on the phone about Ornstein's manuscripts to Pauline, who was concerned about their being destroyed by mice in the New Hampshire barn where many were stored, and Perlis wanted to convince the Ornsteins that the scores would be better off at Yale University, where they would be properly cared for. She made it clear that Yale would be most interested in accommodating them. Perlis, however, was not ready for what she would find: "On that quiet February afternoon in 1972 in Boston, the stillness and light had the strange suspended quality reserved for the time just before snowfall. There, in Severo Ornstein's dining room, were boxes and cartons and brown paper bags filled with music manuscripts—sixty years of Leo Ornstein's creative life."[31]

Soon thereafter Perlis caught up with Ornstein, and during the 1970s conducted several lengthy interviews with him, including one on videotape. She also became active in efforts to bring Ornstein's name back from obscurity. With Pauline Ornstein, Peter Ornstein, Perlis, and later Severo Ornstein as key players, they began a push on several fronts: to find performers who might program Ornstein's music, to get his compositions published, and to get them issued on recordings.

The first break occurred through Pauline's efforts. Early on she contacted the cellist Paul Olefsky, who had taught at the Ornstein School of Music when he was a student at the Curtis Institute in Philadelphia. Olefsky had gone on to win the Naumburg Prize in 1948 and to become the youngest Principal Cellist in the history of the Philadelphia Orchestra, before leaving to establish a solo career. Through Peter, Olefsky received copies of the Cello Sonata, Op. 52, the cello *Preludes* and the *Quintette*. He decided to program all three for a concert at the Northfield Mount Hermon Chamber Music Workshop and Festival on August 4, 1972. The *Quintette* performance did not materialize, however, probably because as Pauline speculated earlier, "I cannot believe that the pianist can learn all these works in time." In the same letter Pauline could not contain her excitement about the concert: "At last! At last! Something is happening."[32]

Happen it did, apparently to great success. At least that is the word Pauline sent to Peter, even though she and Leo were not there to witness it.[33] We do know that the violist of the quartet that was rehearsing the *Quintette* was sufficiently enamored with the cello *Preludes* that he wanted to transcribe them for viola and perform them in a series of concerts in Europe.

For the concert Leo agreed to write a lengthy statement about recent developments in music, which according to Pauline, "seemed to have created something of a sensation."[34] In one sense Ornstein's statement is a critique of musical experimentalism that was prevalent in the 1970s. Ornstein drew a hard and fast line between experiment and music. He made it clear that he was "not interested in experiment for experiment's sake. I am only interested in music. No experiment, however ingenious can justify itself if it does not produce significant music." Lest there be any question who Ornstein had in mind, he made that clear: "It seems to me that the younger generation is almost exclusively involved in experimentation rather than in producing a good musical composition." Ornstein also observed that he found many of these composers' explanations of what they were doing more interesting than what they did. The rest of the statement is a reiteration of themes that Ornstein had voiced for over sixty years, that he writes what comes into his head, that he has no idea where the ideas come from or even why some music moves people, that he is uninterested in whatever theoretical principles may be behind them, that he certainly works from no particular theoretical premise. In essence music is subjective and any criticism or discussion of it must necessarily be subjective.

For an audience living in the puritanical throes of serialism, atonalism, and other experimental approaches, where composers and critics stressed constantly that one *should* like such music, no matter how troubling or bleak, a statement such as Ornstein's, coming from one of the major radical figures of early modernism, must have seemed heretical. The effect was comparable to the closing hymn in a New England Puritan service: After a minister had railed for three hours about the agonies awaiting "sinners in the hands of an angry God," the emotional release the congregation derived from belting out a hymn at full voice, stretching and bending it as the leader lined it out, all but annihilated the desired results of the service.[35]

Olefsky promised a performance of the *Quintette* within a year, but that did not materialize. The concert did open some other doors, however. At Pauline's urging, the National Endowment for the Arts sent a representative to the recital, who was sufficiently impressed to contact Kenneth Schermerhorn, the conductor of the Milwaukee Symphony Orchestra, who was preparing a series of concerts on American music. Schermerhorn was interested, and the Milwaukee Symphony performed Ornstein's *Nocturne* in 1982.

Once the Ornstein material was at Yale, both Perlis and Harold Samuel, Director of the Music Library at Yale University, began to consider ways to bring it to life. In November 1973, Perlis presented a paper on Ornstein at a conference of the American Musicological Society in Chicago. Wanting music to illustrate her talk, she turned to a young graduate student at Yale, William Westney, who recorded *Three Moods* for her. The paper was an immense success, in part because of Westney's recording: "My talk was a complete success—not because of me but because the music and the material were so interesting." Perlis's modesty about her talk should not shield its importance, however. An expanded version of it was published in *Notes* in 1975 as "The Futurist Music of Leo Ornstein."[36] In this article, the first extended discussion of Ornstein since the 1920s, she brought him back to life for a post–World War II generation. Using sources from the time she described Ornstein's meteoric career in the 1910s and discussed his compositions, placing them into a stylistic context, particularly in relation to twentieth-century modernism. The article contains several musical examples of Ornstein's compositions as well as photographs and early publicity announcements, and at the end Perlis provides a catalog of the Ornstein compositions at the Yale University Music Library. The article was seminal: it reintroduced Ornstein and for years served as the principal source of information on him.

Perlis's work was especially important to William Westney, who remembers vividly the moment that he discovered Ornstein's music: "I was walking down Wall St. in New Haven, encountered Vivian by chance, and she told me how she had recovered these amazing manuscripts that had been stored in a barn for decades. She thought a lot of the piano scores looked really good and urged me to take a look at them. Which I did a few days later and could tell just by eye-balling them how much fun they would be to play, in the same way that Ravel and Prokofief are fun to play. So I felt very lucky that I bumped into Vivian that day."[37] Perlis conveyed Westney's excitement over the discovery: In reference to an upcoming Naumberg competition, she wrote, "His plan is to use Three Moods for his American section, and he is so taken with the music (as I am) that he will play The Moods and hopefully other pieces at Yale soon."[38]

Westney was on the cusp of a major career. He soon was awarded a Fulbright to study in Italy, where he won top prize in the Radiotelevisione Italiana auditions, followed by first prize in the Geneva International Competition. Since then he has concertized in both Europe and the United States.

Westney was featured in two of the most important events of the Ornstein revival, the first modern recording of Ornstein's music, and the revival of his Piano Concerto, at Yale University on December 11, 1976, in celebration of Ornstein's eighty-fifth birthday.[39] For the latter Westney joined the Yale Symphony Orchestra under the direction of C. William Harwood. To Pauline the Concerto, along with the *Quintette*, had been the major pieces upon which the Ornstein revival rested, and after several abortive attempts it was coming to fruition.

The performance generated considerable publicity: it was one of several events that spurred Harold Schonberg to feature Ornstein in a lengthy article in the *New York Times*, "A Musical Futurist Rediscovered."[40] Schonberg's opening line dramatically put Ornstein's career into perspective: "In the beginning—before Aaron Copland, before Henry Cowell, before Virgil Thomson—there was Leo Ornstein. Ornstein was the first publicized American avant-gardist composer."[41] Perlis's article had brought Ornstein into the consciousness of the musical-scholarly community. Schonberg's article, which detailed his career and included a lengthy telephone interview, ended Ornstein's oblivion for the entire American musical world.

Schonberg followed up with a detailed review of the performance itself. For those who had either missed or forgotten his earlier article, Schonberg recapped some of Ornstein's life and career, but he was only lukewarm about the Concerto. He himself took a modernist position, expressing concern that it "looked backwards as much as forward" and wondered whether a dichotomy to compose works such as the Concerto and the Piano *Quintette* along with "wild and propulsive dissonance" "may have accounted for its rapid disappearance [from the repertoire]." Schonberg praised highly Westney's performance, although he was less effusive about the piece. He saw it as a period piece, not something that he expected to enter the repertoire.[42]

Schonberg's discussion of the Concerto does touch on one of its weaknesses. Like the *Quintette*, it is eclectic. It has echoes of Eastern Europe, Russian Romanticism, some Debussy, some Scriabin, spiked with American modernism. It is essentially episodic, juxtaposing sudden changes in mood and tempo with little or no transition. Ornstein's lyrical melodic gift is apparent, as is his prodigious virtuosity. Like many virtuoso concerti, there is little let-up for the pianist, and at times the solo part overwhelms that of the orchestra. The real reason that the Concerto is not musically the success of the *Quintette*, however,

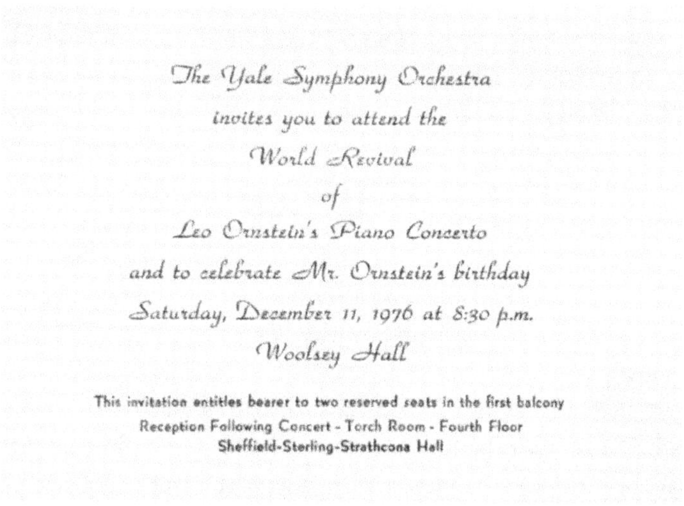

*The Yale Symphony Orchestra
invites you to attend the
World Revival
of
Leo Ornstein's Piano Concerto
and to celebrate Mr. Ornstein's birthday
Saturday, December 11, 1976 at 8:30 p.m.
Woolsey Hall*

This invitation entitles bearer to two reserved seats in the first balcony
Reception Following Concert - Torch Room - Fourth Floor
Sheffield-Sterling-Strathcona Hall

FIGURE 8.2. Piano Concerto revival invitation.

is less that Ornstein could not control the materials formally for a large work, but that he tried too hard to do so. The *Quintette* succeeded precisely because he allowed his musical instincts full rein. As the composer himself admitted, "The *Quintette* is not a polite piece." Ornstein's formal shortcomings in the *Quintette* are compensated by the emotional exuberance of his imagination. He does not allow himself that freedom in the Concerto, and consequently a hesitancy is apparent that Ornstein's own innate musical spontaneity could not overcome.

Meanwhile events were stirring on the West Coast. Independent of Peter Ornstein's and Vivian Perlis' efforts, Charles Amirkhanian at radio station KPFA in Berkeley, California, had discovered Ornstein and was planning an extended program based on his findings. While a student at Fresno State College Amirkhanian's sister had given him a copy of George Antheil's autobiography *Bad Boy of Music*, which mentioned Ornstein.

"Up to that point I hadn't heard a note of either composer [Antheil or Ornstein]."[43] But Amirkhanian was intrigued. He eventually found recordings of some of Antheil's music in San Francisco, where Amirkhanian had gone to graduate school at San Francisco State. Soon after starting work at KPFA he was able to contact Antheil's widow, which led to an Antheil revival program in 1970, followed by one on Dane Rudhyar. For the Rudhyar program Amirkhanian had a young pianist from Los Angeles, Michael Sellers, perform. Buoyed by the success of the program, Sellers suggested some other composers of the early twentieth century, such as Ornstein or Ruth Crawford. Amirkhanian remembered Ornstein from Antheil's autobiography, and to his surprise, he discovered a number of Ornstein's published scores in the University of California, Berkeley library, which he sent Sellers. Even more surprising Sellers received a letter from Temple University that Ornstein was still alive. Through Gilbert Chase (the exact route is not clear), Amirkhanian was put in touch with Vivian Perlis, who supplied Ornstein's New Hampshire phone number. "So I called, and I said, Hi, I'm preparing a memorial program about you, and I see you are not dead."[44]

On December 11, 1972, Amirkhanian aired a special one-hour program on Leo Ornstein, on KPFA, entitled "A Tribute to Leo Ornstein." The program, designed to celebrate his eightieth birthday, contained a lengthy biographical narrative, mostly taken from Martens, extended excerpts from telephone interviews with both Leo and Pauline that Amirkhanian had conducted five days previously, and featured a complete performance of the *Poems of 1917* by Michael Sellers. This may have been the first complete performance of this work; Ornstein played only individual selections when he was concertizing, and to our knowledge no one else had attempted them publicly. The program represented a major breakthrough in the Ornstein revival. It was the first time ever that Ornstein's music had been heard on the radio, and the first time since the 1930s that Ornstein's music was presented and discussed in any length and depth to a major metropolitan area.

As Amirkhanian admitted, it is difficult to gauge audience reaction to a radio program: "With radio you tend not to get much reaction until years later you run into people who say they remembered something, but not many people take the effort to write. If you do something stupid you'll hear from them, but if it's good, maybe not."[45] Yet the program was sufficiently successful, and Amirkhanian was sufficiently enamored with Ornstein that he programmed several other specials later in the 1970s and 1980s. The most elaborate was a planned appearance with Ornstein in 1988 for a series that Amirkhanian put together, "Speaking of Music," which will be discussed later.

Sellers had grown up in Chicago, graduated from Northwestern University, and studied at the Manhattan School of Music with Rudolf Ganz, a friend of Ornstein to whom he had dedicated *A la chinoise*. Ganz was interested enough in the piece that he performed it often and at the suggestion of Leopold Stokowski made an orchestral arrangement of it. We don't know whether Ganz had mentioned Ornstein to Sellers, but Sellers had by the 1970s moved to Los Angeles, gotten to know Dane Rudhyar, and begun to champion twentieth-century composers. He had made the first recording of Rudhyar's piano music. On May 16, 1974, he gave a recital at the New School for Social Research in New York City. The New School had been a center for modernist musical activity since the 1920s, with Charles Seeger and Henry Cowell both active either in lecturing, teaching courses, or conducting there. The recital featured works by Dane Rudhyar,

Debussy, and Ornstein, including the *Poems of 1917* and *Wild Men's Dance*. Sellers had already performed an evening of Rudhyar's music in 1972 so New York audiences were familiar with his championing of twentieth-century eclecticism.[46]

Sellers continued to program Ornstein, with performances in San Francisco, Washington, D. C., New Haven, and further appearances on KFPA. He also made several efforts to program the Concerto. He contacted Seiji Ozawa, Conductor of the Boston Symphony Orchestra, André Previn at the Pittsburgh Symphony, Gerhard Samuel at the Cincinnati University Conservatory of Music, and Dennis Russell Davies at the St. Paul Chamber Orchestra about performances. Previn, Samuel, and Davies expressed interest, but ultimately no performances occurred.[47]

In June 1974, Severo, still having the Sellers performance at the New School in his ears, wrote to Sellers that Ornstein had just completed his Fifth Piano Sonata, *Biography in Sonata Form*, and suggested that Sellers might want to consider recording it. Sellers was sent the manuscript to examine, and he took an immediate liking to it: "The sonata is indeed tremendous. In many respects it is most remarkable. The sonata is like a juicy actor's part. It has a tremendous range from great brilliancy utilizing the full spectrum of keyboard color and sonority, but it also has great depth and breadth. It is comparable to 'Hamlet' and it works."[48] Ornstein apparently concurred: "It may very well be the soundest piece I have written for piano."[49] Sellers was given the opportunity to premiere it, and the piece was dedicated to him. He did this on June 23, 1977, at the International Festival-Institute at Round Top, a music festival in Round Top, Texas, near Austin, founded by the pianist James Dick. Dick, popular in Texas musical circles, was able to secure sufficient support from local patrons to make the festival into a significant musical event.

The sonata was one of Ornstein's major compositions from the 1970s. It was big, in four movements, and lasted approximately fifty minutes. The four movements were

1. Vigor-Passion
2. Youth's Melancholy
3. Some Flashbacks
   —Spring on the Banks of the Dnieper
   —Foreboding of Childhood's End—Last Moments on the Swing
   —Early Sorrows
   —Far Away and Long Ago (W. H. Hudson)
   —Agony & Ecstasy of Approaching Manhood
4. Metamorphosis

Ornstein stressed that the Sonata was not an autobiography, specifically indicating that such interpretation would be wrong. According to Ornstein it was not about events, in spite of the programmatic details of the second movement: "The 'Biography in Sonata Form' does not deal with events. It presumes to be a work of art, not an inventory of incidents. It does deal with self, but only to the extent that we cannot escape ourselves. The past here is sensed through a mist, a haze, or curtain of time which erases all but intangible feelings. These can linger long after the events themselves may be almost forgotten." To Ornstein the Sonata was "a music interpretation of an imaginary life, probably a composite of many lives."[50]

In spite of Ornstein's disclaimers it is difficult not to notice autobiographical connections, be they as specific as the banks of the Dnieper, precisely where Ornstein spent the first ten years of his life. One of the most traumatic events in Ornstein's life was his journey to St. Petersburg to begin study at the Conservatory at age eleven. Ornstein not only left his family, to whom he was close, but his entire culture: he moved from the small-town world of the Jewish Pale to the thriving city of imperial Russia. In the world of nineteenth-century czarist Russia, Ornstein was cut off from all that he had known except the eighty-eight keys of the piano. One can, of course, only speculate what metamorphosis the last movement is about; for Ornstein there were many—St. Petersburg, immigration to America, discovery of his modernist style, heady success in Europe, followed by almost immediate success in America, retraction as a composer, and then disappearance from the world stage.

Yet if we take Ornstein at his word, we can understand the meaning of the sonata. Ornstein provides the clue: it is a late-twentieth-century manifestation of the inner world of W. H. Hudson. Hudson grew up in the nineteenth century, the son of English immigrants in Argentina. As a young man he returned to England, and many of his writings are about life in South America. The past, however, is viewed through a hazy mist, of a world far removed from Victorian London. The area that is now Uruguay, where his family lived, did not become the British colony that English settlers such as Hudson's father believed it would, and much of Hudson's writing is about a world that was lost. His first important work, usually called *The Purple Land*, fully titled, *The Purple Land That England Lost*, establishes these themes, as does his autobiographical memoirs to which Ornstein specifically refers, *Far Away and Long Ago*. Significantly Hudson's memoirs came out in 1917, just as Ornstein was undergoing his own identity crisis. Ornstein could easily relate to the sense of dual or even multiple identities that Hudson wrote about, as he could the sense of loss and distance from a world that remained only in a veil of memories and feelings. Like many Jewish immigrants

Ornstein seldom talked about his life in Russia, but like many Jewish immigrants the world that no longer existed, literally after the Russian Revolution, was never quite forgotten. Even in old age, to a man in his eighties, childhood on the Dnieper River evoked memories and pangs of ecstasy and sorrow.

A third independent front in the Ornstein revival opened in New York and Boston. Marthanne Verbit, who had studied at Boston University, the Eastman School of Music, and Juilliard, made an immediate splash in 1971 when she appeared in an Alice Tully Hall debut in an all-Scriabin concert, followed by a repetition of the recital in Wigmore Hall in London. The Boston-based artist quickly gained a reputation as one who played out-of-the-ordinary twentieth-century music, which was soon further confirmed when she became interested in the music of Cyril Scott. In reading about Scott's music she came across the name Leo Ornstein and was curious. Finding virtually no Ornstein music available she turned to Donald Garvelman, "the provider of offbeat piano music, for those pianists interested in offbeat music." Garvelman was the publisher of Music Treasures Publications and owned an extensive collection of piano music. "I met him when I was playing all Scriabin and he helped a lot. I called him up and said, "who is Leo Ornstein," and he said "ohhhh."[51] From Garvelman Verbit obtained a copy of Ornstein's Fourth Sonata, which she soon had ready for performance.

The Scriabin concerts landed her a recording contract with Genesis, who had heard a tape of Verbit's Scriabin's recital and was interested in her doing an LP of Scott. The Genesis contract called for her to perform a second recording of music of her own choice, and for that she decided to record Ornstein's Fourth Sonata. "Once I learned this piece and recorded it, it was a calling card for me," and she programmed it frequently. Her first performance was at KFPA, in a program Charles Amirkhanian put together. Amirkhanian knew people at Genesis Records, and he had played Verbit's Cyril Scott recording; he asked Verbit to come out and play something live for his programs. "I played the Ornstein at the time because I had just learned it and was going to record it."[52]

While we can trace a connection from Pauline to Paul Olefsky and from Pauline to Peter Ornstein to Vivian Perlis to William Westney to the Rothko and Ford Foundations, Charles Amirkhanian's interest, the involvement of Michael Sellers, and Marthanne Verbit's discovery of Ornstein seem to have occurred totally outside this loop. There was a spontaneous eruption of interest in Ornstein's music in at least three places, at Yale with Vivian Perlis and William Westney, on the West Coast with Charles Amirkhanian and Michael Sellers, and in New York with Marthanne Verbit, and all led to multiple performances, recordings, and publicity. Connections were made: Amirkhanian and Verbit met each other, everyone met Perlis. Ornstein's time, it appeared, had come.

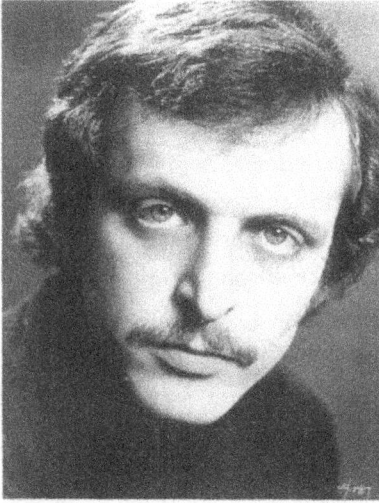

FIGURE 8.3A, B, C. Three pianists important to the Ornstein revival: William Westney, and Marthanne Verbit, top. Michael Sellers with Leo Ornstein, below.

The paths of Verbit and Westney crossed in one important event that occurred in New York, the Ninetieth Birthday Concert in honor of Ornstein at Merkin Hall on December 11, 1982. Yale University sponsored the concert, with the Head of the Music Library, Harold Samuel, and Verbit jointly producing it. The idea itself seems to have come from Marthanne Verbit. She had given the New York premiere of Ornstein's Fourth Sonata the year before in a recital in Merkin Hall that featured the works of mostly early twentieth-century composers,[53] and she had approached Lydia Kontos, Director of Merkin Concert Hall, and the publicity firm of Woerner/Bobrick Associates about the concert. She had also taken the initiative to involve Westney and the violinist Daniel Stepner, who had secured other string players.[54] Merkin demanded an extensive publicity commitment for the event, with the consequence that it was heavily advertised and widely reviewed. The program consisted of the *Hebraic Fantasy*, with Stepner and Verbit, the Viola Fantasy No. 1, a piece that according to the program was actually composed in 1920 but only notated in 1980, with Patricia McCarty and Verbit, *A la chinoise, Morning in the Woods*, and the Fourth Sonata, played by Verbit, *Three Moods*, played by Westney, and the Piano *Quintette*, played by Stepner, Dianne Pettipay, McCarty, David Fink, and Westney.

Critics were there in abundance: Andrew Porter from the *New Yorker*, Peter G. Davis from *New York Magazine*, Robert Kimball from the *New York Post*, and two from the *New York Times*, Edward Rothstein and Donal Henehan. Reviewers came to no clear consensus, although all agreed that Ornstein's intuitive, improvisatory, emotional skill was on full display. Porter and Rothstein were troubled by the works' lack of coherence; Porter found the music "undisciplined, derivative, conventional." To Davis "even the most complicated scores have an appealingly direct naiveté and a more improvisatory character," and "Ornstein communicates with a virile voice that sounds like no one else's." Prior to the concert Donal Henehan had written a lengthy article about Ornstein, whose title was reminiscent of Schonberg's some six years before, "An Old Anarchist Returns." Henehan tried to address the chasm separating the assessments symbolized by Porter and Davis. Henehan noted that Ornstein was writing simultaneously with Schoenberg, and that Ornstein represented the polar opposite of Schoenberg, a "composing school that rejected all methodical approaches." Henehan then goes on to associate such a school with the futurists, although he admits that Ornstein's approach had little in common with the futurists proper. Yet Henehan raises the broader question, to what extent should Ornstein's music be assessed on principles of formalism if he rejected them? Henehan himself thought of Ornstein as "a kind of musical Kropotkin working in a society of Lenins."[55]

As part of the increasing interest in Ornstein's music that developed in the 1970s, the multiple efforts to get Ornstein's music recorded were particularly important, for in the world of the 1970s any sustained interest in Ornstein's music needed more than occasional performance on the concert stage. Recordings were critical, and in all three of the principal circles of interest developing around Ornstein, those centered on William Westney, Michael Sellers, and Marthanne Verbit, recordings emerged, although the path to the vinyl disc for the different performers was as varied as the rediscovery of Ornstein himself.

Bringing a recording to fruition involved a particularly complex set of negotiations as funding had to be secured, commitments from recording companies arranged, and performers and recording companies matched. And like the performances themselves, there was no single coordinated attack, but rather recording efforts emerged on several fronts simultaneously, at times overlapping, but mostly completely independent of each other. The path to Marthanne Verbit's Ornstein recording was the most straightforward, as it was a logical step within her contract with Genesis and her emerging reputation as an advocate of twentieth-century music. More labyrinthine was the trail that led to other Ornstein recordings.

In the 1970s there were a number of smaller record companies producing new classical works, Orion, CRI (Composers Recording International), ACE (American Composers Alliance), as well as some of the larger labels such as CBS and Nonesuch. As we have seen, Pauline had originally approached Roger Hall at CBS, who had expressed interest, but ultimately nothing came of that effort. Peter Ornstein had been able to interest Oliver Daniel, who was on the Board at CRI, in recording Ornstein, and Harold Samuel at Yale had determined from Roger Hall, who had joined the staff at Yale University, that ACE was likely to be interested.

For a twentieth-century composer who was not a household name, however, virtually all of the labels expected a subvention, and the first task for all involved was to find money, through private funds or a foundation grant, to subsidize the recording. Here help came from an unexpected source.

In 1970, at age sixty-six, Mark Rothko, one of the premier American painters of the twentieth century, committed suicide. He had suffered a heart attack two years previously and was in failing health. Before he died he set aside $2.5 million to establish the Mark Rothko Foundation, designed "to help mature, elderly painters and sculptors, composers and writers." In an interview in the *New York Times* Bernard Reis of the Marlborough-Gerson Gallery, Rothko's principal dealer, close friend, and Treasurer of the Foundation, added, "We have no ground rules yet, but we envision the fund as a sort of a Guggenheim of older men and women." Reis went on to explain that they expected to disburse $100,000 a year at the beginning, and then gave an address where applicants could write.[56]

The foundation was tailor-made for Ornstein. Whether Pauline saw the article in the *Times* or whether she was informed about the foundation from another source is not clear. Carter Harmon, Peter Ornstein's brother-in-law, apparently knew Morton Feldman, who was the composer on the Board of the Rothko Foundation, and word may have gotten back to Pauline through that route. In any event she seems to have initiated contact in the fall of 1972. That letter has not survived, but a handwritten letter from Theodore Stamos, dated November 18, 1972, clearly a reply to Pauline, asks for more specific information regarding which pieces of Ornstein's that Leo wishes to have recorded, and what the approximate costs would be.[57]

At this point Severo became more involved in the Ornstein revival. On February 28, 1973, he wrote to Stamos, explaining that because of his parents' illness his mother asked him to try and provide the information that the Foundation requested. Admitting that he was a relative novice in this area, he indicated that he was pursuing the cost issue. He confirmed that CRI was indeed interested in doing a recording, and that, although there were a number of pieces that made good candidates for recording, he favored the Piano *Quintette*.[58] Stamos quickly replied that cost information would be helpful, and he also let Severo know that Morton Feldman, "the musician member of the Board," was "most enthusiastic about this project."[59]

Severo worked quickly and by March 23 had put together a list of suggested pieces and an estimate of costs of recordings. He recommended the String Quartet (unspecified as to which, presumably, Op. 99), the Piano *Quintette*, the *Six Preludes* for Cello and Piano, the Cello Sonata (presumably Op. 52), and the *Hebraic Fantasy*. He estimated that a recording could be done by CRI for about three thousand dollars, although he stated that due to extra performers and rehearsals, a recording of the *Quintette* might run six thousand dollars. He also mentioned Schermerhorn's interest in the *Lysistrata* Suite and suggested that a recording of that might be possible.

Severo met with Stamos the following week, and by April 3 the Board of the Rothko Foundation had awarded three thousand dollars to Ornstein for a recording "to be made by whomever your father chooses as best qualified to do it." The question of performers had already come up, as indicated by a letter of March 30 from Severo to Bernard Reis, the Treasurer of the Rothko Foundation, giving contact information for Paul Olefsky and Michael Sellers. Pauline had been in contact with Olefsky about a possible recording of the Cello Sonata, the *Preludes*, and possibly the *Quintette*,[60] and had mentioned both Olefsky and Sellers to Reis. Because of the absence of dates on most of Pauline's letters, the exact sequence is unclear, but before the money was awarded she apparently had written to Reis making inquiries. She had heard from Olefsky and Beeson and Carter Harmon of CRI, wanting to know if money might be forthcoming. She had also been in touch with Orion Records. Reis had apparently suggested to Pauline that a recording include an early work, and for this she was hopeful that Sellers might record the *Three Moods*.[61]

Morton Feldman had also suggested that Reis contact Harmon at CRI to determine if CRI was interested in following through with a recording, pending Leo's approval, and whether CRI would be willing to undertake distribution of the record. Harmon responded positively but was unable to give a definitive answer pending a meeting of the CRI Board within the month.[62]

Olefsky and CRI were interested, the money was there, but the project almost immediately hit a snag. The CRI Board needed to approve the recording, which included examining the score and passing on the content. Complicating the situation was an extended trip to Israel, beginning in May, that Olefsky had planned. There clearly was not time to put the recording together before then, and some question remained regarding the pieces. The three thousand dollars would not likely cover the Quintette, and Leo had suggested the cello pieces instead. Now there was not time for them either.[63] Olefsky proposed that the Quintette recording be done in Israel, but that met resistance from both Pauline and CRI.[64] As a consequence the CRI recording was put on hold.

In the meantime Severo had been in touch with Giveon Cornfield of Orion Records in Malibu, California, which was affiliated with the Yehudi Menuhin Foundation. Due to other commitments Olefsky had decided not to record the preludes, and Severo had contacted his old friend Bonnie Hampton, cellist, and her husband, the pianist Nathan Schwartz, both of whom were teaching at Stanford.[65] Hampton and Schartz had not only formed the Hampton-Schwartz Duo, but were founding members of the Francesco Trio, which had won a Naumberg award. Severo saw them as a nucleus to make possibly two recordings, one of the Cello Sonata and cello Preludes, and another of the Quintette. They were interested, but matters quickly fell apart. Cornfield had offered Severo, as agent for Leo Ornstein, a standard Orion contract, which spelled out the terms of the agreement in considerable detail. Prompted in part by Pauline, Severo entered into further negotiations attempting to clarify many points. With Cornfield's approval he rewrote the contract, which Cornfield accepted in principle, with only minor revisions. Severo then raised further questions regarding whether the contract should be with the composer or the performers, Orion's commitment regarding distribution and promotion, the number of records that would be pressed, how long they would be kept in inventory, whether the original costs covered subsequent pressings, the problem of copyright as the Quintette was not copyrighted (he was in error on that; it had been when Coolidge accepted it), what both wholesale and retail prices would be, and why the added cost of doing the recording in the Bay area rather than Los Angeles.[66]

This was too much for Cornfield. Exasperated he wrote to Severo, "Thank you for your prodigious correspondence. I have come to the conclusion that this project no longer interests me: it is far too complicated for my liking, and for a record that I know will sell poorly, it is simply not worth the effort. Contemporary American composers simply don't sell (the few that do are exclusive with Columbia.) The Orion catalog is certainly not in need of enlargement per se, and I am not in search of an additional headache."[67] Curiously that was not the end of this project, as we will see.

Between Severo's last letter to Cornfield and Cornfield's reply, further bad news came from Bonnie Hampton. The violinist in the Francesco Trio, David Abel, had taken seriously ill with pneumonia, and Nathan Schwartz had developed a bronchial infection. An April recording date was thus out of the question, and then Ron Erickson, the other violinist who was also to perform in the *Quintette*, was due to leave for Europe. Hampton indicated that in spite of these problems she was still interested in making an Ornstein recording. Severo found the entire episode of putting together the pieces frustrating, but he remained determined. Even before these most recent events he had vented his feelings to Hampton: "Christ it's hard to get anything to happen—so much arranging! Oh well—the end product will be worth it."[68]

Another event in the spring of 1975 seems to have turned matters with Orion around and opened up new possibilities for Ornstein. On May 21, 1975, Leo received the Marjorie Peabody Waite Award of the National Institute of Arts and Letters. The award was given every three years to a composer for significant lifetime achievement. The music section of the Institute consisted of thirty-nine members at the time, including Milton Babbitt, Leonard Bernstein, John Cage, Elliott Carter, Aaron Copland, Richard Rodgers, and Ornstein's old student, Andrew Imbrie.

Armed with this award and the cash prize that went with it, Severo wrote back to Cornfield, indicating that in addition to a CRI recording that was part of the award, there was a small cash prize, which he hoped could be used for the Hampton-Schwartz recording. Realizing that he had pushed too hard earlier, Severo suggested a contractual alternative, that Orion sign the contract directly with Hampton and Schwartz, and that he would simply provide the money. This worked, and in the summer of 1975 Hampton and Schwartz recorded the Cello Sonata, Op. 52, and three of the cello *Preludes*; the limitations of an LP recording preventing the entire set from being put on disk.

Cornfield issued one other Ornstein recording in the 1970s, but Severo did not initiate this. Charles Amirkhanian had suggested to Michael Sellers, who had been featured on Amirkhanian's 1972 radio special on Ornstein, that he consider recording some Ornstein music. Sellers then approached Severo in June 1974 about a recording of Ornstein's early piano music. He proposed that he could contribute a "couple of hundred dollars," and if about $700 could be raised, he would discuss it with Orion. Severo felt this was doable.[69] In October Sellers replied that he had been in contact with Cornfield, who expressed interest in the project, although fees had increased, so that Sellers needed $800 from the Ornstein family. Severo quickly agreed, and the project went forward, with Sellers recording the *Poems of 1917*, *Three Moods*, *A la chinoise*, and *Wild Men's Dance*. By early 1976 it had been completed, and the record was released in March.[70]

The Sellers recording did create some consternation within the Ornstein circle. In 1976 Jack O'Brien, a former teacher at the Ornstein School, had seen the Schonberg article in the *New York Times* and reestablished contact with the Ornsteins. O'Brien got in touch with Sellers, Westney, and Perlis and worked to arrange a major concert for Sellers in New York. He also spearheaded a new committee, the Committee for the Rediscovery of Leo Ornstein, and made contacts with musicians and radio producers in the Boston area, attempting to interest Roland Nadeau, Chairman of the Music Department at Northeastern University, and John Beck, Manager of Station WGBH, to produce a documentary on Ornstein.[71]

In spite of O'Brien's work on behalf of Sellers the two became estranged. According to O'Brien, Sellers simply stopped communicating with him.[72] Sellers was at this time completing his Orion recording, and soon an ad for it appeared in *Clavier Magazine*. Disturbing to O'Brien was the address for ordering the LP, the Leo Ornstein Rediscovery Society. O'Brien was concerned that people would perceive the society as supporting one performer over others. Pauline had written to O'Brien of a rivalry between Westney and Sellers, apparently over the Concerto, the *Quintette*, and the *Three Moods*, and warned O'Brien not to involve the Ornsteins in it.[73] O'Brien viewed the committee as central to the Ornstein revival effort and wanted nothing to undermine it: "I think there is a nucleus of a prestigious committee at this point that they would expect the efforts to be directed toward Mr. Ornstein's music. That would mean promoting *all* records and the efforts of the several performing artists who have shown special interest in Mr. Ornstein's music."[74] The committee itself seems not to have survived beyond 1978.

Leo and Pauline had early identified the *Quintette*, the Concerto, and the Cello Sonata and *Preludes* as pieces they most wanted to see recorded, the *Preludes* in part because they "made a big stir at the festival last summer," Pauline referring to Paul Olefsky's performance in 1972. Severo's efforts with Bonnie Hampton, Nathan Schwartz, and Giveon Cornfield had achieved at least part of that goal: the Cello Sonata and some of the preludes were on disc. Sellers had succeeded in getting out an LP of some of the more important early piano music. The Concerto had to wait another thirty years before it was recorded, and then in a two-piano version. The *Quintette* was the first to appear, but the path to the vinyl disc was labyrinthine. At this time Pauline thought the *Quintette* recording could be financed with money she anticipated receiving in a settlement of her stepmother's estate.[75] Pauline's father, Severo Mallet-Prevost, had left his estate to his second wife, Laeta Hartley, with instructions that it was to devolve to Pauline on Laeta's death. Late in life Laeta changed the terms of her will, leaving the estate to one of her nurses. The Ornsteins challenged this change of will on the grounds that Laeta was no longer capable of independent judgment and reached an out-of-court settlement. Whether any money was eventually used for a *Quintette* recording is unclear. Severo believes that Leo would not have allowed it.[76]

After it was apparent that the Juilliard had little interest in the *Quintette*, and the Ornsteins were informed of the Rothko grant, a relatively straightforward plan was conceived: Paul Olefsky, who had considered programming the *Quintette* at the Northfield Festival in 1972 would pull together a group, and CRI would record it, the cost financed by the Rothko money. Olefsky's trip to Israel in the summer of 1973, however, quickly put that idea in jeopardy. Olefsky did express interest in recording it in Israel, but Pauline was not convinced that the idea was a good one. She was concerned whether Olefsky could accomplish it in the time he would be there, and whether the quality of the recording would be good enough for CRI.[77]

Pauline next suggested that Sellers might be interested in the *Quintette* and wondered if he could put together a group on the West Coast. By this time it was clear that CRI was interested in Ornstein's music and had sent an estimate of costs for the recording. Their estimates, however, were based on Olefsky's original plan of preceding the recording with a live performance, which meant musicians' and rehearsal fees would be lower.[78] At the same time Amirkhanian contacted Fred Kameny at Turnabout Records suggesting that they consider having Sellers, with a group from Los Angeles that had recently done the quintets of both Amy Beach and Arthur Foote, record Ornstein's *Quintette*.[79] Turnabout, however, did not pick up the suggestion.

Pauline also believed that the *Quintette* might be recorded through Yale University, which she hoped would receive a grant from the Ford Foundation. As we will see a recording of the *Quintette* did eventually materialize, but not through Olefsky. Even before Ornstein received the check from the Rothko Foundation, Bernard Reis at the Foundation had been in contact with Carter Harmon of CRI records about an Ornstein recording, and Harmon had responded positively.[80] When the Olefsky plans fell through, Perlis contacted Westney and took on the role of co-producer of the recording. She and Westney then engaged Daniel Stepner, who acted as leader of the string quartet. The recording was made June 10–18, 1975, and included Westney performing *Three Moods* in addition to the *Quintette*.[81] It was the first commercial recording of any Ornstein music.

Thus in a period of two years, 1975–1976, Ornstein's music, which had lain virtually unnoticed for forty years, was suddenly available on four LP's, with four different performers. The Ornstein revival had happened primarily because of the efforts of the Ornstein family itself, Pauline, Peter, and Severo, with the enthusiasm of the performers, Westney, Sellers, Verbit, Hampton, and Schwartz, and others who worked actively to promote Ornstein's music, in particular Charles Amirkhanian and Vivian Perlis. Momentum continued into the early 1980s with important milestones noted on the radio and in concerts. Amirkhanian marked Ornstein's eighty-eighth birthday with a special concert devoted to his music at KPFA on December 11, 1980, and on October 20, 1988, an even more elaborate program on Ornstein in his series "Speaking of Music," for which Amirkhanian attempted to have Ornstein on stage, but at the last minute the elderly composer decided the travel was too much. Amirkhanian did arrange a telephone interview with Ornstein, and the program featured Marthanne Verbit performing Ornstein's Fourth Sonata.[82] Earlier Verbit had also organized a live broadcast in Boston for Ornstein's eighty-eighth birthday. The program appeared on Robert J. Lurtsema's popular show "Morning Pro Musica," on WGBH-FM, and had the title "Ornstein Orgy."

Yet in spite of the efforts of Amirkhanian, Verbit, Perlis and others, the momentum of the Ornstein revival seemed to be slowing in the 1980s. Many of the original goals were accomplished: Ornstein's music was programmed in recitals, it was recorded, and it appeared on the radio. Ornstein himself had been recognized with the Marjorie Peabody Waite award. Yet no further recordings had been made since the flurry of activity in the mid-1970s, and Ornstein's music was still difficult to obtain. Peter Ornstein, who had been so instrumental at the beginning, was no longer heavily involved, and Pauline, the first spearhead, was seriously ill and would not live much longer.

Ornstein himself did little to help, and in some cases his reluctance to travel hurt his visibility. In 1988 Lawrence Wescheer of the New Yorker wanted to do a major profile on him and planned to travel by train with Ornstein from Green Bay to San Francisco, where Ornstein was to appear live on the Exploratorum's Speaking of Music series. Wescheer was to write about the trip and about Ornstein. Ornstein had tentatively agreed to appear on the series, and travel arrangements had been made. It was a highly anticipated event. Marthanne Verbit was to meet Ornstein, and a reunion was planned with Andrew Imbrie, as well as the New Yorker profile being written. At the last minute Ornstein declined, however, claiming that travel at his age was too difficult. Amirkhanian, disappointed, agreed to do the telephone interview.[83]

At this point in the Ornstein revival Severo stepped in to fill one of the principal lacunae, the absence of publications. Many of Ornstein's works had been published earlier in the twentieth century by a number of firms, but by the 1970s most of the scores were no longer available. In addition there were many Ornstein pieces, both old and new, that had never seen publication. In 1976 Harold Samuel at the Yale Music Library recommended that Leo sign a contract with Paul Kapp of Joshua Corporation, an affiliate of the General Music Publishing Company, which was associated with BMI, to publish his music. At first the Ornsteins were reluctant: the offer called for Ornstein to turn over one hundred of his pieces to Joshua, and BMI would guarantee to publish eighteen within the next three years. They were concerned that "he was representing himself as the future 'publisher of the music of Leo Ornstein,'" and that "he was only going to publish a few small works but control so many others." Samuel tried to reassure them that indeed both points were true, but that he would be the publisher, and that eighteen works represented a significant commitment in costs and service—music still had to be engraved by hand in 1977—and that they would be better off with that deal than any other offers. In addition Samuel rejected firmly Pauline's suggestion that the Yale Library could act as a clearinghouse for performers interested in obtaining copies of Ornstein's music.[84]

Pauline and Leo expressed further reservations to Severo about the deal, about what a "work" meant, about the problem of control, about whether everything was going to be published, and how it would be published, and Severo expressed concern "that they were somehow letting greed for the big show prevent *any* show from happening."[85] One can probably assume that the issue was less of greed than Pauline's unwavering conviction about the value of Ornstein's music. Sustaining her throughout the efforts to get Leo before the public was the belief that once it was out, there would be a groundswell of demand for it. She saw Ornstein's works as a moneymaker for any publisher, rather than as a significant risk for a composer who still remained somewhat on the fringes of American musical culture.

Samuel and Severo prevailed, and an agreement was reached with Kapp. True to his word Kapp began to publish Ornstein's music, and in 1979 Kapp reported that he had published eleven pieces, including the *Six Preludes for Cello and Piano*, which Leo and Pauline had urged him to print. Kapp also tried to reassure Severo, who had offered to help with the project as Pauline's health was declining, that "I'm proud to say that in the short time we have been associated with your father and mother more has been done in connection with the publication and dissemination of your father's music than has ever been done before by any agency whatsoever."[86]

Kapp also undertook to issue two recordings of Ornstein's music, under the Serenus Recorded Editions, a label that was part of General Music Publishing. He had "pulled together the strands of the Boston recording of the Quartet No. 3," a relatively new piece that Ornstein had composed in the 1970s, the recording of which Pauline had originally financed, but which needed major editing, and Kapp had recorded entirely at his expense the six cello preludes, performed by Italo Babini, cellist, and Elizabeth Parisot, pianist.[87]

Kapp was precisely who Ornstein needed: a publisher willing to take a risk, to invest time and expense to not only print his music, but to promote it through recordings as well as advertising. Kapp even made the trek to visit the Ornsteins in Brownsville, Texas, in 1978.[88] The situation did not endure, however, as Kapp suffered a stroke and then died in 1984.[89] With Kapp's death, General Music Publishing died as well.

At this point Severo took matters into his own hands. He had retired from his position at Xerox PARC in 1983 and had been instrumental in founding the organization Computer Professionals for Social Responsibility. Now he was ready to make "the break with our second careers (as political reformers), and . . . [embark] on a third—which will be the attempted rescue of my dad's music from the obscurity into which he has allowed it to fall, thanks to his perversely reclusive nature."[90] With characteristic Ornsteinien energy, Severo began a blitzkrieg of letters. In one day he wrote letters to Leonard Bernstein, the Foundation for the Community of Artists, Nancy Clark of the American Music Center, Harold Samuel, Yale Music Library, Richard Warren at the Yale Collection for Historical Sound Recordings, Robert Beaser, Elizabeth Ostrow of New World Records, Betsey Foley at St. Norbert College, the Fromm Music Center at Harvard University, and Robert Minkoff, who was connected to the Bay Area Lawyers for the Arts.[91] September 12 is only an example of Severo's determination; he had been sending letters to various people since that January. His purpose was simple: to get "further works published, performed and recorded."[92]

In 1987 Severo began to digitize Ornstein's music. In 1980, while working with John Maxwell, a graduate student from MIT, he developed the first screen-based, interactive music notation program written for computer. Although Xerox did not market Mockingbird, Severo realized the potential of printing music with a computer, and he established Poon Hill Press to publish his father's music.[93] Both Charles Amirkhanian and Vivian Perlis, however, suggested that Severo first contact some of the larger publishers to see if they might be interested in taking on Ornstein. He contacted Schott and its affiliate European American Music, but both indicated that in essence their schedules were full.[94] Poon Hill Press then began by publishing Ornstein's complete piano music in thirteen volumes,

FIGURE 8.4. Severo Ornstein (right), John Maxwell, and Mockingbird. *Photo courtesy the Ornstein family.*

FIGURE 8.5. Leo and Pauline in Brownsville, Texas, shortly before moving to Wisconsin. *MSS 10, The Leo Ornstein Papers, Irving S. Gilmore Music Library, Yale University.*

274 ILL LEO ORNSTEIN

followed by chamber and vocal works, which continues today. Since then Severo has also made much of Ornstein's music available online, including both scores and audio, at the web site of Poon Hill Press (Poonhill.com).[95]

When one reaches their late eighties, life becomes at best unpredictable, and such was the case with Leo and Pauline. In 1979 Pauline fell and broke her hip. This made living in their relative isolation in Brownsville, Texas, difficult, and they decided to move to Madison, Wisconsin, where Edith lived at the time. Severo and Edith packed them up in a Winnebago, and for a time they lived with Edith, then rented an apartment in De Pere (Green Bay), Wisconsin. During those years Edith lived partly in De Pere and partly in Madison. Soon after arriving in Wisconsin, however, Pauline developed colon cancer, and in 1985 she died.

Pauline's death was devastating to Ornstein. "Of course since Pauline died . . . my whole life has been totally shattered."[96] Eleanor Lasee, who cared for Ornstein in his old age, recalled, "he missed her a lot and he talked about her a lot, just that he missed having her there and how much he loved her."[97] For a period of time he quit composing entirely, but soon he bounced back, musically at least, and between the ages of ninety-five and ninety-seven completed two major compositions, his Seventh and Eighth Piano Sonatas. These are both large-scale works, and in one sense summarize his stylistic eclecticism: they cannot be attached to any style, but within their prevailing lyricism they show a tightness of motivic integration that earlier sometimes eluded Ornstein. Like the Fifth Sonata, *Biography in Sonata Form*, the Eighth is programmatic, the program suggesting autobiography. The opening movement is entitled "Life's Turmoil and a Bit of Sorrow," and the final movement more generally "Disciplines and Improvisations." The middle movement, "A Trip to the Attic—a Tear or Two for a Childhood Forever Gone," consists of four short, simple, independent units: "The Bugler," "A Lament for a Lost Toy," "A Half Mutilated Cradle—Berceuse," and "First Carousel Ride and Sounds of a Hurdy-Gurdy." The movement as a whole forms a striking contrast to the more expansive driving virtuosity of the rest of the work. Ornstein himself observed, "Some may object to the middle four Vignettes as an intrusion; others may find them a distinct contrast and relief from the brusqueness of the rest of the sonata."[98] The "vignettes" also suggest that even in his winter years Ornstein remained haunted by his childhood, by the pain felt from the removal from his home in Kremenchug, and his placement in the Conservatory in St. Petersburg. Ornstein's real-life event parallels strikingly that of Charles Foster Kane in Orson Welles's film *Citizen Kane*, and Ornstein's Eighth Sonata may be his own cry, "Rosebud."[99]

After the Eighth Sonata Ornstein continued to compose, but no more large works came from his pen. He did, however, receive further recognition. To celebrate his ninety-fifth birthday, St. Norbert College in De Pere, Wisconsin, held "A Leo Ornstein Festival of Music," featuring performances of *Three Moods* and Piano Sonata No. 4 by William Westney, the *Six Preludes* for Cello and Piano, by Howard Karp, piano, and Parry Karp cello, *Five Songs*, by Seoung Lee Wilson, mezzo soprano and H. Thomas Hurley, piano, *Two Pieces* for Flute and Piano by Helen Schmidt, flute, and Elaine Becker, piano, and the String Quartet No. 2, Op. 99, by the Pro Arte Quartet. The event included a panel discussion, "American Values and the Music of Leo Ornstein," moderated by Vivian Perlis, with Severo Ornstein, Parry Karp, and William Westney on the panel, and Leo Ornstein was awarded a Doctor of Humane Letters by the college.

In 1993 he went into a serious depression, and for over a year was essentially unresponsive. It seemed the end was near, a not unreasonable assumption about a man 101 years old. Yet after a year and a half, he suddenly began talking and communicating with people, as if nothing had happened. Although his composing days were over, Ornstein lived another seven years. He died peacefully on February 24, 2002, 108 years old.

9 ║║║ Modernist Dilemmas, Personal Choices

And so the questions still remain: What prompted Leo Ornstein's unexpected stylistic epiphany? Why did he turn his back on a lucrative and wildly successful concertizing and composing career only to disappear into obscurity? As quoted remarks from early on and interviews from late in his life attest, Ornstein liked fame. He enjoyed attention. He thrived in stimulating company. He came to life in front of a camera. Pauline's summarial statement from the early 1970s that most people in the music profession were "self-inflated and uneducated due to the very nature of their occupations" needs to be read as her assessment and not one articulated by Ornstein himself. Although Pauline often spoke for her husband, and was accustomed to using "we" when voicing opinions, there is nothing in extant documents to suggest Ornstein himself felt such wholesale disdain.

Accounts of Ornstein's 1913 stylistic epiphany differ enough to raise numerous questions regarding exactly what was composed, where, and when. For those who share the modernist value of primacy, this becomes a central issue, but it should not overshadow other, perhaps more important issues. A percussive approach to the piano had been introduced at least two years earlier by Béla Bartók with his *Allegro barbaro*. We don't know whether Ornstein had any opportunity to hear this work prior to his second trip to Europe in late summer 1913. Later on during this trip, however, he played unnamed pieces by Bartók for Calvocoressi's lectures on modern music, along with works of Schoenberg, Debussy, and Ravel. If the percussive focus of *Wild Men's Dance* was not completely new, its level of dissonance and mood of total abandonment were. It is possible that Ornstein's "wild men" were informed by Bartók's barbarians, but even more likely by the Frankfurt Group's focus upon the "dance," and their cry of "energy," which he made his own.

The year 1913 left its mark on more people and places than one young Russian-American pianist-composer. In artistic circles, 1913 was famous for the Armory Show in New York, and in musical circles for the riotous spring reception accorded Igor Stravinsky's ballet *Le Sacre du printemps* in Paris. *Le Sacre* made news throughout the music world. It is almost a certainty that Ornstein, either on his own or through the efforts of Mrs. Tapper, knew of the event. Ornstein's inquiry of Roger Quilter in May 1914 whether the English composer had heard "many of the 'Russian Ballet' performances," and whether he "like[d] the 'Nightingale' of Stravinsky" bespeaks a familiarity with that composer's works a year later.[1] While he would not have had an opportunity to experience the *Le Sacre* prior to composing his own "futurist" works, Ornstein did acknowledge later that Stravinsky was among his favorite composers. Perhaps the world mood was just right to inspire similar rhythmically charged, dissonant music in three different places, England, France, and the United States, simultaneously. Certainly ideas, musical and otherwise, are not the exclusive property of a single individual or region; they often cross borders unannounced.

Almost as quickly as Ornstein became "inured" to his new style (to use his word), he moved away from it. As early as 1915, just after Ornstein's concertizing career took flight and he had become a household name, he left his most dissonant idiom and the aesthetic that would become central to the 1920s ultramodernists: the one that had brought him his initial fame in London in 1914. While audiences clamored for his radical showstoppers for years, *Wild Men's Dance* most especially, Ornstein was already pursuing what he described as a more "expressive" style. Still drenched with dissonances and relentless rhythms, the melodies that had previously just been hinted at in the moments between the crashing blows were now given greater space to breathe. Lyricism came to the fore, and Ornstein luxuriated, sometimes even wallowed, in it. Critics were alternately perplexed and disappointed, a few were grateful. No doubt, those most eager to establish a distinct American musical modernist movement felt betrayed. The boy wonder who had emerged from nowhere to lead their musical charge seemed, just as unexpectedly, to be calling for retreat. If others were unwilling to fall in line with him this time, it wasn't necessary: Ornstein was going to follow his muse, just as he had before.

Ornstein's confession that his Op. 31 Violin Sonata had led him to the edge of chaos appeared to many to be an inadequate explanation for abandoning the cause of the ultramoderns. Although his cutting-edge colleagues had eagerly embraced him when he championed the strange sounds that had come unbidden into his head in 1913, they were not inclined to follow him into a realm that smacked of melodiousness and sentiment, even if in the 1930s and 1940s this is precisely where the larger musical community eventually moved. Romantic lyricism was too closely associated with late German orchestral music, the tone poems of Strauss, the symphonies of Mahler and Bruckner, to be of much use to a group eager to forge a distinct identity. It would be generous to suggest that Ornstein presciently anticipated the limited appeal of extreme dissonance and systematized compositional processes and once again was ahead of the curve in charting a course that lead ultimately to late-twentieth-century neo-Romanticism. But calculation and forethought, especially when it came to aesthetic issues, were not Ornstein's style. For good or ill, he was and always would remain beholden to his intuitive, instinctive approach to composition.

In one sense Ornstein's creative trajectory brought him to a compositional crisis strikingly similar to what Schoenberg had encountered around 1909, as the underpinnings of tonality evaporated and Ornstein's increasingly dissonant works, particularly Op. 31, seemed to him a dead end.[2] Yet while he and Schoenberg briefly found themselves occupying similar stylistic space Ornstein chose a completely different path out of the dilemma that the collapse of structural tonality created. He never wavered in his belief in the importance of intuition, and he firmly eschewed any theoretical framework that might inhibit the free flow of ideas. Likewise he shied away from any intellectual justification founded on science, experimentalism, or mathematical explication, so important to many twentieth-century composers. In retrospect Schoenberg's solution, to ground his activity in a new theoretical system, has become, if not the only path, at least a broad avenue trod by many composers and historians. At the time, however, Ornstein's solution, to elevate intuition and reject system, seemed as viable as any, and a number of composers embraced it to varying degrees, among them Dane Rudhyar, Ruth Crawford, Carl Ruggles, and to an extent Charles Ives.[3]

The fate of composers who chose the intuitive path, however, suggests that it was not viable. Virtually every composer of this school, including Ornstein, had by the 1930s abandoned not only a radical modernism but in large measure composition itself. Admittedly, the reasons composers quit were not purely aesthetic but were in some cases economic, political, and personal. Nevertheless their choices suggest problems inherent in the musical premises on which they worked.

Ornstein's compositional trajectory differs from the other composers of the intuitive school in two ways: First, he moved away from his extreme modernist idiom around 1915, well before most composers had even discovered theirs, and second, benefiting from an amazing longevity, he did return to composition in the 1970s. His solution to this dilemma of musical modernism was also one that few others were prepared to take. Beyond privileging intuition, Ornstein aligned his work with his Russian heritage to provide a justification for a musical style that seemed to eschew many of the tenets of modernism, and he simultaneously challenged the notion of musical progress prevalent in the early twentieth century. Ornstein himself characterized the latter as a move from an "experimental" to an "expressive" style.[4] As a result ultramodern musicians and critics reacted vehemently, setting in motion a series of judgments that in many ways not only sealed Ornstein's historical fate but influenced the way twentieth-century music was valued.

The notion of progress had been integral to American thinking throughout the nineteenth century. It inspired westward migrations and became a source of national pride with the many scientific and technological developments of the same time. In music it affected the ultramodern circle in the United States, resurfaced with particular force after the Second World War, and was embedded in the writing of musical history throughout much of the twentieth century.

In 1926 *Musical America* asked the question: "Has music made any real progress in America? ... primarily I mean has our country advanced in a creative sense?" *Musical Courier* dismissed Ornstein's Sonata for Two Pianos for its reversion to an earlier style: "This sort of thing is not progression but retrogression," and when the piece appeared five years later, rewritten as his Piano Concerto, Lawrence Gilman lamented, "Mr. Ornstein, judging from this concerto, . . . appears to be advancing very rapidly backwards." Fifty years later Harold Schonberg used almost the same words to describe the Ornstein's Piano *Quintette*, as "eclectic music that looked back as much as forward," and attributed this tendency to Ornstein's disappearance from the modernist scene in the 1920s.[5]

The notion of progress often masqueraded as "advancement," a word used frequently in the nineteenth century,[6] or through negative application of an antonym such as "conventional," the word both Rosenfeld and Cowell used to dismiss Ornstein's later works.[7] Another typical assessment was David Ewen's, which dismissed the *Quintette* because it "lacks any original viewpoint or fresh outlook."[8] When originality is highly valued in Western culture, and when the idea of progress is so closely connected to originality, especially in a modernist aesthetic, it becomes difficult to separate originality of a composition, an aesthetic issue, from originality of style, a historical issue. Often with Ornstein's music, criticisms of his compositions were essentially criticisms of his style. But there were other problems that Ornstein's compositions present, specifically formal ones, especially when he moved to larger compositions.

During the twentieth century the idea of progress was an important measure of a composer's historical stature. Cyril Scott had articulated such in 1916: "What insures immortality in art is the capacity on the part of the artist to create something new,"[9] and in the second half of the century Leonard Meyer considered the issue in a famous article, "Forgery and the Anthropology of Art."[10] Recent historiography seldom discusses progress as such, but the idea of historical evolution has at least since the time of Guido Adler shaped much twentieth-century writing about music. Later serial composers, especially, justified their activity through the notion of progress. Ernst Krenek, who came to the United States in 1938, located serialism squarely within both progress and a unilinear view of evolution: "Atonality, then appears as a state of the musical language that must be accepted as the result of evolution so long as the existence of a permanent motivating force behind the chain of historical events is acknowledged—a force which because of its one-way directedness is identified with progress."[11]

As musical modernism evolved, Ornstein's apparent sins became even more glaring. Ornstein not only turned his back on the *modernism cum progress* aesthetic, but in continuing along his intuitive path, he eschewed formalism as well. He thus left himself open to the criticisms of both conservatives and radicals. This was particularly apparent as Ornstein's style evolved in the late teens and early twenties. At first critics were uncertain of both the direction his music was taking and its formal structure. On hearing Ornstein's Piano Sonata, Op. 54, now lost, the anonymous writer for *Musical Courier* expressed his confusion about both its historical placement and its form: "The sonata is one of his new works and seems to mark a still further step forward in the Ornstein development—if one may use a paradox, a forward step backward; not that the daring composer shows sign of waxing conventional, but there is a certain formal lack of form both in melody and harmony that some of his first ultra works did not suggest."[12] It is perhaps noteworthy to observe that as long as Ornstein's pieces were brief, dissonant outbursts of energy, questions regarding their formal structure were not raised by critics.

By 1920 Paul Rosenfeld had assumed the role of chief interpreter of musical modernism and had, along with A. Walter Kramer and Frederick Martens, become Ornstein's most vocal champion. Yet Ornstein was confined by Rosenfeld's "doctrine" of modernism; he was confined by an insistence on steely newness. By the close of the second decade of the century, Ornstein perceived ultramodernism as restrictive, anti-intuitive, mannered, and dishonest for himself. If, as Ornstein claimed repeatedly, the musical idea determined the medium or style, then to insist upon a single artistic rhetoric was, for Ornstein, to ignore the needs of the music.

But beyond Rosenfeld's and modernism's single-minded pursuit of newness, Ornstein was also troubled by the "virtue" of modernism. In Gdal Saleski's 1927 book *Famous Musicians of a Wandering Race*, Ornstein is quoted as saying: "Nothing irritates me more than to have a composer claim the modernity of his music as a virtue. A statement of this kind is rank heresy, since the sincere composer does not choose a medium—the medium chooses him. He is compelled to use it."[13]

Ornstein was consistent in his valuation of a personal, intuitive musical expression above the intellectual formulation. He eschewed systems and formalism. Whether this was in response to Henri Bergson's popularity at the time, or whether it reflected an interest in Kabbalism via his readings of William Blake, is impossible to determine. Ornstein doesn't say. But in this regard he is lock step with Debussy, Schoenberg, and Busoni, all of whose early-twentieth-century writings rail against formalism, rules, and regulations. His resistance to altering, modifying, correcting, or revising a composition, unless guided by "musical instincts" or an "emotional urge,"[14] speaks to this intuitive principle. Ornstein's most dissonant and modern mode of expression was only valuable to him when it was a natural discourse. When it ceased being that, it ceased being his dominant voice. While Ornstein accepted his aesthetic evolution as a part of the creative process, the modernist in-crowd had difficulty with his "defection."

For Ornstein, the only way for his music to grow and develop was to follow his own inner voices. For him, progress meant turning to what others described as a more conservative style, although there is still plenty of dissonance in his music. Rosenfeld and others saw him as turning his back on modernism. If Ornstein thought about it at all, he probably saw them as not keeping up with him. Ultimately, Leo Ornstein composed for himself and refused to be compromised by outside pressures. While Rosenfeld and his circle lost their poster child *du jour*, Ornstein turned his back on fame and claimed himself—a remarkably bold thing to do. And the modernist tastemakers, they turned to others to carry their colors.

Yet before Ornstein lost the favor of modernists by in effect displaying that same independent streak that made him the modernists' favorite in the first place, he had played a role in shaping American modernism whose significance has remained unnoticed by historians. Whatever the historical verdict on Ornstein as a composer, his activities in the 1910s cause us to reexamine the way the story of musical modernism has been written. First, most histories that address the question see Ornstein and Ives as two isolated individuals, each pursuing his own muse, either in relative solitude, as was the case with Ives,[15] or if done in public in the case of Ornstein, as a distinct, singular aberration, drawing some sort of public principally out of curiosity and amusement, but having little effect on the ultimate course that musical modernism took. While Ives truly remained out of the public eye until 1921, we have seen that Ornstein's efforts on behalf of musical modernism were neither isolated nor solitary. Ornstein was a focal point around which an active modernist movement began to unfold in the United States. Writers, artists, and other musicians formed a coterie to advance a modernist agenda, in which Ornstein was the very public face. Many of these people around Ornstein had specific ties to other groups, the Stieglitz circle in particular. In effect, musical modernism did not stand apart from the broader modernist movement sweeping America in the 1910s; Ornstein was in the inner circles of that movement, in fact, was one of the central orbs around which people in many different areas circled. Because of Ornstein the early history of musical modernism and its connection with the other arts needs to be reconsidered.

A second area demanding revision is the portrayal of national leanings that characterized American musical modernism. In effect, American musicians threw off the yoke of German Romanticism by turning to France. French expatriate musicians such as Edgard Varèse, Carlos Salzedo,[16] and Dane Rudhyar (born Daniel Chennevière) were seminal in the emergence of modernism in the 1920s, and American composers such as Aaron Copland helped change the musical landscape by going to France rather than Germany to study.

Yet with Ornstein another nationality must be added to this mix. On his second trip to Europe in 1913–1914 Ornstein not only created a stir in London with his first public concerts of his modernist works, but formed a close relationship with a group of composers there known as the Frankfurt Five: Roger Quilter, Balfour Gardiner, Percy Grainger, Norman O'Neill, and Cyril Scott. This group had an aesthetic agenda that closely conformed to Ornstein's,[17] and while the extent that it confirmed to Ornstein the rightness of what he was doing, or actually affected his own aesthetic direction is unclear, nevertheless it was the aesthetics of the Frankfurt Five that Ornstein brought back to America. Ornstein showed his support and respect for their musical ideas for several years by programming their music, particular that of Scott, in his concerts. We know that Ornstein would have returned to Europe and especially to England had not World War I forced a permanent change in his plans.

|||

Until his later years Ornstein was anything but the shy, hermitic figure he has come to be portrayed. As far as can be determined Ornstein got along exceedingly well with musicians, those he met in Europe—Bauer, Calvocoressi, Quilter, Scott—and those he knew in the United States, including Franz Kneisel, Hans Kindler, Horatio Parker, Leopold Stokowski, Vera Barstow, Greta Torpedie, and Ethel Leginska, to name only a few.[18] He enjoyed successful relationships with those in the leading musical societies that emerged in the 1920s. He was a respected presence. As a pianist, Ornstein was recognized as belonging to the most talented elite.

On the other hand, Pauline was not completely at home in such company. Perhaps she felt limited by her own lack of formal education. Although she chided musicians as "uneducated," she never went to high school herself and didn't finish the course of study at the Institute.[19] Not graduating from high school was not unusual for women of her day. Her attitude of superiority, however, calls attention to the situation and makes one wonder what she meant by "uneducated." It is possible that early on Pauline sought the validation that Leo provided when it came to all things musical. His pedigree was unassailable.

Fairness insists that we avoid explaining Leo's unexpected but total retirement from the public arena solely as Pauline's doing. History has shown just how easy it is to demonize a spouse, more often than not a wife, and to characterize a full panoply of missteps or unfortunate choices made by the genius subject as reactions to an overreaching, frustrated, demanding, and personally unfulfilled partner. Neither author wants to contribute to that practice. As biographers, however, we are required to interpret what we have discovered. Eight years of research leave little doubt regarding the single most powerful catalyst for the significant changes that occurred in Leo Ornstein's life starting in December 1918.

In a letter from the late 1970s, Pauline wrote to her son and daughter-in-law in an attempt to shed light on her early life, which she acknowledged was likely "something of a closed book by the time you arrived." Pauline referred to her experiences playing with orchestras as a soloist: "the crowning glory was when I played Beethoven's 'Emperor Concerto' with symphony in Carnegie Hall." She mentioned her preference for playing chamber music and her own efforts to form a trio, which "didn't last too long because I married Dad."[20] She recalled times she'd played with members of the Kneisel Quartet, which were likely private events, perhaps even ones associated with the Institute where Kneisel's group was the resident quartet. The Christmas Eve day concert in 1916 on which Pauline Mallet-Prevost performed Beethoven's Concerto was underwritten by her father and was part of the People's Symphony Concerts series. Severo Mallet-Prevost was president of the Symphony for thirty-five years, from 1913 to 1948, and a trustee of the organization. The concert became a family affair; on that particular day Mrs. Severo Mallet-Prevost joined in the chorus of singers.[21]

Even with his powerful connections in the music world, however, the senior Mallet-Prevost could not control reviews. A small piano recital given a few weeks earlier, likely in part to accustom Pauline to playing in public, garnered polite, if less than flattering reviews. Regarding her performance of Mozart's Sonata in C Minor an anonymous reviewer observed "She presented a dignified program with a sincere attempt at its proper performance; but a number of features in her playing stand in the way, at present, of a proper performance. One is her failure to grasp the essential qualities of style in the music she undertakes. . . . Miss Mallet-Prevost's touch sounded sometimes hard yesterday, and there were moments when her treatment of the instrument seemed violent. It is possible that she had not considered duly the acoustics of that small audience room [the Princess Theatre], its unusual brilliancy of resonance, and modified her delivery accordingly. . . . The audience showed a friendly interest in her playing and was liberal in applause."[22]

If Pauline Mallet-Prevost Ornstein harbored virtuosic ambitions, her scattered interests and limited hours of "application," both referred to in Mrs. Tapper's written assessments of her work, precluded her making the necessary commitment to developing her talents fully. Pauline's family had a residence in Paris, but she never took advantage of her European ties to further a musical education. In this regard Pauline's life course was not different from many talented women of her generation who seldom had the opportunity to focus upon cultivating any single aspect of their being beyond that of mother and homemaker. Even Ruth Crawford Seeger, a woman of extraordinary talent and unusual focus, who did use a Guggenheim fellowship to study music in Germany prior to her marriage to Charles Seeger, took a decades-long detour from her own original compositional work to raise a large family. During that time she devoted any leftover creative energies to her husband's musical projects; focusing on her own work was simply impossible. At the very moment Crawford Seeger appeared to be rediscovering her pre-mother/wife musical persona, and considering returning to composition, she died.

Pauline's effort to publish a book, *What Is Music?* was thoroughly rejected by the reader and publishing house as "commonplace."[23] This is not unexpected given the complete absence of any kind of systematic training or reading in aesthetics, acoustics, or philosophy. Daniel Gregory Mason had described the young Miss Mallet-Prevost's work in theory at the Institute as "diligent" and "very earnest,"[24] but this may have not been enough to write an insightful book on music. Pauline did develop clear talents for teaching piano to young people, teaching teachers of young people, and administering all aspects of the Ornstein School of Music. But as Damrosch had pointed out in his commencement address of June 1910, teaching was not accorded the same kind of respect that being an author, composing, or touring as a virtuosic performer earned. She likely felt intimidated by the heady company Ornstein kept, just as she had felt uncomfortable with the equally high-placed social circles of her own parents, which she had rejected. When it came to artistic vision and accomplishment, and the ability to navigate the highest echelons of the wider arts scene, Leo and Pauline were simply in different leagues.

Family lore has it that Ornstein sought total escape from the concertizing world to devote himself exclusively to composing, and Pauline unquestionably helped him achieve this goal, if it had, indeed, been one.[25] But if giving up the virtuoso career was the motivation for the action, it is curious that Ornstein continued his marathon practice sessions each day while tucked away in his studio in the woods of New Hampshire or in his house in Philadelphia. One wonders why he kept himself in fighting form if he had no interest in concertizing, or if he were truly lazy. Was practicing simply a habit, the only life he knew? Surely one way to guarantee *not ever* being asked to perform would be to allow one's technique to wither. But Ornstein didn't choose to do that. On the contrary, he continued to practice. Severo remembers sitting next to his father at the keyboard moving match sticks from one pile to another as Leo completed dozens or hundreds of repetitions of particular passages; it was one way he and his sister got to spend time with their dad. The experience, no doubt, contributed to Severo's own considerable skills as a pianist. Additionally, on numerous occasions throughout the twenties and thirties Ornstein grew weary of the teaching life and took active steps to revive his performing career. As advertisements demonstrate, he made himself available for concerts as late as the 1937–1938 season, and then gave some with the Stradivarius Quartet. But nothing more came of this.

Over the years, other reasons have been offered to explain why Leo would make such a dramatic and unexpected professional choice as to leave his public career. Some are plausible; others are not. Among those fitting the latter category is the explanation that Ornstein left the performing circuit because his hands were too small. This was repeated so often that it's possible even Ornstein himself began to believe it. But it simply doesn't hold up. Not only were his hands not small, he had from early in his career been capable of ripping through Ravel's *Gaspard de la nuit* and Liszt's *Mephisto Waltz* and programmed these works regularly.[26] Works by Liszt and Scriabin were part of his standing arsenal of pieces. His repertoire had never been restricted because of hand size or any physical limitation. Waldo Frank made specific reference to Ornstein's "large, beautiful hands," and Ornstein's speed and agility were regularly commented upon in the press.[27] His technique and musicianship were cause for awe. It is true that compared to Rachmaninoff, one of Ornstein's contemporaries, almost any pianist's hands would be considered small, but virtuosi managed quite well to sustain careers with hands smaller than Rachmaninoff's, and so did Ornstein. While a large hand can be an advantage, fingers that are too long can also get in the way. The stretch of the hand, and the agility of the pianist to move quickly around the keyboard, is paramount. Ornstein's technique was exceptional, his performances breathtaking. Clearly he hadn't been handicapped for his first twenty-five years.

Questions surrounding Ornstein's move away from the public concert arena, and his shift toward a more expressive compositional style became conflated in the minds of Ornstein's contemporaries. And indeed the two seemed to have some common root cause even if they were separated by almost five years. In a review of Paul Rosenfeld's book *Musical Portraits* that appeared in *The Nation* on October 13, 1920, Henrietta Straus followed up on Rosenfeld's "speculation as to what has occasioned that decline in Ornstein's genius which has been so marked of late." Accepting Ornstein's "transition from adolescence to manhood, a flinching from the hostility of the world, too much concertizing, happiness attained through love" Straus offered yet another explanation. Without naming Pauline Mallet-Prevost, Straus's speculation suggests the impact the New York debutante and her milieu may have had on the "the outlaw European Jew."

Straus observed, "Ornstein has, for the last few years, been living in a distinctly non-Jewish atmosphere." She then asks: "Is it not possible that in losing contact with that spiritual soil in which his being had root and was nourished he has lost that in which he found his greatest stimulus and freedom?"[28]

Where did Ornstein's conscious choices begin and those of others end? Ultimately each of us is responsible for the choices we make, or don't make, and so was Ornstein. But along the way we meet people who either encourage us to take chances and broaden ourselves and grow, or oppositely who encourage us to shy away from challenges, to turn back, to seek safety, at all costs—perhaps because it is what those people are most comfortable doing themselves.

In encouraging near-total retreat, ostensibly so that Leo could devote himself to composition, and in directing him toward a career in teaching, Pauline Mallet-Prevost championed safety. And over the years she became the embodiment of it. In doing this for her husband, she also guaranteed what was most comfortable for herself. At a time of war, a flu pandemic, and the incipient Red Scare, the cautious course was not an unintelligent one. In addition, the Mallet-Prevosts' money and social situation, whether needed or sought by Ornstein, made an alliance with such a family not unattractive. This reality was at least noted by friends and associates alike. Without suggesting that Ornstein calculatedly married Pauline Mallet-Prevost, for whom he clearly felt a great deal of affection, he simply couldn't have been blind to the security she offered, to say nothing of the legal assistance her father could provide if needed, and which Ornstein availed himself of with the publication of his song "The Corpse." As critics demanded even more revolutionary musical works and pressured Ornstein to expand his compositional output well beyond his instinctive, intuitive abilities it would seem, the appeal of security and the opportunity to pull back if he were to elect that course must have been extraordinary. Security is seductive.

But in choosing safety Leo gave up much, likely more than he bargained for or imagined, if he imagined anything at all.[29] The safe harbor became more a place of exile, or more accurately a series of exiles: the farm in New Hampshire; the teaching studio in Philadelphia; the trailer park in Brownsville, Texas—none without their allures, and the house in New Hampshire genuinely appealing but isolating still. Over the years, Leo wrote of his utter frustration at being marooned in Brownsville, and even Pauline wrote, "dad wants to jump on the next train to California."[30] Having seen pictures of the California coast sent to him by his son, Leo acknowledged his restlessness: "Looking at the incredible seascape on Route 1, a picture of which you sent us, I could not but wonder why we have bogged ourselves down here and are missing such great beauty when we could live somewhere within the vicinity and have it accessible." But as far as picking up and heading to California, Leo noted: "mother is not much help. She has always liked what is." For years his walks along the Gulf Coast shoreline and compos-ing provided his only solace: "We went over to Boca Chica this morning and the beach is beautiful[,] but Brownsville is really deadly and if it weren't for working I'd be pretty well out of my mind."[31]

Prior to his marriage, Leo had been extremely close to his family. A short article that appeared in *Musical America* September 29, 1917, leads with the sen-tence: "Leo Ornstein adores his parents and is very anxious to live with them when in New York." It seems, however, that Ornstein's relentless practicing hab-its had caused neighbors to "complain bitterly about the noises," with the upshot that the Ornsteins "moved to Riverside Drive." But the situation persisted even though the location changed, and "the apartment had to be exchanged for another one six months later, and for the same reason." To save his parents from a third move simply to accommodate his professional routine, Ornstein rented "a small apartment on the top floor of a nine-story building" where his only furniture was "his grand piano, a writing table, a few chairs and some towels."[32] The lease speci-fied hours during which Leo could practice, thus allowing him a place to work uninterrupted, and a place to live with his family without imposing upon them. That the nearly twenty-four year old traveling virtuoso preferred to reside with his family when not on the road, when he could have afforded to live elsewhere and on his own, reflects a solid and caring family constellation.

But Leo's interactions with his extended family changed significantly and forever upon his marriage. Ornstein's relatives have spoken of feeling as if Pauline drove a wedge between them and Leo. They refer to her smothering over-protectiveness, their sense of her running interference when none was necessary. It's likely they were also frustrated that she had convinced Leo to curtail his very lucrative performing schedule, in a sense to hide his talent, which also meant there was less money to be showered on family members; they lost the cachet of claim-ing a relation to the notorious musician who was turning so many heads across the nation.

Leo's brother Manus, a physician, was the single Ornstein sibling who main-tained anything close to the relationship that he and Leo had once enjoyed, even though Aaron, another of Leo's older brothers, had pursued a career as a piano teacher, and Leo had a twin sister, Lisa.[33] The Leo-Manus relationship continued after the Ornsteins closed their Philadelphia school and moved near Manus and his family in Manhattan. Manus helped Leo through a period of depression that followed soon after that move, and so provided both professional and personal attention that Leo needed. Not only did the two brothers stay close, but Manus's son, Peter, was good friends with Leo's children, Severo and Edith. Why this single familial connection continued is difficult to say. It did, more or less, endure. But regardless of what Leo's siblings believed, Pauline wasn't alone in driving a wedge; Leo went along. Perhaps he felt embarrassed by his immigrant family and parents who clung to Old World ways; perhaps he felt they didn't appreciate the influence of his debutante wife. And it seems quite clear they didn't. Maybe he felt he had to make a choice, and he chose his wife.

But more devastating to Leo professionally than pulling him away from his family, Pauline appears to have actively discouraged commerce with the most nourishing stream of inspiration for her husband's creative work: the multiple people in multiple places and disciplines across the arts world, those she found "self-inflated and uneducated." Why this occurred, we don't know. Ornstein thrived both as a pianist and a composer while in London and Paris, and then when he returned to New York. He was at the center of the nascent modernist scene and appeared to enjoy his position there. Not until years after he turned away from the public did anyone hear he had been dissatisfied with his career. Given all the prose generated by and about Ornstein, one might expect at the very least quiet murmurings. The silence makes his action all the more perplexing.

Intuitive creators need stimulation. Improvisational artists need ideas off which they can bounce. Jazz players listen and respond to what's being said. When Ornstein had these things in place his productivity seemed endless. Music flowed from his head, his fingers, and his pen. When they disappeared, his output all but did the same. Despite Pauline's sincere efforts on Leo's behalf, it would appear that she didn't understand fully all that was essential to his creativity; a less generous reading might conclude that she chose to ignore it. Perhaps Pauline's needs were greater, and Leo understood that, and he selflessly capitulated. But not always, and notions of Ornstein as a selfless nurturer of others do not hold up against the picture painted of him by his family.[34] Tales of Leo's explosive temper, scenes where he traumatized his children by threatening to leave the family, and his obvious dissatisfactions with farm life, the teacher's studio, and the isolation of the trailer park—all bespeak a person frustrated with limitations, whether imposed from without or within, or a combination of both.

Composition was never a disciplined activity for Leo. He was no Beethoven, laboriously copying out exercises and working over a musical idea until it suited his larger needs or intentions. Quite the opposite, Leo spoke often and at length about the ways music simply came to him, and how he eschewed intervening in the process. The improvisational quality of Ornstein's most effective, brief programmatic piano pieces—*Wild Men's Dance, Three Moods,* "Impressions of Notre Dame"—which is the genre in which he excelled, and the obvious difficulties he encountered writing more expansive works underscore this reality. Leo rejected working at composition, the same way he had resisted working for his theory and harmony courses with Percy Goetschius, and his history lecture courses with Waldo S. Pratt and Henry E. Krehbiel at the Institute. For Ornstein, "composition" was a spontaneous, instinctive releasing of the sounds he heard in his head. That some of them got caught in written form and others got lost didn't change their mode of conception, but the process goes a long way to explaining the difficulties he encountered when he began to receive commissions for larger, more expanded works.

Ornstein never took a single composition course at the Institute, although a full complement of courses existed and Pauline actually enrolled in one. Arthur A. Loesser performed a simple "Romanza" that Pauline had composed as part of the "Work of the Composition Classes" recital on May 20, 1911. The "grade III" work was grouped with another elementary piece by Miss Anna H. S. Malmquist under the rubric "Homophonic forms for pianoforte."[35] Although anecdotal remarks exist that claim Leo could compose contrapuntally, no music exists to support this assertion. While fugal writing is learned, and Ornstein disdained such formal constraints, it can with practice become a natural part of one's compositional arsenal. On the other hand, one has only to consider Bach's fugues to appreciate what must have been his instinctive inclination for the procedure.

Once Ornstein had turned from his most futuristic style, the music streaming through Leo's inner ear was predominantly lyrical and homophonic, though, granted, still highly dissonant. Occasionally two melodies might overlap for a brief period, one more as a sound heard from a distance, but that would be the extent of the interaction or musical relationship. Without contrapuntal techniques, Ornstein had to seek other solutions to unify his expanded works. Even Brahms's and Schoenberg's pieces that are integrated through continuous (developing) variation included passages of polyphony. The absence of counterpoint, whether by design or necessity, created problems for Ornstein's works in the larger forms.

Clearly, Leo's concertizing schedule of the late-teen years didn't provide much opportunity for composing. Critics began to notice a certain staleness in his music. Spontaneous creation also needs time and a conducive environment to flourish, and both were in short supply with the schedule he kept. Pauline aggressively advocated on behalf of "downtime" for Ornstein. At the end of 1918 with a world reeling from the war, a pandemic, and the first rumblings of the Red Scare, which must have made the Russian musical anarchist nervous, he needed the safe harbor she provided. But time and quietude were only a part of the picture. Ornstein also needed the closeness of artists, writers, and musicians who were similarly inclined to create—conversations over books, paintings, and ideas that cause the synapses to fire, the kinds of motivation that only friendly competition can provide. Pauline was less willing or able to provide this. Her behavior likely had many causes.

Without diminishing her considerable pedagogical and administrative talents, Pauline was not a particularly creative artistic individual herself. She clearly was in awe of Leo's musical gifts, and later in life regularly compared him to Bach, which, given that much of the fame of the Baroque master rested upon his contrapuntal achievements, made the comparison particularly jarring. It must, however, have been extremely difficult for her to empathize with her husband's creative process. According to Severo, his father thought of Pauline as "a bit of a pedant," and he accepted the situation.[36] Whether Leo fully appreciated the ramifications of her pedantry for his own life is not clear.

In addition, by all accounts Pauline was not comfortable or secure in social situations. Recognizing and accepting that others might be able to supply one's spouse with what one cannot oneself is extremely difficult, even for those with the least of egos. If Pauline had fully appreciated and accepted Leo's need for artistic stimulation and involvement, would she have been able to see that he received such nurturing, given her own desperate need to have him to herself: could she have shared him, could she have invited others in?[37] The answer appears to be no; she couldn't even share him with her own children.

Both children have referred to feeling as if they were satellites orbiting a closed system, "always looking for a way into the circle."[38] When the children were young, their Nanny, Ida Hackett, took them to Old Orchard, Maine, during the summers while Pauline and Leo stayed in the city and taught. The parents would join the three for long weekends. Edith described Nanny as "real, very real, and always there," as compared with her parents. In Pauline and Leo's personal and professional worlds, the children were ancillary.

This reading was reinforced by Leo Ornstein in an interview conducted by his niece Holly Carter in 1986. When she asked her granduncle whether having children was a profound experience, rather than respond with the expected "of course," Leo proffered that "keeping the cycle going" answered some kind of biological "urge." "After all [we] might be carrying out nothing but what nature has already endowed us with." The perpetuation of the species was dependent upon it. In reflecting upon their decision to have children, Leo mused, "I don't think Pauline ever thought of having a child, or anything of the sort. I think she was pretty content." Ultimately they "decided that we ought to have the experience perhaps."[39] From the distance of many years, and based upon the clear professional and personal successes of both children, each of them has come to terms with their upbringing. They've even developed a remarkable degree of objectivity.

Characterizing her own existence as likely "an experiment," and her brother's as perhaps "a mistake," Edith concluded that probably her parents "shouldn't have had children."[40]

Pauline was, however, rocklike in providing Leo with a type of stability that he craved. With the death of Mrs. Tapper he sought out another maternal figure, one who had some connection with the piano world, a person who shared his commitment to music and Mrs. Tapper, someone who knew where he'd come from. Pauline provided these things. As Edith Ornstein Valentine has observed of her parents: "He was looking for a mother and she was looking for someone to be a lifelong partner."[41] Both, it seems, found that aspect of what they needed.

Biographers spend years, sometimes lifetimes, attempting to get to know their subjects, talking with them (if they're lucky), tracking down those who knew them, reading everything that was ever written by or about the person, in the case of composers, listening to and reading through their music, speaking with performers, visiting favorite haunts with the hope of divining some elusive insight, becoming acquainted with the events, the places, the forces that might have acted upon them. And so it has been with our efforts on behalf of Leo Ornstein. We have crossed the country numerous times for a conversation with a student, or friend, or nurse, or relative. We've scoured archives, asked and fielded questions, been interviewed ourselves, and enlisted the aid of researchers and performers both here and continents away. Along with Leo's son, Severo Ornstein, we've become something of a clearinghouse for all things Ornsteinian. We've come to understand that every informant, however well intentioned and generous, offers a uniquely skewed perspective on a subject, and that every source is biased.

After eight years we've learned much about Leo Ornstein: sometimes the sheer quantity of information we possess takes our breath away. But while we ostensibly know more about the man, his music, and his milieu than we did when we began in 1998, there is still much we don't know, and likely never will. In this regard we are like Ornstein himself who in an interview explained that by the time he reached the age of 94 he "had hoped some disclosure would be made to me." He concluded wistfully, "I realize now that I shall die as unwittingly as I was born, and essentially know nothing at all about the things one really wants to know."[42]

Neither Ornstein nor Pauline kept good records. On the contrary, they destroyed many documents and habitually neglected to date those they kept. However, even if they had fastidiously archived personal papers, they might not tell us what we wanted to know. Written documents, although they appear truthful and objective, are incomplete and remarkably inadequate resources when it comes to understanding people, their motivations, and behaviors. They may or may not tell a researcher what happened, but they usually can't tell why something happened. Sometimes that which is most important speaks loudest with its absence and silence. To complicate the Ornstein biographers' task, as if the absence and incompleteness of records were not enough, Ornstein lived the equivalent of two lifetimes, 108 years, across two continents, and three centuries.

Having spent close to a decade with the man, we can't help but wonder whether Leo's disappearance from the public sphere around 1920 had anything to do with a dawning recognition of his own limitations. Was he aware of them? Did he fear confronting them? Had he been so elevated by his champions that he couldn't acknowledge in public what he needed? Did Ornstein disguise limited compositional skills (not musical ideas) behind a rhetoric that dismissed formalism, systems, and compositional intent? Critics were not completely misguided in the late teens when they observed a certain sameness creeping into Ornstein's pieces; a number of the piano works sound similar. But many of his later works, especially the *Quintette* for Piano and Strings (1927), the Cello *Preludes* (1929–1930), Sonata No. 5 in the form of a biography (1974), the *Poem* for Flute and Piano (1979), and Sonata No. 8, written in 1990, when the composer was ninety-seven years old, were inspired, and when Ornstein was at his best his music could be alternately thrilling and poignant.

We assume great composers have a distinctive voice, a unique way of thinking in music that informs even the smallest gesture, and that a piece will be identifiably theirs regardless of the genre or medium. To that degree they have a sonic fingerprint; it brands their works. In the best of all worlds their voice emerges from a mastery of all aspects of their art. But one wonders whether Ornstein's complete dependence upon only the continuous sounds flowing through his head impeded fully mastering his craft as a composer. Was he a prisoner of his own widely disseminated views about the instinctive act, the intuitive outpouring? Given his fame, could he have sought instruction in composition if he'd wanted it? Did he cease to grow? Did he hide behind Pauline? Did he and Pauline hide behind each other?

The dynamics of relationships are usually not understood by any but the principals in them. And even they may not know or be able to articulate how or why things work. It seems possible that in making herself central to Leo's very existence, and by pulling him away from so many people, Pauline encouraged, promoted and, in common parlance, "enabled" Leo to grow more dependent (to take the safe course) to a degree he hadn't as the touring virtuoso. Although, as a child, he had had much done for him, by 1914 he had also learned to do much for himself. The globe-trotting, fiery young man, full of energy and ideas and unlimited promise, who crisscrossed the continent many times, handled reporters with panache, worked with those inside and outside the music world, dined at manor houses, and regularly delivered the goods in thousands of concerts, amassing a sizeable bank account along the way, shrank to the size of the world with which he'd surrounded himself. This happened slowly, but surely. By the 1970s his world was the width of a trailer.

Who or what is responsible for his removal? At least at one time, Leo Ornstein had possessed the power and agency to direct his own life course. It is possible he used Pauline as a foil for decisions he ultimately would have made on his own, but this is impossible to know. Perhaps it is safest to suggest that while he was not a hapless victim of a controlling spouse, for unknown reasons he didn't demand the room he needed to grow or even to breathe. Perhaps he didn't want to. Perhaps he didn't know how. Perhaps he didn't realize what had happened until it was too late.

Sometimes those closest to a situation have the greatest difficulty seeing, especially when their own relationship to events is fraught and unresolved; but not always. In an e-mail to the authors written in September 2005 Severo Ornstein waxed philosophical on the complex man who was his father: "I wish myself that I knew more of his former life, days, friends, but he was quite reticent about his past and if mother hadn't clued us in, we would have never had any idea from him. In some ways, tempestuous giant though he obviously was at one time, he was also a very prosaic little man who just happened to have this enormous waterfall of music constantly pouring into his head. Something of a perpetual enigma to all of us, as well as himself."[43]

Ornstein's gradual departure from the public scene had as much to do with personal choices, his and others, and most especially with the appearance of Pauline in his life, as it did with real or imagined physical limitations, political exigencies, stylistic changes and the aesthetic dilemmas they wrought, or critical reception of his music, all of which have been offered up at various times as explanations for his disappearance. That the man possessed brilliance and extraordinary pianistic gifts is beyond question. That he composed a unique body of powerful and beautiful musical works has become increasingly clear to a whole new generation of performers and listeners. That he elected to alter his life course in ways that defy easy understanding is another of his bequests. Ultimately he had choices, and either by omission or commission, he exercised them.

APPENDIX: TABLE OF COMPOSITIONS
Compiled by Steven Leinbach

GUIDE TO THE TABLE

If the date of the piece is listed as 19__/pre- (e.g., many early works listed only by Martens have been dated 1918/pre-), it generally means that the source has not actually put a date of composition on it, and we are dating it with reference to the source's date of publication.

The abbreviation 19__/or pre- means that the piece was written on or before the given date (e.g., Dec. 1920/or pre- means that the piece was written in or before Dec. 1920).

If there is no source next to a piece of information [e.g., the Date column for the Clarinet Nocturne reads "1952; 1946 (Oberlin)," with no reference next to the "1952"], it should be assumed that what is listed immediately after the name of the piece is the source.

In the case of compositions that have been irretrievably lost, we have tried to include as much descriptive information as possible from the primary sources; otherwise we have tried to be as brief as possible in notes to this table, which can be found on p. 318.

LIST OF ABBREVIATIONS

Add: refers to addenda to Clank/Crumb and Martens; in the former case it is an update to the Yale Catalog to encompass recently acquired works; in the latter case it is two pages of advertisements from publishers after the main text of the book

Ampico: list of Ampico recordings by Ornstein in Severo Ornstein's holdings

CC: Archival Collection, MSS 10, Ornstein Manuscripts (New Haven: Yale University Library), processed by Cindy Clank, 1974; revised and updated by Thomas Crumb, 1978.

CJM: *Canadian Journal of Music*

E: James Alfred Eastman, *A Bibliography of Leo Ornstein* (typescript), New York City, 1935

M: Frederick H. Martens, *Leo Ornstein: The Man—His Ideas, His Work*

MA: *Musical America*

MC: *Musical Courier*

MGG: *Die Musik in Geschichte und Gegenwart*

MO: *Musical Observer*

MS: *Musical Standard*

P: Vivian Perlis, *The Futurist Music of Leo Ornstein* (high numbers)

Reis: Claire Reis, *Composers, Conductors, and Critics* (New York: Oxford University Press, 1955)

VV: Carl Van Vechten, *Music and Bad Manners*

R: Paul Rosenfeld, "Ornstein" in *The New Republic*

S: Severo Ornstein's Index, piano music

SC: Severo Ornstein's Index, chamber music

SO: Severo Ornstein's Index, orchestral music

SV: Severo Ornstein's Index, vocal music

S#: Number in Severo Ornstein's Thematic Index

Y: Leo Ornstein Papers, Irving S. Gilmore Library, Yale University, MSS 10, http://webtext.library.yale.edu/xml2html/music.ornstein.nav.html

PIANO WORKS

TITLE	DATE	S#	COMMENTS
13th Psalm, Op. 27 (E-17)	1913 (M-23)	—	Part of E's "List of Unidentified Scores"; E is the only source to confirm that this is a piano work (others do not describe it); this work is also mentioned by MGG-703 and a Philadelphia Orchestra program (Feb. 13/14, 1925)
4 Untitled Pieces (Y)	1963–1967	—	Designated "F" through "I" on manuscript
A Chromatic Dance[1] (S-7)	Dec. 29, 1978	151	The number in parentheses refers to the volume number in *The Piano Music of Leo Ornstein*, ed. Severo Ornstein (Woodside, Calif.: Poon Hill Press, n.d.)
A Dream Almost Forgotten (S-5)	Feb. 24, 1977	110	
A la chinoise, Op. 39[2] (aka Impressions of Chinatown)	Mar. 1916/ pre- (MC, Mar. 30)	060	Also exists in orchestrated version, also by B&H, which is not at Yale (P-735); R-313 refers to "Eighteen Preludes"—A la chinoise, Op. 39; M-73 dates this to 1911, but this is almost surely incorrect
A la mexicana, Op. 35, No. 1[3] (CC-Add)	ca. 1918 (M-77)	059	Merkin and S-3 agree with the Op. No.; R-313 and M-77 list these as Op. 48; No. 9 not at Yale (P-750)
A Long Remembered Snow (S-5)	1964	102	At Yale as Comp. 19 = 25 = 42
A Moment of Retrospect (S-8)	?	156	At Yale as Comp. 10 = Comp. 32
A Morning in the Woods (S-5)	Sept. 29, 1971	106	
A Paris Street Scene at Night, Op. 4, No. 3[4] (M-Add)	1912/pre- (CC-Add)	—	M makes much of the usefulness of Op. 4 as instructional pieces
A Reverie (S-7)	Apr. 21, 1979	150	
A Small Carnival (S-6)	July 31, 1978	115	

PIANO WORKS

TITLE	DATE	S#	COMMENTS
An Allegory (S-1)	pre-1918	007	Apparently not at Yale but published by S
An Autumn Improvisation (S-7)	Nov. 15, 1978	119	
An Autumnal Fantasy (S-7)	Oct. 13, 1978	118	
Bagatelle (S-4)	Feb. 1952	100	At Yale as Comp. 2 = 33 (S-4); CC lists a Bagatelle No. 1 with no year
Ballade (S-5)	Dec. 21, 1976	108	
Barbaro: A Pantomime (S-7)	Nov. 30, 1978	120	
Barcarolle, Op. 3, No. 1 (E-17)	?	—	
Barcarolle, Op. 6, No. 4 (CC)	?	008	S-1 agrees with the Op. No.; judging from the Op. No., it seems fairly likely this piece was written before 1910
Berceuse (MA, Mar. 18)	Mar. 1916/pre-	—	
Burlesca (a Satire)[5] (S-5)	Sept. 23, 1976	107	Dedicated to William Westney
Burlesques (of Richard Strauss)[6] (M-77)	ca. 1918	—	Later orchestrated (incomplete) (P-750)
Calory Rag	Jan. 1917/pre-	—	An (apparently) untitled piece written especially for a luncheon L.O. had (ca. end of Jan. 1917) with some New York City police officers
Cossack Impressions, Op. 14[7] (M-62)	ca. 1914	055	In two volumes
Danse arabe (M-73)	1914; Apr. 1916/pre- (Metzer-352)	—	
Dwarf Suite, Op. 11[8] (Suite des gnomes) (M-74)	1913; Apr. 1914/pre- (NY Times, Apr. 8)	052	See MA, Apr. 8, 1916, for L.O.'s explanation of the title and MC, Mar. 29, 1917, for a bit about the circumstance under which the piece was written. "Professor Theodore Leschitizky gewidmet."

PIANO WORKS

TITLE	DATE	S#	COMMENTS
Eleven Short Pieces, Op. 29 (M-69)	Apr. 1914/ pre- (MS, Apr. 18)	—	Subtitled "Scenes of Parisian Life"
Evening's Sorrow (SI-CC-5)	Oct. 30, 1968	104	At Yale as Comp. 26a; called one of Three Landscapes, but no others apparent (S-5); CC-12 suggests that Some New York Scenes might be the other two landscapes
Five Pieces, Op. 17 (P-749)	ca. 1913, also S-1	003	Considering that the movements have titles like Volga, Potok, and Doumka (CC-10), it seems that this and what M-62 calls "Suite Ukraine, Op. 17," are the same piece. Ms at Yale has on first page "A mon père Aaron Ornstein." At end signed "Song without Words" (Box 2a, Folder 4)
Four Fantasy Pieces (S-16)	1960–1961?	440–442	No. 2 is not at Yale (P-750). Ms signed "Dec. 1961"
Four Intermezzos (S-11)	1965–1968	320–323	P-748 lists five of these, with all but the fourth (1965) dating from 1968
Four Legends	1960–1982	350–353	First two Legends are at Yale
Galop fantastique (M-73)	1914	—	
Humoresque (M-77)	1918/pre-	—	Transcription of Dvořák
Impressions of Notre Dame, Op. 16⁹ (*Deux impressions de Notre Dame*) (M-64)	ca. 1914 (S-2), also CC-8; Mar. 1914/pre- (*NY Times*, Mar. 30)	056	Sound of Bells Floating through the Atmosphere; The Gargoyles (M-64). Along with The Bells, The Monk, and the Midnight Mass, this piece forms part of Four Religious Impressions (M-67), which appear to be lost
Impressions of Switzerland (*Quatre impressions de la Suisse*), Op. 27 (M-19)	1913	—	Four Hands; Sunrise, The Forest, The Mountains, Sunset (E-17); the Op. No. (which is apparently also that of the 13th Psalm) is recorded by E-17, not M

PIANO WORKS

TITLE	DATE	S#	COMMENTS
Impressions of the Thames, Op. 13, No. 1[10] (*Impressions de la Tamise*) (M-68)	Mar. 1914/ pre- (NY Times, Mar. 30)	053	R-313 agrees with the Op. No.
Impromptu—A Bit of Nostalgia[11] (S-10)	Nov. 11, 1976	303	
Impromptu—An Interlude (S-10)	Oct. 27, 1976	302	
Impromptu— Epitaph[12] (S-10)	Oct. 3, 1976	301	Called "Impromptu—At the Grave of a Dead Infant" at Yale
Impromptu (S-10)	1950s	300	At Yale as Comp. 24 = 31
Improvisata (M-73)	1914; Jan. 1915/pre- (MA, Jan. 30)	—	
In the Country[13] (S-3)	1924	063	
Journal (S-11)	1987–1988	330– 336	Exact dates can be found on S-11; published by S
Just a Fun Piece (S-7)	June 29, 1978	114	
Melancholie (M-30)	1909 (MA, Apr. 8, 1916)	—	This may be part of the Russian Suite or the Nine Miniatures
Memories from Childhood[14] (S-4)	1925	066	
Metaphors, 1–15 (S-8)	1959–1978?	200– 215	
Mindy's Piece (S-5)	1967	103	"Written for a granddaughter when a child" in pencil on manuscript (Y)
Mindy's Piece No. 2 (P-748)	1967	—	
Moments Musical (after Schubert), Op. 51, No. 1[15] (S-4)	1918; 1918/ pre- (M-77)	071	M-77 calls this a recent work
Musings of a Piano[16] (S-3)	1924	065	

PIANO WORKS

TITLE	DATE	S#	COMMENTS
Nine Arabesques, Op. 42[17] (CC-7)	ca. 1918 (M-77); 1918 (Verbit); Oct. 1917/ pre- (MA, Oct. 13)	062	
Nine Miniatures, Op. 7, No. 1[18] (S-4)	1915; Feb. 1916/pre- (MO)	072	Mentioned as early as May 1915 (MC, May 26); apparently not at Yale but published by S
Nine Vignettes (CC-12)	Fall and winter 1977	380– 388	All but No. 9 dated in manuscript
Nocturne No. 1 (P-748)	ca. 1922	153	
Nocturne No. 2 (P-748)	1922	004	P-750 refers to incomplete orchestrated versions of two Nocturnes, presumably these
Nocturne, Op. 1, No. 2 (CC-13)	ca. 1905 (P-748)	001	This work is signed "Liova Oranoff" (S-1)
Piano Concerto (Two Piano Version) (S-17)	?	553	Changes were made to the concerto in Dec. 1976 in Westney's hand (CC-19)
Piano Sketch Books[19] (S-4)	1939	068	Two volumes of children's pieces, combined by S. into one
Pièce Pour Piano, Op. 19, No. 1 (P-749)	Oct. 1913 (S-17)	550	Piano four hands
Poems of 1917, Op. 41[20] (S-3)	1917	061	Dedicated to Leopold Godowsky; CC-10 agrees with the Op. No.; M-77 lists this as Op. 68. According to MC, Sept. 19, 1918, composed in Montreal. MC has lengthy program, from Waldo Frank.
Prelude in C-sharp Minor (MC, Nov. 7)	Oct. 1918/ pre-	—	Work is mentioned by MC as early as Oct. 24; almost certainly same as Prélude tragique

PIANO WORKS

TITLE	DATE	S#	COMMENTS
Prélude tragique[21] (CC-14)	1918, 1924	069	Piano four hands; apparently recorded for Ampico in Aug. 1925. See Prelude in C-sharp Minor
Preludium (MA, March 9)	Feb. 1918/ pre-		
Pygmy Suite, Op. 9[22] (M-60)	1914 (S-4)	070	S-4 agrees with the Op. No.
Russian Sketches (MA, Jan. 26)	Jan. 1918/ pre-	—	Played by Ornstein at his Jan. 15, 1918 recital; according to the source, it was written by "one Vladimirsky, who, according to rumor, is as much Ornstein as was a certain enigmatic Vannin"; unclear if this is related to any of L.O.'s other, similarly titled works
Russian Suite, Op. 12[23] (*Suite russe*) (M-61)	1911/pre-	058	M-61 claims that L.O. played this in New York in 1911 and Norway in 1913
Sarabande, Op. 4, No. 2 (M-Add)	1917/pre-	—	This was likely also published in 1912; held by Eastman School of Music
Scherzino, Op. 5, No. 2[24] (M-77)	1909; May 1916/ pre- (MC, May 18)	051	CC-14 lists 1918, but this is clearly impossible in light of the review from MC two years earlier; Jamestown Journal (Dec. 15, 1916) refers to this as a "credible effort of a boy of fourteen"
Scherzo, Op. 3, No. 2 (E-17)	?	—	
Seeing Russia with Teacher[25] (S-17)	1925	552	Piano four hands; in two volumes
Serenade, Op. 5, No. 1[26] (M-77)	1918/pre– (S-2)	050	Martens (Nov. 1917) describes these two pieces as early works

PIANO WORKS

TITLE	DATE	S#	COMMENTS
Seven Fantasy Pieces (M-71)	Dec. 1915/ pre- (MC, Dec. 16)	—	Metzer-353 suggests this might also be known as Seven Sketches; in that case the date of composition should read March 1915/pre- (*NY Times*, March 1); the MC review calls this Seven Fantastic Pieces
Seven Moments musicales, Op. 8[27] (M-61)	1907/pre-	—	
Shadow Pieces (*Pièces à silhouette*), Op. 17 (M-68)	Apr. 1914/ pre- (MS, Apr. 18)	—	Dance of Shadows, Shadows Pursued (M-69) vs. Dancing Shadows, Shadows in Pursuit (MS, Apr. 18); note that this and the Five Piano Pieces have the same Op. No.; MS agrees with this Op. No.
Six Lyric Fancies, Op. 10[28] (M-61)	1910? ("when the composer was fourteen"; Martens)	—	Yale does not have all the movements (CC-Add); held by Eastman School of Music
Six Tragic Sketches, Op. 48[29] (P-750)	?	—	The Op. No. suggests that this was written ca. 1917; MC, Sept. 27, mentions a piece "Grotesques, Op. 48" just published by B&H
Six Water Colors, Op. 80[30] (S-4)	1921	067	The newly published piece was reviewed in MA, Apr. 32
Solitude (S-6)	Aug. 5, 1978	116	Originally titled "Departure" (CC-11)
Some New York Scenes (S-5)	Mar. 11, 1971	105	
Sonata for Two Pianos, Op. 89 (CC-14)	Summer 1921 (MC, Aug 4)	—	Philadelphia Orchestra, Feb. 13/14, 1925, program notes dates this precisely to 1921; according to MC, Aug. 4, Ornstein put "the finishing touches" on this piece in the late summer of 1921
Sonata No. 4[31] (S-12)	1918	360	CC-4 lists this publication date as 1920

PIANO WORKS

TITLE	DATE	S#	COMMENTS
Sonata No. 5 (Biography in Sonata Form)[32] (S-12)	May 24, 1974	361	S-12 claims only the first movement was published by Joshua
Sonata No. 6 (S-13)	June 4, 1981	362	
Sonata No. 7 (S-13)	Aug. 1988	363	
Sonata No. 8 (S-13)	Sept. 23, 1990	364	
Sonata, Op. 25 (M-76)	1914; March 1914/pre- (NY Times, March 30)	—	Subtitled "The Tragedy of a Soul;" Four Movements: Tragedy, Love, Mystery, Retrospection (M-76). NY Times mentions a Sonata, Op. 28, but likely a typo since that is the Op. No. of the String Quartet. R-84 mentions this Sonata as well
Sonata, Op. 35 (E-17)	?	—	
Sonata, Op. 54 (MC, 1917 Dec. 6)	Oct. 1917/pre- (MC, Nov. 22)	—	Four movements: Allegro appassionata, Marche funèbre, Allegretto, Animato (MC, Feb. 6, 1919); LA Times, Nov. 28, 1917, and MC, Dec. 12, 1918 suggest that this was one of L.O.'s more conservative works
Sonatina, Op. 15 (M-62)	1909 (MC, Mar., 30, 1916), also MA, Jan. 29, 1916, & MC, Feb. 17, 1916; 1910 (MC, Apr. 6, 1916); 1905 (MO, Feb. 1916)	—	Andante con Tristezza, Burlesca, Appassionata, Allegretto (Montreal Star, Feb. 14, 1916); the date of 1905 seems somewhat unlikely since, going by the 1895 birth date that was then in use, he would have been ten years old; according to MA, Feb. 17, 1916: "The spirit of the composition is unruffled; the finale, pleasantly impressionistic. In parts it suggests César Franck; certainly it carries very little suggestion of its own author as he appears today"; Philadelphia Orchestra program notes, Feb. 13/14, 1925, claim that L.O. wrote five sonatinas (though it does not say that they are necessarily for solo piano)

PIANO WORKS

TITLE	DATE	S#	COMMENTS
Suicide in an Airplane (P-749)	1913	006	Based on an article in the NY Times, Apr. 2, 1913
Suite Belgium (M-77)	ca. 1918	—	
Tarantelle (S-8)	1963?	155	CC-11 refers to an undated Tarantelle, perhaps the same piece; there are two at Yale
Tarantelle diabolique (S-5)	July 29, 1960	101	At Yale as Comp. 6
Tartar Dance (P-750)	?	—	
The Cathedral, Op. 37, No. 2 (MO, Dec. 1915)	Dec. 1915/ pre-	—	M-67 incorrectly calls this Op. 38, No. 2; this is an instructional piece, especially written for this periodical; found in the office holdings; Three Russian Impressions shares the Op. No.
The Deserted Garden (S-7)	Dec. 6, 1982	152	
The Masqueraders (M-74)	ca. 1916; May 1916/ pre- (R.)	—	Inspired by the Andreyev play (R-85)
The Night (VV-234)	Dec. 1915/ pre- (NY Times, Dec. 6)	—	Attributed to "Vannin"; M-29 refers to this piece as At Night, but corrects himself on p. 71; NY Times (Dec. 6, 1915) suggests that the Vannin pieces are more conservative than Ornstein's other works
The Recruit and the Bugler (S-7)	Aug. 24, 1978	117	
The Waltzers (VV-234)	Dec. 1915/ pre- (NY Times, Dec. 6)	—	Attributed to "Vannin"
Three Burlesques, Op. 30 (M-69)	Apr. 1914/ pre- (MS, Apr. 18)	—	
Three Moods, Op. 22 (M-69)	ca. 1914; Mar. 1914/pre- (NY Times, Mar. 30)	005	Anger, Grief, Joy

PIANO WORKS

TITLE	DATE	S#	COMMENTS
Three Preludes, Op. 20[33] (M-68)	ca. 1914 (S-2), Mar. 1914 /pre- (NY Times, Mar. 30)	057	CC-10 agrees with the Op. No.
Three Tales (CC-12)	1977	111–113	A Rendez-vous at the Lake (June 30, 1977), A Fantasy (July 29, 1977), A Midnight Waltz (June 9, 1977)
To a Grecian Urn (S-8)	?	154	
Two Improvisations, Op. 95 (CC-14)	1921, also CC-14	551	Piano four hands; consisting of Berceuse triste (missing) and Valse buffon (P-749); A. W. Kramer implies in MA, Jan. 7, that there may have been an orchestral version of the latter
Two Lyric Pieces[34] (S-3)	1924	064	Yale appears to have just the second piece, Waltz; both are published by S
Untitled (CC-13)	?	—	Unfinished; no further information
Valley of Tears (Impressions of Norway) (M-77)	1918/pre-	—	Seems likely that this was written ca. 1913–14, considering that his other "Impressions" were written during or not long after his European trip
Valse diabolique[35] (S-6)	Jan. 22, 1977	109	
Valse gallope (MC, Dec. 6, 1916)	Dec. 1916/ pre-	—	
Valse in G Major, Op. 4, No. 1[36][37] (M-Add)	1917/pre- (M-B)	—	This was likely also published in 1912; held by Eastman School of Music
Various untitled works (CC-13)	1950–1972	—	Numbered 1–42

PIANO WORKS

TITLE	DATE	S#	COMMENTS
Waltzes, 1–17 (S-14)	1958–1980?	400–416	CC-13 lists fifteen waltzes, "mostly between 1950–1972"; later (14) she lists a set of seven waltzes from ca. 1979 and "miscellaneous" from 1980
Wild Men's Dance, Op. 13, No. 2[38] (*Danse sauvage*) (P-749)	ca. 1913 (S-2); Mar. 1914/pre- (NY Times, Mar. 30)	054	aka Wild Man's Dance; S-2 agrees with P-749 on Op. No.; M-63 calls this Op. 3, No. 2, likely a typo

WINDS

TITLE	INSTRUMENT	DATE	S#	COMMENTS
Andante and Allegro, Op. 57 (M-86)	Flute, Piano	1918/ pre-	—	"Still in MS or the process of gestation" (Martens, 86)
Ballade for Clarinet (S-C3)	Clarinet, Piano	?	617	
Ballade for Saxophone[39] (S-C2)	Saxophone, Piano	1955?	609	Exists in alternate versions for clarinet and viola (CC-15)
Five Etchings (Philadelphia Orchestra Notes, Feb. 13/14, 1925)	Flute, Clarinet, Bassoon	1925/ pre-	—	We have never seen this piece mentioned by any other source
Intermezzo[40] (CC-15)	Flute, Piano	1959	604	
Nocturne[41] (S-C1)	Clarinet, Piano	1952	600	
Poem (CC-15)	Flute, Piano	Feb. 1979	605	"Worked on but never published by Joshua" (S-C1)
Prelude (S-C1)	Flute, Piano	195?	603	
Prelude and Minuet in Antique Style (S-C1)	Flute, Clarinet	1946?	602	aka Ancient Style (CC-15)

STRINGS

TITLE	INSTRUMENT	DATE	S#	COMMENTS
Barcarolle and Scherzo, Op. 3 (M-86)	Violin, Piano (?)	?	—	
Cello Sonata No. 1, Op. 52[42] (S-C2)	Cello, Piano	1915–1916	612	M-86 claims a total of four cello sonatas were written (as does Kramer in MA, March 1, 1919); R-313 lists two additional sonatas, Opp. 45 and 78; Philadelphia Orchestra Notes, Feb. 13/14, 1925, claims that there were three cello sonatas; L.O. talks of writing a sonata for cello and piano as early as the summer of 1915 (MO, Aug. 1915)
Cello Sonata No. 2[43] (CC-16)	Cello, Piano	ca. 1920	613	S-C2 claims this was never published; originally entitled Rhapsody, emended to Sonata No. 2; one large movement, extended work; Yale, Box 4, Folder 10
Cello Sonatina (M-86)	Cello, Piano	1918/ pre-	—	"[N]ot yet come from press" according to M
Composition No. 36 (S-C3)	Cello, Piano	?	619	
Five Pieces, Op. 75 (M-86)	Cello, Piano	1918/ pre-	—	"Still in MS. or the process of gestation" (Martens, 86)
Four Pieces, Op. 55 (M-86)	Violin, Piano	1918/ pre-	—	"Still in MS. or the process of gestation" (Martens, 86)
Hebraic Fantasy[44] (S-C1)	Violin, Piano	1929	601	Written for Alfred Einstein's 50th birthday party
Miniature String Quartet[45] (M-Add)	String Quartet	1918/ pre-	—	

STRINGS

TITLE	INSTRUMENT	DATE	S#	COMMENTS
Piano Quintet, Op. 49 (R-313)	Piano, Strings	July 1911/ pre- (MA, July 8); 1914 (M-27)	—	A. W. Kramer mentions a quintet as early as 1911 (MA, July 8); "The quintet has come before the notice of Dr. Horatio Parker, who has expressed himself most favorably about it." Op. No. seems very high for a work written this early, however; R-313 attests to this piece as well; MA (June 10, 1916) mentions that L.O. was at work on a quintet that summer
Piano Quintette, Op. 92 (CC-17)	Piano, Strings	1927 (S-C2)	610	CC-17 lists this as Op. 92 and gives the date as 1929, which is impossible, as the premiere was in Jan. 1928
Russian Festival (MA)	Violin, Piano	ca. 1919		A transcription of said movement from the Russian Choruses by Arthur Hartmann
Russian Lament	Cello, Piano (?)	Apr. 1922/ pre-	—	Mentioned by Hans Kindler in MA, Apr. 15; presumably a cello transcription of the eponymous piece from the Russian Choruses
Six Preludes[46] (S-C2)	Cello, Piano	1930–1931	611	A review in the NY *Herald Tribune* (Apr. 13, 1931) claims that the preludes are "dated this year"
String Quartet No. 1, Op. 28[47] (S-C3)	String Quartet	1913 (M-19); Dec. 1914/ pre- (MA, Dec. 12)	616	S-C3 claims this was unpublished, while MA, Dec. 12, claims the piece is "in preparation" by Schott; CC-16 lists two String Quartets, Op. 28 and Op. 99, in addition to the third (1976)

STRINGS

TITLE	INSTRUMENT	DATE	S#	COMMENTS
String Quartet No. 2, Op. 99 (S-C2)	String Quartet	1928	608	S-C2 lists this as Op. 28; MA, Aug. 2, 1919, mentions that L.O. had spent the summer working on a new quartet—could it have been this one?
String Quartet No. 3 (S-C2)	String Quartet	1976	615	
String Quintet (M-19)	String Quintet	1913	—	
Three Russian Impressions, Op. 37[48] (M-86)	Violin, Piano	Apr. 1916/ pre- (MC, May 4)	—	Three parts: Olga, Natascha, Sonja; Yale has the second movement; other two held by Eastman School of Music. Mentioned in NY *Herald Tribune*, May 14, 1916. To be presented on concert with premiere of Op. 26. MC, May 18, 1916, refers to latter named four pieces. Latter two sources suggest that they are for violin solo
Two Barcarolles, Op. 43[49] (M-86)	Violin, Piano	1918/ pre-	—	Consisting of June Barcarolle (transcription of Tchaikovsky) and a transcription of Rubinstein; M-86 calls them "recently published"; held by Eastman School of Music
Two Miniatures, Op. 9 (M-86)	Violin, Piano	May 1916/ pre- (MC, May 18)	—	A transcription of the piano miniatures; according to CJM the two pieces in question are called Melancholie and Mazurka
Untitled, Op. 33, Nos. 1 & 2 (S-C3)	Cello, Piano	?	620	P-748 mentions this as well; according to S-C3 it shares its Op. No. with Drei Lieder

STRINGS

TITLE	INSTRUMENT	DATE	S#	COMMENTS
Viola and Piano No. 1 (Moderato)	Viola, Piano	Oct. 26, 1980		Not the same as the Viola Fantasies
Viola Fantasy No. 1	Viola, Piano	1972?	606	Merkin claims it was written ca. 1920 and notated in 1980. Copyist's score dated Nov. 1980
Viola Fantasy No. 3 (CC-16)	Viola, Piano	Oct. 23, 1972	607	
Violin Sonata	Violin, Piano	After 1918		Slow movement only, at Yale; "North Conway, N.H."
Violin Sonata, Op. 26^{50} (M-Add)	Violin, Piano	1915	—	
Violin Sonata, Op. 31^{51} (S-C2)	Violin, Piano	May– Aug. 1915	614	MC, May 26, announces that the work is to be published shortly by Fisher; MC, Sept. 16, suggests that he wrote it during that summer; in an interview in MO, Aug. 1915, L.O. calls this "one of my most recent efforts"; according to MC, May 26, this was scheduled to be performed "in several leading music venues next winter"
Violin Sonatina, Op. 60 (M-85)	Violin, Piano	1918/ pre-	—	Incomplete
Violin Sonatina, Op. 74 (M-85)	Violin, Piano	1918/ pre-	—	Incomplete
Waltz (S-C3)	Violin, Piano	?	618	

VOCAL

TITLE	INSTRUMENT	DATE	S#	COMMENTS
30th Psalm (R-313)	Chorus	1920/pre-	—	This is possibly R's error and he is actually referring to L.O.'s setting of the 13th Psalm
Aimless I Wander (MC, Feb. 6)	Voice, Piano	Feb. 1919/ pre-	—	Unclear if this is part of another, larger work
America[52] (CC-Add)	Chorus	1930/pre-	702	Words by Martens; the published version is for voice and piano
Drei Lieder, Op. 33[53] (M-87)	Voice, Piano	1915/pre-	—	Cradle Song (Wiegendliedchen), A Vision of Glory (In goldener Fülle), Alone in the Forest (Waldseligkeit); words by Paul England inspired by words of R. Strauss's Songs, Op. 49 (VV-242); songs 1 and 3 include a violin acc. (CC-5); song 1 has S# 704; work shares its Op. No. with S# 620; only Cradle Song is at Yale
Five Songs, Op. 17 (S-V1)	Voice, Piano	1927–1928	700	
Four Blake Songs, Op. 18 (M-87)	Voice, Piano	1918/pre- (see notes)	—	Spring, My Silks in Fine Array, Memory, Hither Come, Mad Song; R-313 agrees with the Op. No.; these songs are also attested to by Rosenfeld, May 27, 1916

VOCAL

TITLE	INSTRUMENT	DATE	S#	COMMENTS
Four Songs (NYPL)	Voice, Piano	May 1918/ pre- (MA, May 4)	—	The Raindrop (aka The Rain, aka Raindrops), The Fountain, The Nightingale, The Song of a Mother (aka the Mother Croon) (vocalise); formerly owned by Eva Gauthier; the final song is dated Feb. 3, 1918—unclear if this refers to that song or the entire cycle; held by NY Public Library in MS
Four Songs without Words (S-V1)	Voice, Piano	1928	701	CC-6 lists 2 and 3 as 1928, but 1 and 4 are undated
Lullaby (S-V1)	Voice, Piano	?	705	Possibly related to the NY Public Library's "Mother Croon"? (see Four Songs above)
Mother Croon (MA, May 4)	Voice, Piano	May 1918/ pre-	—	Possibly the same as the Song of a Mother in the Four Songs at NY Public Library; the source refers to it as an "early written" vocalise
Mother o' Mine[54] (M-86)	Voice, Piano	1910/pre-	706	Words by Kipling
She Stoops in Visions of the Night (M-88)	Voice, Piano	1918/pre-	—	
Six Russian Songs, Op. 76 (M-88)	Voice, Piano	1918/pre-	—	Words by Pushkin

VOCAL

TITLE	INSTRUMENT	DATE	S#	COMMENTS
The Corpse[55]	Voice, Piano	1918; pre-1918 (CC-5)	703	Words by L.O.; published by Henry Cowell in New Music, Apr. 1928
There Was a Jolly Miller Once[56] (M-86)	Voice, Piano	1910/pre-	708	"while still an East Side schoolboy"
Three Moorish Songs (MC, Dec. 12)	Voice, Piano	Dec. 1918/ pre-	—	Unclear if this is part of another work
Three Russian Choruses, Op. 61[57] (S-V2)	Chorus	1918/pre-	709	Russian Lament, Russian Winter, Russian Festival (CC-5); see P-750 for more on the publication; Russian Festival was transcribed for violin by Arthur Hartmann and published by B&H ca. 1919
Twenty Songs (M-86)	Voice, Piano	1910/pre-	—	Written "while still an East Side schoolboy" (M-86)
Two Oriental Songs[58] (P-750)	Voice, Piano	1918/pre- (M-Add)	—	Tartar Lament; Gazal, Arab Love Song; words by Martens; Gazal is not at Yale

ORCHESTRAL

TITLE	INSTRUMENT	DATE	S#	COMMENTS
A la chinoise (M-81)	Orchestra	ca. 1917	—	MC (May 31, 1917) reports that L.O. spent the summer of 1917 doing the orchestration
Burlesques of Richard Strauss (M-81)	Orchestra	1918/pre-	—	M-81 claims that this was scheduled to be performed in the "coming season"
Dance of the Fates (S-O)	Orchestra	1936–1937	822	
Evening Song of the Cossack[59] (CC-Add)	Chamber orchestra	1923	—	Arr. Nicolaj Hanson; an orchestration of the eponymous first Cossack Impression?
Five Songs, Op. 17 (S-O)	Voice, Orchestra	post-1928 (S-O); 1929 (Reis)	823	Words by Waldo Frank; orchestration of the Five Songs for Voice and Piano; songs 1, 3, and 5 date from 1927, 2 from 1928, and 4 is undated; S-O agrees with the Op. No.
Incidental Music for Lysistrata (S-O)	Chamber orchestra (Reis)	1930?	825	
Life of Man (R-313)	Orchestra	1918/pre- (Martens)	—	After Andreyev (R-313)
Lysistrata Suite (S-O)	Orchestra	1930 (P-747); 1930 (Reis)	826	S-O claims the suite doesn't relate to the complete incidental music
Marche funèbre (MC, Oct. 24)	Orchestra	Dec. 1918/pre-	—	Orchestration of movement of the Dwarf Suite
Nocturne and Dance	Orchestra	1936	821	Premiere, St. Louis Symphony Orchestra, Feb. 12, 1937

ORCHESTRAL

TITLE	INSTRUMENT	DATE	S#	COMMENTS
Pantomime Ballet (R-89)	Orchestra	1930 (IC)	—	R-89 agrees with the dates for this work and the one below
Pantomime "Lima Beans" (P-750)	Chamber orchestra (Reis)	1931 (IC)		P-750 claims this is incomplete; according to Reis, the piece also requires alto, tenor, and bass and puppets
Piano Concerto, Op. 89 (NY Herald Tribune, Feb. 18)	Piano, Orchestra	pre-1921 (S-O); 1923 (Gojowy), also Grove's and Reis (see notes)	824	Philadelphia Orchestra program, Feb 13/14, 1925, dates the Sonata for Two Pianos to 1921. Sonata extensively revised when made into concerto. M-77 mentions a piano concerto, Op. 44 (in C-sharp minor), in four movements and "built up on Tschaikovskian lines." Almost all sources relating to the performance of the Op. 89 concerto (including the Philadelphia program) refer to it as L.O.'s "Second Piano Concerto"
Sinfonietta (R-271)	Orchestra	1918/pre- (Martens)	—	
Symphony (P-750)	Orchestra	1932/pre- (Reis); 1936 (IC)		Incomplete; Charles Amirkhanian claims it dates from 1934; "In preparation" according to Reis
The Faun (VV-234)	Orchestra	June 1916/pre-	—	"Henry Wood had [it] in mind for performance before the war"; Kramer (in MA, Dec. 12, 1914) says something similar about "a number of orchestral pieces"

ORCHESTRAL

TITLE	INSTRUMENT	DATE	S#	COMMENTS
The Fog (M-27)	Orchestra	1914; 1915 (Reis)	—	After Andreyev (R-313)
Two Nocturnes (Reis)	Orchestra	1924	—	P-750 claims these are incomplete orchestrations of the two Nocturnes for Piano; no information whether these might be related to the existing Nocturne for Orchestra

1. GMP, 1980 (P-14)
2. B&H, 1918 (S-3); Joshua, 1945 (Stanford)
3. B&H, 1919; Joshua, 1947 (S-3)
4. Ditson, 1912 (CC-Add)
5. Joshua-EMI, 1978 (S-5)
6. B&H, 1917 (?) (MA, Oct. 13, 1917)
7. Hansen, 1914 (P-748)
8. Schott, 1915 (S-2); Joshua (Merkin)
9. Schott, 1915; Joshua, 1941 (S-2)
10. Schott, 1920; Joshua, 1948 (S-2)
11. Joshua-EMI, 1978
12. Joshua-EMI, 1978
13. Schirmer, 1924 (S-3)
14. Schirmer, 1925, renewed in 1953; Joshua
15. B&H, 1918 (S-4)
16. Schirmer, 1924 (S-3)
17. B&H, 1921 (S-3); B&H, 1917 (MA, Oct. 13, 1917)
18. Fischer, 1915 (S-4); Fisher, 1940 (NY Public Library)
19. Elkan-Vogel, 1939; Elkan-Vogel, "Listen to the Drum" was reprinted in *Collection of Contemporary Classics—Easy Pieces from the Contemporary Literature* (World Cat)
20. Fischer, 1918 (S-3)
21. Fischer, 1924 (P-14); B&H (P-735)
22. BMC, 1914 (S-4)
23. Hansen, 1914 (S-3)
24. B&H, 1918 (S-2)
25. Schirmer, 1925 (P-11)
26. B&H, 1918 (S-2)
27. Norsk Musik Forlag, 1913 (MGG, 407)
28. Schmidt, 1911 (ESM)
29. B&H, (1917) (P-750)
30. Fischer, 1921 (S-4)
31. Schirmer, 1918 (S-12)
32. Joshua (S-12), (1974)
33. Schott, 1914 (P-10)
34. Fischer, 1924 (S-3)
35. Joshua-EMI, 1978 (S-6)
36. Ditson (M-Add), 1912 (?)
37. Ditson (M-Add), 1912 (?)
38. Schott, 1915; Joshua, 1942 (S-2)
39. Joshua, 1978 (S-C2)
40. Joshua, 1978 (S-C1)
41. Elkan-Vogel, 1952 (S-C1)
42. Fischer, 1918 (S-C2)
43. Fischer (Reis)
44. Joshua, 1978 (S-C1)
45. B&H, 1917 (?) (MA, Oct. 13, 1917)
46. Joshua, 1975 (S-C2)
47. Schott (?), (MA, Dec. 12, 1914, and NY *Times* list it as "in preparation")
48. Ditson, 1916 (CC-Add)
49. B&H, 1917 (MA, Oct. 13, 1917)
50. B&H, 1917 (P-748)
51. Fischer, 1915; Joshua, 1981 (CC-Add)
52. Fischer, 1931 (CC-Add)
53. Fischer, 1915 (S-V1)
54. Fischer, 1916 (S-V1)
55. *New Music*, 1928 (S-V1)
56. Fischer, 1916 (S-V1)
57. Assoc. Music (1& 2), 1928; B&H (3), 1918 (S-V2)
58. Fischer (1918) (M-Add)
59. Hansen, 1923 (CC-Add)

NOTES

INTRODUCTION

1. Jeremy Eichler, "A Virtuoso Who Favors the Fringe," *New York Times*, March 24, 2002, "Arts & Leisure," 29, 32.

2. Ibid., 32

3. Ibid., 29.

4. In the nineteenth and early twentieth centuries, Jews were allowed to live only in certain parts of Jewish Russia. That area was called "the Pale."

5. Hamelin is quoted as saying, "I would like to play in Carnegie once again before I die," a remark author Jeremy Eichler characterized as being said "with palpable frustration." (Eichler, "Virtuoso," 32).

6. In 1975 William Westney made the first modern recording of the music of Leo Ornstein. It contained *Three Moods*, and along with Daniel Stepner, Michael Strauss, Peter John Sacco, and Thomas Mansbacker, the *Quintette* for Piano and Strings, Op. 92. Since then, Michael Sellers, William Westney, Janice Webber, Marthanne Verbit, Jeanie Golan, and Alan Feinberg have recorded various piano works by Ornstein. See chapter 8 for a discussion of their roles in the reemergence of Ornstein's music. Without their early efforts it is likely Marc-André Hamelin would not have known of the existence of Ornstein's music. In our early work for this book, it was these recordings that argued the case for Ornstein's worthiness as the subject of a full-length biography. Hamelin's emergence as an Ornstein advocate has only strengthened our conviction that we are right.

7. A recent CD featuring music of Ornstein, George Antheil, and Henry Cowell is entitled *The Bad Boys*, Hat Hut Records, ART CD 6144.

1. JACOB TITIEV'S STORY

1. See Institute of Musical Art, "Lectures, Recitals and General Occasions, October 15, 1906 through June 4, 1907," "Twelfth Students' Recital, Saturday morning, May 4, 1907," "Lectures, Recitals and General Occasions, October 12, 1908 through June 3, 1909," and "Fifth Students' Recital, Wednesday morning March 10, 1909," the Lila Acheson Wallace Archives and Library of the Juilliard School. In 1907 "Master Leo Orenstein" played the Andante and Rondo: Allegretto of a Mozart C Major Concerto. In 1909 he played Schumann's Andante and Variations, B-flat Major, Opus 46, for two pianos with Miss Irene Schwarcz.

2. See Institute of Music Art, "Lectures, Recitals and General Occasions, October 18, 1909 through June 6, 1910," "First Students' Recital, Friday afternoon December 10, 1909," Lila Acheson Wallace Archives and Library of the Juilliard School. Here Leo Ornstein played Three Studies by Chopin: Opus 10, Nos. 3 and 5, and Opus 25, No. 5.

3. Titiev's story, which he titled "Without a Guide," exists in two separate parts: the first goes up to the time of the pogroms, and the second begins with the Ornstein family's departure from Russia and immigration to the United States. For a long time we had only the first half of the story. We are grateful to the Ornstein and Titiev families for helping us piece them together. The journal is currently in the possession of Titiev's grandson, Robert Titiev.

4. Ibid., 3.

5. Ibid., 4–5.

6. Ibid.

7. Ibid., 6.

8. Ibid.

9. Ibid., 7.

10. Ibid., 10.

11. As is easily imagined, the difference in age between Jacob and his classmates contributed to numerous social problems for Titiev.

12. Ibid., 16–17.

13. Ibid., 15.

14. Ibid., 23.

15. Ibid., 25.

16. Ibid., 86.

17. Ibid., 90–93. At one point after becoming engaged to Rose, Jacob attempted to break off his engagement. But his future mother-in-law convinced him that any difficulties Jacob detected with his future bride could be worked out. Clara Ornstein prevailed, and Jacob and Rose were married.

18. Given Ornstein's thorough embrace of dissonance in his most famous pieces, this story suggests that a significant departure from his childhood aesthetic took place.

19. Ibid., 94.

20. Ibid. Titiev does not expand upon the reasons for the elder Ornsteins' objections, but one can imagine numerous possibilities including their fear that Jacob was applying too much pressure to their child, or leading young Leo into a too secular life for the orthodox parents' tastes. One also wonders just how much the parents objected, as Leo's brother Aaron had started taking piano lessons some time before, presumably with his father's consent.

21. Ibid., 94–95.

22. Ibid., 95–96.

23. Ibid., 96.

24. Ibid., 97–99.

25. Ibid.

26. Ibid., 103–121.

27. Ibid., 121–122. Gabrilowitch was a virtuoso pianist who in the 1920s became conductor of the Detroit Symphony Orchestra. For all of Jacob's comments regarding Abraham Ornstein's reluctance to encourage Leo's musical education, ultimately it was Leo's father who took him to St. Petersburg.

28. Since Jews living in the Pale were already ostracized and only marginally Russian, Jacob's disavowal of his nationality was less dramatic than it might have been for non-Jews. Jacob's rejection of Judaism, however, put him in an unusual position of being without a religious or national identification.

29. In 1880 approximately 5,000 Jews immigrated from Russia and the Slavic areas; in 1907 the number reached 258,000. http://nkasd.wiu.k12.pa.us/VHS/discushellis.html. Accessed July 3, 2004.

30. Being rejected by his Jewish friends meant that Titiev was truly a person without any refuge, practical or emotional. This would have energized his efforts to leave the country.

31. This passage suggests a significant source of tension between Titiev and the Ornstein family: religious practice. Abraham and Clara's orthodoxy must have clashed with Jacob's atheism on numerous occasions, and one wonders whether Clara eventually regretted having pressured Jacob to honor his engagement to her daughter, Rose. It must also have been extremely difficult for Leo's parents to entrust so much of their youngest son's early musical activity to a son-in-law who held their religious traditions in such contempt. Family dynamics left much to be desired. Titiev's account is troubling in that kosher accommodations would likely have been kept very clean and hygienic. It is likely that the squalor he describes has nothing to do with Abraham's insistence on keeping kosher, but rather on the crowded conditions in general. Titiev appears to use the situation to take another swipe at religion.

32. Given the absence of dates from Titiev's journals, and the impossibility of ascertaining Leo's precise date of birth, it is difficult to know how long Leo was in Petrograd, or how old he was when he was there. Our best guess is that Leo attended the conservatory for approximately two years, between 1903 and 1905, and was met by Jacob sometime in January 1906. This would mean Leo was enrolled when he was less than ten years of age, and left after having just turned twelve the month earlier.

33. We have not located any record of this informal recital by Leo beyond Jacob's account. Given the appearance of an article by Arthur Brisbane in June 1910, it is likely that this encounter occurred sometime in spring 1910. See Brisbane, "The Great Power of Music," *New York Evening Journal*, June 11, 1910, 12.

34. Arthur Brisbane joined the staff of William Randolph Hearst's *New York Evening Journal* in 1897. The "editorials" Titiev refers to likely became Brisbane's story "The Great Power of Music," which appeared in that paper on June 11, 1910. This story and Ornstein's early years at the Institute will be considered in greater detail in chapter 2.

35. Beatrice Fairfax was the pen name of Marie Manning, a journalist and advice columnist for the *New York Evening Journal*. She also wrote short stories that appeared in *Harper's Magazine*. No story on Leo Ornstein written by Fairfax prior to the Volpe Symphony concert has been located at this time.

36. Titiev does not clarify who "we" refers to. Given Tapper's resources and Titiev's ambitions for Leo, however, it could easily be the two of them. There is no way to corroborate Titiev's claim of how many people were turned away.

37. Ornstein had been scheduled to give nearly forty concerts in Norway, but they were canceled because of the political situation. It may be that Titiev knew of arrangements for this tour, but never learned that it had been canceled.

2. FROM INSTITUTE TO BANDBOX

1. In the first decades of the twentieth century Arnold Dolmetsch (1858–1940) heightened the American public's awareness of earlier musical practices when he headed a department at Chickering & Sons (1905–1911) that specialized in early-keyboard instrument making. In 1915 he published a monograph entitled *The Interpretation of the Music of the XVII and XVIII Centuries Revealed by Contemporary Evidence* (London, 1915). At the same time, Wanda Landowska, Polish keyboardist, touring virtuoso, and writer on early music, advocated playing Bach on the harpsichord. She became a champion of historically informed performances long before the idea was taken up by others. In the late 1940s and early 1950s, Edgard Varèse also directed a chorus, the Greater New York

Chorus, whose repertoire drew heavily upon early music from both Europe and America and included such infrequently programmed composers as Perotin and Billings. The early music revival really gained steam in the 1960s as part of larger social and political movements that revalued simplicity, a "return to nature," and indigenous art.

2. See Michael Broyles, *Mavericks and Other Traditions in American Music* (New Haven, Conn.: Yale University Press, 2004), 131–132, for a discussion of the conflicts Reis's democratic ideas about music caused with Varèse, founder of the ICG. In Reis's own words she sought to reach "the man on the street." One can only imagine Varèse's reception to such an agenda. See additionally Claire Reis, "Contemporary Music and the Man on the Street," *Eolian Review* 2, no. 2 (1923), 24–27.

3. Between spring 1906 and spring 1910 Ornstein listed four addresses on his Institute records: in April 1906, 214 Henry Street; for the 1906–1907 school year it was 10–12 Attorney Street; for 1907–1908 he gave 60 Second Avenue as his address; and for his final year 1909–1910, 17 Attorney Street. While Leo seemed to move more times than many, even a family as well placed as the Mallet-Prevosts also moved frequently by today's standards.

4. Frank Damrosch, *Institute of Musical Art: 1905–1926*, privately printed for the Juilliard School of Music, 1936, 83.

5. The exact dates of Ornstein's European sojourns have not been pinned down. A. Walter Kramer refers to the "Summer of 1910" as the time Tapper and Ornstein departed for Europe. No clues are given for their return. By then, Bertha Feiring Tapper had resigned from the Institute to concentrate on private teaching and so would not have been constrained by a school calendar. Her private students would await her return regardless. See Kramer, "Leo Ornstein, Pianist: A Study," *Musical America* 14, no. 8 (July 8, 1911), 23.

6. Frank Damrosch personally signed all of Leo's and Pauline Mallet-Prevost's grade transcripts for the years they were at the Institute. We assume that this was typical of Damrosch's involvement in all students' work, although rules concerning personal privacy did not allow us to consult any other pupil's records. We are extremely grateful to Jeni Dahmus and Jane Gottlieb, Archivist and Vice President for Library and Information Resources, respectively, at the Juilliard School for their help in locating records and making them available to us.

7. His father was Jewish, and his mother was Lutheran.

8. See Andrea Olmstead's *Juilliard: A History* (Urbana: University of Illinois Press, 1999), chapters 1 and 2, for an overview of the early years of the Institute for Musical Arts and Frank Damrosch's role in its founding. The Olmstead book, the Juilliard Archives, and George Martin's *The Damrosch Dynasty* (Boston: Houghton Mifflin, 1983) are the principle sources consulted for the discussion of the Institute. Years later Juilliard's requirement of American citizenship and its association with Jewish students and foreign faculty became contentious issues.

9. See James Francis Cooke, "The Advent of Endowed Institutions in America," *Etude* 24 (February 1906), 58, cited in Olmstead, *Juilliard: A History*. A few years' statistics reveal the gender imbalance: 1908's graduating class included 13 males of 52 students or 25%; 1909's graduating class had a total of 56 students, with 10 of them male or 17.85%. In 1910, the year Ornstein graduated, there was a total of 85 students, and 22% of them were male. This percentage dropped in 1912, when of a class of 52 only 8% were male. The entry of the United States into World War I in 1917 would have an effect on all institutions' male student enrollments.

10. See Olmstead, *Juilliard: A History*, pp. 25–26, for a complete list of the inaugural faculty.

11. Lectures, Recitals, and General Occasions, 1909–10, Lila Acheson Wallace Archives and Library of the Juilliard School. The emphasis is original to Damrosch's text. Damrosch's use of the male pronoun "his" is in keeping with the dominant cultural practice at the time. Considering the overwhelming female enrollment at the Institute, however, one might wonder whether Damrosch was directing his remarks to Ornstein in particular. The capitalization appears in Damrosch's text, which is preserved in the Lila Acheson Wallace Archives.

12. No other student in the Institute's first fifteen years of existence played a complete piano concerto at the commencement program. See Commencement Program, June 6, 1910, Lila Acheson Wallace Archive and Library of the Juilliard School.

13. As noted above, over the years of Ornstein's study at the IMA he registered four different addresses. The family came to the United States with a position waiting for the senior Ornstein at a synagogue. While the Ornsteins were not prosperous at first, relatives in the larger community meant they never lived in squalor. Their trajectory was upward and swift. See Brisbane, "The Great Power of Music."

14. On Ornstein's initial admissions record from April 1906, his age is given as "12?," which coincides with the 1893 birth year. He would be sixteen years old at the June 1910 commencement.

15. Frederick H. Martens, *Leo Ornstein: The Man—His Ideas, His Work* (New York: Breitkopf & Härtel, 1918), 17, originally from Brisbane, "The Great Power of Music," 12. The capital letters are in the original. It is hard to know upon what Brisbane based his remarks regarding Leo's potential as a "musical creator" unless it was from Jacob Titiev, since according to the records of concerts and recitals given at the Institute, none of Ornstein's early works were ever performed there. See folders entitled "Lectures, Recitals, and General Occasions," Lila Acheson Wallace Archives and Library of the Juilliard School. It is equally impossible to ascertain precisely whom Brisbane might have had in mind with his remarks regarding exploitation, although Titiev comes to mind.

16. See also Kramer's article "Leo Ornstein, Pianist: A Study" for reference to this event.

17. In preparation for founding the Institute, Damrosch had "visited conservatories at Paris, Brussels, Amsterdam, Berlin, Leipzig, Vienna, Stettin, Cologne and London" (Damrosch, *Institute of Musical Art*, 8).

18. Ibid., 55.

19. According to Olmstead, Dr. H. Holbrook Curtis presented the lectures on singing, Walter Damrosch those on Beethoven, and Waldo Selden Pratt "the three-term 'History of Music' lectures." See Olmstead, *Julliard: A History*, pp. 31–32, for course offerings. Numerous detailed course outlines exist among the Lila Acheson Wallace Archives and Library of the Juilliard School. As becomes clear, the Institute involved some of the most important musicians and scholars in New York at the time.

20. For an example of Thomas Tapper's philosophical/moralistic approach to music and music education, see his 1896 work "Music Talks with Children," which can be read in its entirety online at the Project Gutenberg eBook, http://library.beau.org/gutenberg/1/4/3/3/14339. Accessed June 9, 2005.

21. Ibid. The Lila Acheson Wallace Archives at the Juilliard School contain the syllabi for Tapper's lecture courses. See catalog entitled "Lectures, Recitals, and General Occasions."

22. See Leo Orenstein, progress reports, Lila Acheson Wallace Archives and Library of the Juilliard School.

23. See ibid. for Damrosch's assessment that Leo needed to become more regular in his attention to the lecture courses.

24. The cover page of his book *First Year Melody Writing* (1911) lists Tapper as "Lecturer in New York University. *Second Year Harmony* (1912), and *First Year Counterpoint* (1913) list him as Thomas Tapper, Litt.D. and "Lecturer in New York University, in the Cornell University Summer School, and in the Institute of Musical Art of the City of New York." *Key to First Year Harmony with Additional Exercises* (1915) lists no affiliations, but then neither does it include his honorary "Litt.D." In 1914 Tapper coauthored *Essentials in Music History*, with Percy Goetschius, who was then head of theory and composition at the Institute and one of Leo's instructors.

25. Damrosch, *Institute of Musical Art*, 78.

26. See "Dr. Tapper Dead; Writer on Music," *New York Times*, February 25, 1958, 27. Tapper received an honorary doctorate from Bates College in 1911. Nowhere does Ornstein comment upon Tapper's role in his work or life, so the extent of. Tapper's participation in the young pianist's training must remain speculation. It is likely that because of Leo's absences from his lectures, Tapper attempted to fill in the gaps in Ornstein's knowledge of the materials he covered, perhaps during their summers together at Blue Hill. Ornstein's records indicate that he did not do particularly well in the exams for the lecture courses, and that Damrosch was concerned that he find a way to attend more of them. See Leo Ornstein student record, Lila Acheson Wallace Archives and Library of the Juilliard School.

27. Pauline Mallet-Prevost Ornstein, *Reminiscences from Here, There, and Everywhere*, unpublished typescript, 2–3. Pauline performed an entire Mozart Concerto in C Major on a December 10, 1909, recital; whether this is the concerto referred to in the passage above is unknown. Given Ornstein's prior training and obvious level of accomplishment, it may not be particularly noteworthy that he could sight-read a Mozart concerto. Not having a precise date for this exchange and not knowing the quality of his performance is also problematic. As noted above, Ornstein had played the Andante and Allegretto from a C Major Mozart Concerto on a student recital on May 4, 1907. Pauline may not have been aware of this event, as she only enrolled for the first time at the Institute in October 1908. Pauline's remarks may be more revelatory of her own limitations than of Ornstein's prodigious gifts at this point. Her progress report for the year 1909–1910 includes the following assessment from Mrs. Tapper: "Application as good as divided interests allow." She was, however, an excellent student in theory and ear-training and earned 94 percent in her lecture exams. See Pauline Mallet-Prevost progress reports, Lila Acheson Wallace Archives and Library of the Juilliard School.

28. Martens, *Leo Ornstein*, 15. Percy Goetschius's remarks on Ornstein's work in his theory classes range from "Very earnest. Work fairly good" in 1906–1907, to "Fair" in 1907–1908, to "Very good. May be re-examined for fourth practical" in 1909–1910. According to his transcript, Ornstein took no courses with R. Huntington Woodman. Besides Goetschius, his only other teacher of theory was Forrest J. Cressman, who graded his work "Fair" and "Very diligent." See student records in the Lila Acheson Wallace Archives and Library of the Juilliard School.

29. Leo Ornstein's complex attitude toward performing and Pauline's role in directing and shaping his career away from the stage will be considered in greater detail later in this

study. While Ornstein was a student at the IMA, he took no composition courses, although a graded curriculum in composition was offered. While his grades in his theory courses were among his weakest, Pauline's grades in theory and composition were strong and consistently in the high ninetieth percentile. See student records, Lila Acheson Wallace Archives and Library of the Juilliard School.

30. Martens, *Leo Ornstein*, 16.

31. Ornstein, *Reminiscences*, 1.

32. See A. Walter Kramer, "Bertha Feiring Tapper: Altruist," *Musical America* 22, no. 21 (September 25, 1915), 9; Albert D. Jewett, "Mrs. Thomas Tapper," *The Musician* (October 1915), 632, 675. A brief, anonymously written death announcement had appeared in the September 11, 1915, *Musical America*, 35. Ornstein seems never to mention the role Damrosch had in his musical education.

33. When Chadwick took over the directorship of the NEC in 1897, he invited Helen Hopekirk (1856–1945), a Leipzig student colleague, to join his faculty. She came and taught there until her death.

34. See *Memoirs of Waldo Frank*, ed. Alan Trachtenberg, introduction by Lewis Mumford (Amherst: University of Massachusetts Press, 1973), 65. In the fall of 1914, Ornstein would have been twenty years old. Frank's comments about Leo's "large, beautiful hands" will become important later in this biography. Frank had accompanied fellow Tapper student and Ornstein classmate Clair Raphael (Reis) to this event. The Institute provided Ornstein with important contacts, not only with well-placed faculty, but with peers who would, like Reis, assume pivotal positions in New York's modern music scene in the twenties. Reis's relationship to the International Composer's Guild likely explains Ornstein later being named a member of that society's advisory board.

35. In Paul J. Carter, *Waldo Frank* (New York: Twayne, 1967), 27, the article is erroneously cited as appearing in *The Outlook*. As Frank records in his notebooks, the piece was just 1,500 words in length. See Waldo Frank Papers, Annenberg Rare Book and Manuscript Library Collection, University of Pennsylvania.

36. The Kneisel Hall Chamber Music School is the oldest chamber music festival in America. Established in 1902, it celebrated its 103rd year in 2005. The school ceased functioning for a time after Kneisel's death in 1926, but was restarted by his daughter Marianne in 1953.

37. The Tappers and Franz Kneisel would have known each other from the Institute, and perhaps even earlier from their days in Boston. They made similar moves from Germany and Austria to Boston, and then to New York.

38. Parker began work on *Mona* in 1908, so Ornstein may have had numerous opportunities over a period of years to observe its gestation. The opera premiered at the Metropolitan Opera in New York on March 14, 1912, and had a total of four performances. Like his second opera *Fairyland*, it never found a place in the standard repertoire.

39. Tapper's Saturday afternoon group classes in the city provided similar opportunities for her students although the quality of performances would have been significantly different among the young amateurs.

40. "The Firs and Felsted: Sunset Maine," undated typescript, Deer Isle–Stonington (Maine) Historical Society.

41. The authors located the house in summer 2004. It is presently owned by William and Elana Anderson.

42. According to records located by Elvira Bass of the Blue Hill Historical Society, the Tappers did not live in their house "Tapper's Woods" during the years 1913 and 1914. Instead they rented it to the Frank Rutan family. How much or what part of those years they rented it out is not clear. It is possible that Tapper and Ornstein made other arrangements for lodging in Maine. Frederick Martens writes: "In the summer of 1913, Ornstein once more crossed the ocean in company with Mrs. Tapper and went directly to Paris" (*Leo Ornstein*, 19). Letters from Leo to Roger Quilter definitively place Ornstein in Blue Hill the summer of 1914. Starting in the summer of 1915 and continuing through 1918, Ornstein's summering habits are mentioned in *Musical America* and *Musical Courier*. In *Making Music Modern: New York in the 1920's* (New York: Oxford University Press, 2000), Carol Oja refers to "Dane Rudhyar, who met Ornstein during the summers of 1917 and 1918 at Seal Harbor, ME" (23). Seal Harbor lies south of Bar Harbor, Maine, which is east of Deer Isle and Blue Hill and easily accessible using the many ferries in the area.

43. Theodore Parker had studied with George Whitefield Chadwick, who encouraged him to go to Munich to work with one of his own former teachers, the eminent organist, theorist, conductor, composer, and composition pedagogue Joseph Rheinberger.

44. With the outbreak of World War I, the destination for American composers moved from Germany to France and specifically to the American Conservatory at Fontainebleu where Nadia Boulanger taught. But German instruction retained its cachet up until that time.

45. Martens claims that Tapper and Ornstein went to Europe in the spring of 1910, but it was at the earliest summer of that year, as Ornstein was still a student at the Institute through the spring term and performed at Mendelssohn Hall as part of graduation events in June 1910 (*Leo Ornstein*, 16). His attendance at the Salzburg Festival, which took place late in July and throughout August, would also support a later date for this first trip. The Salzburg Festival in 1910 to which Martens refers was among a series of music and drama festivals mounted by the Vienna Philharmonic and the Mozart-Stiftung irregularly starting in 1877. Although plans for an annual festival were being discussed at the time of Ornstein's visit, World War I interrupted their coming to fruition until 1920. The festival focused upon the works of Mozart. It is not known with whom Leo played Brahms.

46. Kramer, "Leo Ornstein, Pianist: A Study." At a recital in honor of Mme. Teresa Carreno given on March 11, 1910, at the Institute, Ornstein had played works of Chopin and Leschetizky. It is possible he played the pedagogue's own work for him when he visited later that year. See "Lectures, Recitals, and Other Occasions," Lila Acheson Wallace Archives and Library of the Juilliard School, October 18, 1909, through June 6, 1910, 58.

47. The 1906 cast of *Don Giovanni* included Johanna Gadski as Donna Elvira, Geraldine Farrar as Zerlina, and Lilli Lehmann as Donna Anna. In 1910 Antonio Scotti joined the cast as the Don, and Karl Muck conducted. See www.wyastone.co.uk/nrl/pvoce/7921c.html for information on Lehmann's role at the Salzburg Music Festival. Accessed June 20, 2005.

48. In subsequent years his age would be listed anywhere from two to five years younger than he actually was. Whether this was a conscious attempt to take advantage of his youthful looks and exaggerate his prodigiousness, one can't be certain. Given the absence of any birth certificate there is ample room for honest mistakes.

49. *New York Times*, March 5, 1911, X2 and X3.

50. *New York Times*, March 6, 1911, 7. See also Carl Van Vechten, *Music and Bad Manners* (New York: Knopf, 1916), 232, for clarification: "Concerts by serious artists seldom took place outside of recognized concert halls, nor did they occur on Sunday nights." In 1911 Van Vechten was "assistant to the musical critic of the *New York Times*."

51. "Leo Ornstein's Recital: New Prodigy Makes His Appearance at the New Amsterdam," *New York Times*, March 6, 1911, 7. If Ornstein's programming is any reflection of his preferences, he did not prefer Beethoven. Among programs for which we have works listed, Beethoven's name appears only thirteen times, and nine of these performances take place between November 1918 and March 1919. Each time Leo performed Op. 57, the *Appassionata*.

52. *New York Times*, March 30, 1911, 20.

53. *New York Times*, April 1, 1911, 22.

54. *New York Times*, April 2, 1911, X13.

55. Given that Mahler was diagnosed with his ultimately fatal illness in February, 1911, it is not certain that the concert even took place, or if it did with Mahler at the podium.

56. "The Philharmonic Society," *New York Times*, April 3, 1911, 9.

57. Van Vechten, *Music and Bad Manners*, 236.

58. *New York Times*, May 14, 1911, 3.

59. *New York Times*, May 22, 1911, 11.

60. *New York Times*, October 1, 1911, 8.

61. *New York Times*, October 15, 1911, 10.

62. In 1902 Volpe had organized the Young Men's Symphony Orchestra with the express purpose of training students in orchestral music; it was the first organization of its kind in the nation and folded into the Volpe Symphony Orchestra in 1904. See www.miami.edu/advancement/NamedBuildingsGables.doc. Accessed June 22, 2005.

63. *New York Times*, October 1, 1911, 8.

64. "Music Here and There," *New York Times*, March 24, 1912, A9.

65. "Volpe Symphony Gives Last Concert: Leo Ornstein and Miss Margarete Kellner Soloists in Carnegie Hall," *New York Times*, March 27, 1912. Unsigned review. Based upon remarks Van Vechten includes in his book *Music and Bad Manners*, where he states that he did not hear of Ornstein between his earliest New Amsterdam Theatre concert and the Bandbox ones of 1915, he is not the author of this article (233). Edward MacDowell lived from 1860 to 1908. His second concerto dates from 1886.

66. See *Musical Courier*, February 7, 1912, and May 1, 1912. Anderson's firm is at 5 West 38th Street in New York.

67. "Stroud Week at Aeolian Hall" *New York Times*, April 23, 1912, 5.

68. *Lyric Fancies for the Pianoforte by Leo Ornstein* (Boston: Arthur P. Schmidt, Boston, 1911). Their 1911 date makes them among Ornstein's earliest published works. We are grateful to Ms. Jeni Dahmus of the Lila Acheson Wallace Archives and Library of the Juilliard School for compiling a list of Bertha Feiring Tapper's students for us. Of the four young women dedicatees, only Miss Mallet-Prevost's first name is missing. Whether this is indicative of a special relationship between the composer and Pauline is unknown. Soon after Pauline Ornstein died in 1985, Leo Ornstein dedicated No. 5 of his *Six Journal Pieces*: "For my beloved wife." Severo Ornstein has numbered this piece S334–1 and dates its composition sometime between 1987 and 1988. These are the two works we have found that bear a dedication to Pauline. Martens refers to Ornstein's "Russian Suite," another

early work, being played in concerts in New York in 1911, although at this time no mention has been found in reviews of that year. The work numbered Op. 12, Nos. 1–7, was published in 1914 by Wilhelm Hansen in Leipzig. It appeared as *Suite russe*, perhaps reflecting Ornstein's time in Europe and the provenance of the publishing house.

69. In his book on Carlos Salzedo, another musician who summered in Maine, author Dewey Owens observed "Maine *is* a musical summer camp." See *Carlos Salzedo: From Aeolian to Thunder, a Biography* (Chicago: Lyon & Healy, 1992), 21–23.

70. At this time no score for a mazurka in B-flat minor by Ornstein can be located. There are copies of mazurkas in both E-flat major (No. 3 of *Cossack Impressions*, ca. 1914) and B minor (No. 2 from *Nine Miniatures*, ca. 1915). See *Catalog and Thematic Index of Works for Solo Piano by Leo Ornstein* compiled by his son Severo Ornstein (Woodside, Calif.: Poon Hill Press), 1998.

71. Who instigated the recording sessions is not known. For the Grieg and Poldini see Columbia A 1445. For the Chopin see Columbia A 1473. They were issued in February and March 1914 while Ornstein was in Europe. While the quality of these recordings is poor, as is typical of early acoustic recording, it is good enough to hear Ornstein's remarkable facility on the keyboard, his easy speed, and his expressive, emotional approach to the repertoire.

72. A. Walter Kramer, "Has Leo Ornstein Discovered a New Musical Style?" *Musical America* 21, no. 4 (December 12, 1914), 5. This piece comes from a set of six pieces called *Dwarf Suite*, his Op. 11. It was dedicated to Theodore Leschetizky

73. Edvard Grieg's *Lyrische Stücke*, Op. 54, was composed in 1891. In 1905 Peters published Grieg's arrangement of four of his pieces as a *Lyric Suite for Orchestra*. "March of the Trolls" was one of the four piano pieces arranged for the suite.

74. Mr. Wesley Weyman gave a student recital at the Institute of Musical Arts on April 23, 1908, at which he played the third piece from this same set, *Bénédiction de Dieu dans la solitude*. Since attendance at piano recitals was required, and this program took place in the morning when Ornstein was free of his regular school responsibilities, we can assume that he heard at least this selection of Liszt's *Harmonies poétiques et religieuses*. Attendance was taken and commented upon in yearly progress reports if it was an issue. See "Lectures, Recitals, and Other Occasions," 1907–1908, p. 59, Lila Acheson Wallace Archives and Library of the Juilliard School.

75. "Ornstein's Ultra-Modernism and Expert Pianism," *Musical Courier* 70, no. 15 (April 14, 1915), 31. Unsigned article.

76. "Leo Ornstein Hoists the Banner of Musical Futurism," *Current Opinion* 61 (July 1916), 30–31. His more lyrically driven old manner of composing would not completely disappear but become part of his new voice.

77. Charles L. Buchanan, "Futurist Music," *The Independent*, July 31, 1916, 160.

78. Van Vechten, *Music and Bad Manners*. 236.

79. Leo Ornstein, interview by Vivian Perlis, Yale University Oral History American Music (OHAM) Project, December 8, 1972, Waban, Massachusetts. Quoted in Perlis, "The Futurist Music of Leo Ornstein," *Notes* 31, no. 4 (June 1975), 737. Ornstein's reference to himself as eighty is in keeping with his assumption that he was born in 1892.

80. Ornstein's latter-day recollection is the only one that mentions Tapper's reactions or her involvement in the stylistic epiphany. This is curious given the number of accounts that appeared closer to the actual event, and raises the question why Ornstein didn't refer to her in his earliest tellings of the story.

81. "The Last of the Original 20th Century Mavericks, Leo and Pauline Ornstein speak with Vivian Perlis," Yale University Archives of Oral History American Music. Interview conducted at Sierra Mobile Park, Lot #32, off I-18, Brownsville, Texas, November 19 and 20, 1977.

82. The study of stemmatics in scholarship focuses upon the sources of our information and how information is disseminated. Multiple repetitions of the same information may give the impression that many scholars independently concur with the truthfulness of a fact, when in reality they may simply be repeating a single source. This can result in the efficient dissemination of accurate information or equally widespread misinformation.

83. These pieces were eventually published as Op. 16, Nos. 1 and 2, by Joshua Corporation of Dobbs Ferry, N.Y., in 1941. See Martens, *Leo Ornstein*, 19. This narrative agrees with the 1977 interview.

84. Vannin was a pseudonym that Ornstein used in the 1910s for mostly short, simple piano compositions. When we interviewed Ornstein in June 1998, the 104-year-old composer had no memory of Vannin or any works composed by this "third voice."

85. Leschetizky's commenting on *Wild Men's Dance* raises further the question of when Ornstein wrote this piece. Its similarity to aspects of Ravel's *Valses nobles et sentimentales* leads one to recall that Ornstein had had an opportunity to hear much of the French composer's works in the time since he had arrived in Europe. Certainly Ravel's piano music became an important part of Ornstein's programs in the years that followed. Ornstein had not played Ravel on any of the student recitals at the IMA.

86. Martens, *Leo Ornstein*, 20.

87. Ibid. Though trained initially as a violinist, Bauer was an English-born musician, who after studying with Paderewsky devoted himself to the piano and enjoyed a worldwide reputation for his technical abilities and extraordinary interpretive gifts. Starting in 1892 he based himself in Paris. As a result of his international fame, Bauer knew Europe's most important musicians.

88. See Charles Timbrell, "Walter Morse Rummel," *Grove Music Online*, ed. L. Macy. www.grovemusic.com. Accessed July 12, 2005.

89. Members of *Les Apaches* included "the Catalan pianist Ricardo Vines . . . writers Tristan Klingsor and Léon-Paul Fargue, the painter Paul Sordes, the conductor Désiré-Emile Inghelbrecht, and composers André Caplet, Maurice Delage, Manuel de Falla, Florent Schmitt, and Déodat de Severac. . . . It was in this circle of artistic acceptance that [Ravel] tried out some of his first masterworks." Regarding Ravel's involvement with this group see newyorkphilharmonic.org/programNotes/0304_Ravel_Sheherazade3Poems .pdf. Accessed July 12, 2005.

90. Maurice Ravel (1875–1937) dedicated each of his *Miroirs* to a different member of *Les Apaches*. No. 4, "Alborada del gracioso," is dedicated to Michel Dimitri Calvorcoressi. Additionally, Ravel set a number of Calvocoressi's poems. Calvorcoressi was thoroughly committed to modern music. In addition to his advocacy of Ravel, he was an occasional correspondent of Stravinsky's and a champion of Mussorgsky.

91. Valerie Langfield, *Roger Quilter: His Life and Music* (Suffolk: Boydell Press, 2002), 45–46.

92. It may or may not be telling that in this account Ornstein refers to *Danse sauvage* as *Wild Men's Dance*, the more likely title he would have given the piece had it been composed in New York prior to his visit to Paris. It may also be he used the English title

in this account because that's what it was commonly called in the United States by 1917 when he was talking to Martens.

93. Calvocoressi was an extremely talented linguist and translator. In addition to English and French, he also read and spoke Greek and Russian.

94. It is likely he drew from his acquaintances among *Les Apaches*.

95. From this remark, it appears that Ornstein was more interested in composing than performing.

96. See Martens, *Leo Ornstein*, 20–22. Bartók's ground-breaking *Allegro barbaro* (1911) may have been one of these piano pieces. Its newly percussive treatment of the piano would have made it a noteworthy example of that which was most modern. In 1927, Ornstein would label the first movement of his *Quintette* for Piano and Strings "Allegro barbaro." Selections from Scott's *Jungle Book* would regularly appear on Ornstein's recitals once he was back in the United States.

97. Ibid., 22.

98. Ibid.

99. Langfield, *Roger Quilter*, 6. For a photograph of Bawdsey Manor and the Quilters' London home at 74 South Audley Street, see Langfield's book, photographs following page 204. We are sincerely grateful to Ms. Langfield for sharing letters from Leo Ornstein to Roger Quilter that she discovered while doing research for her biography. They filled an important lacunae in the narrative of Ornstein's life.

100. Langfield hypothesizes that "to be 'musical'" was a euphemism for being homosexual. Quilter was indeed homosexual, although the number or names of his partners is undetermined beyond a relationship with Robert Allerton.

101. Ibid., 22.

102. As Langfield explains, in 1907 Percy Grainger traveled to Norway and met Grieg, a composer he idolized. While there he "played and sang some of Quilter's songs . . . which pleased Grieg greatly. [Upon] Grainger's suggestion, Quilter promised to send Grieg some of his music." Quilter's connection to Grieg, and Ornstein's own through Mrs. Tapper, gave the two men an important musical link. Ibid., 27.

103. Ibid., 16.

104. Stephen Lloyd, "Grainger and the 'Frankfurt Group,'" *Studies in Western Music* (University of Western Australia) 16 (1982), 111–118, quotation on 112–113.

105. Ornstein's *Lyric Fancies* and *Miniatures*, pieces written prior to his second trip to Europe, are extremely lyrical and not primarily focused on vertical sonorities. See Lloyd, "Grainger and the 'Frankfurt Group,'" 115–116, for a discussion of these qualities in the music of the Frankfurt Group in general and Cyril Scott in particular.

106. Langfield, *Roger Quilter*, 20.

107. Martens, *Leo Ornstein*, 23. The identity of the precise Arthur Shattuck referred to in this passage has not been determined.

108. Ibid. Given the Quilter's long list of friends and associates it is not possible to definitively identify the painter Martens alludes to. Based, however, upon Langfield's description of Major Benton Fletcher, "a noted artist and author" who was also "a popular guest at dinner parties, interesting, witty, [and] good-looking," he is a likely candidate. See Langfield, *Roger Quilter*, 28.

109. Ibid. The immediate transferal of idea or image to sound would be the composer's analogous experience. Ornstein appears to have worked very much this way.

110. It was part of the ethos of the Frankfurt Group to assist each other arrange performances. According to Stephan Lloyd, Balfour Gardiner was especially helpful in

promoting his cohorts' music: "Gardiner . . . was born into a wealthy family of merchants, though his inherited wealth was put to excellent and unselfish use. He was ever one to put his friends' music and needs before his own, and the Group's finest hour was in many ways the eight concerts in 1912 and 1913 which Gardiner organized, financed, and in part conducted. Not without good cause did Grainger call him the 'Good Angel of British Composers'" (Lloyd, "Grainger and the 'Frankfurt Group,'" 117).

111. It is not known what piece Ornstein is referring to.

112. "A 'Futurist' at the Piano," *London Times*, March 28, 1914, 6.

113. R. C., "Futurist Music: Wild Outbreak at Steinway Hall: Pale and Frenzied Youth," *Daily Mail*, March 28, 1914, 1a.

114. The author is not identified, but would appear to be Ornstein himself, or perhaps Bertie Landsfield, who Ornstein referred to in his letter to Quilter as writing some kind of biographical piece, one presumes for this recital.

115. The Bach pieces were inserted at the suggestion of Roger Quilter. It appears that perhaps Ornstein's initial inclination to play only futurist music might have been the wiser course to take.

116. U.A., "A 'Futurist' Recital: Mr. Ornstein's 'Impressions,'" *Daily Telegraph*, March 28, 1914, 7. The Corybants come from Greek mythology. They attended the goddess Cybele by dancing wildly for her during her nightly journeys.

117. Algernon Ashton (1859–1937) was a Leipzig-trained pianist/composer who was Professor of Piano at the Royal College of Music.

118. R. C., "Futurist Music Hissed: Hostile & Derisive Audience," *Daily Mail*, April 8, 1914, 3.

119. U.A. "Steinway Hall," *Daily Telegraph*, April 8, 1914, 8.

120. U.A. "More 'Futurist' Music: Mr. Leo Ornstein's Agility as a Pianist," *London Times*, April 8, 1914, 10.

121. U.A., "M. Leo Ornstein: A Futurist Recital," *Musical Times* 55, no. 855 (May 1, 1914), 331.

122. U.A. "Hissing Defended," *Musical Courier*, May 6, 1914, 52.

123. Ornstein's unusual posture at the piano was cause for critical remarks while he was a student at the IMA. In a report from January 21, 1910, Frank Damrosch wrote "Bad position and movements of head growing worse." See "Lectures, Recitals, and Other Occasions" 1909–1910, Lila Acheson Wallace Archives and Library of the Juilliard School.

124. C.N., *The Musical Standard*, April 18, 1914, 374–375.

125. Van Vechten, *Music and Bad Manners*, 238.

126. MS 70603 f 156, May 18, 1914.

127. Langfield's letter #157, May 29, 1914, Leo Ornstein, Blue Hill, Maine, to Roger Quilter, 7 Montagu Street. One wonders if Ornstein was aware of Mendelssohn's immense popularity among the British public in the mid-nineteenth century, and that those feelings continued strong into the early years of the twentieth century.

128. Quilter was, in fact, called to report for a medical exam years later when the pool of able-bodied young men had been decimated by the horrendous death tolls suffered by the English, but his poor health kept him from being accepted.

129. Langfield's letter #162, August 25, 1914, Leo Ornstein, Blue Hill, Maine, to Roger Quilter.

130. Martens, *Leo Ornstein*, 27.

131. See the Statute of Liberty–Ellis Island Foundation (SOLEIF) site for Ellis Island immigrant records. Lucian Swift Kirtland arrived August 25, 1916, on the *Baltic*. He registered his age as thirty-four, his marital status as single, and his residence as Poland, Ohio. In 1918 Kirtland published *Samurai Trails: A Chronicle of Wanderings on the Japanese High Road*. Based upon the dates of the letters in our possession Kirtland was in New York at least from January 30, 1915, through April 29, 1915. He could have come earlier and stayed later. During that period he resided at 137 West 12th Street, in what is now known as Greenwich Village. Percy Grainger came to the United States in 1914, but there is no record of Ornstein's meeting him at any time.

132. Add MS 70598 f 114–17, 30 Jan 1915, Lucian Swift Kirtland 137 West 12th Street, NYC letter to Roger Quilter, 7 Montagu Street, London W1.

133. The four concerts were held January 26, February 7, February 28, and March 16.

134. Langfield's letter #118, April 29, 1915, Lucian Kirtland, 137 West 12th Street, New York City, to Roger Quilter. We have found no documentation of an Ornstein concert in Rio, although if it had taken place in a private home, it is possible that no mention would appear in the press.

3. CIRCLES AND TRIANGLES AND NETWORKS AND NETS

1. See Ornstein's letter to Roger Quilter of May 29, 1914: "I wish I could have been with you in Oxford when you saw the boys[,] it must have been lots of fun."

2. Undated signed autograph letter in authors' possession. Peter is the son of Leo's brother Manus. We are grateful to Peter's daughter, Holly Ornstein Carter, for sharing her father's letters with us.

3. Ornstein, interview with his niece, Holly Carter.

4. Questions related to Leo and Pauline's relationship and more especially Leo's personal choices will be discussed in the final chapter.

5. The precise years of Raphael Reis's work with Tapper are uncertain. In an article that appeared in *Eolian Review* 2, no. 2 (March 1923), 28, Reis states that she worked with Tapper between 1908 and 1910. These years would coincide with Ornstein's last two years of study at the Institute and concur with Raphael Reis's own remarks in her book *Composers, Conductors, and Critics* (New York: Oxford University Press, 1955) that she "spent the next two years at the Institute of Musical Art" (21). But as Carol Oja has observed, "among Reis's papers is a photograph of Tapper, stating on the back that Reis studied with her from 1906 to 1913 (Reis-NN, box 1a)." See "Women Patrons and Crusaders for Modernist Music: New York in the 1920s," in *Cultivating Music in America: Women Patrons and Activists since 1860*, ed. Ralph P. Locke and Cyrilla Barr (Berkeley: University of California Press, 1997), 258, fn. 42. Raphael Reis may very well have studied privately with Tapper after 1910, when Tapper left the Institute. The only question really is when she began study. If it was as early as 1906, she would have known Leo from the time of his arrival in the country, making her one of his very earliest acquaintances.

6. Reis, *Composers, Conductors, and Critics*, 35.

7. Ibid., 21.

8. See ibid., 18–19, for a discussion of the "brilliant center for the arts" that was Berlin.

9. Waldo Frank to Claire Reis, September 21, 1956, Reis-NN (box 2), as quoted by Oja in "Women Patrons and Crusaders for Modernist Music," 244–245.

10. Waldo Frank was an accomplished amateur cellist, a fact that would have been known to Ornstein over their many years of friendship. What is not known is whether any of Ornstein's many cello pieces were written with Frank in mind. Certainly Ornstein developed into a sensitive writer for the instrument. Correspondence with Leo's son Severo clarifies that during Waldo's visits to the family compound in New Hampshire in the 1930s and 1940s, Waldo Frank did not play cello either for or with Ornstein: "I would have known and been stunned if he had. Dad never played when the family had visitors— unless he went up to his studio to practice" (letter, September 13, 2005).

11. Reis, *Composers, Conductors, and Critics*, 21.

12. It is reasonable to assume that had he been at the London concerts, some mention would have been made in his voluminous correspondence. To date we have turned up nothing that refers to Rosenfeld's hearing Ornstein in London in 1914.

13. See Charles L. P. Silet, *The Writings of Paul Rosenfeld: An Annotated Bibliography* (New York: Garland, 1981), xxii. See Paul Rosenfeld, "Grand Transformation Scene— 1907–1915," ibid., 356–357, quoted by Silet, xxii.

14. Ibid., xxiii. Ten years later Aaron Copland would return from his three years of study in France with a similar goal in mind.

15. Rosenfeld spent most of the months of July and August 1915 and 1916 in Blue Hill, Maine.

16. It is likely that this comprehensive course morphed into a series of articles entitled "How My Music Should be Played and Sung: A Series of Papers Devoted to the Character and Idiom of My Latest Works, Describing Essential Requirements for Their Adequate Understanding and Providing Suggestions for Mastery of Their Technical Difficulties." See *The Musical Observer*, January 1916, 9–11, for the first of these articles. It contains yet another explanation regarding Ornstein's stylistic epiphany, which he refers to as "My Musical Awakening."

17. Paul Rosenfeld to Claire Raphael, signed autograph letter, August 6, 1915. See MNY Amer. Claire Reis Collection Box 5 at the New York Public Library for the Performing Arts. A typed transcription of this letter exists in the collection. It has incorrectly transcribed the date as August 16, 1915. One has to wonder whether Ornstein really envisioned Steinway Hall for this event intended to attract an audience of sixty or seventy. Steinway Hall, then on 14th Street, had a main auditorium of 2,000 seats. It had been the home of the New York Philharmonic until Carnegie Hall was built in 1891. Perhaps he planned to use one of the smaller rooms where pianists tried out instruments. Steinway Hall moved to its current location at 109 West 57th Street in 1922. It is likely that Ornstein assumed that his infamous concerts at Steinway Hall in London provided some kind of entry into the related facility in New York.

18. In addition to Kramer's being a violinist, chamber musician, and composer, he was also a writer and would eventually become editor of *Musical America*. It is no coincidence that many extended pieces on Ornstein were published in that widely circulating music magazine.

19. Henry J. Wood had been present at Ornstein's London recitals and been one of the few enthusiastic listeners. Correspondence from Wood to Quilter from March 13, 1919, refers briefly to that time: "I have heard from Mr. Ornstein [what could he play at one of my symphony concerts. . . . shall never forget the impression his recital at Steinway Hall made upon me." Add MS 70603 f 100–1 13 March 1919, Henry J. Wood, Apple Tree Farm House, Chorley Wood Common, Herts, letter to Roger Quilter. It is located in the British Library, London.

20. Just a month after Kramer's article appeared, Thomas Vincent Cator responded with a letter to *Musical America* 21, no. 9, that appeared on January 2, 1915, 24–25. In it he proposed a reharmonization of Ornstein's *Impressions* "according to the best principles . . . with chords that are logically related to one another." Needless to say, Cator's suggestions eliminated the very qualities of Ornstein's music that made it distinctive. Kramer's allusions to modern French composers is curious given Ornstein's regular programming of Debussy and his avowed respect for Ravel. One wonders whether Kramer heard a resemblance between Ornstein's music and theirs and felt compelled on his own to claim no influence of the French masters upon his young friend.

21. A variation on this explanation includes Ornstein's assertion that once written down he never changed a note. As we discovered when creating the critical edition of Ornstein's *Quintette* for Piano and Strings, such a process, which may have worked for the briefer piano works, did not hold for this larger work. There is much evidence of Ornstein's having revisited and revised the *Quintette*, and sometimes the changes were significant and over very lengthy passages.

22. See "Ornstein Lecture-Recital," *Philadelphia Ledger*, January 22, 1934, for a review of Ornstein's demonstration of his improvisational skills. The Leo Ornstein Papers, MS 10, Irving S. Gilmore Music Library, no page number.

23. Kramer's insistence that Ornstein's music is not like contemporary Frenchmen's suggests that the man doth protest too much.

24. Kramer, "Has Leo Ornstein Discovered a New Musical Style?"

25. Signed autograph letter, Leo Ornstein to Waldo Frank, December 7, 1914. Ornstein invites Frank to "come up on Sunday at five in the afternoon to 85 West 87th Street room 14. (Mr. Jewett's Studio)." Clearly the men were in the very earliest stages of their friendship. The letter is addressed to "My dear Mr. Frank" and signed "With kind regards, Leo Ornstein." Waldo Frank Papers, Annenberg Rare Book and Manuscript Library Collection, University of Pennsylvania. Letters between Waldo Frank and both Leo and Pauline Ornstein are collected in two folders in Box 21, "Correspondence."

26. Frank records this information in one of his many notebooks. This notebook contains titles of articles, dates of completion, numbers of words, and information on if and when a piece was published. If published, Frank provides the name and date of the publication. See Waldo Frank Collection, Box 47, Annenberg Rare Book and Manuscript Library Collection, University of Pennsylvania.

27. Signed autograph letter, Leo Ornstein to Waldo Frank, February 25, 1915, from the Correspondence folders of the Waldo Frank Papers, Annenberg Rare Book and Manuscript Library Collection, University of Pennsylvania.

28. See Silet, *The Writings of Paul Rosenfeld*, for the most thorough listing of Rosenfeld's critical works. Rosenfeld dedicated his 1924 book *Port of New York* to Ornstein.

29. What became of the plans for Steinway Hall is not known. It is likely that given the late date of the initial discussions, the hall had already been booked. The Reis recitals took place on four Sunday evenings: March 5 and 19 and April 2 and 16. See David Joel Metzer, "The Ascendancy of Musical Modernism in New York City, 1915–1929" (Ph.D. diss., Yale University, 1993), 352.

30. Frank introduced Rosenfeld to Alfred Stieglitz. The Rosenfeld-Stieglitz relationship lasted until their deaths, just one month apart. Silet has characterized Rosenfeld's attachment to Stieglitz as "filial" (xxvi).

31. Frank mentored the Harlem Renaissance writer Jean Toomer and became close friends in the process. In 1920 the two traveled together through the southern states. Toomer's affair with Frank's wife, Margaret Naumberg, soon thereafter strained the marriage, which after the birth of their child Thomas in 1922 ultimately ended in divorce in 1926. Frank took responsibility for the failure of the marriage because of his own numerous infidelities, of which he had kept Naumberg informed. Toomer became close friends with Rosenfeld, and in 1925 he and Rosenfeld summered in Maine together. The two men also visited Stieglitz and Georgia O'Keeffe at their Lake George summer home, "The Hill." Frank would ultimately marry twice more. It is unknown what Ornstein thought of these particular relationships or even of their precise nature. According to his son, Severo, after a visit by Frank to the Ornstein's home in New Hampshire, sometime after Frank's separation from his second wife Alma Magoon, whom he had married in 1927, "Dad said (shaking his head) that he simply couldn't understand someone who would get divorced." Shortly after his 1943 Reno divorce, Frank married Jean Klempner. As to the topic of homosexuality, Severo recalled, "it never came up that I recall. But promiscuity once you were married, was decidedly a no-no" (letter, September 13, 2005).

32. On two occasions, at least, Rosenfeld's harsh criticisms of Frank's novel caused major rifts in their friendship. See "The Novels of Waldo Frank," The Dial 70 (January 1921), 95–105; and "Waldo Frank's Dream," The Nation 148 (May 20, 1939), 590.

33. Claire Raphael Reis was an essential player in the formation of both societies.

34. Martens, Leo Ornstein, 27. Whether these were public or private events is unknown. No record of these concerts has been found at this time.

35. A final paragraph of the brief remarks commented upon a talk entitled "The Song Singer's Art," which was given by a Mr. Max Heinrich at the same meeting. See A.W.K. (A. Walter Kramer), "'Bohemians' Hear Ornstein." Musical America 21, no. 2 (November 14, 1914), 14.

36. From 1905 to 1917 Stieglitz managed the "Little Galleries of the Photo-Secession" at 291 Fifth Avenue, which became known as "The 291."

37. According to Ornstein's daughter, Edith Ornstein Valentine, it was auctioned by the Phillips Auction house in New York in 2003 (telephone conversation, August 14, 2005).

38. See Ruth E. Fine, John Marin (Washington, D.C.: National Gallery of Art, 1990), 84–89.

39. "The Crags" was the name of the Mallet-Prevost–Ornstein summer cottage in North Conway, New Hampshire. Stieglitz and O'Keeffe had a similarly named family retreat at Lake George in New York, "The Hill."

40. Leo's daughter Edith Valentine reported that from their New Hampshire home close to the Saco River, her father liked to climb nearby Moat Mountain best of all (phone conversation, August 14, 2005).

41. According to family correspondence, in the 1970s Leo and Pauline considered buying property in Maine, and even engaged a realtor to help them find something suitable. But ultimately their desire for warmer climes led them farther south.

42. E-mail correspondence with Severo Ornstein, November 1, 2005.

43. Ibid.

44. Interview with Edith Valentine, July 27, 2003.

45. We are grateful to Ms. Marin for her gracious hospitality and many insights regarding the Marin and Zorach friendship which she shared with us during an interview

on July 16, 2004, at the former home of John Marin at Cape Split in Addison, Maine, which she now owns.

46. William Zorach was born on February 28, 1887, in Eurburg (now Jurbarkas), Lithuania. The Zorachs came to the United States in 1891 as one of many Russian Jewish families who escaped an inhospitable environment, like the Ornsteins fifteen years later. The Zorachs settled in Port Clinton, Ohio, just outside Cleveland. Between 1910 and 1911 Zorach traveled to Paris to study art. In December 1912 he married Marguerite Thompson, whom he had met in Paris, and in 1913 they both had paintings in the Armory Show in New York City, where they had settled.

47. See *Art Is My Life: The Autobiography of William Zorach* (Cleveland: World, 1967), 58–59, for Zorach's discussion of his summer in Stonington. Stonington is on Deer Isle and just minutes away from Sylvester's Cove where Ornstein had summered. It is also the place where the ferry docked and where earlier Ornstein had met Frank when he came to Maine for a visit.

48. In the 1920s William Kroll taught at the Institute of Musical Art, the same institution from which Ornstein graduated in 1910.

49. The Kroll painting is owned by the University of Virginia Art Museum. For information on it and on Leon Kroll see *Leon Kroll: A Spoken Memoir*, ed. Nancy Hale and Fredson Bowers (Charlottesville: University Press of Virginia, 1983).

50. Rosenfeld's citing of Ornstein's cry of "energy, energy" recalls Stephen Lloyd's discussion of Grainger and the Frankfurt Group: "In one respect 'energy' was a musical characteristic of the Group (especially with Grainger at the fore). Its symbolic manifestation was in the 'English Dance', a title shared by Grainger, Scott, Gardiner and Quilter" ("Grainger and the 'Frankfurt Group'"). Ornstein's most famous piece was, of course, a dance as well, *Danse sauvage.*

51. Signed autograph letter, Paul Rosenfeld to Claire Reis, July 25, 1915, on stationery from the Blue Hill Inn in Blue Hill Maine, New York Public Library, Claire Reis Papers.

52. Rosenfeld to Sherwood Anderson, signed typed letter, June 24 [1920], Newberry Library, Chicago, Anderson Collection, An, Box 27, Folder 1372. There is no evidence of what business Ornstein might have had in mind. He was not trained to make a living outside of music. It is possible his father-in-law could have found a position for him.

53. Ibid.

54. See Silet's *The Writings of Paul Rosenfeld* for a complete listing of books, articles, and extant letters.

55. The same material had appeared a year earlier as one of Rosenfeld's "Musical Chronicle" articles in *The Dial* (March 1922), 332–336.

56. See Paul Rosenfeld, *An Hour with American Music* (Philadelphia: J. B. Lippincott, 1929), 61–62.

57. Ibid., 62.

58. Ibid., 64.

59. Ibid., 65.

60. Ibid., 67.

61. Silet, *The Writings of Paul Rosenfeld*, 28.

62. Typed letter, Paul Rosenfeld to Sherwood Anderson, 29 November [1920], Newberry Library, Chicago, Sherwood Anderson Papers, Box 27, Folder 1392.

63. Signed typed letter, undated. Written from North Conway, N.H., and signed "With love, Leo." Waldo Frank Papers, Annenberg Rare Book and Manuscript Library Collection, University of Pennsylvania.

64. Signed autograph letter, Leo Ornstein to Waldo Frank, no date. Waldo Frank Papers, Annenberg Rare Book and Manuscript Library Collection, University of Pennsylvania.

65. See Notebook III, 91, Waldo Frank Papers, Annenberg Rare Book and Manuscript Library Collection, University of Pennsylvania.

66. Silet, *The Writings of Paul Rosenfeld*, 71.

67. Typed letter, Leo Ornstein to Waldo Frank, undated except for "Monday morning." Waldo Frank Papers, Annenberg Rare Book and Manuscript Library Collection, University of Pennsylvania. This letter almost certainly dates from before Leo's marriage in December 1918. Once married, extent letters from Leo to Waldo usually conclude with Leo's sending greetings from Pauline.

68. Frank and Naumberg married because of Margaret's position as a teacher, and the pressure they both felt that she be respectably married rather than merely cohabitating. Having entered into marriage with this understanding, neither of them was constrained by traditional notions of fidelity to one's spouse. If entries in Frank's notebooks are accurate, clearly he felt no such restrictions. Naumberg's affair with Jean Toomer suggests she took advantage of their arrangement as well.

69. Typed letter, Leo Ornstein to Waldo Frank, undated. The reference to proofs from Fischer, which were only available in 1917—the work was published in 1918—and the directions to Deer Isle, where Leo regularly summered, make this letter relatively easy to date as summer 1917. Although telephone lines were installed as early as 1911 in Deer Isle, it would seem that Leo did not have easy access to a phone—hence his request that Waldo inform him ahead of time when he was leaving.

70. The appellation appears in letters as well as in the inscription of a photograph of Frank, which he gave to Ornstein. It is now in the possession of Leo's daughter Edith.

71. Typed letter, Rosenfeld to Anderson, Westport, July 19, 1923, Sherwood Anderson Papers, Newberry Library, Chicago, Ill.

72. The entry appears on page 93 of book VII, Sept. 1918–May 1922. See Waldo Frank Papers, Annenberg Rare Book and Manuscript Library Collection, University of Pennsylvania. Frank's handwriting is often very difficult to decipher, hence the ellipses. While not all the details may be accurate to Jacob's experience, the basic story line is: Jacob felt great resentment toward a family he believed did not appreciate all that he had done for them. He left a thriving business in Russia, arrived in America with no job prospects, and tried his hand at a number of careers. He studied pharmacy in night school and eventually owned his own; he did despair of a loveless marriage and ungrateful children and ultimately left his family.

73. Ibid., 106.

74. Add MS 70599 f103, Roger Quilter letters. According to Quilter's biographer, Valerie Langfield, Florence Koehler was an "expatriate American jeweler and painter . . . who lived in London. . . . [S]he and Quilter often played duets and attended concerts together" (Langfield, *Roger Quilter*, 44).

75. Signed typed letter, Paul Rosenfeld to Waldo Frank, The Blue Hill Inn, Blue Hill, August 6, 1916, Waldo Frank Papers, Annenberg Rare Book and Manuscript

Library Collection, University of Pennsylvania. There are no additional letters in either Frank's or Rosenfeld's collections that shed light on what is being referred to. The cause of Leo's "biliousness" is not explained, although it likely that, with Mrs. Tapper's death, he was not invited to stay at the Tappers' summer home any longer, thus losing access to the studio Mrs. Tapper had built for him.

76. This would not seem to be supported by Leo's using the term "engaged" when he described the situation to his son Severo years later. As Severo recalls, "I'm pretty sure he spoke of its being three years. I remember the number because it struck me as an extremely long time" (e-mail, November 2, 2005).

77. See the *New York Times*, December 12, 1918, 15, for an announcement of their engagement, and a follow-up story in the same paper, December 14, 1918, 17, that speaks of their marriage the day before. See also *Musical Courier* 77, no. 25 (December 19, 1918), 9, and *Musical America* 29, no. 8 (December 21, 1918), 35.

78. Correspondence with Severo Ornstein, June 22, 2004, regarding his parents' religious beliefs.

79. Carter, *Waldo Frank*, 8 (unnumbered page).

80. Frank's interest in political affairs may also have contributed to his rift with Rosenfeld, who believed that the arts should be free of political entanglements. Rosenfeld's romantic notions regarding the purity of art made him appear old school to musicians and artists, who became increasingly politically active throughout the 1930s.

81. "S. Mallet-Prevost Legal Leader, 88," *New York Times*, December 11, 1948, 15.

82. See letters from Severo Mallet-Prevost to Waldo Frank in the Waldo Frank Papers, Box 18, signed typed letter of November 21, 1930, and November 1, 1931, Annenberg Rare Book and Manuscript Library Collection, University of Pennsylvania.

83. *Time Exposures* by Search-Light (pen name of Waldo Frank) (New York: Boni & Liveright, 1926, 144–146). Frank's connections with the Stieglitz circle and the famed photographer may well have informed the title of his book.

84. From Frank's *Memoir of Waldo Frank*, 134, quoted in Carter, *Waldo Frank*, 31.

85. Black notebook in Waldo Frank Papers, Box 47, Annenberg Rare Book and Manuscript Library Collection, University of Pennsylvania. See entry for 1917. According to biographer Paul J. Carter, in the fall of 1917 "Frank was stricken by an illness that was incorrectly diagnosed as appendicitis and [then had] an unnecessary operation [that] nearly killed him. He did not fully recover until September, 1918" (*Waldo Frank*, 31).

86. An excerpt of the "Prelude" was reprinted in *Musical Courier* 77, no. 12 (September 19, 1918), 42.

87. See Frederick H. Martens, "Introductory," *Poems of 1917* by Leo Ornstein. (New York: Carl Fischer, 1918).

88. Signed typed letter, Leo to Waldo, undated but prior to late summer 1917: Dear Waldo: "Thank you a thousand times for the Prelude. . . . And now what about the individual poems? The sooner you can let me have them the sooner they can be put into press. I have had a number of letters from my publishers. They are most anxious to get started on them so that they may be out for the late summer market. Love, Leo." Waldo Frank Letters, University of Pennsylvania Library, Philadelphia.

89. Ibid.

90. The program for a June 20, 1918, concert for the New York State Music Teacher's Association lists Ornstein as playing two unspecified *1917* poems. An October 18, 1919, concert program refers to *1917* (four excerpts), and a February 1, 1922, concert at Jordan Hall in Boston has Ornstein playing "Dirge" ("A Dirge of the Trenches"), which was the

sixth number of the set. It is likely that in the years following the war, audiences did not want to be reminded of the worldwide catastrophe. An advertisement for the sheet music erroneously stated that the pieces were "played in public for the first time by the composer . . . at Aeolian Hall on Saturday Afternoon, October 18th, 1919." See *Musical Courier* 79, no. 17 (November 6, 1919), 26, for the advertisement.

91. Radio interview with Charles Amirkhanian, December 11, 1972. We are grateful to Mr. Amirkhanian for sharing tapes of this broadcast with us.

92. "Books and Authors," *New York Times Book Review*, January 21, 1923, BR 18.

93. A note written in Pauline's hand on the "List of Works" cataloged at Yale's Irving S. Gilmore Music Library explains that the five songs mentioned "are the same five songs later arranged for orchestra at Stokowsky's [*sic*] request." See List of Works of Leo Ornstein, "Vocal Works," 2.

94. Line taken from song no. 1: "Dawn beyond windows/Morning beyond my soul."

95. Line taken from song no. 5: "Shades of tremulous color."

96. See signed typed letter, Leo Ornstein to Waldo Frank, August 22, 1929 for mention of the songs and Anderson's performance, Waldo Frank Papers, Annenberg Rare Book and Manuscript Library, University of Pennsylvania.

97. See Nancy Van Norman Baer, "The Ballets Suedois: A Synthesis of Modernist Trends in Art," in *Paris Modern: The Swedish Ballet 1920–1925*, ed. Nancy Van Norman Baer (San Francisco: Fine Arts Museums of San Francisco; distributed by the University of Washington Press, Seattle, 1995), 10. Van Norman Baer points out that given de Maré's interests, "the intentional pictorial emphasis of Ballets Suedois productions is hardly surprising" (12).

98. A similar situation existed early in Meredith Monk's career. The discipline-bending work of Ms. Monk meant multiple critics attended her performances.

99. Robert M. Murdoch, "Gerald Murphy, Cole Porter, and the Ballets Suedois Production of *Within the Quota*," in *Paris Modern*, 111–112.

100. Lee Brown, "Now They're Saying It in Swedish," *Dance Lovers Magazine*, February 1924, 23, quoted in Van Norman Baer, *Paris Modern*, 28.

101. Ibid., 28.

102. See Gail Levin, "The Ballets Suedois and American Culture," in *Paris Modern*, 124.

103. Waldo Frank, *Our America* (New York: Boni and Liveright, 1919), 214.

104. See Levin, "The Ballets Suedois and American Culture," 124.

105. "Extended techniques" is the term used to describe any unconventional use of an instrument or the voice to produce "musical" sounds. With the piano, this could include playing parts of the instrument other than the keyboard, for instance, strumming the strings inside, or patting or tapping the case, or attaching bolts and screws to sounding parts.

106. Ibid., 124.

107. See Edmund Wilson, *Letters on Literature and Politics: 1912–1972*, ed. Elena Wilson (New York: Farrar, Straus and Giroux, 1977), 522–523.

108. See Edmund Wilson to Van Wyck Brooks, January 2, 1962. The letter continued: "I had been so much depressed myself by my negative feelings nowadays—I think that this country is a mess and I don't approve of anything that the government is doing—and the mainly negative character of my Civil War book, that it quite bucked me up to read anything so affirmative and so imaginatively colorful as Waldo on Cuba." Quoted in Wilson, *Letters on Literature and Politics*, 622–623.

4. THE BANDBOX AND AFTER

1. The International Exhibition of Modern Art at the 69th Regiment Armory in New York City in 1913 became known as the Armory Show. Probably the most important single event in American art, certainly the most significant event in the establishment of modernism in America, the Armory Show for the first time gave Americans a full sense of the new currents in Europe. It created a sensation. An estimated 87,000 people saw it in New York, and it made headlines in all the New York newspapers. After its New York run the Armory Show traveled to Boston and Chicago, where it met a similar reception. Altogether an estimated 300,000 people saw the show.

2. www.wayneturney.20m.com/washingtonsquare.htm. Accessed July 27, 2005.

3. "Very Modern Music," *Musical Courier* 70, no. 5 (February 3, 1915), 29.

4. A.W.K. (Walter Kramer), "Ornstein Plays His Own Music," *Musical America* 21, no. 13 (January 30, 1915), 43. In this article Kramer explains "I had heard Mr. Ornstein play his 'Impression[s] of the Thames' and 'Wild Men's Dance' several times prior to last Monday," but does not say where. This may be a reference to the private performance at Tapper's in November 1914 (see Kramer, "Has Leo Ornstein Discovered a New Style," 5).

5. In Norway Tapper studied piano with the Norwegian pianist and composer Agathe Backer-Grøndahl. We have been unable, however, to establish any relationship between her and the Danish composer and conductor Launy Grøndahl.

6. The list of pieces is taken from the review "Schoenberg Most Conservative Composer at Boston Concert," *Musical Courier* 71, no. 24 (December 16, 1915), 18, and from Metzer, "The Ascendancy of Musical Modernism in New York City, 1915–1929," 253. Regarding identification of Ornstein compositions, many have not survived because he never wrote them down, as he would often carry a piece in his head for years before committing it to paper (Pauline Ornstein, *Reminiscences*, 46). In Yale's Ornstein collection there are numerous instances of multiple copies of individual pieces with different names, which is probably the result of pieces being written down long after they were created and Ornstein forgetting or confusing their original names.

7. Anonymous reviewer, *New York Herald* (February 8, 1915), 6.

8. Anonymous reviewer, *Musical Courier* 70, no. 9 (March 3, 1915), 57.

9. A.W.K., "Ornstein Plays His Own Music."

10. "Mr. Ornstein's Recital," *New York Times*, January 22, 1915.

11. "Very Modern Music," *Musical Courier* 70, no. 5 (February 3, 1915), 29.

12. H.F.P., "Ornstein Presents His 'Dwarf Suite,'" *Musical America* 21, no. 15 (February 13, 1915), 26.

13. Anonymous reviewer, *Musical Courier* 70, no. 9 (March 3, 1915), 57.

14. Kramer, "Ornstein Plays His Own Music."

15. Anonymous reviewer, *Musical Courier* 70, no. 6 (February 10, 1915), 29.

16. A.W.K. (Walter Kramer), "Ornstein Presents More of His Music," *Musical America* 21, no. 18 (March 6, 1915), 6.

17. A.W.K. (Walter Kramer), "Ornstein Completes Cycle of Recitals," *Musical America* 21, no. 20 (March 20, 1915), 39.

18. "Ornstein's Ultra-Modernism and Expert Pianism."

19. "A Futurist and Ultra Modern Program," *Musical Courier* 70, no. 12 (March 24, 1915), 41.

20. *New York Herald*, March 20, 1915, 2; *New York Tribune*, March 14, 1915, section III, p. 7.

21. "To my fellow Hebrew citizens we are indebted for bringing Mr. Leo Ornstein to Toronto" ("Music and Drama," [Toronto], *Saturday Night*, May 8, 1915, 6).

22. Ibid.

23. "Moderns Superbly Played by Ornstein," H.F.P. (Horatio Parker), *Musical America* 27, no. 13 (January 26, 1918), 30.

24. Frederick Corder, "On the Cult of the Wrong Notes," *Musical Quarterly* 1, no. 3 (July 1915), 381–386; "Leo Ornstein's Music," *Musical America*, 29, no. 9 (January 2, 1916), 24–25; Lawrence Gilman, "Drama and Music," *North American Review* 201, no. 713 (April 1915), 593–597; James Huneker, "Seven Arts," *Puck* 77, no. 1989 (April 7, 1915), 11.

25. "Ornstein Augments Futurist Music," *Musical Courier* 70, no. 21 (May 26, 1915), 35.

26. "Ornstein's New Works," *Musical Courier* 71, no. 11 (September 16, 1915), 29.

27. Ibid.

28. Harriete Brower, "Leo Ornstein, An Ultra Modern Pianist and Composer," *Musical Observer* (August 1915), 467.

29. Kramer, "Bertha Feiring Tapper: Altruist."

30. Signed autograph letter, Paul Rosenfeld to Philip Skinner Platt, July 15, 1915. Letter in Paul Rosenfeld Papers, YCAL 25, Series II, Correspondence, Box 7, Folder 120. Beinecke Rare Books Library, Yale University.

31. The Cort Theater recital was on December 5. The Boston recitals occurred on November 16 and December 7, 1916, then on January 11, February 9, and February 22, 1917.

32. H.F.P., "'Advanced Thinkers' Applaud Ornstein," *Musical America* 23, no. 7 (December 11, 1915), 51.

33. Curiously, many years later, when asked directly, "Who is Vannin," Ornstein had no recollection of the name whatsoever. Leo Ornstein, personal interview with the authors, Green Bay, Wisconsin, June 26, 1998. A man of 105 can be forgiven such memory lapses, but even then Ornstein's memory for distant events was keen. We don't believe he was being disingenuous; possibly he did not want to remember.

34. "Leo Ornstein, Long Haired and Noisier," *New York Herald*, December 6, 1915, part 2, 11; Charles Buchanan, "Ornstein and Futurist Music," *Vanity Fair* 5, no. 6 (February 1916), 48.

35. "Sunday Busy in Musical Events," *New York Times*, December 6, 1915, 9; "Pianist Ornstein in a Futurist Recital," *New York Sun*, December 6, 1915, reprinted in *Musical Courier* 71, no. 24 (December 16, 1915), 9; "Leo Ornstein Long Haired and Noisier," *New York Tribune*, December 6, 1915, 11.

36. Titiev, Journal, 263.

37. Ibid.

38. G.F.H. (Gilbert F. Haywood), "Ornstein in Two Providence Recitals," *Musical America* 23, no. 9 (January 1, 1916), 18.

39. Varèse founded the "New Symphony Orchestra" in 1919, for the avowed purpose of introducing new music to the public. Although he had backing from prominent patrons in New York, critical reaction to the first two concerts was so negative the musicians revolted, demanding a change in programming. Refusing to compromise, Varèse abandoned the venture. See Broyles, *Mavericks and Other Traditions in American Music*, 120; see also Oja, *Making Music Modern*, 30–32.

40. Reis, *Composers, Conductors, and Critics*, 35.

41. Ibid.

42. A.W.K. (Walter Kramer), "Ornstein Heard in Ultra Tone-Poems," *Musical America* 23, no. 23 (April 8, 1916), 22.

43. Curiously Barstow and Ornstein did not play the Violin Sonata, Op. 31. Instead they performed an earlier violin sonata by Ornstein, Op. 26, which was somewhat less radical.

44. Comment on "brilliant player," in "Leo Ornstein Compels Wonder and Admiration in Chicago," *Musical Courier* 72, no. 13 (March 30, 1916), 32. "Splendid technique" in "Chicagoans Hear New Works Played at Symphony Concerts," *Musical Courier* 72, no. 17 (April 27, 1916), 8. "Splendid pianist" in Farnsworth Wright, "Ornstein Once More Astonishes Chicago," *Musical America* 23, no. 26 (April 29, 1916), 60.

45. Eric De Lamarter, "Pianists Three and Their Gentle Ways," *Chicago Tribune*, part eight, March 26, 1916, 1.

46. Anonymous reviewer, "First Futurist Concert in City Has Great Value: Leo Ornstein Amuses and Educates Large Audience—Brilliant Player," *Montreal Daily Star*, February 14, 1916, 2.

47. Comment about "vaudeville trick," in H.F.P., "Ornstein Descends to Classic Level," *Musical America* 23, no. 13 (January 29, 1916), 40; "noise that poured" in Wright, "Ornstein Once More Astonishes Chicago," *Musical America* 23, no. 26 (29 April 1916), 60; "Parts of" in "Leo Ornstein's Exotic Pianism," *Musical Courier* 72, no. 4 (January 27, 1916), 63.

48. Titiev, Journal, 265.

49. "Personalities," *Musical America* 24, no. 6 (June 10, 1916), 26; "Ornstein and Barstow Heard in Concert at Beverly," *Musical Courier* 73, no. 8 (August 24, 1916), 31.

50. Laura Van Kuran, "Music Teachers of the State Sound Optimistic Note," *Musical America* 24, no. 9 (July 1, 1916), 2–3; "Ornstein Bookings," *Musical Courier* 73, no. 10 (September 21, 1916), 26.

51. "Ornstein and Barstow Heard in Concert at Beverly," *Musical Courier* 73, no. 8 (24 August 1916), 31.

52. This total is calculated by using distances provided by the computer program *Microsoft Streets and Trips, 2005*. Because *Streets and Trips* calculates highway miles, it is not exact relative to railroad miles, but does give a reasonably close approximation of the number of miles Ornstein would have covered in this time.

53. "Ornstein's Many Engagements," *Musical Courier* 73, no. 21 (November 23, 1916), 45 (list of engagements); "Vera Barstow Delights Fall River Music Lovers," *Musical Courier* 74, no. 5 (February 1, 1917), 45; *Fort Worth Star-Telegram*, January 31, 1917, 7; "Leo Ornstein's Double," *Musical Courier* 74, no. 7 (February 15, 1917), 39; "Advance Bookings," *Musical America* 25, no. 14 (February 3, 1917), 51.

54. "Leo Ornstein Heard," *New York Times*, March 5, 1917, 9; "Ornstein, A Truly Great Artist," *Musical Courier* 74, no. 10 (March 8, 1917), 72.

55. J.O.J., "The Three Arts, Impressions of Leo Ornstein, the Disturbing Composer-Pianist," *Baltimore Evening Sun*, February 10, 1917, reprinted in *Musical Courier* 74, no. 11 (March 15, 1917), 7.

56. "Montreal Finds War Solace in Music," *Musical America* 25, no. 23 (April 21, 1917), 9.

57. *Buffalo Courier*, October 4, 1916, 5.

58. "Ornstein-Barstow Recital in Buffalo," *Canadian Journal of Music* 3, no. 7 (October 1916), 320–321, 326.

59. Richard L. Stokes, "Futurist Pianist Gives an Amazing Performance: Leo Ornstein's 'Wild Men's Dance' Applauded by St. Louis Audience, While Paris and London Wanted to Mob Him," *Saint Louis Post-Dispatch*, October 22, 1916, 3.

60. Louise Dooley, "Ornstein, The Eccentric, Charms Large Audience," *The Constitution* (Atlanta), November 3, 1916, 10.

61. *Atlanta Georgian*, November 3, 1916, 7.

62. Comment "frantically applauded," in M.M.F., "Ornstein in San Jose," *Musical America* 27, no. 6 (December 8, 1917), 13; "jumped to their feet," in *San Francisco Call*, November 2, 1917, quoted in "Leo Ornstein, Musical Rebel, Wins Auditors," *Musical Courier* 75, no. 20 (November 15, 1917), 10.

63. Britt Craig, *Atlanta Constitution*, November 1, 1916, quoted in Steve Goodson, *Highbrows, Hillbillies and Hellfire: Public Entertainment in Atlanta 1880–1930* (Athens: University of Georgia Press, 2002), 171–172.

64. Anonymous reviewer, "Leo Ornstein, Today's Artist, Sees South the Home of Melody," *Houston Chronicle*, October 29, 1916, 28.

65. Goodson, *Highbrows, Hillbillies and Hellfire*, 172.

66. "Ornstein Stirs Up Deer Isle," *Musical Courier* 77, no. 15 (August 11, 1918), 23.

67. "Piano Plays as 'Soloist,'" *New York Times*, June 5, 1918, 9; "Ornstein to Play Own Works for Teachers," *Musical Courier* 76, no. 25 (June 20, 1918), 30. *Musical Courier* also states that he was to perform his Sonata, Op. 52, but there is no mention of a cellist. This could have been a typographical error, Op. 54 being intended.

68. M.M.F., "Ornstein in San Jose," *Musical America* 27, no. 6 (8 December 1917), 13.

69. Anonymous reviewer, "Ornstein Conquers Los Angeles," *Musical Courier* 25, no. 20 (November 15, 1917), 29.

70. *San Francisco Call*, November 2, 1917, quoted in "Leo Ornstein, Musical Rebel, Wins Auditors," *Musical Courier* 75, no. 20 (November 15, 1917), 10.

71. Anonymous reviewer, "Ornstein Erratic but Gifted Pianist: Performance of Young Russian Shocks Sensibilities of Audiences, But Genius Thrills," *Sacramento Bee*, November 23, 1917, 14.

72. What remains unclear is whether a young man only four years younger than Ornstein heard him in California. Henry Cowell was in the San Francisco Bay area at that time and may have already met Ornstein in New York in 1916. Later Cowell would have a major impact on new music on the West Coast when he founded the New Music Society of California in 1925. Ornstein's 1917 visit awakened the Californians to their first taste of ultramodern music and likely paved the way for Cowell's more extended efforts in the next decade.

73. Comment "the most discussed," in J.O.J., "The Three Arts, Impressions of Leo Ornstein, the Disturbing Composer-Pianist," *Baltimore Evening Sun*, February 10, 1917, reprinted in *Musical Courier* 74, no. 11 (March 15, 1917), 7; "the most spectacular," in Jeanne Redmann, "Ornstein Concert: Sensational Pianist Repeats His Surprises," *Los Angeles Times*, November 28, 1917, section II, 3.

74. The Armistice ending World War I was signed early on November 11, 1918, and went into effect later that day. No one could have known that at the beginning of the season, however.

75. "Influenza Stops Concert Events," *Musical America* 38, no. 24 (October 26, 1918), 4.

76. James Gibbons Huneker, "Symphony Society Opens Its Season," *New York Times*, November 1, 1918, 13.

77. Advertisement, *Musical Courier* 76, no. 28 (June 6, 1918), 27.

78. Anonymous reviewer, "Ornstein to Play Own Works for Teachers," *Musical Courier* 76, no. 25 (June 20, 1918), 30.

79. Ella Smith, "Leo Ornstein Fails to Play His Own Music," *Milwaukee Journal*, November 26, 1918, 4.

80. "November Demands on Ornstein," *Musical Courier* 77, no. 19 (November 7, 1918), 24.

81. Anonymous reviewer, "Leo Ornstein, Pianist," *Musical Courier* 77, no. 21 (November 21, 1918), 16.

82. "Leo Ornstein's Activities," *Musical Courier* 77, no. 22 (November 28, 1918), 22a.

83. Ibid.; "Ornstein's Songs," *Musical Courier* 77, no. 24 (December 12, 1918), 43.

84. "Leo Ornstein to Wed Society Girl," *New York Times*, December 12, 1918, 15; "Leo Ornstein Marries," *New York Times*, December 14, 1918, 12; "Leo Ornstein Married," *Musical Courier* 77, no. 23 (December 19, 1918), 9, "Ornstein's Romance Has Swift Climax," *Musical America* 29, no. 8 (December 21, 1918), 35.

85. "February and March Will Be Busy Months for Leo Ornstein," *Musical America* 29, no. 15 (February 8, 1919), 11.

86. Anonymous reviewer, "Philadelphia Orchestra," *Philadelphia Inquirer*, March 8, 1919, 9; F.L.W. "Stokowski Gives Novel Compositions," *Philadelphia Public Ledger*, March 8, 1919, 9.

87. G.M.W., "Philadelphia Gasps, Then Applauds First Ornstein Orchestral Works," *Musical Courier* 78, no. 11 (March 13, 1919), 31.

88. Signed typed letter, Leo and Pauline Ornstein to Severo Ornstein, undated but probably written in the 1970s.

89. R.G.M., "Alda and Ornstein Interest Montreal," *Musical America* 30, no. 6 (June 7, 1919), 29.

90. "Ornstein in Joint Recital with Rosen," *Musical Courier* 78, no. 21 (May 22, 1919), 17.

91. Anonymous reviewer, "New York Concerts of the Past Week: Leo Ornstein, Pianist," *Musical Courier* 77, no. 24 (December 12, 1918), 25.

92. A.W.K. (Walter Kramer), "Ornstein Rouses Intense Admiration," *Musical America* 29, no. 7 (December 14, 1918), 29.

93. Anonymous reviewer, "Ornstein's Los Angeles Recital," *Musical Courier* 75, no. 21 (November 22, 1917), 52.

94. Anonymous reviewer, "Leo Ornstein at Aeolian Hall," *Musical Courier* 73, no. 22 (November 30, 1916), 27.

95. Anonymous reviewer, "Huneker's Description of Ornstein Recital," *Musical Courier* 78, no. 6 (February 6, 1919), 43.

96. Anonymous reviewer, "Another Ornstein Success," *Musical Courier* 80, no. 21 (May 20, 1920), 42.

97. Anonymous reviewer, "Ornstein Mobbed in Phialdelphia," *Musical Courier* 79, no. 14 (April 3, 1919), 41.

98. "Ornstein Will Make Seventy Appearances," *Musical Courier* 81, no. 13 (September 23, 1920), 12; "Ornstein Booked for Extensive Western Tour," *Musical Courier* 79, no. 11 (September 11, 1919), 15.

99. "Ornstein Booked for Extensive Western Tour."

100. "Leo Ornstein to Remain at Home," *Musical Courier* 80, no. 6 (February 5, 1920), 37.

101. Since the above summaries are only general, it is not clear in many cases in which cities Ornstein performed, and consequently reviews or records of his concerts are difficult to obtain. Additionally not all newspaper records from the early twentieth century have survived.

102. "The Musical Courier's Summer Directory of Musicians," *Musical Courier* 79, no. 1 (July 3, 1919), 50; "Leo Ornstein Busy Composing," *Musical America* 30, no. 21 (September 21, 1919), 29. Reference to Ornstein's canceling his tour is in "Personalities," *Musical America* 30, no. 24 (October 11, 1919), 16.

103. The conservative tenor of critical comments can be assessed in H.F.P.'s reference to the "Scriabin rubbish": "Audience Engrossed in Composer-Pianist's Futuristic Offerings," *Musical America* 30, no. 26 (October 25, 1919), 5; and Richard Aldrich's observation about *Three Moods*, "the musical basis is not there" (Aldrich, "Music," *New York Times*, October 19, 1919, 22). See also anonymous reviewer, "Ornstein, Apostle of Music with Punch, Plays Discordantly," *New York Herald*, October 19, 1919, 11.

104. Jeanette Cox, "Goldmark's 'Requiem' a Feature of Chicago Symphony's Sixth Program—Leo Ornstein, as Soloist Plays the MacDowell Concerto," *Musical Courier* 79, no. 22 (December 11, 1919), 52.

105. Anonymous reviewer, "Musical News in Brief," *Musical Courier* 79, no. 17 (November 6, 1919), 16.

106. "Music from Cincinnati," *Philadelphia Inquirer*, December 11, 1919, 3; "Ornstein's Sensational Boston Notices," *Musical Courier* 70, no. 3 (January 15, 1920), 55.

107. Anonymous reviewer, "Ornstein Triumphs with Boston Symphony," *Musical Courier* 80, no. 4 (January 22, 1920), 53.

108. Anonymous reviewer, "Leo Ornstein, Pianist," *Musical Courier* 79, no. 19 (November 20, 1919), 8.

109. "Ornstein Winner of Rare Tribute," New Orleans *Times-Picayune*, January 24, 1921, 3.

5. IDENTITY

1. *Musical America* 27, no. 26 (October 26, 1918), 4.

2. www.pbs.org/wgbh/amex/influenza/timeline, accessed June 7, 2004.

3. According to a *Musical Courier* story of November 21, 1918, Ornstein had to postpone a November 16th concert "to take to his bed," presumably the day after his Tuesday, November 12th, concert because of "an approaching attack of influenza." See "Tuesday, November 12: Leo Ornstein, Pianist," 16. The anonymous writer found his "unusually fine work all the more praiseworthy" in light of Ornstein's presumed weakened condition. The previous week he had played two successful concerts: the first with Walter Damrosch on November 1, when he performed the MacDowell D Minor Concerto, and a solo recital at the Brooklyn Institute of Arts and Sciences on November 6. An article that appeared in *Musical Courier* 77, no. 22 (November 28, 1918), just one week after that, which referred to an impending case of the flu, begins: "Leo Ornstein, who has entirely recovered from the nervous breakdown from which he suffered recently" (22). In light of these reports and no additional information, it is impossible to ascertain the cause of Ornstein's very brief performing hiatus.

4. www.infoplease.com/ipa/A000461.5.html, accessed June 6, 2004.

5. www.stanford.edu/group/virus/uda/index.html, accessed June 6, 2004. Some sources put the number of Americans dead at 800,000. Other sources narrow the total

number dead to somewhere between 25 and 37 million. The global population in 1918 stood at 1.8 billion.

6. A.W.K. (Kramer), "Leo Ornstein, Pianist: A Study."

7. *Musical Courier* 64, no. 6 (February 7, 1912), and several subsequent issues.

8. The phrase "young Russian pianist" appeared in "Music Here and There," *New York Times*, March 24, 1912; in an advertisement for a concert at Aeolian Hall on December 7, 1912, preserved among the letters of Pauline Ornstein, in the possession of Severo Ornstein; and in "Ornstein's Futurist Music," *Boston Globe*, December 5, 1915, 39.

9. "Futurist Music: Wild Outbreak at Steinway Hall," *Daily Mail* (London), March 28, 1914, 1a; "Echoes of Music Abroad," *Musical America*, 19, no. 22 (April 4, 1914), 11.

10. Advertisement in *Musical Courier* 70, no. 21 (May 16, 1915), 39.

11. *New York Times*, December 12, 1918, 15.

12. Marjory Markress Fisher, "Futurist Music a Logical Outcome of the Age, Declares This Modernist," *Musical America* 26, no. 16 (August 18, 1917), 27. It should be noted that although she was an art critic, Mrs. Herrington had considerable background in music, having studied piano with Louis Elson and having attended the New England Conservatory for three years.

13. "Leo Ornstein Discusses Futuristic Music," *Musical Courier* 70, no. 12 (March 24, 1915), 30.

14. "Leo Ornstein Heard," *New York Times*, March 5, 1917, 9. The anonymous writer refers to Ornstein as "the former 'cubist' prodigy of the piano." The early Stieglitz Group included painters John Haviland, John Marin, Katharine Rhoades, and Abraham Walkowitz among others, many of whom adapted Cubist techniques.

15. The set was published in 1914 in Leipzig by Wilhelm Hansen. The seven pieces are titled "Doumka," "Extase," "Barcarolle," "Mélancolie," "Danse burlesque," "Berceuse," and "Chanson pathétique."

16. *Suite Ukraine*, Op. 17, may very well be the same set of pieces as Five Pieces, Op. 17. Given the information available at this time, it is impossible to be certain.

17. *Musical Courier* 78, no. 20 (November 14, 1918), 5.

18. Rupert Hughes, *Contemporary American Composers, A Study of the Music of This Country, Its Present Conditions and Its Future, with Critical Estimates and Biographies of the Principal Living Composers and an Abundance of Portraits, Fac-Simile Musical Autographs, and Compositions* (Boston: L. C. Page, 1900), 34–35.

19. Theodore Baker, *Über die Musik der nordamerikanischen Wilden* (Leipzig: Breitkopf and Härtel, 1882).

20. http://dlib.nyu.edu/dram/Objid/14453, accessed June 11, 2004. Johnson observes that "it may be significant that Dvorak's Symphony No. 9, 'From the New World,' also using native American materials, had appeared two years earlier." The five movements of the suite are titled "Legend," "Love Song," "In War-time," "Dirge," and "Village Festival."

21. See Geoff Kuenning's quotation of MacDowell in his program notes to the Suite as they appear at http://fmg.www.cs.ucla.edu/geoff/prognotes/macdowell/indianSuite.html, accessed June 11, 2004.

22. Given the suddenness of Ornstein's substitution, one wonders if Gabrillowitsch was stricken with the flu, or perhaps simply avoiding a large concert hall to reduce his chances of contracting the virus, or whether something else completely different caused

his change of plans. The October 31st performance took place just as concert halls were being reopened after their preventative closures.

23. The first quote is from James Gibbons Hunneker, "Symphony Society Opens Its Season," *New York Times*, November 1, 1918, 13, the second from "Symphony Society; Leo Ornstein, Soloist," *Musical Courier* 78, no. 19 (November 7, 1918), 8.

24. "MacDowell Honored by Leo Ornstein," *Musical Courier* 80, no. 5 (January 29, 1920), 10.

25. Ibid.

26. "Leo Ornstein, Today's Artist, Sees South the Home of Melody," *Houston Chronicle*, October 29, 1916, 28.

27. Ibid.

28. "Leo Ornstein, Volunteer, Refused by the Examining Board," *Musical Courier* 65, no. 18 (November 1, 1917), 43.

29. "Personalities," *Musical America* 36, no. 6 (June 9, 1917), 24.

30. According to Robert K. Murray, "giving or lending of money to a proscribed revolutionary organization was to be regarded as proof of advocacy or membership." See Robert K. Murray, *Red Scare: A Study in National Hysteria, 1919–1920* (Minneapolis: University of Minnesota Press, 1955), 250. How performing for such organizations was viewed, and which organizations might be defined as such, was not clear.

31. Julian F. Jaffe, *Crusade against Radicalism: New York during the Red Scare, 1914–1924* (Port Washington, N.Y.: National University Publications, Kennikat Press, 1972), 5.

32. Quakers had been pacifists since their founding. In the postwar environment, their three-hundred-year tradition of nonviolence was reinterpreted as subversion. Another avant-garde musician of the time, Charles Seeger, in effect lost his position at the University of California because of his pacifist beliefs, even though Seeger was from an upper-class New England family. For comments on Seeger and pacifism see Broyles, *Mavericks and Other Traditions in American Music*, 126; see also fn. 26, p. 347.

33. Todd J. Pfannestiel, *Rethinking the Red Scare: The Lusk Committee and New York's Crusade against Radicalism, 1919–1923* (New York: Routledge, 2003), 13–14.

34. www.u-s-history/com/pages/h1345.html, accessed June 12, 2004. Over 2,000 people were prosecuted because of the Espionage and Sedition Acts until they were repealed in 1921.

35. A. Mitchell Palmer, "The Case against the 'Red,'" *Forum* 63 (1920) 63, 173–185.

36. Murray, *Red Scare*, 205–207.

37. For instance, J.O.I. wrote, "That Ornstein is an anarchist there is no gainsaying" (J.O.I., "Impressions of Leo Ornstein, the Disturbing Composers-Pianist," *Baltimore Evening Sun*, February 19, 1917, quoted in *Musical Courier* 71, no. 11 [March 15, 1917], 7).

38. Wendell Pritchett, *Brownsville, Brooklyn: Blacks, Jews, and the Changing Face of the Ghetto* (Chicago: University of Chicago Press, 2002), 14–15.

39. "Leo Ornstein's Many Engagements," *Musical Courier* 76, no. 17 (February 14, 1918), 8, refers to the same management also booking Efrem Zimbalist and Sophie Braslau, two performers closely associated with Hurok.

40. Pritchett, *Brownsville, Brooklyn*, 35.

41. "Leo Ornstein's 'Calory Rag,'" *Musical Courier* 74, no. 5 (February 1, 1917), 42.

42. Pauline Ornstein, *Reminiscences*, 13. This is confirmed in a letter from Paul Rosenfeld to Sherwood Anderson, typed letter, Paul Rosenfeld to Sherwood Anderson, June 24, 1920, in Sherwood Anderson Papers, Newberry Library, Chicago, Ill., Box 368. We will not comment on the irony of Ornstein's being considered waspish.

43. Pauline Ornstein, *Reminiscences*, 12.

44. This figure represents almost 12 percent of the total population. See www.wzo .org.il/home/politic/pale.htm, accessed June 14, 2004. The Pale continued until the 1917 Bolshevik Revolution, when policies confining Jews to this area were discontinued.

45. Recorded recollections of the experience, from the distance of more than eighty years, are filled with an immediacy and pain that are palpable. Ornstein, interview with Holly Carter in 1986.

46. It is difficult to ascertain the degree to which Abraham Ornstein supported or encouraged his son Leo to become a part of the new American culture. Different accounts give credit to Ornstein's attendance at the Institute of Musical Arts to Leo's father or to Leo's more progressive brother-in-law, Jacob Tetiev, who was the driving force behind the Ornsteins' emigration from Kremenchug.

47. The reason given by Ornstein's family for his attendance at the Friends School was its flexibility of schedule, which gave the young pianist ample opportunity to practice.

48. E-mail from Severo Ornstein to Denise Von Glahn, June 24, 2004.

49. Daniel Gregory Mason, "Is American Music Growing Up? Our Emancipation from Alien Influences," *Arts and Decoration* 14, no. 1 (November 1920), 40.

50. Michael Broyles, *"Music of the Highest Class": Elitism and Populism in Antebellum Boston* (New Haven, Conn.: Yale University Press, 1992), 69.

51. For a general discussion of anti-Semitism in the late nineteenth century see John Higham, "Anti-Semitism in the Gilded Age: A Reinterpretation," *Mississippi Valley Historical Review* 43, no. 4 (March 1957), 572.

52. For a discussion of Henry Adams's anti-Semitism in the 1890s see Richard Hofstadter, "The Folklore of Populism," in *Antisemitism in the United States*, ed. Leonard Dinnerstein (New York: Holt, Rinehart, and Winston, 1971), 61.

53. The quotations are from Josiah Strong, *Our Country: Its Possible Future and Its Present Crisis* (New York: Baker and Taylor, 1885), 205, 211, and the discussion of Strong is from Neil Baldwin, *Henry Ford and the Jews: The Mass Production of Hate* (New York: Public Affairs, 2001), 33–35.

54. Lothrap Stoddard, *The Rising Tide of Color against White World-Supremacy* (New York: Charles Scribner's Sons, 1926), 299, 271. For a similar although less inflammatory statement, see Kenneth L. Roberts, *Why Europe Leaves Home* (New York: Arno Press, 1977; originally published 1922), 97.

55. Broyles, *Mavericks and Other Traditions in American Music*, 133–134. See also Olivia Mattis, "Edgard Varèse and the Visual Arts" (Ph.D. diss., Stanford University, 1992), 176.

56. Baldwin, *Henry Ford and the Jews*, 64.

57. Ibid., 80.

58. Robert Singerman, "The American Career of the *Protocols of the Elders of Zion*," *American Jewish History* 71, no. 1 (September 1981), 54–55.

59. Albert Lee, *Henry Ford and the Jews* (New York: Stein and Day, 1980), 25.

60. Ibid., 26.

61. Sergei Nilus, *The Protocols of the Learned Elders of Zion* (Kiev, 1917); this was the fourth edition of Nilus's book, which originally appeared in 1905.

62. Baldwin, *Henry Ford and the Jews*, 82. Houghton probably urged De Borgy to work with Brasol on the translation.

63. Ibid., 144–145.

64. www.holocaust-history.org/short-essays/protocols.shtml, accessed June 12, 2004.

65. The extent that the *Protocols* directly influenced Mason's thought is not clear, but given the timing of his article and the notoriety of Ford's publications, they likely emboldened his decision to make this very public statement.

66. *Musical Courier* 94, no. 4 (January 28, 1926), 30.

67. Paul L. Rosenfeld in *The New Republic*, May 27, 1916, 84. Unbeknown to Rosenfeld, his suggestion that Ornstein gave voice to the Russian Jew and somehow captured the experience of the proletariat, a term closely associated with socialism, might have given Ornstein cause for concern just a year later as the Red Scare mentality began to take hold. Rosenfeld credits Ornstein with being able to make his audiences feel that which they hadn't before, a dangerous power if others construed it to be working against American ideals.

68. Paul Rosenfeld, *Musical Portraits: Interpretations of Twenty Modern Composers* (New York: Harcourt, Brace and Howe, 1920), 267.

69. Ibid., 268–269, 273. Rosenfeld's contrasting of gabardine and silk are none-too-subtle references to Ornstein's changed social status. Gabardine is a sturdy woven fabric, often with a rough texture, that is used to make coats, jackets, and suits. The twisted weave is extremely durable. Silk, on the other hand, is a fine, soft, elegant fabric associated with luxury. The first fabric is practical, the second is extravagant. Between 1916 and 1920, Ornstein had married a Park Avenue debutante; he had come a long way from the day he disembarked the *Campania*.

70. Paul Rosenfeld, *Musical Chronicle 1917–1923* (New York: Harcourt, Brace, 1923), 220–221.

71. Ibid., 221.

72. Rosenfeld, *An Hour with American Music*, 62–63.

73. *Musical Courier* 80, no. 7 (February 12, 1920), 23. It is not clear which cello sonatas *Musical Courier* has in mind. Only one cello sonata has survived, Op. 52, which was then referred to as Sonata No. 1. There was a Sonata No. 2, which was originally called a Rhapsody, but it was never published and is no longer extant. The existence of a Sonata No. 3 is unknown beyond this reference. In 1931 Ornstein wrote a set, *Six Preludes for Cello and Piano*, which was originally intended as another cello sonata.

74. Deems Taylor, "Music," *New York Evening World,* February 18, 1925.

75. "Its Slavic flavor is unmistakable and there are moments when the idioms of Stravinsky and Borodin are strongly suggested. Much of the work has the flavor of Tartar dances"; *Musical America* 90, no. 7 (February 12, 1925), 40.

76. Henry Cowell, *Musical America* 61, no. 23 (March 28, 1925); "America Takes a Front Rank in Year's Modernist Output," 4.

77. W. J. Henderson, *New York Sun*, February 18, 1925, 21.

78. A.W.K. (Kramer), "Ornstein Rouses Intense Admiration."

79. Alexander Knapp, "The Jewishness of Bloch: Subconscious or Conscious?" *Proceedings of the Royal Musical Association* 97 (1970–1971), 108.

80. From unpublished typed pages, untitled, in a folder of letters of Ornstein, in possession of Severo Ornstein. The *Quintette* will be discussed in more detail in chapter 7.

81. Derek B. Scott, "Orientalism and Musical Style," *Musical Quarterly* 82, no. 2 (summer 1998), 326–327.

82. Ibid., 329–330.

83. H. T. Craven, "Contemporary Organization Gives Premiere of Ornstein's Quintet," *Philadelphia Record*, January 3, 1928, n.p., clipping in folder from Severo Ornstein folder "Old Stuff."

84. "Ornstein-Bartók Works Are Heard," *Musical America* 47, no. 13 (January 14, 1928), 33.

85. Abraham Zvi Idelsohn, *Jewish Music in Its Historical Development* (New York: Tudor, 1948), 473–474.

86. Van Vechten, *Music and Bad Manners*, 241.

87. Martens, *Leo Ornstein*, 12.

88. Roy Eastman, *Cincinnati Times-Star*, March 29, 1917.

89. Martens, 47, 12.

90. David Metzer observes that Ornstein's melodies tend to have a narrow range and use modal and whole-tone scale patterns and characteristic Eastern intervals such as the augmented second. See Metzer, "The Ascendancy of Musical Modernism in New York City, 1915–1929."

91. Interview with Frank Patterson, *Musical Courier* 84, no. 11 (March 16, 1922), 58.

92. Baldwin, *Henry Ford and the Jews*, 211.

93. *Musical Courier* 99, no. 3 (January 28, 1926), 30.

94. Frank misses the mark regarding Ornstein's immigration by one year—it was 1906; the uprising in 1905 was a revolt, not a revolution, Leo's family was implicated only insofar as they were Jewish, and "some cellar synagogue" was the Bialostoker Synagogue, one of the most important in New York.

95. Frank, *Time Exposures*, 142–145.

96. Lazare Saminsky, "East Meets West," *Modern Music* 4, no. 22 (January–February, 1927), 21.

97. Lazare Saminsky, *Music of Our Day, Essentials and Prophecies* (Freeport, N.Y.: Books for Libraries Press, 1930; reprinted 1970), 157–157.

98. See comments of David Ewen, *Composers of Today: A Comprehensive Biographical and Critical Guide to Modern Composers of All Nations* (New York: H. W. Wilson, 1934), 182, and Henry Cowell, Introduction to Cowell, ed., *American Composers on American Music, A Symposium* (Stanford, Calif.: Stanford University Press, 1933), 4–5.

99. Gdal Saleski, *Famous Musicians of a Wandering Race: Biographical Sketches of Outstanding Figures of Jewish Origin in the Musical World* (New York: Bloch, 1927), 357–358.

100. Heyman Zimel, "Ornstein, Modernistic Composer," *B'nai Brith Magazine* 41 (1927), 455–456.

101. Maury Klein, "Life on the Lower East Side," *American History Illustrated* 7, no. 7 (1972), 25.

102. Waldo Frank, *The Jew in Our Day* (New York: Duell, Sloan and Pearce, 1944), 29–30.

103. Waldo Frank was not born Jewish but converted to Judaism.

104. Quoted in Saleski, *Music of Our Day*, 358. Saleski does not specify his source.

6. THE TURNING POINT

1. Van Vechten, *Music and Bad Manners*, 238.

2. Paul Rosenfeld, letter to Sherwood Anderson, 24 June (1920), Newberry Library, Chicago, Anderson Collection, Box 20, Folder 31.

3. "Personalities," *Musical America* 24, no. 6 (June 10, 1916), 26.

4. According to Edith Valentine, Leo's daughter, her father was especially fond of the New Hampshire setting: "In the summertime we would leave Philadelphia, where we

lived, and head for our summer home in the heart of New Hampshire's White Mountains. Of all the places in the world, this area is nearest and dearest to my father."

5. "Ornstein Busy on New Sonata," *Musical Courier* 83, no. 5 (August 4, 1921), 13.

6. "Portrait of a Concert Manager," *New York Times*, February 9, 1947, section II, 7; "Arthur Judson Dies at 93," *New York Times*, January 29, 1975, 38.

7. Quoted by Linda Whitesitt, "'The Most Potent Force' in American Music: The Role of Women's Music Clubs in American Concert Life," in *The Musical Woman*, vol. 3: 1990, ed. Judith Long Zaimont (Westport, Conn.: Greenwood Press, 1991), 664.

8. "Ornstein Busy on New Sonata," *Musical Courier* 83, no. 5 (August 4, 1921), 13.

9. "Miss Leginska Plays in Recital with Ornstein," *New York Tribune*, December 31, 1921, 6; A. Walter Kramer, "Leginska-Ornstein, December 30," *Musical America* 25, no. 11 (January 7, 1922), 17.

10. "Evelione Taglione's Charming Manner Wins Audience," *Musical Courier* 84, no. 6 (February 9, 1922), 49.

11. Henry Levine, "Monteux Introduces Schrerer Work in Rich Week of Music in Boston," *Musical America* 25, no. 17 (February 25, 1922), 33.

12. Fourteen or fifteen pianists participated, depending on which reports one reads. A photograph of all the participants shows fifteen plus Damrosch, who conducted. "A Platoon of Pianists," *Musical Courier* 83, no. 26 (December 29, 1921), 21.

13. The Harrisburg concert occurred on December 8, the Philharmonic Society Concert was announced for January 4, 1922. Program Booklet, Philharmonic Society of Philadelphia, November 18–21, 1921, 184.

14. Advertisements placed in *Musical Courier* 87, no. 18 (October 23, 1923), 8, and *Musical America* 86, no. 11 (March 15, 1923), 35.

15. Advertisement in *Musical Courier* 88, no. 5 (January 31, 1924), 62.

16. "Ornstein Busy on New Sonata," *Musical Courier* 83, no. 5 (August 4, 1921), 13.

17. "Ornstein Program Greatly Enjoyed," *Jacksonville Courier*, November 18, 1924, 8.

18. H. T. Craven, "Philadelphia Hears Ornstein Concerto," *Musical America* 61, no. 18 (February 21, 1925), 40; S.L.L. "Orchestra Plays Ornstein Concerto," *Philadelphia Public Ledger*, February 14, 1925, 5; "Music—By Lawrence Gilman," *New York Herald Tribune*, February 18, 1925, 13.

19. David L. Saul, "Reproducing Pianos," in *Encyclopedia of Automatic Musical Instruments*, ed. Q. David Bowers (Vestal, N.Y.: Vestal Press, 1972), 323–334. The device was first called the Mignon. Later a hyphen was added: Welte-Mignon.

20. Correspondence with L. Douglas Henderson of ARTCRAFT Music Rolls, March 19, 2005. For a general description of how rolls were made see Robbie Rhodes, "How Piano Rolls Were Made," www.waterex.com.au/player/rollmade.html, accessed June 21, 2005.

21. Robbie Rhodes, "Dynamic Range of the Ampico B—Hickman Data," *Mechanical Music Digest Archives*, April 2001, http://mmd.foxtail.com/Archives/Digests/200104/200 1.04.23.12.html, accessed June 22, 2005. Rhodes observes that Hickman's method was similar to that used on the Bösendorfer SE and the Yahama Diskclavier, late-twentieth-century reproducing pianos, the principal difference being the Bösendorfer and the Yamaha used a photoelectric cell rather than contact points to measure speed. For Ornstein this new development mattered little, as all but three of his rolls were cut prior to 1926. Those last three, of Robert Schumann's *Kreisleriana*, Op. 16, numbers 2 and 8, and Leschetizky's *Barcarola*, Op. 39, no. 3, were made on March 17, 1926, and it is not clear if the Hickman dynamic recorder was in place then.

22. Later Arthur Rubinstein would be added to that list.

23. Information taken from the company's ledger, now in possession of Alan Mueller. Information compiled by Jim Edwards, past President of the Chicago Chapter of the Automatic Musical Instruments Collector's Association.

24. Robert Plumb, "Recording Techniques," *New York Times*, March 21, 1954, XX13.

25. "Ornstein and Knabe-Ampico in Concert," *Musical Courier* 72, no. 22 (June 1, 1916), 9.

26. "Godowsky versus Godowsky's Record," *New York Globe*, October 11, 1916, reproduced in the Ampico advertisement, "The Affair at the Biltmore," *New York Times*, October 15, 1916, p. 2. The ad appeared many other times in various newspapers. According to both Artes Orga, "Pianola to Reproducing Piano: 3, A Plaine and Easie Introduction," www.mvdaily.com/articles/1999/02/ppiano14.htm, accessed June 23, 2005, and Saul, "Reproducing Pianos," this was the first demonstration.

27. "Ornstein and Orchestra in an Ampico Concert," *Musical America* 30, no. 1 (May 3, 1919), 20; "Rivoli to Hear Leo Ornstein on Ampico," *Musical Courier* 79, no. 4 (July 24, 1919), 13.

28. Signed typed letter, Arthur Rubinstein to Severo Ornstein, March 9, 1972.

29. Arthur Rubinstein, *My Many Years* (New York: Alfred A. Knopf, 1980), 54.

30. Display ad, "Futurist Pianist Amazes Audience at the Biltmore with His Ampico-Knabe Reproductions," *New York Times*, June 4, 1916, X4.

31. Jeff Miller, "A Chronology of AM Radio Broadcasting, 1900–1920," http://members.aol.com/jeff560/chrono1.html, accessed June 24, 2005. The De Forest quotation is taken from "The Complete Lee de Forest," www.leedeforest.org/broadcaster.html, accessed June 24, 2005.

32. Acoustic recordings had a frequency range of approximately 250–2,500 Hz, whereas electrical techniques could record 50–6,000 Hz and a much wider dynamic range. Although components, such as the condenser microphone, had already been developed, Henry C. Harrison at Bell Labs developed a complete recording system in 1925. The first recording of this machine, licensed by the Victor Talking Machine Company, was of Stokowski and the Philadelphia Orchestra. "Sound Recording Research at Bell Labs," http://history.acusd.edu/gen/recording/bell-labs.html, accessed June 24, 2005.

33. This and the following description of the company's last years are taken from "The American Piano Company," a case study at Harvard Business School, 1934, www.playerpianogroup.org.uk. See also a summary of much of this information by Julian Dyer, "Demise of American Piano Company," online Mechanical Music Digest Archives, http://mmd.foxtail.com/Archives/Digests/200104/2001.04.12.05.html, accessed June 24, 2005.

34. Bowers, *Encyclopedia of Automatic Musical Instruments*, 660.

35. Rubinstein, *My Many Years*, 54.

36. Henderson, e-mail message, March 20, 2005. According to Henderson, Charles Foster Stoddard, credited with being the inventor of the Ampico, had a hearing loss and no interest in music whatsoever. He approached it strictly as a businessman, his main asset being connections and the ability to raise capital. After Ampico collapsed, Stoddard went into the restaurant business. There is even some question as to what extent Stoddard actually invented the Ampico mechanism or transferred patents from others, particularly Lewis B. Doman and Clarence Hickman.

7. THE PHILADELPHIA YEARS

1. "Camille Zeckwer, Composer, Is Dead," *Philadelphia Inquiry*, August 8, 1924, 23. Zeckwer died of complications following throat surgery.

2. The Zeckwer-Hahn Academy, which used that name alternatively with the Philadelphia Musical Academy, began offering Bachelor's degrees in 1950, and with further mergers, changed its name in 1976 to the Philadelphia College of Performing Arts. In 1987 it merged with the Philadelphia College of Art to create the University of the Arts. In 1924–1925 Charlton Lewis Murphy was briefly Director of the Academy.

3. Comments of Ornstein come from a letter from Leo Ornstein to Edmund Wilson, n.d., Edmund Wilson Papers, Beinicke Rare Books Library, Yale University, YCAL MSS 187, Box 53, Folder 1418.

4. Both the issue of Ornstein's desire to demonstrate financial independence and his losses in the stock market are uncorroborated statements from Ornstein's son, Severo. There is little doubt that the Ornsteins did receive help from Pauline's family: land in New Hampshire and a car given to them in 1941 are two examples. In the 1930s the Ornsteins and the Mallet-Prevosts (Severo Mallet-Prevost and his new wife, Laeta, whom he married in 1930) spent part of the summers together at their summer home in New Hampshire, "The Crags."

5. "Ornstein to Continue Playing," *Musical Courier* 89, no. 15 (October 9, 1924), 23.

6. Advertisement in *Musical Courier* 89, no. 17 (October 23, 1924), 13.

7. *Catalogue of the Philadelphia Musical Academy, Season 1929–30*. The catalogs of the Academy, beginning in 1929, are in the library of the University of the Arts, Philadelphia.

8. *Piano Sketch Books*, vol. 5 of *The Piano Music of Leo Ornstein* (Woodside, Calif.: Poon Hill Press), n.d.

9. E-mail message from Severo Ornstein, September 26, 2005.

10. Ornstein, *Catalog*, 19.

11. Ibid., 6.

12. Ibid., 17.

13. "Course in Language and Literature of Music by Leo Ornstein," photocopy of flyer in possession of Severo Ornstein.

14. *Musical America* 54, no. 7 (April 10, 1934), 38; copy of program for recital, in possession of Cedric Elmore.

15. *Musical Courier* 109, no. 1 (July 14, 1934), 39.

16. "Passing Tones of the Ornstein School of Music," n.d. The date of 1938 is inferred from the reference that this was the third year of operation of the school. According to the newsletter, it was to be a monthly publication, but no other copies have survived. Wadlemer Dabrowski composed music for the play *Noah*, and Charles Swier composed the one-act opera *The Dark Kingdom*.

17. Copy of Ornstein School of Music Brochure, Season 1940–1941, in possession of Severo Ornstein.

18. Signed autograph letter, Leo Ornstein to Mrs. Jasper Elmer, April 29, 1941.

19. Signed typed letter, Leo Ornstein to Mildred P. Smith, October 22, 1935. Signed typed letter (carbon copy), Leo Ornstein to Julia Shanaman, July 28, 1938. Letter in possession of Cedric Elmer, son of Julia Shanaman.

20. E-mail, Elizabeth Kessler to Denise Von Glahn, June 5, 2003. Most faculty would not get Ornstein's fees, of course, but if he taught twenty pupils per week, that would be

$180. Pauline's teaching load probably brought in at least another $100, likely more. If the Ornstein School had 400 pupils, the average cost per lesson was four dollars, and the school received 40 percent, deducting the Ornsteins' students and assuming that not all students took lessons each week, the income would probably come to roughly $480 per week, making a total revenue stream of approximately $3,000 per month. Since teacher's salaries are already accounted for, the only expenses would be rental of the building and general operating costs. Assuming expenses at approximately $1,000 per month, this meant a profit of about $2,000. This was a considerable amount in 1940.

21. Program, "Commencement Week, June 16–June 23 [1951], The Ornstein School of Music." Program in possession of Cedric Elmer.

22. "Andrew Imbrie, 'Portrait of a Contemporary Composer,'" an oral history conducted in 1998 and 1999 by Caroline C. Crawford, Regional Oral History Office, Bancroft Library, University of California, Berkeley, 2000.

23. Olga Samaroff, born Lucie Hickenlooper, was a concert pianist, critic, and teacher who married Leopold Stokowski in 1910. Ornstein would have known Samaroff both through Stokowski and possibly through her reviews of Ornstein's own concerts.

24. "Andrew Imbrie, Portrait."

25. Lewis Porter, John Coltrane, His Life and Music (Ann Arbor: University of Michigan Press, 1998), 33–34.

26. These comments are drawn from the authors' personal interviews with Ornstein students Lily Friedman, conducted on June 26, 2003, and Andrew Imbrie, conducted July 8, 2001, and from e-mail correspondence with Elizabeth Kessler, June 2003.

27. Interview with Lily Friedman.

28. Leo Ornstein, "How My Music Should be Played and Sung," Musical Observer 12, no. 12 (December 1915), 713–715; vol. 13, no. 1 (January 1916), 9–16.

29. Leo Ornstein, "Modern Principles of Piano Technic," Musical Observer, "First Paper," 21, no. 2 (February 1922), 14–15; "Second Paper," 21, no. 3 (March 1922), 14–15; "Third Paper," 21, no. 4 (April 1922), 14–15; "Fourth Paper," 21, no. 5 (May 1915), 12–13; "Fifth Paper," 21, no. 6 (June 1922), 50–51; "Sixth Paper," 21, no. 7 (July 1922), 9–10; "Seventh Paper," 21, no. 8 (August 1922), 11–12; "Eighth Paper," 21, no. 9 (September 1922), 11–12; "Ninth Paper," 21, no. 10 (October 1922), 13–14; "Tenth Paper," 21, no. 11 (November 1922), 12–13. With pedagogical articles such as this, there is the possibility that Pauline had a hand (no pun intended) in writing them.

30. E-mail message, Elizabeth Kessler to Denise Von Glahn, June 3, 2003.

31. Interview with Andrew Imbrie, June 8, 2001.

32. "Andrew Imbrie, Portrait."

33. Interview with Andrew Imbrie.

34. Interview with Lily Friedman, July 7, 2003.

35. "Andrew Imbrie, Portrait."

36. Temple University web site, www.temple.edu/tyler/history.html, accessed October 18, 2005.

37. "Gift to Establish Fine Arts College," New York Times, July 3, 1935, 15.

38. Ibid.

39. Erin Cusak, "Tyler Move Threatens Identity," Temple News, October 11, 2005, www.temple-news.com/media/paper143/news/2005/09/13/Opinion/Tyler.Move.Threatens.Identity-983243.shtml, accessed October 18, 2005.

40. Claire Reis, *Composers in America: Biographical Sketches of Contemporary Composers with a Record of Their Works* (New York: Macmillan, 1947), 274.

41. Gilbert Chase, *America's Music, From the Pilgrims to the Present* (New York: McGraw-Hill, 1955), 573.

42. Pauline Ornstein, Perlis interview, 1972.

43. Signed typed letter, Pauline Ornstein to Waldo Frank, May 17, 1937, Waldo Frank Papers, University of Pennsylvania.

44. Ornstein, interview with Holly Carter, 1986.

45. Edith Valentine, interview with authors, June 30, 2003.

46. For a description of Severo's role in the Internet, see Katie Hafner and Matthew Lyon, *Where Wizards Stay Up Late: The Origins of the Internet* (Carmel, Calif.: Touchstone Books, 1996); see also Severo's own account, *Computing in the Middle Ages: A View from the Trenches 1955–1983* (La Vergne, Tenn.: Lightening Source, 2002).

47. Leo Ornstein, interview with Vivian Perlis, Yale University Oral History America Project, December 8, 1972.

48. Phone conversation with Edith Valentine, August 14, 2003.

49. Referred to by the children as "the big house."

50. This would be in the late 1950s, although exact dates are not certain. E-mail to authors from Severo Ornstein, July 16, 1998; phone conversation with Edith Valentine, August 14, 2003.

51. Cyrilla Barr, *Elizabeth Sprague Coolidge: American Patron of Music* (New York: Schirmer, 1998), 353.

52. Severo Ornstein, interview, Woodside, Calif., July 3, 2001.

53. The International Society for Contemporary Music (ISCM) was founded in Salzburg in 1922. Concerts sponsored by various national societies provided forums for important premieres. It is not known whether the group sponsoring this particular concert in Philadelphia was part of the larger organization or a local group. No information on such a group has been located.

54. Henry Prunières, "News and Comments of the Current Week in Music," *New York Times*, December 1, 1929, section XI, 10; F. D. Perkins, "League of Composers Gives 4th Sunday Concert," *New York Herald Tribune*, January 13, 1930, 10.

55. *Musical Courier*, January 19, 1928, 22.

56. Henry Prunières, "News and Comments of the Current Week in Music," *New York Times*, December 1, 1929, section XI, p. 10.

57. From unpublished typed pages, untitled, in folder of letters of Ornstein's, in possession of Severo Ornstein. They were probably written in the 1970s. We know that Ornstein modified much of the piece, as numerous sketch revisions attest.

58. For a discussion of new music organizations see R. Allen Lott, "New Music for New Ears," *Journal of the American Musicological Society* 76, no. 2 (1983), 266–86; Metzer, "The Ascendancy of Musical Modernism in New York City, 1915–1929"; Oja, *Making Music Modern* and "Women Patrons and Crusaders for Modernist Music: New York in the 1920s," among others.

59. Linton Martin, "Modern Music Has a New Year Party," *Philadelphia Inquirer*, January 2, 1928, 12.

60. F. D. Perkins, "Recital Given by Belgians and Leo Ornstein," *New York Herald Tribune*, January 13, 1928, 15.

61. Ornstein's concerts included works by Bach, Haydn, Schubert, Chopin, Mendelssohn, Schumann, Liszt, and Grieg, as well as Schoenberg, Korngold, Ravel, Debussy, Scriabin, and Albéniz. In 1916 he added works by Bartók and Busoni to his repertoire.

62. *Three Moods*, one of his most famous pieces, was written out only in 1949 for a memorial concert for Paul Rosenfeld. Ornstein had been playing it for decades.

63. Leo Ornstein, interview by Vivian Perlis, November 19–20, 1977.

64. "Leo Ornstein Discusses Futurist Music," *Musical Courier* 78, no. 12 (March 24, 1915), 30.

65. Ornstein's musical training centered on the piano. He never studied another instrument, nor was he formally trained in orchestration or composition beyond rudiments he picked up at a very young age in harmony and theory courses. As he grew acquainted with string instruments, however, he discovered that writing for them tapped into a lyric strain that came to be one of his strengths as a composer. This discovery was aided by collaborations with string players, including his previously mentioned work with violinist Vera Barstow, with whom he played his Violin Sonata, Op. 26. In the latter 1910s and early 1920s, Ornstein also appeared frequently with Hans Kindler, principal cellist with the Philadelphia Orchestra, and dedicatee of the Cello Sonata, Op. 52. In old age, Ornstein recalled Kindler's comment that, although the composer did not actually play the instrument, he wrote for it as if born with a cello between his knees. Ornstein himself explained his understanding of the violin and the cello as a gift from God. Leo Ornstein, personal interview, Green Bay, Wisconsin, June 26, 1998.

66. See opening and then measures 29 and 37 for the beginnings of the motivic material. See measures 75, *Meno mosso*, and 191, *Andante*, for more lyrical thematic material. The lyrical theme introduced at measure 191 will return later in the Quintette.

67. Ornstein's *Quintette* premiered on a program that was part of a series of concerts featuring the music of Bartók, who was then making a six-week tour of the United States. In the holograph of Ornstein's score at the Library of Congress, the indication "Allegro barbaro" in the first movement is written in a heavy scrawl that is different from the other writing on the page. Perhaps Ornstein was paying homage to Bartók's now famous piano work "Allegro barbaro" written in 1911, with a last minute addition to his own score.

68. The *Quintette* is available in a modern edition, *Leo Ornstein, Quintette for Piano and Strings*, Critical Edition with Introduction, coedited by Denise Von Glahn and Michael Broyles (Ann Arbor, Mich.: MUSA [Music in the United States of America], vol. 13, in conjunction with A-R Editions), 2005. An unedited version, along with many other Ornstein pieces, is also available in pdf format at www.otherminds.org/ornstein/index.htm.

69. See measure 27: a pedal tone followed by a tritone and diminished chord; measure 34: an E-flat pedal tone followed by a tritone and a diminished chord. Various pedal tones occur at measure 37, G; measure 55, F; measure 62, E; measure 69, E-flat; measure 72, D; measure 75, D-flat. The descending pattern of pitches outlined in this series might suggest that Ornstein was aiming for D-flat as a pitch center. The movement ends, however, on a quadruple *forte* E-flat minor chord. We believe, for example, that the D-flat pedal at measure 75 (reh. 13), in a movement whose final sound is an E-flat chord, reflects Ornstein's commitment to spontaneity more than it does any theory that might make a rational tonal plan out of the harmonic materials of this movement.

70. "Expressive" is Ornstein's own word for his style of composition that featured greater lyricism. Expressive pieces would be in contrast to his more dissonant and

rhythmically driving works, which had dominated his more "futurist" style. He called these "experimental."

71. The viola plays the tritone G-sharp–D; Violin II plays the major seventh A–G-sharp. The first violin enters on the last beat of the m. 2 on a high E. It is difficult to hear any harmonic relationship between the closing of the first movement and the opening of the second movements in these initial sounds.

72. In the recollected theme Ornstein modifies not only the note values but also the key. That choice underscores Ornstein's lack of dependency on tonal centers. The return of a familiar theme is enough to connect the two movements in the listener's ear.

73. A similar motion from B-flat to C-sharp, this time in the first and second violins, occurs at measure 63. In neither case, however, does the C-sharp imply long-range functional harmonic significance as might a pitch that is lingered upon in a more tonal piece. C-sharp gains importance only in retrospect when it emerges as the most important pedal tone in the closing *Languido* passage starting at measure 173. Even here, as the piece is winding down to its final denouement, and C-sharp appears to be the point of resolution, the pedal is interrupted on three occasions with brief forays to B-flat, A, and C (as the lowest note in a left-hand piano pattern in mm. 83–121, A, was an important pitch). If A and C are interpreted as lower neighbors to B-flat and C-sharp, the rising gesture cited in measure 6 emerges in the pedal tones of the closing measures of the piano part. Whether this was a part of Ornstein's thinking is difficult to say. Given the C-sharp minor closing chord, however, such a reading seems reasonable.

74. See measure 53, violin I, and measure 75, piano, for an example of a theme undergoing harmonic, metrical, and timbral modification.

75. Ornstein's formal training in composition was limited and occurred when he was very young. It is possible that he regarded fugal writing as too intellectual and anti-intuitive, rejecting it as a manifestation of "formalism"; it is also possible he rejected it because he wasn't particularly good at it.

76. Ornstein's brief sections of counterpoint do not require large-scale planning, nor long-range compatibility of materials, that a fully realized fugue insists upon, nor is there any need for their lines to harmonize, as in tonal counterpoint.

77. One might hypothesize that the half-step motion between the C-sharp minor chord that ends the second movement and the complex centeredness on D that begins the third is an extension of Ornstein's focus on minor seconds within the *Quintette*.

78. Additional sections of polyrhythm occur in the movement when the opening melody reappears at measures 27–34, and at measures 157–160, 275–282, and 323–330. Single, very brief sections of polyrhythms occur in each of the first two movements: Movement I, measures 101–103; Movement II, measures 44–46. Regardless of the quantity of polyrhythms, however, all movements are characterized by numerous meter changes. Rhythmic unpredictability and tension contribute to the energy of the music.

79. F. D. Perkins, "Recital Given by Belgians and Ornstein," *New York Herald Tribune*, January 13, 1928, 15.

80. On the New World Records recording of the *Quintette* by the Lydian String Quartet, the first movement takes 13 minutes and 48 seconds, the second movement takes 10 minutes and 25 seconds, and the third movement takes 14 minutes 50 seconds. *Leo Ornstein Piano Quintet, String Quartet No. 3*, Lydian String Quartet, Janice Weber, piano. New World Records, 80509-2.

81. From unpublished typed pages, untitled, in possession of Severo Ornstein. Leo Ornstein probably wrote them in the 1970s for program notes.

82. Prunières, "News and Comments of the Current Week in Music," 10, noted the resemblance in 1929, not long after the work's premiere. Ernst Bloch (1880–1959) was Swiss born but became an American citizen in 1924

83. See Ernst Bloch, *Quintet for Piano and Strings* (New York: G. Schirmer, 1924), third movement, reh. 20, p. 94.

84. "Old Greek Play at Walnut," *Philadelphia Inquirer*, April 29, 1930, 8.

85. "League of Composers Again Commissions New Scores," *Musical Courier* 111, no. 7 (October 19, 1935), 6.

86. "Golschmann Introduces New Score by Ornstein in St. Louis Concerts," *Musical Courier* 115, no. 10 (March 6, 1937), 3.

87. "Programs of the Current Week," *New York Times*, December 6, 1936, X10F; D. Perkins, "League of Composers Gives 4th Sunday Concert," *New York Herald Tribune*, January 13, 1930, 10; Moses Smith, "Easter Concerts by Boston Orchestra," *Musical Courier* 115, no. 15 (April 10, 1937), 27; "Notes Here and There," *New York Times*, March 14, 1937, 180; http://proquest.umi.com/pqdweb?sid=1&RQT=511&TS=106234 9604&clientId=1360&firstIndex=30, accessed August 31, 2003.

88. Photograph caption, *New York Times*, November 12, 1933, X7.

89. Undated letter from Pauline Ornstein to Waldo Frank, in the Waldo Frank Papers, Annenberg Rare Book and Manuscript Library Collection, University of Pennsylvania. Context suggests 1929 or 1930.

90. "Programs of the Week," *New York Times*, November 11, 1932,

91. Signed typed letter, Pauline Ornstein to Waldo Frank, June 26, 1936, Waldo Frank Papers, Annenberg Rare Book and Manuscript Library Collection, University of Pennsylvania.

92. *Musical America* 63, no. 3 (February 10, 1937), 183.

8. RETURN FROM OBLIVION

1. It should be noted that none of the performances at the Ornstein School of Music were of the piano pieces. On February 15, 1949, three of Ornstein's *Russian Choruses* were sung; on April 5, 1949, Ornstein's *Suite in Classic Styles* for Flute and Piano was performed; and at Commencement, June 16, 1950, his *Nocturne* for Clarinet and Piano was performed.

2. Henry Cowell, "Current Chronicle," *Musical Quarterly* 35, no. 2 (April 1949), 292.

3. *Musical Courier* 93, no. 1 (January 7, 1926), 29. It should be pointed out that in the same column J.F.P., cited as the author of the Ornstein comment, also asked, "For the matter of that, what has become of Stravinsky, the hero of last season."

4. Cowell, *American Composers on American Music: A Symposium*, 4.

5. John Tasker Howard, *Our American Music*, 3rd ed., revised (New York: Thomas Y. Crowell, 1946), 505; Chase, *America's Music*, 1955 ed., 572, 1966 ed., 578; H. Wiley Hitchcock, *Music in the United States: A Historical Introduction* (New York: Prentice Hall, 1969).

6. Harold Schonberg, "A Musical Futurist Rediscovered," *New York Times*, March 14, 1976, D51.

7. Telegram, Pauline Ornstein to Music Division, Library of Congress.

8. Signed typed letter, Pauline Ornstein to Peter Ornstein, n.d., probably 1969.

9. Signed typed letter, Severo Ornstein to Elliott Carter. In an e-mail to the authors, September 14, 2005, Severo confirmed that he believed it was addressed to Carter.

10. Telephone interview with Charles Amirkhanian, September 18, 2005.

11. The anonymous review is enclosed in a letter from Donald R. Hammonds to Peter Ornstein, September 15, 1969. Hammonds make it clear to Peter that the review is *"for your eyes only"* (emphasis original).

12. Signed typed letter, Jack Behrens to Ornstein, October 1, 1969. Behrens is currently Director of Academic Studies at the Glenn Gould School of the Royal Conservatory of Music, Toronto, Canada. While teaching at California State University, Bakersfield, 1970–1976, Behrens programmed some of Ornstein's music on lecture recitals on twentieth-century music and at one point considered proposing to make an LP. E-mail messages, Jack Behrens to authors, August 9, 2005, and August 11, 2005.

13. Signed typed letter, Pauline to Peter Ornstein, n.d. probably 1969.

14. E-mail message from Severo Ornstein to Michael Broyles, August 8, 2005. The exact date of this recording is not known. Johannesen's performance was given at the League of Composers' memorial concert for Paul Rosenfeld in New York City on January 23, 1949.

15. Signed autograph letter, Pauline Ornstein to Peter Ornstein, January 22, 1970.

16. Copy of typed letter, Peter Ornstein to Pauline and Leo (Ornstein), February 15, 1970. The last page(s) of the draft is/are missing, so we do not know what else it contained.

17. Signed autograph letter, Pauline (Ornstein) to Peter and Barbara (Ornstein), January 22, 1970. The article is "Ford Fund to Assist Publishing and Recording of New Music," *New York Times,* January 2, 1970, 33.

18. Signed autograph letter, Pauline Ornstein to Peter Ornstein, n.d.

19. Signed autograph letter, Pauline Ornstein to Peter Ornstein, July 29, 1970.

20. Raymond Ericson, "Boulez Outlines Orchestral Plans," *New York Times,* January 28 1971, 42.

21. The letter exists only in a rough typed draft. Boulez's response below indicates that it was sent.

22. Olin Downes, "Music: The Philadelphia Orchestra," *New York Times,* February 18, 1925, 12.

23. Signed typed letter, Pierre Boulez to Mrs. Leo Ornstein, March 10, 1971.

24. Signed autograph letter, Pauline Ornstein to Peter Ornstein, March 13, 1971.

25. Signed autograph letter, Pauline Ornstein to Peter Ornstein, n.d.

26. Vivian Perlis, *Charles Ives Remembered: An Oral History* (New Haven, Conn.: Yale University Press, 1974); 2nd edition (New York, W. W. Norton, 1976); 3rd edition (Chicago and Urbana: University of Illinois Press, 2002).

27. Authors' interview with Vivian Perlis, New Haven, Conn., June 10, 2003.

28. Authors' e-mail interview with Vivian Perlis, August 29, 2005.

29. E-mail interview with Vivian Perlis, August 29, 2005.

30. Vivian Perlis, "Mystery Man of American Music," *Vision* 5, no. 2 (February 1985), 11–12.

31. Ibid.

32. Signed autograph letter, Pauline Ornstein to Peter Ornstein, July 23, 1972.

33. Signed autograph letter, Pauline Ornstein to Peter Ornstein, August 10, 1972.

34. Ibid. Pauline enclosed a carbon copy of the statement to Peter in the letter.

35. This was no hypothetical problem. Puritan ministers complained specifically about this situation. See Broyles, "*Music of the Highest Class*," 40–42. The phrase "sinners in the hands of an angry God" is the title of a sermon by the Puritan minister Jonathan Edwards.

36. "The Futurist Music of Leo Ornstein," *Notes* 31, no. 4 (June 1975), 735–750.

37. William Westney, e-mail interview with authors, September 6, 2005.

38. Signed typed letter, Vivian Perlis to Leo and Pauline Ornstein, November 13, 1973.

39. At the time it was believed that Ornstein was born on December 11, 1892.

40. *New York Times*, March 14, 1976, D14.

41. Schonberg does concede, "It is true that Charles Ives was writing at this time, but Ives was unknown.

42. "Harold C. Schonberg, "An Octogenarian's Eclectic Sounds," *New York Times*, December 13, 1976, 48.

43. Authors' telephone interview with Charles Amirkhanian, September 18, 2005.

44. Ibid.

45. Ibid.

46. Donal Henehan, "Sellers Offers Rudhyar's Music," *New York Times*, April 18, 1972, 56.

47. Signed typed letter, Thomas W. Morris (Boston Symphony Orchestra) to Michael Sellers, October 26, 1976; typed letter, Michael Sellers to Severo Ornstein, February 20, 1977.

48. Signed typed letter, Michael Sellers to Severo Ornstein, October 21, 1974.

49. Signed autograph letter, Leo Ornstein to Marthanne Verbit, September 9, 1980 (written by Pauline Ornstein).

50. Program note that accompanied the first performance.

51. Telephone interview, authors with Marthanne Verbit, September 22, 2005.

52. Ibid.

53. Theodore W. Libbey, Jr., "Piano: Anne Verbit Recital," *New York Times*, November 15, 1981. In addition to Ornstein she played a Verdi paraphrase and works of Liszt, Schoenberg, Stravinsky, Scriabin, Casella, and Busoni.

54. Signed typed letter, Marthanne Verbit to Leo Ornstein, April 12, 1982. Over the years Daniel Stepner became one of the more important performers in the Ornstein Renaissance. He was first violinist on the first recording of the *Quintette*, made in 1975, the second recording done in 1994, and the String Quartet No. 3, done in 1995. Harold Samuel had the difficult task of raising sufficient funds, and as Yale University sponsored the concert, was responsible for contracts and many details such as an after-concert reception. According to the program the concert itself was funded from grants from BMI, Xerox Corporation, where Severo then worked, Severo Ornstein and his wife Laura Gould, and an "anonymous donor."

55. Andrew Porter, "Musical Events," *New Yorker*, February 14, 1983; Peter G. Davis, "Marathon Man," *New York Magazine*, December 27, 1982–January 3, 1983; Robert Kimball, "American Treasure Rediscovered," *New York Post*, December 11, 1982; Edward Rothstein, "Concert: Yale Presents Works of Leo Ornstein," *New York Times*, December 10, 1982; Donal Henehan, *New York Times*, December 5, 1982. These articles are photocopies from the files of Woerner/Bobrick Associates. Piotr Kropotkin was a Russian writer and political theorist. Born a prince, he embraced the cause of

peasants and was known as an anarchist. Cut off from political influence by Lenin, he predicted that the Bolshevik state would essentially descend into tyranny.

56. Alden Whitman, "2 Funds Aiding Older Americans Who Are in the Arts," *New York Times*, February 10, 1971, 34.

57. Signed autograph letter, Theodore Stamos to Leo Ornstein, November 18, 1972.

58. Signed typed letter, Severo Ornstein to Theodore Stamos, February 28, 1973.

59. Signed typed letter, Theodore Stamos to Severo Ornstein, March 13, 1973.

60. Notes by Severo Ornstein on Theodore Stamos letter to Pauline, November 18, 1972.

61. Signed autograph letter, Pauline Ornstein to Severo Ornstein, n.d. Pauline throughout her letter refers to "Mrs. Reis," a salutation echoed by Severo in his letter to Bernard Reis of March 30, and one wonders if she is confusing him with Claire Reis. Severo himself wondered if Reis was the son of Claire (notes by Severo on Stamos letter to Pauline, November 18, 1972). They appear unrelated, unless distantly. Claire had a son, Arthur, Jr., and a daughter, Hilda. Neither had a child named Bernard.

62. Signed autograph letter, Bernard Reis to Severo Ornstein, April 11, 1973.

63. Signed typed letter, Severo Ornstein to Paul Olefsky, May 9, 1973.

64. Signed autograph letter, Pauline Ornstein to Severo Ornstein, n.d.

65. Both Schwartz and Hampton taught at Stanford University in the 1970s.

66. Carbon copy of typed letter, Severo Ornstein to Giveon Cornfield, November 29, 1973, February 15, 1974, and February 26, 1974.

67. Signed typed letter, Giveon Cornfield to Severo Ornstein, March 20, 1974.

68. Carbon copy of typed letter, Severo Ornstein to Bonnie Hampton, November 29, 1973.

69. Carbon copy of typed letter, Severo Ornstein to Michael Sellers, June 3, 1974.

70. Signed typed letter, Severo Ornstein to Michael Sellers, November 13, 1973; signed typed letter, Giveon Cornfield to Severo Ornstein, December 24, 1975; signed typed letter, Giveon Cornfield to Severo Ornstein, February 27, 1976.

71. Signed typed letter, Jack O'Brien to Pauline Ornstein, April 19, 1978.

72. Ibid.

73. Signed autograph letter, Pauline Ornstein to Severo Ornstein [July 1, 1976].

74. Signed typed letter, Jack O'Brien to Pauline Ornstein, April 19, 1978.

75. Signed autograph letter, Pauline Ornstein to Severo Ornstein, n.d.

76. E-mail to authors from Severo Ornstein, November 30, 2005.

77. Signed autograph letter, Pauline Ornstein to Peter Ornstein, April 30, 1973

78. Signed autograph letter, Pauline Ornstein to Severo Ornstein, n.d.

79. Signed typed letter, Charles Amirkhanian to Fred Kameny, January 22, 1975.

80. Signed autograph letter, Bernard Reis to Carter Harmon, April 11, 1973.

81. Information on recording date taken from the LP, CRI SD 339.

82. Promotional material in papers of Charles Amirkhanian.

83. Signed typed letter, Charles Amirkhanian to Leo Ornstein, September 7, 1988; signed typed letter, Charles Amirkhanian to Edith Valentine, September 7, 1988.

84. Carbon copy of typed letter, Harold Samuel to Leo and Pauline Ornstein, January 21, 1977.

85. Signed typed letter, Severo Ornstein to Harold E. Samuel, January 26, 1977.

86. Signed typed letter, Severo Ornstein to Paul Kapp, December 2, 1979; response, signed typed letter, Paul Kapp to Severo Ornstein, December 8, 1979.

87. Kapp to Ornstein, December 8, 1979. The recordings are Serenus Corporation SRS 12089 and Serenus Corporation SRS 12090.

88. Signed typed letter, Paul Kapp to Severo Ornstein, December 8, 1979.

89. "Paul Kapp," *New York Times*, May 16, 1984, D26.

90. Copy of letter from Severo Ornstein to Harold Samuel, September 12, 1987. It should be noted that Severo never abandoned his career as a political reformer and continues to be active today.

91. Copies of all letters are in the collection of Severo Ornstein.

92. Copy of letter from Severo M. Ornstein to Fromm Music Center, September 12, 1987.

93. Poon Hill Press, 2200 Bear Gulch Rd, Woodside, Calif. 94062. Poon Hill is the name of the home that Severo and his wife Laura Gould own in Woodside, California.

94. Signed typed letter, Severo Ornstein to Peter Hanser-Strecker, Schott and Co., February 13, 1988; reply, Peter Hanser-Strecker to Severo Ornstein, February 29, 1988; signed typed letter, Ronald Freed, European American Music, to Severo Ornstein, Schott and Co., March 15, 1988.

95. http://poonhill.com.

96. Taped interview, Ornstein with Holly Carter, 1986.

97. Authors' interview with Eleanor Lasee, June 30, 2003.

98. Introduction to the score of the Eighth Piano Sonata, Poon Hill Press.

99. "Rosebud" was the last word that Orson Wells, who portrayed Charles Foster Kane in the movie *Citizen Kane*, uttered. The mysterious reference was the name of a sleigh that Kane left behind when he was taken from his family to be schooled in the East.

9. MODERNIST DILEMMAS, PERSONAL CHOICES

1. Langfield's letter #157, May 20, 1914, Leo Ornstein to Roger Quilter (see chapter 2).

2. Terrance J. O'Grady, "A Conversation with Leo Ornstein," *Perspectives of New Music* 23 (Fall–Winter 1984), 127.

3. This does not mean, of course, that these composers did not carefully craft their works.

4. Authors' interview with Leo Ornstein, Green Bay, Wisconsin, June 26, 1998.

5. "Mephisto's Musings," *Musical America* 42, no. 7 (June 6, 1926), 8; "New York Concerts, *Musical Courier* 84 (January 5, 1922), 58; Lawrence Gilman, "Music," *New York Herald Tribune*, February 18, 1925, 13; Harold C. Schonberg, "A Musical Futurist Rediscovered," *New York Times*, March 14, 1976, D15.

6. W. L. Hubbard, ed., *History of American Music* (Toledo, Ohio: Irving Square, 1867; rev. 1908), 87.

7. Ironically, Ornstein may have suffered because he was ahead of his time. Many, in fact most, composers turned away from the ultramodern approach in the 1930s and again in the 1970s, but to do it in 1916 was for most observers inexplicable.

8. Ewen, *Composers of Today*, 182.

9. Cyril Scott, "The Connection of the War with Art and Music," *Monthly Musical Record* 46, no. 543 (March 1916), 69.

10. Leonard Meyer, "Forgery and the Anthropology of Art," *Yale Review* 52, no. 2 (December 1962), 220–233, reprinted in *Music, the Arts, and Ideas: Patterns and Predictions in Twentieth-Century Culture* (Chicago: University of Chicago Press, 1967), 54–67.

11. Ernst Krenek, "Tradition in Perspective," *Perspectives of New Music* 1 (Fall 1962), 32.

12. "Leo Ornstein, Pianist," *Musical Courier* 77, no. 24 (December 12, 1918), 25. As we have noted, Ornstein had the habit of carrying works around in his head for many years before committing them to paper, and in some instances by the time he got around to it he could no longer remember the piece. Op. 54 is one of those. In Ornstein's case the presence of an opus number does not necessarily mean that it was published.

13. Saleski, *Famous Musicians of a Wandering Race*, 361–362.

14. O'Grady, "A Conversation with Leo Ornstein," 130.

15. This is not to say that Ives was unaware of new forces in the musical world around him, just that the musical world was unaware of him at the time.

16. Salzedo was Basque-Spanish, but spent much of his childhood in France early before coming to the United States.

17. See chapter 2 for a discussion of the aesthetic orientation of the Frankfurt Five.

18. According to a letter written by Henry Cowell to Ellen Veblen that is quoted in Michael Hicks's biography of Cowell, at a concert in January 1920 where Cowell substituted for an ill Ornstein, Ethel Leginska "publicly announced that Henry Cowell was a better composer than Ornstein." The authors have not found corroborating evidence of Cowell's claim in any public record. See Michael Hicks, *Henry Cowell: Bohemian* (Urbana: University of Illinois Press, 2002), 104–105.

19. See signed autograph letter, undated to "Dearest Children." Likely from the 1970s, in possession of Severo Ornstein.

20. Ibid.

21. The concert took place Sunday afternoon, Christmas Eve Day, at 3:15.

22. "Three Artists in Recitals," *New York Times*, December 6, 1916, 7.

23. Typed letter from anonymous reviewer to Peter Ornstein.

24. See student records for Miss Pauline Mallet-Prevost from the Institute of Musical Art of the City of New York 1908–1909, 1909–1910, Lila Acheson Wallace Archives and Library of the Juilliard School.

25. There are numerous remarks scattered among Ornstein's many interviews that support the notion he wanted to pull back on the number of concerts he was giving, although none suggests he wanted to abandon a virtuoso career completely.

26. The authors observed Ornstein's hands in their interview with him. Even at his advanced age, his hands were supple, expressive, and certainly of adequate size. It may be that Ornstein felt he had to keep practicing to maintain his flexibility, but this is an issue quite aside from the size of one's hand and still doesn't explain why he would keep practicing if he wanted to give up performing.

27. Trachtenberg, *Memoirs of Waldo Frank*, 65.

28. Review of *Musical Portraits* by Henrietta Straus, *The Nation* 111, no. 2884 (October 13, 1920), 411–412.

29. The same spontaneous quality that characterized his creative work may very well explain his surprise marriage.

30. Signed autograph letter, n.d., Pauline to "Dearest Children," in possession of Severo Ornstein. A reference in the letter to a doctor advising Pauline to continue "what I am doing for another 84 years" suggests that the letter was written in 1976.

31. Signed autograph letter, Leo Ornstein to Severo Ornstein, March 3, 1976, in possession of Severo Ornstein. The Boca Chica Highway goes from Brownsville, Texas, to Port Isabel and then to Padre Island in the Gulf of Mexico.

32. See *Musical America* 26, no. 22 (September 29, 1917), 4.

33. It is often assumed that twins share an unusually close bond, although fraternal twins much less so than identical twins. There is no mention of Lisa in any of the Leo Ornstein letters or papers that survive.

34. Severo Ornstein described his father as affectionate toward his mother but not considerate.

35. Malmquist's work was entitled "Allegretto." The two Grade III works were the most elementary of the grades represented on the recital, which consisted of no Grade IV pieces at all, but six each of Grade V and VI pieces. By Grade V students were expected to write fugues, and with Grade VI entire sonata movements for an instrument. See "Lectures, Recitals, and General Occasions," October 10, 1910, through June 1, 1911, Lila Acheson Wallace Archives and Library of the Juilliard School.

36. E-mail correspondence from Severo Ornstein to authors, July 22, 2005.

37. In a personal interview with Edith Valentine, July 27, 2003, Edith quoted her father as saying, "My wife wanted me all to herself."

38. Telephone interview with Edith Valentine, August 14, 2005.

39. Ornstein, interview with Holly Carter, 1986.

40. Telephone interview of Edith Valentine with authors, August 14, 2005.

41. Telephone interview of Edith Valentine with authors, September 12, 2005.

42. Ornstein, interview with Holly Carter, 1986.

43. E-mail correspondence, Severo Ornstein to authors, September 13, 2005.

BIBLIOGRAPHY

"The American Piano Company." Case study at Harvard Business School, 1934. www
.playerpianogroup.org.uk. Accessed June 24, 2005.

Baer, Nancy Van Norman. "The Ballets Suedois: A Synthesis of Modernist Trends in
Art." In *Paris Modern: The Swedish Ballet 1920–1925*. Edited by Nancy Van Norman
Baer. San Francisco: Fine Arts Museums of San Francisco; distributed by the
University of Washington Press, Seattle, 1995.

Baker, Theodore. *Über die Musik der nordamerikanischen Wilden*. Leipzig: Breitkopf &
Härtel, 1882.

Baldwin, Neil. *Henry Ford and the Jews: The Mass Production of Hate*. New York: Public
Affairs, 2001.

Barr, Cyrilla. *Elizabeth Sprague Coolidge: American Patron of Music*. New York: Schirmer, 1998.

Brisbane, Arthur. "The Great Power of Music." *New York Evening Journal*, June 11, 1910, 12.

Brower, Harriete. "Leo Ornstein, An Ultra Modern Pianist and Composer." *Musical
Observer* (August 1915), 467.

Broyles, Michael. *Mavericks and Other Traditions in American Music*. New Haven, Conn.:
Yale University Press, 2004.

———. *"Music of the Highest Class": Elitism and Populism in Antebellum Boston*. New Haven,
Conn.: Yale University Press, 1991.

Buchanan, Charles L. "Futurist Music." *The Independent*, July 31, 1916, 160.

———. "Ornstein and Futurist Music." *Vanity Fair* 5, no. 6 (February 1916), 48.

C.N. *Musical Standard*, April 18, 1914, 374–375.

Carter, Paul J. *Waldo Frank*. New York: Twayne, 1967.

Cator, Thomas Vincent. "Letter to." *Musical America* 21, no. 9 (January 2, 1915), 24–25.

Chase, Gilbert. *America's Music, From the Pilgrims to the Present*. New York: McGraw-Hill,
1955, 1966.

Collins, Brian. *Peter Warlock: The Composer*. Cambridge: Scholar Press, 1996.

"The Complete Lee de Forest." www.leedeforest.org/broadcaster.html. Accessed
June 24, 2005.

Cooke, James Francis. "The Advent of Endowed Institutions in America." *Etude* 24
(February 1906), 58.

Corder, Frederick. "On the Cult of the Wrong Notes." *Musical Quarterly* 1, no. 3 (July
1915), 381–386.

Cowell, Henry, ed. *American Composers on American Music: A Symposium*. Stanford, Calif.:
Stanford University Press, 1933.

Cox, Jeanette. "Goldmark's 'Requiem' a Feature of Chicago Symphony's Sixth Program—
Leo Ornstein, as Soloist Plays the MacDowell Concerto." *Musical Courier* 79, no. 22
(December 11, 1919), 52.

Damrosch, Frank. *Institute of Musical Art: 1905–1926*. New York: Privately printed for the
Juilliard School of Music, 1936.

Dolmetsch, Arnold. *The Interpretation of the Music of the XVII and XVIII Centuries Revealed by Contemporary Evidence.* London: Novello, 1915.

Dyer, Julian. "Demise of American Piano Company." Mechanical Music Digest Archives. http://mmd.foxtail.com/Archives/Digests/200104/2001.04.12.05.html. Accessed June 24, 2005.

Eichler, Jeremy. "A Virtuoso Who Favors the Fringe." *New York Times,* March 24, 2002, "Arts & Leisure," 29, 32.

Ewen, David. *Composers of Today: A Comprehensive Biographical and Critical Guide to Modern Composers of All Nations.* New York: H. W. Wilson, 1934.

Fine, Ruth E. *John Marin.* Washington, D.C.: National Gallery of Art, 1990.

"The Firs and Felsted: Sunset Maine." Deer Isle–Stonington (Maine) Historical Society.

Fisher, Marjory Markress. "Futurist Music a Logical Outcome of the Age, Declares This Modernist." *Musical America* 26, no. 16 (1917), 27.

Frank, Waldo. *The Jew in Our Day.* New York: Duell, Sloan and Pearce, 1944.

———. *Memoirs of Waldo Frank.* Edited by Alan Trachtenberg. Introduction by Lewis Mumford. Amherst: University of Massachusetts Press, 1973.

———. *Our America.* New York: Boni and Liveright, 1919.

"A Futurist and Ultra Modern Program." *Musical Courier* 70, no. 12 (March 24, 1915), 41.

G.F.H. (Gilbert F. Haywood). "Ornstein in Two Providence Recitals." *Musical America* 23, no. 9 (January 1, 1916), 18.

Gilman, Lawrence. "Drama and Music." *North American Review* 201, no. 713 (April 1915), 593–597.

Goodson, Steve. *Highbrows, Hillbillies and Hellfire: Public Entertainment in Atlanta 1880–1930.* Athens: University of Georgia Press, 2002.

Hafner, Katie, and Matthew Lyon. *Where Wizards Stay Up Late: The Origins of the Internet.* Carmel, Calif.: Touchstone Books, 1996.

Hale, Nancy, and Fredson Bowers, eds. *Leon Kroll: A Spoken Memoir.* Charlottesville: University Press of Virginia, 1983.

H.F.P. (Horatio Parker). "'Advanced Thinkers' Applaud Ornstein." *Musical America* 23, no. 7 (December 11, 1915), 51.

———. "Audience Engrossed in Composer-Pianist's Futuristic Offerings." *Musical America* 30, no. 26 (October 25, 1919), 5.

———. "Moderns Superbly Played by Ornstein." *Musical America* 27, no. 13 (January 26, 1918), 30.

———. "Orstein Descends to Classic Level." *Musical America* 23, no. 13 (January 29, 1916), 40.

———. "Ornstein Presents His 'Dwarf Suite.'" *Musical America* 21, no. 15 (February 13, 1915), 26.

Hicks, Michael. *Henry Cowell: Bohemian.* Urbana: University of Illinois Press, 2002.

Higham, John. "Anti-Semitism in the Gilded Age: A Reinterpretation." *Mississippi Valley Historical Review* 43, no. 4 (March 1957), 572.

"Hissing Defended." *Musical Courier,* May 6, 1914, 52.

Hitchcock, H. Wiley. *Music in the United States: A Historical Introduction.* New York: Prentice Hall, 1969.

Hofstadter, Richard. "The Folklore of Populism." In *Antisemitism in the United States.* Edited by Leonard Dinnerstein, 58–63. New York: Holt, Rinehart, and Winston, 1971.

Howard, John Tasker. *Our American Music.* 3rd edition, revised. New York: Thomas Y. Crowell, 1946.

Hubbard, W. L., ed. *History of American Music.* Toledo, Ohio: 1867, rev. 1908.

Hughes, Rupert. *Contemporary American Composers, A Study Of the Music Of This Country, Its Present Conditions and Its Future, with Critical Estimates and Biographies of the Principal Living Composers and an Abundance of Portraits, Fac-Simile Musical Autographs, and Compositions.* Boston: L. C. Page, 1900.

Huneker, James Gibbons. "Seven Arts." *Puck* 77, no. 1989 (April 7, 1915), 11.

Idelsohn, Abraham Zvi. *Jewish Music in Its Historical Development.* New York: Tudor, 1948.

Jaffe, Julian F. *Crusade against Radicalism: New York during the Red Scare, 1914–1924.* Port Washington, N.Y.: National University Publications, Kennikat Press, 1972.

Jewett, Albert D. "Mrs. Thomas Tapper." *The Musician* (October 1915), 632, 675.

Klein, Maury. "Life on the Lower East Side." *American History Illustrated* 7, no. 7 (1972), 25.

Knapp, Alexander. "The Jewishness of Bloch: Subconscious or Conscious?" *Proceedings of the Royal Musical Association* 97 (1970–1971), 108.

A.W.K. (A. Walter Kramer). "Bertha Feiring Tapper: Altruist." *Musical America* 22, no. 21 (September 25, 1915), 9.

———. "'Bohemians' Hear Ornstein." *Musical America* 21, no. 2 (November 14, 1914), 14.

———. "Has Leo Ornstein Discovered a New Musical Style?" *Musical America*, no. 21, no. 4 (December 12, 1914), 5–6.

———. "Leo Ornstein, Pianist: A Study." *Musical America* 14, no. 8 (July 8, 1911), 23.

———. "Ornstein Completes Cycle of Recitals." *Musical America* 21, no. 20 (March 20, 1915), 39.

———. "Ornstein Heard in Ultra Tone-Poems." *Musical America* 23, no. 23 (April 8, 1916), 22.

———. "Ornstein Plays His Own Music." *Musical America* 21, no. 13 (January 30, 1915), 43.

———. "Ornstein Presents More of His Music." *Musical America* 21, no. 18 (March 6, 1915), 6.

———. "Ornstein Rouses Intense Admiration." *Musical America*, 29, no. 7 (December 14, 1918), 29.

Krenek, Ernst. "Tradition in Perspective." *Perspectives of New Music* 1 (fall 1962), 32.

Kuran, Laura Van. "Music Teachers of the State Sound Optimistic Note." *Musical America* 24, no. 9 (July 1, 1916), 2–3.

Langfield, Valerie. *Roger Quilter: His Life and Music.* Woodbridge, Suffolk: Boydell Press, 2002.

Lee, Albert. *Henry Ford and the Jews.* New York: Stein and Day, 1980.

"Leo Ornstein Busy Composing." *Musical America* 30, no. 21 (September 21, 1919), 29.

"Leo Ornstein Hoists the Banner of Musical Futurism." *Current Opinion* 61 (July 1916), 30–31.

"Leo Ornstein, Pianist." *Musical Courier* 77, no. 24 (December 12, 1918), 25.

Levin, Gail. "The Ballets Suedois and American Culture." In *Paris Modern: The Swedish Ballet 1920–1925.* Edited by Nancy Van Norman Baer, pp. 118–127. San Francisco: Fine Arts Museums of San Francisco. Distributed by the University of Washington Press, Seattle, 1995.

Lloyd, Stephen. "Grainger and the 'Frankfurt Group.'" *Studies in Western Music* (University of Western Australia) 16 (1982), 111–118.

Lott, R. Allen. "New Music for New Ears." *Journal of the American Musicological Society* 76, no. 2 (1983), 266–286.

Martens, Frederick H. "Introductory." *Poems of 1917 by Leo Ornstein.* New York: Carl Fischer, 1918.

———. *Leo Ornstein: The Man—His Ideas, His Work.* New York: Breitkopf & Härtel, 1918.

Martin, George. *The Damrosch Dynasty.* Boston: Houghton Mifflin, 1983.

Mason, Daniel Gregory. "Is American Music Growing Up? Our Emancipation from Alien Influences." *Arts and Decoration* 14, no. 1 (November 1920), 40.

Mattis, Olivia. "Edgard Varèse and the Visual Arts." Ph.D. dissertation, Stanford University, 1992.

Mellquist, Jerome, and Lucie Wiese. *Paul Rosenfeld: Voyager in the Arts.* New York: Creative Age Press, 1948.

Metzer, David Joel. "The Ascendancy of Musical Modernism in New York City, 1915–1929." Ph.D. dissertation, Yale University, 1993.

Meyer, Leonard. "Forgery and the Anthropology of Art." *Yale Review* 52, no. 2 (December 1962), 220–233. Reprinted in *Music, the Arts, and Ideas: Patterns and Predictions in Twentieth-Century Culture,* 54–67. Chicago: University of Chicago Press, 1967.

Miller, Jeff. "A Chronology of AM Radio Broadcasting, 1900–1920." http://members.aol .com/jeff560/chrono1.html. Accessed June 24, 2005.

"M. Leo Ornstein: A Futurist Recital." *Musical Times* 55, no. 855 (May 1, 1914), 331.

M.M.F. "Ornstein in San Jose." *Musical America* 27, no. 6 (December 8, 1917), 13.

Murdoch, Robert M. "Gerald Murphy, Cole Porter, and the Ballets Suedois Production of *Within the Quota.*" In *Paris Modern: The Swedish Ballet 1920–1925.* Edited by Nancy Van Norman Baer, 108–117. San Francisco: Fine Arts Museums of San Francisco, distributed by the University of Washington Press, Seattle, 1995.

Murray, Robert K. *Red Scare: A Study in National Hysteria, 1919–1920.* Minneapolis: University of Minnesota Press, 1955.

Ogorzaly, Michael A. *Waldo Frank: Prophet of Hispanic Regeneration.* Lewisburg, Penn.: Bucknell University Press, 1994.

O'Grady, Terrance J. "A Conversation with Leo Ornstein." *Perspectives of New Music* 23 (fall-winter 1984), 126–132.

Oja, Carol. *Making Music Modern: New York in the 1920s.* New York: Oxford University Press, 2000.

———. "Women Patrons and Crusaders for Modernist Music: New York in the 1920s." In *Cultivating Music in America: Women Patrons and Activists since 1860*. Edited by Ralph P. Locke and Cyrilla Barr. Berkeley: University of California Press, 1997.

Olmstead, Andrea. *Juilliard: A History*. Urbana: University of Illinois Press, 1999.

Orga, Artes. "Pianola to Reproducing Piano: 3, A Plaine and Easie Introduction." www.mvdaily.com/articles/1999/02/ppiano14.htm. Accessed June 23, 2005.

"Ornstein Busy on New Sonata." *Musical Courier* 83, no. 5 (August 4, 1921), 13.

Ornstein, Leo. "How My Music Should be Played and Sung: A Series of Papers Devoted to the Character and Idiom of My Latest Works, Describing Essential Requirements for Their Adequate Understanding and Providing Suggestions for Mastery of Their Technical Difficulties." *Musical Observer* 12, no. 12 (December 1915), 713–715; 13, no. 1 (January 1916), 9–16.

Ornstein, Leo, and Pauline Ornstein. "The Last of the Original 20th Century Mavericks, Leo and Pauline Ornstein Speak with Vivian Perlis." Interview in Vivian Perlis Archives of Oral History American Music, Yale University. Sierra Mobile Park, Lot #32, off I-18 Brownsville, Texas, November 19–20, 1977.

Ornstein, Pauline Mallet-Prevost. *Reminiscences from Here, There, and Everywhere*. Lila Acheson Wallace Archives and Library, Juilliard School of Music.

Ornstein, Severo. *Catalog and Thematic Index of Works for Solo Piano by Leo Ornstein*. Woodside, Calif.: Poon Hill Press, 1998.

———. *Computing in the Middle Ages: A View from the Trenches 1955–1983*. La Vergne, Tenn.: Lightening Source, 2002.

"Ornstein's Ultra-Modernism and Expert Pianism." *Musical Courier* 70, no. 15 (April 14, 1915), 31.

Owens, Dewey. *Carlos Salzedo: From Aeolian to Thunder, a Biography*. Chicago: Lyon & Healy, 1992.

Palmer, A. Mitchell "The Case against the 'Red.'" *Forum* 63 (1920), 173–185.

Perkins, F. D. "Recital Given by Belgians and Ornstein." *New York Herald Tribune*, January 13, 1928, 15.

Perlis, Vivian. *Charles Ives Remembered: An Oral History*. 3rd edition. Urbana: University of Illinois Press, 2002.

———. "The Futurist Music of Leo Ornstein." *Notes* 31, no. 4 (June 1975), 735–750.

———. "Mystery Man of American Music." *Vision* 5, no. 2 (February 1985), 11–12.

Pfannestiel, Todd J. *Rethinking the Red Scare: The Lusk Committee and New York's Crusade against Radicalism, 1919–1923*. New York: Routledge, 2003.

Porter, Lewis. *John Coltrane, His Life and Music*. Ann Arbor: University of Michigan Press, 1998.

Pritchett, Wendell. *Brownsville, Brooklyn: Blacks, Jews, and the Changing Face of the Ghetto*. Chicago: University of Chicago Press, 2002.

Reis, Claire. *Composers, Conductors, and Critics*. New York: Oxford University Press, 1955.

———. *Composers in America: Biographical Sketches of Contemporary Composers with a Record of Their Works*. New York: Macmillan, 1947.

———. "Contemporary Music and the Man on the Street." *Eolian Review* 2, no. 2 (1923), 24–28.

R.G.M. "Alda and Ornstein Interest Montreal." *Musical America* 30, no. 6 (June 7, 1919), 29.

Rhodes, Robbie. "Dynamic Range of the Ampico B—Hickman Data." Mechanical Music Digest Archives, April 2001. http://mmd.foxtail.com/Archives/Digests/200104 /2001.04.23.12.html. Accessed June 22, 2005.

Roberts, Kenneth L. *Why Europe Leaves Home*. New York: Arno Press, 1977; originally published 1922.

Rosenfeld, Paul. "Grand Transformation Scene—1907–1915." In *The Writings of Paul Rosenfeld: An Annotated Bibliography*. Edited by Charles L. P. Silet, 356–357. New York: Garland, 1981.

———. *An Hour with American Music*. Philadelphia: J. B. Lippincott, 1929.

———. "Musical Chronicle." *The Dial* 72 (March 1922), 332–336.

———. *Musical Chronicle 1917–1923*. New York: Harcourt, Brace, 1923.

———. *Musical Portraits: Interpretations of Twenty Modern Composers*. New York: Harcourt, Brace and Howe, 1920.

———. "The Novels of Waldo Frank." *The Dial* 70 (January 1921), 95–105.

———. *Port of New York*. With an Introductory Essay by Sherman Paul. Urbana: University of Illinois Press, 1961.

———. "Waldo Frank's Dream." *The Nation* 148 (May 20, 1939), 590.

Rubinstein, Arthur. *My Many Years*. New York: Alfred A. Knopf, 1980.

Saleski, Gdal. *Famous Musicians of a Wandering Race: Biographical Sketches of Outstanding Figures of Jewish Origin in the Musical World*. New York: Bloch, 1927.

Saminsky, Lazare. "East Meets West." *Modern Music* 4, no. 22 (January–February 1927), 21.

———. *Music of Our Day, Essentials and Prophecies*. Freeport, N.Y.: Books for Libraries Press, 1930; reprinted 1970.

Saul, David L. "Reproducing Pianos." In *Encyclopedia of Automatic Musical Instruments*. Edited by Q. David Bowers, 255–308. Vestal, N.Y.: Vestal Press, 1972.

"Schoenberg Most Conservative Composer at Boston Concert." *Musical Courier* 71, no. 24 (December 16, 1915), 18.

Scott, Cyril. "The Connection of the War with Art and Music." *Monthly Musical Record* 46, no. 543 (March 1916), 69.

Scott, Derek B. "Orientalism and Musical Style." *Musical Quarterly* 82, no. 2 (summer 1998), 326–327.

Search-Light (Waldo Frank). *Time Exposures*. New York: Boni & Liveright, 1926.

Silet, Charles L. P. *The Writings of Paul Rosenfeld: An Annotated Bibliography*. New York: Garland, 1981.

Singerman, Robert. "The American Career of the *Protocols of the Elders of Zion*." *American Jewish History* 71, no. 1 (September 1981), 54–55.

Smith, Barry. *Peter Warlock: The Life of Philip Heseltine*. Oxford: Oxford University Press, 1994.

"Sound Recording Research at Bell Labs." http://history.acusd.edu/gen/recording /bell-labs.html. Accessed June 24, 2005.

Stoddard, Lothrap. *The Rising Tide of Color against White World-Supremacy.* New York: Charles Scribner's Sons, 1926.

Strong, Josiah. *Our Country: Its Possible Future and Its Present Crisis.* New York: Baker and Taylor, 1885.

Tapper, Thomas. *First Year Counterpoint.* Boston: A. P. Schmidt, 1913.

———. *First Year Melody Writing.* Boston: A. P. Schmidt, 1911.

———. *Key to First Year Harmony with Additional Exercises.* Boston: A. P. Schmidt, 1915.

———. "Music Talks with Children." Project Gutenberg eBook. http://library.beau.org /gutenberg/1/4/3/3/14339. Accessed June 9, 2005.

———. *Second Year Harmony.* Boston: A. P. Schmidt, 1912.

Tapper, Thomas, and Percy Goetschius. *Essentials in Music History.* New York: C. Scribner's Sons, 1929.

Timbrell, Charles. "Walter Morse Rummel." *Grove Music Online.* Edited by L. Macy. www.grovemusic.com. Accessed July 12, 2005.

Titiev, Jacob "Without a Guide." Unpublished manuscript, undated, in possession of Titiev's grandson, Robert Titiev.

Trachtenberg, Alan, ed. *Memoirs of Waldo Frank.* Amherst: University of Massachusetts Press, 1973.

Van Kuran, Laura. "Music Teachers of the State Sound Optimistic Note." *Musical America* 24, no. 9 (July 1, 1916), 2–3.

Van Vechten, Carl. *Music and Bad Manners.* New York: Knopf, 1916.

"Very Modern Music." *Musical Courier* 70, no. 5 (February 3, 1915), 29.

Warlock, Peter. *The Collected Letters of Peter Warlock (Philip Heseltine).* Edited by Barry Smith. Woodbridge: Boydell Press, 2005.

Whitesitt, Linda. "'The Most Potent Force' in American Music: The Role of Women's Music Clubs in American Concert Life." In *The Musical Woman.* Vol. 3: *1986–90.* Edited by Judith Long Zaimont. Westport, Conn.: Greenwood Press, 1991.

Wilson, Edmund. *Letters on Literature and Politics: 1912–1972.* Edited by Elena Wilson. New York: Farrar, Straus and Giroux, 1977.

Wright, Farnsworth. "Ornstein Once More Astonishes Chicago." *Musical America* 23, no. 26 (April 29, 1916), 60.

Zimel, Heyman. "Ornstein, Modernistic Composer." *B'nai Brith Magazine* 41 (1927), 455–456.

Zorach, William. *Art Is My Life: The Autobiography of William Zorach.* Cleveland: World, 1967.

ARCHIVAL RECORDINGS

Leo Ornstein plays Grieg and Poldini: see Columbia Tape A 1445.

Leo Ornstein plays Chopin: see Columbia Tape A 1473.

WEB SITES

http://dlib.nyu.edu/dram/Objid/14453. Accessed June 11, 2004.

http://fmg-www.cs.ucla.edu/geoff/prognotes/macdowell/indianSuite.html. Accessed June 11, 2004.

http://history.acusd.edu/gen/recording/bell-labs.html. Accessed June 24, 2005.

http://library.beau.org/gutenberg/1/4/3/3/14339. Accessed June 9, 2005.

http://members.aol.com/jeff560/chrono1.html. Accessed June 24, 2005.

http://mmd.foxtail.com/Archives/Digests/200104/2001.04.12.05.html. Accessed June 24, 2005.

http://mmd.foxtail.com/Archives/Digests/200104/2001.04.23.12.html. Accessed June 22, 2005.

http://nkasd.wiu.k12.pa.us/VHS/discushellis.html. Accessed July 3, 2004.

http://proquest.umi.com/pqdweb?sid=1&RQT=511&TS=1062349604&clientId=1360&firstIndex=30. Accessed August 31, 2003.

www.holocaust-history.org/short-essays/protocols.shtml. Accessed June 12, 2004.

www.infoplease.com/ipa/A000461.5html. Accessed June 6, 2004.

www.leedeforest.org/broadcaster.html. Accessed June 24, 2005.

www.miami.edu/advancement/NamedBuildingsGables.doc. Accessed June 22, 2005.

www.mvdaily.com/articles/1999/02/ppiano14.htm. Accessed June 23, 2005.

www.newyorkphilharmonic.org/programNotes/0304_Ravel_Sheherazade3Poems.pdf. Accessed July 12, 2005.

www.pbs.org/wgbh/amex/influenza/timeline. Accessed June 7, 2004.

www.stanford.edu/group/virus/uda/index.html. Accessed April 18, 2004.

www.temple.edu/tyler/history.html. Accessed October 18, 2005.

www.u-s-history/com/pages/h1345.html. Accessed June 12, 2004.

www.waterex.com.au/player/rollmade.html. Accessed June 21, 2005.

www.wayneturney.20m.com/washingtonsquare.htm. Accessed July 27, 2005.

www.wyastone.co.uk/nrl/pvoce/7921c.html. Accessed June 20, 2005.

www.wzo.org.il/home/politic/pale.htm. Accessed June 14, 2004.

NEWSPAPERS AND JOURNALS

Atlanta Georgian

Baltimore Evening Sun

Boston Globe

Buffalo Courier

Chicago Tribune

The Constitution (Atlanta)

Current Opinion

Daily Mail (London)

Daily Telegraph

Fort Worth Star-Telegram

Houston Chronicle

The Independent

Jacksonville Courier

London Times

Los Angeles Times

Milwaukee Journal

Montreal Daily Star

The Musical Standard

The Musical Times

The Musician

The New Republic

New York Evening Journal

New York Evening World

New York Globe

New York Herald

New York Sun

New York Times

New York Tribune

Philadelphia Inquirer

Philadelphia Ledger

Philadelphia Public Ledger

Philadelphia Record

Sacramento Bee

Saint Louis Post-Dispatch

San Francisco Call

INDEX

Michael Broyles is Professor of Music in the School
of Music at Pennsylvania State University.

Denise Von Glahn is Associate Professor in the
College of Music at The Florida State University.